FARMERS AS HUNTERS: THE IMPLICATIONS OF SEDENTISM

FARMERS AS HUNTERS

The implications of sedentism

EDITED BY SUSAN KENT

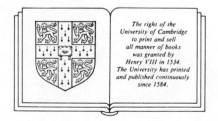

The right of the
University of Cambridge
to print and sell
all manner of books
was granted by
Henry VIII in 1534.
The University has printed
and published continuously
since 1584.

CAMBRIDGE UNIVERSITY PRESS

CAMBRIDGE

NEW YORK   PORT CHESTER

MELBOURNE   SYDNEY

Published by the Press Syndicate of the University of Cambridge
The Pitt Building, Trumpington Street, Cambridge CB2 1RP
40 West 20th Street, New York, NY 10011, USA
10 Stamford Road, Oakleigh, Melbourne 3166, Australia

First published 1989

Printed in Great Britain at the University Press, Cambridge

British Library cataloguing in publication data

Farmers as hunters: the implications of
  sedentism. – (New directions in
  archaeology).
  1. Hunter–gatherer communities
  I. Kent, Susan II. Series
  307.7'72

Library of Congress cataloguing in publication data

Farmers as hunters: the implications of sedentism/edited by Susan
  Kent.
        p.   cm . – (New directions in archaeology)
  Bibliography.
  Includes index.
  ISBN 0-521-36217-2
  1. Agriculture, Prehistoric. 2. Economics, Prehistoric.
  3. Agriculture, Primitive. 4. Land settlement patterns,
  Prehistoric. 5. Hunting and gathering societies. I. Kent, Susan,
  1952– . II. Series.
  GN799.A4F37 1989
  630'.9'01–dc19   88-23470

ISBN 0 521 36217 2

AL

To my parents, Shirley and Theodore,
my brothers, Don and Steve,
and my affinal sisters, Susie and Nancy

CONTENTS

Contents

CONTRIBUTORS

Susan Kent, Old Dominion University, Norfolk, Virginia
Kenneth M. Kensinger, Bennington College, Bennington, Vermont
Abraham Rosman, Columbia University, New York
Paula G. Rubel, Columbia University, New York
Leslie E. Sponsel, University of Hawaii, Honolulu, Hawaii
William T. Vickers, Florida International University, Miami, Florida
P. Bion Griffin, University of Hawaii, Honolulu, Hawaii
John D. Speth, University of Michigan, Ann Arbor, Michigan
Susan L. Scott, University of Southern Mississippi, Hattiesburg, Mississippi
Christine R. Szuter, University of Arizona, Tucson, Arizona
Frank E. Bayham, Chico State University, Chico, California
Helga Vierich, Box 451, Bayview Avenue, P.O. Woodlawn,
   Ontario K0A 3M0

ACKNOWLEDGEMENTS

There are a number of people I would like to thank for their help and encouragement while I was working on this book. I first would like to thank the individual authors for their participation. Each chapter is an original contribution written for this volume. Many authors took the time to read and comment on the other chapters. This interaction among the individual authors makes the book more integrated than are many edited volumes. I also would like to sincerely thank my friends at the University of New Mexico where the book was conceived and written, at the University of Kentucky where it was revised and reviewed, and at Old Dominion University where the final draft was put together.

Chapter 1

Cross-cultural perceptions of farmers as hunters and the value of meat

Susan Kent

The goals of *Farmers as hunters: the implications of sedentism* are to critically analyze the role of hunters and hunting in horticultural societies and to assess the influence of mobility on this role. Cross-cultural and diachronic analyses have proven to be invaluable for hunter–gatherer studies (see for example, Lee and DeVore 1968). However, they have been curiously absent from horticulturalist studies which tend to be more regional in scope. This book represents an attempt to describe, analyze, and interpret how hunters and hunting are incorporated within the culture, behavior, and cultural material of small-scale farming societies. The volume should be viewed as a beginning that may raise more questions than it answers, but it represents a beginning that provides a necessary starting point for future studies.

The aim of this chapter is to explore cross-cultural values and perceptions of hunting in societies with different mobility patterns and economies. These include hunter–gatherers – or food extractors – and horticulturalists who hunt – or food producers and extractors. Two of the most crucial differences between hunter–gatherers and farmers are the use of domesticates and a reduction in mobility (with some exceptions as discussed below). I submit that in most cases mobility is a more influential variable accounting for differences and similarities in culture than is the adoption of domesticates. This is examined below in a section on the origins of complexity. In addition the relationship between subsistence strategies and cultural preferences is investigated in

this chapter. Why many groups consider hunting and meat intrinsically better than gathering or farming and vegetables, despite adequate protein diets, is examined in detail on both culture-specific and cross-cultural levels. The question pursued here is not why meat is so important because it obviously is nutritionally essential for human health (Hayden 1981:397 and others), but why it is consistently deemed more important than plants which are also nutritionally essential for humans.

A cross-cultural method is employed to investigate and understand pan-cultural views of the role of hunting, hunters, and meat in groups with disparate economies and organizations. This method stems directly from my theoretical orientation that presumes the presence of general cross-cultural principles that underlie culture (Kent 1987). These principles are not, however, thought to be innate as the result of human instincts but, instead, are the result of learned culture synthesized and symbolized through a common *Homo sapiens* brain. Most anthropologists view the role of hunters and hunting on a culture-specific level or at least on a subsistence-specific level; i.e., among hunter–gatherers or among horticulturalists. Studies such as those in most of the chapters which follow provide important culture-specific explanations that are of a different level from cross-cultural ones. *Neither is necessarily "right," only different.* The advantages and disadvantages of approaching the topic from a general cross-cultural level are explored in the conclusions to this chapter. The following is intended to provide context and integration for the chapters which follow.

Nomadism and sedentism – a continuum of mobility

Despite previous discussions of sedentism (e.g. Watanabe 1968; Rafferty 1984; Eder 1984; J. Brown 1985; Kent 1986), the concept remains ambiguous. There is sometimes a failure to recognize a basic semantic difference between the terms mobility, sedentism, and nomadism. The terms are used here to denote conditions of group movement. Nomadism is the movement of a group on a landscape and sedentism is the lack of movement. Mobility is simply the movement of a group (not a camp) through space. Nomadism and sedentism, then, denote the amount of movement or mobility involved. There are different degrees and types of nomadism, as noted by Binford (1980), and of sedentism, as noted by Vickers (chapter 5, this volume). Nomadism and sedentism represent the extremes of the mobility continuum. Whether groups whose mobility patterns fall between the two extremes are classified "semi-nomadic" or "semi-sedentary" is, in my opinion, usually rather arbitrary. Below I refer to the Amazonian Siriono as semi-sedentary because they are seasonally sedentary during the dry part of the year. I classify them as such in order to indicate that they are neither totally nomadic nor completely sedentary. Instead about six months of the year they are nomadic and six months of the year they are sedentary. Groups who are less equal in the time spent moving or stationary can be more easily classified.

Sedentism creates new potentials for interpersonal conflicts that cannot be resolved as readily as when groups are mobile. Once sedentary, fissioning and moving to different areas are no longer viable options. Instead, people with restricted mobility must address intragroup conflicts in other ways than through movement. This is often accomplished through the mediation of a sanctioned arbitrator (Carneiro 1967; Lee 1972a and b). In the case of people with permanent residences but who are otherwise mobile, an arbitrator and other features associated with sedentism are not always necessary. Hence, the people are not in my opinion really sedentary – they are nomadic with permanent base camps.

There are other changes necessitated by sedentism, such as refuse disposal patterns, which become, out of necessity, more formal and restricted at sites which are occupied on a permanent basis (Kent 1984). Sites also tend to become larger per capita and dwellings tend to become substantial (see Kent and Vierich this volume, chapter 9; Kent forthcoming). In addition, restricted mobility encourages disease vectors that promote bacterial, viral, and parasitic infections in more sedentary settlements, despite changes in the refuse patterning that usually accompanies sedentism. Long-term residential stability creates a cycle of chronic diseases that significantly affect morbidity and mortality (Kent 1986). Demography and settlement patterns also are affected by sedentism (Hitchcock 1982:185; Hassan 1981; and others). Site structure and content are more complex when movement is infrequent than when it is continuous. This is visible in formal

storage areas, site activity diversification, and other features (Kent and Vierich this volume, chapter 9; Blomberg 1981; Binford 1980).

Keeping the above factors in mind, one can begin to discuss how sedentary "sedentism" is. It is doubtful that many aboriginal societies spent 12 months a year for many decades at a time in a single location. That is a pattern probably more characteristic of societies in constrained spaces with high population densities, such as in restricted valleys and/or particularly in the case of urban centers.

Even though classified as sedentary, Euroamericans as a group do not occupy the same location for decades at a time. For instance, many families take long vacations. They do not spend every month of the year at the same location. Nor is such mobility necessarily a new phenomenon – at the turn of the century less than one-third of Americans from Omaha, Nebraska, lived in the same place after only five years (Chudacoff 1972). A total of 96.2 percent of the males sampled had moved one mile or further from their earlier residence and only 3.8 percent of the sample occupied the same residence for 20 years (ibid. 36–37). Although higher than mobility elsewhere in North America at the time, it shows how unrealistic some definitions of sedentism are when applied only to groups who inhabit the same settlement for 12 months a year over a hundred or more years. Between 1970 and 1975, just 44 percent of North Americans over four years of age resided at the same dwelling at the end of the study as they did in the beginning. During this short five-year period, 15 percent of the people moved to locations outside their original community (Berry and Dahmann 1980:26–28). South African Zulu, as but one of many non-Western examples usually regarded as sedentary, occupy their homesteads for only 15 to 30 years, resulting in few sites occupied longer than one generation (Oswald 1987). Sedentary Tswana settlements in Botswana were traditionally moved every 10 to 15 years (Silitshena 1983:191). Over two-thirds of the 1982 population of one Longana village in Vanuatu (formerly the New Hebrides) had moved into or away from the village over only a 12-year period (Rodman 1985:67). And yet, I think it would be misleading to classify these groups as nomadic.

There are basically two types of nomadism and sedentism. There are nomadic groups with and without permanent base camps, or foragers and collectors (Binford 1980). There are sedentary groups who leave for short periods of time and those who live permanently in one location. Seasonal sedentism characterizes groups that make seasonal trips but return to a permanent camp where they reside for the majority of the year. Examples are the Ainu (Watanabe 1968:71–73) and North American Northwest Coast societies (see below). Permanent, in contrast to seasonal, sedentism characterizes groups who occupy sites more or less year-round for the majority of a year, as do the Zulu, Longanas, Euroamericans, and others. It is productive in my opinion to view sedentism as a situation in which a group spends over six months a year continuously at one locus, even if at other times during the year the group leaves, returning to the community after short, often seasonal, absences.

Mobility and ecology

As will be shown, hunter–gatherers are not exclusively nomadic any more than horticulturalists are exclusively sedentary (i.e., subsistence strategies do not determine mobility; see below and also Kent and Vierich, this volume, chapter 9). It is important to note that mobility appears to affect differences and similarities between groups more than does ecology *per se*. For example, some groups inhabiting the same environment have very different levels of sociopolitical organization as well as very different subsistence strategies. Different groups occupying the same environment include the nomadic Mbuti Pygmies and the neighboring sedentary Bantu farmers (Turnbull 1961), the nomadic Basarwa or "Bushmen" and the sedentary Bantu Bakgalagadi agropastoralists (chapter 9, this volume), and the nomadic Agta and the sedentary Paranan or non-Agta farmers (Griffin, chapter 6, this volume). Sedentary hunter–gatherers tend to share a more similar degree of sociopolitical complexity, technological complexity, and other features with sedentary horticulturalists than they do with mobile but fellow hunter–gatherers (that is, groups with different mobility patterns but with the same subsistence strategies are at different levels of complexity, such as nomadic Basarwa or "Bushmen" hunter–gatherers and sedentary Northwest hunter–gatherers). Similarities do not exist among groups with similar subsistence strategies but do exist among groups with similar mobility strategies.

The ecological approach in archaeology has in the past emphasized subsistence strategies (Watson, LeBlanc, and Redman 1984:115). This economically oriented ecological approach has dominated American archaeology and influenced European archaeology since the end of the 1960s (ibid.). For example, Watson, LeBlanc, and Redman stated in 1984 that many "archaeologists believe as we do that much cultural behavior is in fact dependently related to environmental factors and that ecological hypotheses automatically have considerable plausibility" (ibid. 115). Moreover they later write that the "justification for concern with empirical information about subsistence and paleo-environment is that one must know how a prehistoric society made its living if one is to achieve understanding of that society" (ibid. 131). According to Hayden (1981:346), if "we are to take cultural materialists at their word, subsistence activities are inextricably bound up with every facet of culture and social organization . . ." Because of the prevalence of ecological deterministic thinking in our discipline, we sometimes tend to forget that mobility is not necessarily directly linked to ecology. There are social, political, and ritual reasons also that dictate mobility patterns. In fact, preliminary analysis of 32 Basarwa ("Bushmen") and Bakgalagadi (Bantu speakers) households indicates that in 1987 57.4 percent moved to their present camps for political or social reasons (the latter to be close to or away from kin and friends), whereas 19.2 percent moved for environmental or economic reasons, 19.2 percent moved for a combination of environmental/economic, social, and political reasons, and 3.9 percent moved for undetermined reasons (Kent n.d.a.).

Although mobility has, in the past, been thought of as ecologically determined, it is productive to view mobility as independent of ecology, that is, as independent of the environment or of economics, such as particular subsistence strategies. There are numerous instances where politics, just as one example, has curtailed or otherwise determined the mobility of a group. This includes forced relocations, forced sedentarization, and other patterns (e.g., Lee 1979:363–364; Fahim 1980; among many). To cite another example: in the past, Batswana chiefs dictated that people live in villages away from their agricultural fields so that they could maintain political control over their subjects (Silitshena 1983). This resulted in a second residence at the fields which was occupied during the agricultural season, leading to movement between the two camps. The "existence of nucleated settlements in Botswana owed much to the influence of the chiefs and the power which they exercised in insuring their continued existence" (ibid. 71). When chiefs were weak the people lived permanently near the fields and abandoned their homes in the village and the migration between the two residences (ibid.). Within a specific society, there are social, ritual, political, environmental (e.g., mountains or rivers), and economic factors that together determine a people's mobility pattern. To say that a group moves only for ecological reasons is as incorrect as to say it moves just for social or political reasons. Mobility therefore should not be seen as ecologically determined. Instead, all the components that influence mobility need to be examined equally and none to the exclusion of the others (also see Kent and Vierich, this volume, chapter 9). This can be done only if mobility is examined separately from subsistence strategies and the environment.

Within the same economic strategy, hunting and gathering and species exploitation strategies of foraging societies contrast significantly according to a group's degree of mobility. Hitchcock (1982:204–280) compared nomadic and sedentary Kalahari peoples' hunting and documented differences in such strategies. He observed that sedentary groups exploit a wider variety of animals than do nomadic ones, depend more on smaller animals, and use more traps, ambush hunting, and long-distance hunts, as well as transportation aids such as donkeys and horses (ibid. 204). Meat scavenged from diseased or otherwise dead animals, and insects, are consumed by both nomadic and sedentary peoples, but are much more frequently used among the sedentary households. Perhaps most intriguing, although referring to a small sample, is Hitchcock's observation (ibid. 257) that without a gun and when not on an expedition or trophy hunt, sedentary hunters are less successful than nomadic ones. Also important is the role of garden hunting among horticulturalists which provides frequent opportunities to hunt antelopes, baboons, monkeys, and birds (ibid.). Garden hunting (common in other parts of the world) may offset some of the negative repercussions of any possible lowered hunting skills among sedentary peoples. Sedentary hunters travel as far away as 60 kilometers to procure large species which are brought back on donkeys (ibid.).

Interestingly, Basarwa sedentary food-producers also utilize more plants (116 species) than do nomadic foragers (59 species) and nomadic groups tend to collect roots, tubers, and bulbs more than do sedentary peoples (Hitchcock 1982:217; also see C. Brown 1985 for a related discussion). Less mobile people in the Kalahari tend to use plants that are considered undesirable by more mobile people and long-distance trade is more common among sedentary groups (Hitchcock 1982:222). Research is needed to determine if this is a cross-culturally consistent pattern.

The following discussion contrasts groups with different economics and mobility patterns. Their sociopolitical organization and the value they place on hunting and meat are then compared. The following shows that regardless of the subsistence strategy or mobility pattern, meat and hunting are esteemed over plants and gathering.

Hunting among nomadic hunter–gatherers

In order to understand the role of hunters and hunting in sedentary horticultural societies, which is the goal of this book, it is first necessary to understand their role among nomadic hunter–gatherers. Since I have conducted fieldwork among the San or Basarwa ("Bushmen"),[1] of the Kalahari, I am most familiar with them, and will therefore use them to illustrate this role. Although differences exist, a number of the features germane to the present discussion are shared by other nomadic hunters and gatherers such as the Aché (Hawkes, Hill, and O'Connell 1982) and Hadza (Woodburn 1968). The influence of mobility and economic organization can then be examined among horticulturalist hunters.

The relatively small contribution of meat to certain Basarwa groups' diets, in contrast to vegetable foods, has been documented by a number of researchers. According to Lee (1979:450), gathering provides about two-thirds of the diet. Marshall (1976:93) estimates a similar figure for the !Kung of Nyae Nyae. The ratio of plants to meat consumed by the ≠Kade of the Central Kalahari is 20:1 (Tanaka 1980:70). Although Tanaka's ratio may be a little low for meat (Silberbauer 1981:204), as may be Lee's figures for the !Kung (Draper n.d.:7), the point remains unchanged – vegetable foods constitute the majority of the Basarwa diet. Importantly, Silberbauer (1981:202) who, unlike Tanaka, did not observe the Central Kalahari Basarwa during a drought, noted that "hunters' contributions to the diet are irregular and periods as long as two months may pass without meat; at these times the household relies completely on plant foods." It is interesting that the cultural value placed on meat far exceeds its representation in the diet, just as it does among horticulturalists who hunt, a point to be explored in depth later.

Dobe !Kung men work harder hunting than women do gathering, while contributing less to the diet (Lee 1984:51). Men work as much as two to three times more than females among the \Du\da !Kung (Draper n.d.). Moreover,

> Not all hunters are successful. In fact, on most days of hunting a man will come back empty-handed. And even if an animal is wounded, there is no guarantee that the meat will ever reach camp. As many as half the animals shot by the !Kung either recover from their wounds or run so far that they die out of range of the carrying party. An individual hunter is deemed fortunate if he kills as many as two large antelopes per year [although numerous smaller animals are killed within that time]. (Lee 1984:48)

The correlation between hunting success and social status is minimal and tends not to be emphasized. Basarwa belittle individuals' success in hunting since the accumulation of goods, be it meat or anything else, can create potential inequality. They trade arrows, which distributes the ownership of meat (the person to whom an arrow belongs "owns" the meat even if shot by someone else), and deliberately intersperse periods of successful hunting with periods of inactivity that can last as long as three or more months (Lee 1979:246–249; Silberbauer 1981:244). On those rare occasions when there is conflict over hunting plans, it is usually resolved by making one's view known to all and reaching an acceptable consensus of opinion through public discussions participated in by both males and females (Silberbauer 1981; Lee 1982).

The high value of meat and hunting in horticultural societies has often been attributed to the status of men and a rigid division of labor. Meat and hunting are highly valued among the Basarwa despite a gender division of labor that is not pronounced. Whereas men generally hunt and women gather, women also own arrows and men gather. In fact, men contribute as much as one-fifth of the total plants collected (Lee 1979:247, 450). Women actually "own" and distribute meat from any animal killed by one of their arrows (Lee 1979: 278; Shostak 1981:60). In *hxaro* exchange, women can receive and pass on gifts made and used by men, such as arrows, and men can receive and pass on women's gifts, such as aprons (Wiessner 1982;71).

Hunting among sedentary hunter–gatherers

Unlike most hunter–gatherers, North American Northwest Coast groups are (using the ethnographic present) seasonally sedentary. There are other groups such as the Japanese Ainu I could describe, but I am more familiar with the Northwest Coast Indians as a result of my fieldwork among Coastal Salish speakers and Makah/Ozettes. The Northwest Coast Indians present an interesting case for examining the role of hunting and meat in groups with a similar economic orientation to the Basarwa – hunting and gathering – and a dissimilar mobility pattern – sedentism.

Winters are spent at permanent villages and summers are spent on and off at the villages and at fishing, hunting, and wild-plant-gathering camps. Some of these seasonal camps are temporary and not reoccupied. Others, such as Tatoosh Island, Cape Flattery, Washington, are used for generations where the inhabitants seasonally exploit the offshore halibut beds year after year. Shells from the Ozette archaeological site at Cape Flattery (one of the Makah villages) indicate that the so-called winter village was actually occupied year round by at least some people (Wesson 1982).

As wild plants are to the Basarwa, fishing is to the Northwest Coast groups. Thousands of salmon, herring, smelt, and olachen run seasonally in inland waters to spawn (Drucker

1963:35). Although obviously not identical, in a number of respects harvesting anadromous fish, such as salmon, resembles the gathering of wild plants more than it does hunting (although their processing is entirely different, see Schalk 1977:232–233). This is because one must go to where the fish are running, the locations of which vary between species and seasons just as different wild plant species ripen at various locations and seasons. Moreover, exploiting these periodically abundant resources is often referred to as "harvesting," a term associated with plants. The same is applied also to the collecting of shellfish. As is the case with plants, the harvesting of anadromous fish tends to have less prestige than, for example, mammal hunting (see below).

Obtaining other non-anadromous fish with different behavior, such as lingcod, rockfish, and halibut, might be considered more closely aligned with hunting, although it would be a mistake to take any analogy too far. A different technology based on the non-anadromous species' behavior is employed to obtain them. This includes spears and specialized hooks (e.g., halibut hooks) versus nets and weirs used to procure anadromous fish. These species tend to be less seasonal and more available all the year round. According to Huelsbeck (1983:107), there is a bias in the Northwest Coast literature concerning the seasonality of fishing that under-emphasizes the importance of fresh fish available all the year round, and particularly their frequency in the winter diet (also see Swan 1869:30; Garfield 1966:13).

Whales, seals, sea lions, and otter are hunted to different degrees among various groups (e.g. Makah, including the Ozette, and the Nootka actively hunt whales to a greater extent than do other Northwest Coast groups). Land mammals are also hunted, including deer, elk, and bear, and birds are additionally obtained.

Although variable as to group and season, plants in general are less important than meat in Northwest Coast diets. Seaweed, fern roots, clover, equisetum tubers, salmonberries, strawberries, soapberries, and other berries are collected (Drucker 1965:208; Swan 1869:25). Berries are picked seasonally, often during short trips inland.

As was true for the Basarwa, hunting supplements the gathered or harvested resources (here anadromous fish) while the latter constitutes the bulk of the diet. The Quileute of Washington state provide one example wherein "whether they dwelt on the coast or along rivers inland, [Quileute] lived chiefly on fish [rather than on hunted meat]" (Pettitt 1950:5). Also like the Basarwa, Northwest Coast Indians' resources are seasonal and available at different locations over the landscape. Unlike the Kalahari hunter–gatherers, however, Northwest Coast hunter–gatherers have a different mobility pattern – that of sedentism rather than nomadism.

As among nomadic hunters, hunting, in this case of sea mammals, is considered to be more important and prestigious than fishing among many Northwest Coast groups despite its much smaller contribution to the overall diet (e.g., Suttles 1974:135). The Quinault Indians of Coastal Washington have a

    somewhat romantic aura surround[ing] the pursuit of hunting, whether of the sea mammals or of elk and bear,

and men were fond of relating their hunting experiences. For this reason they looked with a sort of disdain upon men who were not reckoned good hunters and who found it more profitable to spend most of their time fishing. (Olson 1936:41)

Specific animals, such as whales, are shrouded in ritual, myth, and status, and appear in Northwest Coast art on both utilitarian and ritual objects (Kent 1975; Croes 1977). Drucker (1951:49) notes the small contribution that the much talked about and portrayed whale made to the Nootkan diet when he wrote: "That the prestige value of whaling outweighed its economic importance is clear from modern accounts ... Recent whalers, though they hunted diligently ... got but few [whales] in their careers." Killing three whales during a lifetime was most typical, although legends suggest that hunters had been more successful in the past. Jewitt, the shipwrecked sailor forced to be the personal slave of the Nootkan chief Maquinna between 1803 and 1805, observed whale hunting. His journal recorded that in 53 days of hunting, nine whales were hit but only one was successfully killed and brought to shore (Jewitt 1815). Drucker (1951:50) concluded from various ethnohistorical sources that "Clearly the economic reward in proportion to the expenditure of time and energy was slight." As with the Basarwa, Northwest Coast groups spend a relatively large amount of time procuring meat with much effort in terms of time and preparation while receiving a relatively low return for their endeavor compared to the gathering of high-protein anadromous fish, shellfish, and other gathered resources. They nevertheless placed a higher ritual, prestige, and social premium on hunted resources than on harvested resources.

The economic division of labor among Northwest Coast groups is quite dissimilar to that of mobile hunter–gatherers. In general Northwest Coast societies' division of labor is characterized by status-related tasks like whale hunting, limited access to certain specific resources and their locations (often also class/status-related), and occupational specialization. However, the ubiquitous sexual division of labor is still based on a male/hunting–female/gathering distinction. For instance, Coastal Salish speakers relegate gathering wild plants to women, although men also sometimes help as is the case with the Basarwa, while men, and only occasionally women, fish for halibut (Suttles 1974; also see Haeberlin and Gunther 1930). Women gather seaweed, berries, roots, and shellfish while only men hunt (see e.g. Boas 1966:10).

As has been noted by others, sedentism is a major factor responsible for the complexity of Northwest Coast sociopolitical organization (see Schalk 1977;236); a complexity more similar to some also sedentary horticulturalists than to more mobile hunter–gatherers. Characteristics of Northwest Coast culture such as ascribed status, chiefs with hereditary rank and institutionalized power validated through potlatches, redistribution as the economic mode of exchange, a three-class social hierarchy including slaves, and part- and limited full-time specialists are not commonly found among nomadic hunter–gatherers, but are found among some sedentary horticulturalists. As I try to demonstrate more fully below and as the subtitle of this book implies, in the case of the Northwest Coast and other mobility-restricted groups sedentism is a more influential factor in the development and perpetuation of the sociopolitical organization than is their economy in terms of subsistence or storage (e.g., Testart 1982). However, this makes sense only if you separate ecology and economics, particularly subsistence and storage, from mobility and recognize that there are a number of factors that influence mobility. Environmental and economic factors, for example, represent but two such factors. Social, political, and religious factors are equally important; sometimes more important. I additionally show the importance of hunting and hunters among horticulturalists who hunt and how this importance does not differ substantially in magnitude from that among hunters and gatherers.

Hunting among semi-sedentary horticulturalists

Horticulturalists do not have to be sedentary, although mobile farmers are less common than sedentary ones. As Hitchcock and Ebert (1984:343) note, "In the Kalahari, groups do not have to be sedentary in order to practice food production, nor does it necessarily lead to people becoming sedentary. Some of the groups . . . had gardens at several of their campsites. They returned to harvest the crops . . . going from one abandoned campsite to another . . ." (also see, in this volume: Sponsel, chapter 4; Vickers, chapter 5; and Griffin, chapter 6). According to the discussion above and model presented below, a group with a semi-sedentary mobility pattern should have more sociopolitical complexity than a more nomadic society and less sociopolitical complexity than a more sedentary society. A number of Amazonian horticulturalists fall into this semi-sedentary mobility category. One of the more detailed ethnographies of this type of society describes the Siriono of Bolivia (Holmberg 1969).

Among the seasonally sedentary Siriono, members of both sexes participate in cultivation activities, usually in conjunction with hunting or less frequent fishing trips (Holmberg 1969). They are mobile during the rainy season from June to November and stationary during the dry season, December to May (Holmberg 1969).

Siriono gardens are located at varying distances from a settlement. Maize, sweet manioc, camotes, papaya, and other plants are cultivated. Men and women collect wild plants, although women gather more than men who are often busy with hunting (ibid. 67–69). Seasonal fishing with bow and arrow contributes only a little to the diet.

As is true of all the groups discussed here, hunting is considered the most important subsistence endeavor while actually providing a smaller proportion to the diet than domestic and wild plants. "No other activity of the men can match the importance of hunting. The temper of the Siriono camp, in fact, can be readily gauged by the supply of game that is daily being bagged by the hunters; there is rarely ever equaled that joy which follows a successful chase or that discontent which follows an unsuccessful one" (ibid. 51).

Hunters go out on an average of every other day throughout the year, using the days in camp to rest, repair arrows, and perform other activities (ibid. 75–76). During the months of August and September 1941, Holmberg observed that an individual consumed approximately one-half pound of meat per day; for October the mean consumption was about one-third of a pound per day (ibid. 74). He ascribes the monthly variation to seasonal scheduling conflicts with horticulture (ibid. 75). Men average 10 to 12 days a month hunting, the most persistent hunter going out 12 to 19 days a month. Sharing food is mandatory within the nuclear family and is encouraged among the extended family.

Both sexes partake in gathering, horticulture, dressing game, and burden-carrying in contrast to such strictly male tasks as hunting, fishing, and tool and weapon manufacture (Holmberg 1969). Female tasks are child care, twining hammocks and string, weaving including baskets and mats, ceramic pot manufacturing, and collecting water and firewood (ibid. 104). Although it is not identical, men and women have similar status while growing up and as adults (ibid.).

A good hunter enjoys higher status than a poor one, and the informal chief is always one of the group's best hunters (Holmberg 1969:148–150). Even so, the position is usually inherited patrilineally from father to oldest son, provided the latter also is a good hunter and possesses the other abilities deemed necessary for a chief. Important in this discussion is the fact that the hereditary chief requires a combination of ascribed and achieved status that is more similar to sedentary Northwest Coast hunter–gatherers and sedentary horticulturalists than to more mobile nomadic groups. However, at the same time, he has little direct influence. "He is respected for his wisdom and may make suggestions about hunting trips and band movements, but his advice is not always followed. His major prerogative is that of occupying a central position in the large house, and he always heads a polygynous family. He must, however, perform the round of daily tasks that fall to all adult males" (Steward and Faron 1959:428). In this respect the leader is similar to more nomadic hunter–gatherers than to more sedentary horticulturalists or hunter–gatherers. Also important to this discussion is the fact that other semi-sedentary groups are similar in a number of general respects. For example, among the Akwe-Shavante of Brazil: "Without hunting Shavante culture would have been very different, but without gathering, the Shavante could not exist" (Maybury-Lewis 1974:55). Even so, hunting is valued over gathering and "is the most common expression of virility" (Maybury-Lewis 1974:36).

Hunting among sedentary horticulturalists

Comments in this section are limited to only generalized observations and specific issues because hunting among horticulturalists is the focus of the chapters that follow. Consequently, this section is very short. As with the Basarwa, Northwest Coast groups, and Siriono, hunting among sedentary horticulturalists contributes proportionately little to the overall diet, although it constitutes much or most of the dietary protein. As in other sedentary groups, hunting confers male identity and status. It is an endeavor that, despite many hours of pursuit, has a return that is less in terms of calories than that obtained through gathering or cultivation, while also being more unpredictable than either of the two. For instance, Kensinger (1975:25) notes that "Hunting, next to sex, is the major passion of a Cashinahua male" and a man "views himself primarily as a hunter, and only secondarily as a gardener." Moreover, "No meal is complete without meat" and after a large vegetarian meal people will complain of hunger because there was no meat (ibid. 25). This is also true of the Ilongots of the Philippines who begin to grumble about their gnawing "hunger for meat" if they go without it for a week or more (R. Rosaldo 1982).

Hunting not only provides male identity for Peruvian Cashinahua, but unlike more egalitarian societies such as the Inuit[2] or Basarwa, successful hunters are "highly respected and even more highly desired as a lover or as a husband and son-in-law" (Kensinger 1975:29). This respect includes admiration both of the hunter's ability and his knowledge of animals. As was the case with other groups, Cashinahua men also participate in a small amount of nonhunting subsistence activities, particularly in farming and in fishing (Kensinger 1975). Nevertheless, there is still the male/hunting–female/farming dichotomy common to all horticulturalists who hunt.

The importance of sharing meat is paramount because of the day-to-day fluctuation in hunting, which over a long period of time either naturally evens out or artificially evens out through the sharing of meat. For instance, adult male Waorani of eastern Ecuador spend one day out of 6.6 days (or 4.5 days a month) hunting – 7.4 percent of all hunts are unsuccessful and 67 percent of the hunts produce less than 10 kg of meat (Yost and Kelley 1983:214–215). However, during this time period other hunters are more successful and the compulsory community sharing of meat results in everyone getting enough protein for an adequate diet (ibid.). This same pattern requiring sharing is found in all hunting societies and partially makes up for the uncertainty of hunting and the uneven skills of individual hunters. Communal hunting of certain species may also be a feature of some sedentary horticulturalists who hunt (see Speth and Scott, chapter 7, and Szuter and Bayham, chapter 8, this volume).

An evaluation of common explanations for the differential preference for hunting versus gathering

Why are meat and hunting consistently and ubiquitously valued more than plants and gathering or farming? Why is this the case among both nomadic and sedentary hunter–gatherers and among both nomadic and sedentary horticulturalists? Although obviously important as protein and minerals to the diet, meat and its acquisition tend to have a value disproportionate to their economic and nutritional contribution compared to plant and fish resources. Although meat is certainly important for protein, vitamins, and minerals, fish also contains such important nutrients but is rarely endowed with the value that meat is (see Yesner 1980 for a discussion of the similarity of the nutrients, protein, and caloric content of fish and meat). The discussion below does not ask why meat is important, because its nutritional importance is self-evident, but instead asks why meat is *more* important than plants

and why each is not given equal value since humans cannot exist very well without either. The following section examines culture-specific reasons for the discrepancy between cultural preference and status and the economic value of hunters, hunting, and meat in particular societies. These are then compared on a cross-cultural level. This is not to imply that the culture-specific reasons are not valid for particular groups – they just may not be valid on a cross-cultural level, the latter being the focus of this chapter, the former the focus of the chapters which follow. The following is concerned only with ascertaining whether these reasons are consistently and predictably equally valid on a cross-cultural level.

Some anthropologists have attributed the disparity between hunting and gathering, hunters and gatherers, and meat and vegetables to the relatively high risk and uncertainty involved in meat procurement in contrast to the relatively low risk and high certainty in procuring wild or domesticated plants. "Males hunt for meat ... Their endeavors are risky, unpredictable, and often dangerous. Females, by contrast, concentrate on gathering ... plant food ... Their work is less dangerous, success is more predictable. . . ." (Lancaster and Lancaster 1983:34; also see C. Hugh-Jones 1979:170–172). The status of men and hunting is ascribed to what has been considered to be risky. "Because men must sometimes gamble with their lives, power and prestige are the incentive that motivates them to hunt ... and are the reward for being very nearly expendable in terms of the group's ultimate survival" (Sanday 1981:115).

Evidence from a number of studies suggests that the risk involved in gathering tends to be underestimated and that involved in hunting overemphasized. For example, collecting wild fruits has been characterized as hazardous "since a man is liable to fall from a branch while picking the fruits" (Holmberg 1969:65); there are additional dangers involved in chopping down large trees. Certainly gathering and cultivating, including digging up roots and tubers, are not without danger with the potential for encountering snakes and scorpions, stinging ants, and other insects. It additionally has not been demonstrated that hunting is any more dangerous to an individual than gathering or other activities in which people routinely participate (the "real" hunting Kensinger discusses in chapter 2 is not a routine hunting strategy). Most people do not hunt the more dangerous carnivores for meat and when large potentially dangerous species are sought, groups like the Basarwa use poison, enabling them to shoot from a distance (Lee 1979; Kaplan and Hill 1985a; Carneiro 1970a; Krause 1956; etc.).

Furthermore, the uncertainty and risk of availability in terms of gathering or harvesting plants has been underestimated. "The security of plant food gathering, however, should not be over-emphasized. As the following discussion will show, there are a number of factors which affect food availability and foraging strategies. There are cycles in food plant productivity, and there are variations in the success rates of collectors which in part are related to the organization of labor, mobility patterns, and technology" (Hitchcock 1982:207). It is important to note that groups for whom farming is an extremely risky venture still exalt animal products over crops.

The importance in developing hunting skills has also been

invoked as an explanation for the high premium put on hunting, but once again I think this is unsatisfactory at a cross-cultural level of understanding since other activities that require skill do not share the prestige of hunting. These include various tasks, from spearing fish to making baskets. Variations in the hunting skills of individuals also do not seem to be as pronounced as some may think. Boys are typically taught to practice their hunting skills from a very young age. In one Amazonian Indian village the only really poor hunter whose efforts invariably met with failure had spent three to four years of his childhood, a time normally devoted to developing hunting skills, with a Peruvian trader and nonhunter (Siskind 1973a:237). Individual ability is further factored out by Sharanahua hunters with less skill or luck who typically even the odds by hunting more often than the more successful and skilled hunters (ibid.). The same pattern exists in other groups, such as among the !Kung who will stop hunting if overly successful (Lee 1979). The meat distribution pattern common to many groups equalizes available hunting skills as men share meat with households other than their own (Siskind 1973b:101; Lee 1979; and others). In fact in the Philippines, "the reluctance of Ilongots to talk about inequality of skill among hunters is rooted in a view of game as a collective product, publicly appropriated and consumed" (M. Rosaldo 1980:118–119).

The cultural preference for hunting has been attributed to the mundane nature of gathering plants. This was described by Silberbauer:

> Plants have none of the emotive significance of game animals but are discussed and dealt with as a routine necessity of life [among the Basarwa]. The gathering of plants requires much knowledge, which is shared by men, women, and children without esotery, but involves little skill once the specimens are located. Because the immobility of plants reduces the number of variables involved in collection, a gatherer needs to know their location and their season of availability and to have the ability to recognize useful species. The rest is a matter of hard work, and apart from this, the yield of the season is in the hands of N!adima, who cannot be influenced to make it more plentiful. Man's role is that of exploiter only [is that not true also for hunting?]. These aspects, and the fact that plant foods are not exchanged as gifts and thus have less social significance than meat, perhaps explain why food plants are regarded with general emotional neutrality. (1981:94)

Nonetheless, Draper (1975:82) convincingly challenges this biased stereotype in which female foraging roles in hunter–gatherer societies are thought to be individualized, repetitious, and boring in contrast to glamorous male hunting:

> Descriptions of the work of gathering leave the reader with the impression that the job is uninteresting and unchallenging – that anyone who can walk and bend over can collect wild bush food. This stereotype is distinctly inappropriate to !Kung female work, and it promotes a

condescending attitude toward what women's work is all about. Successful gathering over the years requires the ability to discriminate among hundreds of edible and inedible species of plants at various stages in their life cycle. This ability requires more than mere brute strength. The stereotype further ignores the role women play in gathering information about the "state of the bush" – presence of temporary water, evidence of recent game movements, etc. (Draper 1975:82–83)

The biased stereotype of gathering activities is also incorrect for other foraging groups, such as Australian Aborigines to give just one example (Berndt 1981:176–177).

Furthermore, the nonmundane nature of hunting may be questioned in that Aché hunter–gatherers spend over 70 percent of their time hunting just searching for game (Hill and Hawkes 1983:159). The entire concept of the pure joy of hunting in contrast to gathering needs to be objectively reevaluated for, as Siskind (1973a:232) noted, "After slogging through the tropical forest in the rainy season, wading through swamps up to the hips, picking off ticks, and avoiding stinging ants, I would question the idea that hunting is far more joyful than gathering or agriculture." Despite Kensinger's suggestion (chapter 2, this volume) that the pain associated with intense hunting may be similar to the jogger's "high" produced from the release of endorphins, people who jog usually do so every day to reduce additional pain caused by running only once a week or so. This differs from the intense hunting practiced by the Amazonian Cashinahua which occurs more sporadically and requires several days' recuperation (and, in fact, such demanding "real" hunts are much more rare than are the less arduous but more common regular hunts and it is the typical, not special, hunting pattern that is the focus of this chapter). The endorphin high may explain why men embark on the difficult "real" hunts Kensinger describes in chapter 2; but since the majority of Cashinahua hunts tend to be the less arduous or exhilarating type, it does not explain the cultural value attributed to meat and hunting that results from the more common type of Cashinahua hunting. Nor does it explain the hunting found among the Basarwa or Siriono, or Northwest Coast Indians – in other words, the importance of regular hunting on a nonculture-specific, cross-cultural level.

Of particular interest is the fact that the same cultural values and preference for meat are present also among pastoralists, and this cannot be attributed to the excitement of the kill or hunt. Herding, as among the Navajos, is rarely if ever dangerous, and yet caring for domestic animals is the major interest and pastime for pastoralists.

Some have suggested that hunting also takes men out of the local area to places far away not often or consistently visited by women. While hunting, men may meet other peoples, some of whom may be friendly and potential trading partners and others not (e.g., in reference to the Mapuche of Chile, Dillehay 1985, personal communication). According to R. Rosaldo (1982:36), "Illongots say that men surpass women in their 'knowledge' because their distant treks in hunting and raiding have taken them to see more places away from their homes and gardens." Although perhaps true for sedentary groups, it is not a cross-culturally consistent factor, particularly with respect to nomadic hunter–gatherers and horticulturalists. For instance, gathering berries and other activities carried out by women among many sedentary Northwest Coast groups like the Coastal Salish traditionally took them to distant locations (usually with men who would hunt and/or fish while the women gathered). Also, demographic data for the !Kung show "that the space occupied over a lifetime does not differ for the two sexes" and that "!Kung men and women have similar knowledge of the larger hunting and gathering territory within which their kin and affines range. Both men and women range out from the camp in the course of their subsistence work and are equally affected by group moves in search of bush food, game and water" (Draper 1975:86). Moreover, hunting treks away from the village among nomadic and semi-sedentary Amazonian horticulturalists include both males and females.

The question still remains: why the status of hunting and meat? How can we account for emerging studies that indicate, for instance, that in some societies good hunters are reproductively more successful? "All the data suggest that good hunters have higher reproductive success than poor hunters. This increase in fitness is due to both increased survivorship of offspring and increased access to extramarital affairs through which illegitimate offspring are produced" (Kaplan and Hill 1985b:132). Access to protein is not the reason for the high cultural value placed on successful hunters since the strong moral commitment to sharing equalizes the variation in quantity of meat consumption between more and less skilled hunters. In addition, fishing, particularly the mass harvesting of anadromous fish among Northwest Coast Indians as but one example, indicates that access to quality protein alone is not a factor on a cross-cultural level because fish contribute quality protein and other nutrients to a diet but are not accorded the prestige that meat is. It is for this very reason that I also reject the optimal foraging model that suggests that, in cost/benefit terms, meat has a higher value than gathered resources (Hawkes, Hill, and O'Connell 1982).

Is the key the sharing of meat (in contrast to plants) as Silberbauer (1981:94) suggested for the G/wi Basarwa? If so, it is not even a culturally consistent pattern. Among the !Kung, according to Lee (1979:118), and among other Basarwa, according to Hitchcock (1982:222), all food, be it gathered or hunted, is shared. The same is true for the Agta of the Philippines (Estioko-Griffin and Griffin 1981b:146) and for other groups as well. Sharing meat then cannot account for the all-pervasive preference attributed to hunting and meat products.

A common assertion is "Whether men prove their virility by hunting and thus gain wives or offer meat to seduce a woman, the theme is an exchange of meat for sex" (Siskind 1973a:234; also see Holmberg 1969). This is thought to produce competition between men and provide incentives for hunting when women are a scarce commodity (Siskind 1973a:236). Basically Siskind suggests that a

scarcity of sex due to a scarcity of women results in the high prestige and demand for meat, also a scarce resource. In an interesting rebuttal, Kensinger (1983, 1984, and this volume, chapter 2) points out recent studies suggesting that native Amazonian communities typically obtain more than twice the amount of protein recommended for minimal health maintenance. Although perhaps scarce in the eyes of the beholder, among Peruvian Cashinahua meat is special not in the quest for sex *per se* but in interpersonal politics (Kensinger 1984). Women may withhold sex for meat, but they also withhold sex for a multiplicity of other reasons as a way to manipulate their husbands (ibid. 3). Men also withhold meat for sex, may refuse sex or, more commonly, may give meat away to sisters or mothers or to cowives to show displeasure. This, Kensinger states, is not economics but domestic politics, refuting Siskind's postulation of the economy of sex.

The differential status accorded to meat and hunting versus plants and horticulture/gathering becomes even more perplexing when one examines the critical factor in mobility and settlement patterns among both hunter–gatherers and horticulturalists. Hunter–gatherers tend to move on the basis of plant resources and horticulturalists tend *not* to move on the basis of plants – in their case, cultivated crops. "The timing and destination of a move by the ǂKade Basarwa are almost 100 percent determined by vegetable food; hunting conditions and distribution of game hardly figure at all in such decisions" (Tanaka 1980:79; also see Cashdan 1984). There are a number of other examples of hunter–gatherers who move on the basis of plant availability. Just one example is the Shoshoni Indians of the Great Basin who divide their year into the four seasons in conjunction with specific plant species availability, and move accordingly (Steward 1938:19). The exploitation of these plants sometimes involved moves of considerable distances. "Gathering, therefore, entailed erratic movements of the Indians. Individual families wandered from spring to fall as the promise of [plant] foods was greater in one locality or another" (ibid. 20). A number of factors are involved in the moving of horticulturalists' villages, but garden soil depletion, i.e. plants, can be a major one (Hames 1983a). Access to and the availability of plants are not the only reasons why people move but may be a critical factor in non-Arctic societies and certainly is a more critical factor than animals in many societies.[3]

It is the mundane, supposedly low-risk, socially insignificant plants that determine when and where people move in many societies, not animals. And it is mobility that affects sociopolitical specialization, stratification, and hierarchies. One characteristic common to many of the more complex societies (that is, typological chiefdoms and state-level societies) is their sedentism and it is plants which often dictate that sedentism.

The following sections should be seen in the spirit in which they are offered; that is, speculation based on data too incomplete and complicated to present here in detail and not yet globally substantiated. They are meant to stimulate thinking and to suggest directions for research rather than to be a treatise on the subject.

Mobility and cultural complexity

One factor that emerges from the above discussion is that subsistence *per se* is not the instrumental variable in many of the sociopolitical differences between hunter–gatherers and horticulturalists. Nor are hunting or animals *per se* the instrumental variables in differing mobility strategies for either group (plants often are). The following explores the relationship between mobility and sociopolitical complexity from a conceptual viewpoint. This brief discussion is presented in order to examine the subtitle of the book – the implications of sedentism.

Cultural complexity has been studied by many anthropologists. Most agree on a definition but many fewer on an understanding of why and how complexity occurs, the latter being particularly important for this book. Why are horticultural societies more often sociopolitically complex than are hunter–gatherer groups? (Although degrees of complexity are present in hunting-gathering groups, I am unaware of a state-level society that is, or ever was, based solely on hunting and gathering.) The key I think is mobility – nomadism versus sedentism. I also know of no past or present autonomous nomadic state-level society (so-called nomadic pastoralist states were actually possible only when based on sedentary village farmers and never comprised an autonomous nomadic group: Khazanov 1983).

Although the following model of the development of complexity was built on the foundation of many anthropologists' writings, as is true of all research, it is its combined features and emphasis that differentiates it from other models. As with all models, that presented below is purposely parsimonious in an attempt to highlight those variables thought to be most influential in the differences between levels of complexity often found in hunter–gatherer versus horticultural populations. Basically complexity is seen as segmentation or an increase in the parts that make up the whole (Kent 1984).

When population density rises, creating packing, because people cannot or do not want to move into less populated areas, there are several options available, as has been pointed out by demographers, geographers, archaeologists, and ethnographers (see Hassan 1981; Carneiro 1970b and elsewhere; Price and Brown 1985; etc.). The option of importance here is restricted mobility, for whatever reason, resulting in sedentism. The preconditions for the development of complexity occur when increasing sedentism is combined with an environment that has potential for local or introduced predictable and storable surpluses of resources[4] either from continual trade or through diffusion and local adoption.

These preconditions can result in an intensification and localization of resource exploitation (i.e., intensive seasonal resource exploitation like that found on the Northwest Coast or in some types of horticulture). This leads to further sedentism and, importantly, aggregation which result in population increases (Lee 1972a and elsewhere; Hassan 1981; and others). As many have pointed out (Lee 1972b; Carneiro 1967; Flannery 1972; Gold-

schmidt 1980; Kent 1984), sedentary aggregations result in the need for an arbiter, one with enough recognized power to settle community disputes that can no longer be mediated by mobility. Just one of many examples is provided by the Hadza who move "to segregate themselves from those with whom they are in conflict," although there are other reasons why they move (Woodburn 1968:106).

The consequence of an arbiter is paramount – incipient political differentiation that is concomitant with changes in social organization. An individual with the political authority to make decisions (informal as that may be) differs slightly though significantly in social status by being the person consulted when problems arise (Kent 1984:215). Leaders with slightly different status (although not necessarily hierarchical status at first) are imperative for settling disputes and for generally ensuring the smooth running of sedentary aggregations.

Eventually incipient social and political differentiation can lead to increased segmentation (i.e., stratification, hierarchies, gender role differentiation, economic diversification – the latter by way of *in situ* development or trade – and activity area segregation). One example can be seen in newly sedentary !Kung among whom "sex roles are more rigidly defined, and at the same time women's work is seen as 'unworthy' of men" (Draper 1975:96). Gender segregation of activities is also more common in sedentary Navajo where the same process is occurring (Kent 1983).

Segmentation results in the incorporation of pan-societal mechanisms which are necessary to integrate the segments. All of this then leads to organizational (social, political, economic) change. For example, according to the model, an increase in the stratification of the sociopolitical organization of a group results in specialization – the leader being a political specialist – and in the development of incipient hierarchies in both the political and social realms. Once institutionalized, a leader may devise methods to exert control over his/her power and subjects. This can result in control over a group's mobility (see Silitshena 1983). The stratification will eventually influence other aspects of culture (e.g., religious, occupational, and economic specialization and eventually hierarchies of various kinds), behavior (e.g., the organization of space), and cultural material (e.g., the organization of objects and the built environment; see Kent 1984:219 and Kent forthcoming).

Much has to be left out of this very brief and incomplete sketch, but these organizational changes may through time result in institutional changes as in formal educational systems. They also can result in a rigidity of segmentation as in class–caste differentiation, and in the development of formal sanctions as in a police force, written laws, etc. All of these together comprise complexity.

Whereas I am not implying that sedentism is the only variable which causes the development of complex societies, I am saying that it is a primary factor, particularly when coupled with aggregation (also see Flannery 1972; Johnson and Earle 1987; Rowley-Conwy 1983, and the papers in Price and Brown 1985 in which variations on this theme are discussed). The sociopolitical organizational changes which result from sedentism and aggregation may then lead to increased segmentation or differentiation and ultimately complexity. Although this latter part of the model is not appropriate to the small-scale farmers discussed in this chapter or the book, it is included here in order to present the total model of complexity, and particularly to point out the crucial role of mobility, especially its reduction, as occurs in sedentism. This permits the understanding of how and why patterned differences exist between horticulturalist and hunter–gatherer gender roles, division of labor, specialization, and hierarchies.

Thus it can be seen that the major differences in terms of complexity between hunter–gatherers and horticulturalists are organizational differences. These sociopolitical organizational differences result, in my opinion, from dissimilar mobility patterns. As pointed out earlier, a primary though not the only difference between mobility patterns is often the distribution and seasonality of plant (or anadromous fish) resources, not animals (the Arctic perhaps being an exception). In one sense, it may be valid to assert that a plant (and anadromous fish) resource base is more of a critical economic factor in the origin of complexity than meat. In other words, plants rather than animals may be more of a reason for mobility and ultimately complexity than is usually acknowledged. If plants are so important in terms of determining mobility and the development of sociopolitical complexity, why then are they perceived as relatively unimportant in most culture-specific contexts?

As I suggested above, as a society becomes more sociopolitically complex, it becomes composed of more parts which are organized in a system of stratification (i.e., parts or segments in a society), hierarchies (ranked segments), sharp gender role differentiation (separate male and female segments), and strict division of labor (gender-distinct labor segments: Kent 1984). I propose that this segmentation is also generalized to an individual's conception of oneself and the universe wherein the human–nonhuman dichotomy becomes more fixed and exclusive. The difference may be viewed in terms of inclusive versus exclusive categorization (see also Douglas 1970).

Therefore the human–nonhuman animal boundary or lack of it is only a manifestation of an us–them boundary. I suggest that what underlies the need to group while splitting, to be an individual while part of a group, to be one and many, is an innate tension between compartmentalization, or segmentation, and holism (Kent 1987).

The development of language, as a compartmentalizing and categorizing device, accentuated the compartmentalization–holism tension characteristic of humans. The compartmentalization–holism tension, I believe, is the basis for the structuring of cross-cultural relationships and interrelationships in culture, behavior, and cultural material, as I describe elsewhere (Kent 1987 – note that I am referring to cross-cultural and not culture-specific relationships and interrelationships). This tension is responsible for the universality of kinship whereby a lone individual is tied

into a larger group. It is responsible also for the universality of religion whereby a sole person is actually part of a larger entity, system, or universe. Simmel (1950:239) wrote that ultimately all restless evolution of society's forms, from its bold outlines to its minute details, is merely the ever-renewed attempt at reconciling the individual with the group. It is this dialectical tension between compartmentalization and holism that structures the relationships between human and nonhuman animals – a relationship that is manifested in conceptualizations expressed in categorization. Further research is needed to ascertain if the degree of inclusiveness or exclusiveness and rigidity or flexibility of these conceptions and macro-categories is the result of the amount of segmentation or differentiation present within a society as I propose. The distinction between categories is thought to be further influenced by the presence/absence of domesticated animals and market-organized economies with specialized occupations (see discussion below). It is not until the adoption of animal domestication that human–nonhuman distinctions and macro-categories become pronounced and rigid.

Animals beyond economics

Western European culture, from which most anthropologists come, sees animal–human relationships primarily in terms of economics – as food and its acquisition (e.g., meat); as labor (e.g., pack animals, hunting dogs, or plough oxen); or as raw material (e.g., hides, bone, etc.).[5] This is a view not shared by all cultures. I have tried to show that the emphasis and status conferred on hunting, hunters, and meat in horticultural as well as hunter–gatherer societies is not cross-culturally based on general subsistence strategies or mobility patterns. As discussed in a previous section, anthropologists have attempted to attribute the symbolic importance or value of hunting and meat to the economic or social value of animals. Below I try instead to link the symbolic value of hunting and meat to cross-cultural symbolic categories of animals. This is not to belittle the importance of meat in supplying dietary protein and minerals (except for Northwest Coast and other societies where fish tend to contribute an equal amount of protein and minerals to the diet, if not more). It is, however, to state that there is a variable on a cross-cultural level beyond economics influencing the value of hunting and meat in these societies. That variable is also the one property that humans and animals share to the exclusion of plants and inanimate objects. I think this, in many cases, can explain the differential preference accorded to most animals over most plants (but see note 6). This is consciously recognized in some groups. "However, at least in the Vaupés territory, all this preoccupation with animals is not concerned with the zoological species and their economic importance but with their symbolic value," a point acknowledged by the shamans (Reichel-Dolmatoff 1985:140).

In many hunter–gatherer and horticulturalist groups without domesticated animals, both human and nonhuman animals are viewed as having an intellect – that is, sentience, sociability, and intelligence – and a common mythical ancestry with humans. Plants do not usually share this combination of traits with humans.[6] The common animal intellect and common origin are expressed in the conception of hunters and hunting that anthropologists have recorded and interpreted within economic and social terms relevant to Western society. On a general, cross-cultural level I do not think that the relationship between humans and nonhuman or wild animals is an economic one, but that it is instead a symbolic and categorical relationship. If the relationship with animals were primarily economic, hunting would be valued as gathering is. It is only the relationship between plants and humans that is mostly economic; not that between wild animals and humans. This is not to imply that there is never any symbolism attached to plants and humans, only to suggest that the relationship between plants and humans is often more economic than symbolic and that the relationship between animals and humans is often more symbolic than economic.

The symbolic and categorical relationship between humans and animals is exposed when beliefs, myths, and legends are examined rather than calories, grams of protein, or gender roles *per se*. The latter may be important in a culture-specific context but not in a general cross-cultural one, which is the focus of this chapter.

The human–nonhuman dichotomy

Discrimination between human and nonhuman animals is much less distinct and straightforward in societies that hunt than in those that do not. As paraphrased by Lévi-Strauss (1963b:101), Rousseau wrote that it is because humans originally felt themselves identical to all those like them including animals that they acquired the tendency to distinguish humans as they distinguish animals – by using the diversity of species as conceptual support for social differentiation. Thus, only human and nonhuman animals are intellectual in an otherwise nonintellectual world, and they are categorized as such.

According to one !Kung origin myth, "in the beginning people and animals were not distinct but all lived together in a single village led by the elephant . . ." (Lee 1984:106). Kūa Basarwa believe that originally humans could intermarry with animals until the former acquired the bow and arrow and began hunting (Vierich 1985, personal communication). Among the Tlingit, Raven grew up virtually indistinguishable from humans and transformed into his bird form only later to escape a flood that killed all humans (Krause 1956:176). In the Netsilik Eskimo beginning "there was no difference between humans and animals. They lived promiscuously; a person could become an animal and vice versa. Both people and animals spoke the same tongue" (Balikci 1970:210). According to Lummi Coastal Salish speakers, the first deer was transformed from a human (Stern 1934). To the Amazonian horticultural Sharanahua, peccaries were once humans (Siskind 1973b:153; and others). Many other cross-cultural examples are available.

That animals were as intelligent as humans, or more so, at least in the past, if not in the present, might result from the perceived common ancestry that goes beyond the often teleological view of a human–nonhuman animal ancestry common in Western thought. Several examples may illustrate this. For the Ainu, bears are able to provide food and look after the general welfare of humans, wolves provide food for humans and cure serious illnesses, owls foretell specific events, etc. (Ohnuki-Tierney 1974:90–97). It is important to note that despite being used as food, these animals aid humans in ways other fellow humans cannot. Good spirits for the Campa Indians of Peru can assume the guise of certain animal species (Weiss 1972). Tulalip Coastal Salish informants told me in 1980 of their continued belief in the well known concept of animal spirit helpers who give "power" (often abilities) to humans whom the animals choose by having earned their respect or pity. These animals also give humans their spirit song and dance. Here animals are able to help humans in a noneconomic and suprahuman way.

Because of this common intellectual heritage animals not only at one time in the mythical past were as intelligent as humans, or more so, but also are thought to be intelligent today; and it may be this that makes the human–nonhuman animal distinction more vague in many societies than it is in Western European culture or among other groups who do not hunt and have instead domesticated animals (see below for discussion of the latter). For example, G/wi Basarwa anthropomorphize animal behavior. Animals are thought to have customs similar to humans, such as hartebeest customs, and animals possess language and attributes of human personality and character (Silberbauer 1981:64–67). They can be contrary, courageous, cheating, cowardly, insolent, and/or conceited. In addition, the G/wi "project their own values and habits in explaining other types of mammal behavior. The gregarious species of antelope . . . are believed to discuss their migrations in much the same way as does a G/wi band, and the 'nursery' herds of springbok are seen as a parallel to the G/wi custom of leaving the children in the care of a campkeeper during the day" (ibid. 67). Special capabilities of some animals are believed by the G/wi to have been arrived at by rational thought and then institutionalized into species' customs just as human customs developed (ibid. 64). Animals are thought to be able to understand a little of the G/wi language as humans can animal communication, but some animals have knowledge that is beyond humans, such as the length of the rainy season, location of the best rainfall, and when a hunter will or will not be successful (ibid.). Plants on the other hand "have no power of locomotion, do not feel pain or experience pleasure and have neither will nor intelligence" (ibid. 77). Urton (1985:9) notes that it is no coincidence that the South American human–animal metaphors discussed in the book he edited all refer overwhelmingly to asserted similarities between humans and animals. This is in contrast to, for example, Western culture which tends to emphasize the differences between humans and animals.

Among many groups the vagueness of the human–nonhuman animal distinction goes beyond perceived mental and physical similarities to include spiritual ones as well. To Netsilik Eskimos, both humans and animals have souls (Balikci 1970:198). "As with human souls after death, the hunter had to pay homage to the animal he killed by observing a number of rigorous taboos. A failure in any of these observances could turn an animal soul into a crooked spirit . . ." (ibid. 200). According to the Chipewyan, animals are killed only by their consent and an animal must consent to its own death in order for a hunter to be successful (Sharp 1981:226).

Animals and humans can be seen as comprising a single category – there is no distinction between them beyond species-specific characteristics. In some groups, hunters have to give a brief prayer of thanks to the animal just killed for giving up its life so that the hunter and kin may eat. This may be seen as transforming the hunting act of killing from murder to self-sacrifice on the part of the animal so that humans will have food to eat.

The pedagogical role of animals toward humans has often been underestimated (Dillehay 1985, personal communication). Common themes in mythology are animals teaching humans customs, skills, and knowledge which are necessary and often vital for survival. Examples are plentiful – Red Squirrel (in some versions Toucan) made the sacred *He* instrument for all humans according to horticultural Colombian Barasana Indians (S. Hugh-Jones 1979:285). Tlingit hunter–gatherers say, "As Raven lived and acted, so we must also behave" (Krause 1956:174). Humans actually had to be acceptable and accepted by animals before the First Made Person of the Southwestern United States Tewa horticulturalists could originate (Ortiz 1969:14). "The animals gave him [the First Made Person] a bow and arrows and a quiver, dressed him in buckskin, painted his face black, and tied the feathers of the carrion-eaters on his hair," all characteristics of Tewa humans (ibid.). A Mapuche elder said that non-Indians have been in Chile only a short time and therefore know little about animals, while "We have lived here for thousands of years and the animals taught us and we have passed their knowledge from generation to generation" (Dillehay and Gordon 1977:306).

It can then be seen that the human–nonhuman animal dichotomy so sharp in Western civilization is not at all as clear or even present in all societies. Hunter–gatherers and small-scale farmers who hunt do not differentiate between humans and nonhumans in the same way as do Europeans/Euroamericans. Nonhuman animals are seen as having intellectual capabilities that are similar to or sometimes even surpass those of humans.

Creating heterogeneity out of homogeneity

Modern humans are all one species, all *Homo sapiens sapiens*. As observed by Lévi-Strauss (1963b; 1966) and others, distinguishing within the human species – between them and us, individual and group – can be accomplished in nonpluralistic societies only by creating artificial boundaries, e.g., clans, moieties, and others. Culturally defined minorities and races (race being a cultural concept based on physical attributes) in complex societies allow otherwise homogeneous humans to separate and define themselves. Such pluralism does not exist as readily in less sociopolitically complex societies, although the presence of lineages, phratries, and kindreds may be one manifestation of the need to define oneself in relation to others. In these societies, to which belong most groups who hunt, animal species are often used to create an artificial heterogeneity within homogeneity. This is necessary for identities and boundaries in otherwise homogeneous groups (see Lévi-Strauss 1963b).

Elsewhere I have tried to show that there is an innate tension between the necessity of seeing oneself as an individual and seeing oneself as a part of a group (Kent 1987). Lévi-Strauss described this tension:

> All the members of the species *Homo sapiens* are logically comparable to the members of any other animal or plant species. However, social life effects a strange transformation in this system, for it encourages each biological individual to develop a personality; and this is a notion no longer recalling specimens within a variety but rather types of varieties or of species, probably not found in nature ... and which could be termed "mono-individual." (1966:214)

This tension is mediated through creating heterogeneity out of homogeneity so that both individuals and groups exist simultaneously in what would otherwise be a society of individuals and no groups, or a society of one group and no individuals. Neither of these can occur for humans.

I see this phenomenon as related to the necessity for categorization and classification common to language which is then generalized to thought and nonlinguistic conceptions. Although all animals classify the world around them – at least in a rudimentary way as between edible and nonedible, danger and non-danger – none do it to the extent and with the elaboration that humans do. Humans do so in part because of the acquisition and development of complex language which, by its nature, requires complex categorization and classification (Brown 1958; Kent 1984).

The only truly absolute difference between human and nonhuman animals is the possession of culture, including complex language. In those small-scale societies where animals are thought to have culture and, in some, to have actually been the ones to teach originally noncultural humans culture, the distinction between human–nonhuman animals is vague and the level of the dichotomy or segmentation that exists in other more complex groups nonexistent (table 1.1). It is the humanity of animals and inhumanity of humans (i.e., lack of culture) that is often a theme stressed in myths. I submit that in these societies *human and nonhuman animals are in the same macro-category* – that is, a macro-category of intellectual creature. I suggest that humans and animals together form one macro-group of intellectual beings: to distinguish oneself it is necessary only to differentiate between type of animal or species – be it *Homo sapiens, Cervus, Ursus, Odocoileus*, or *Raphicerus*. Of course humans are not the same as rabbits, any more than rabbits are coyotes – but all are parts of a single macro-category of Animal. A dichotomy between human and nonhuman animals is present in groups that have domesticated animals, unlike the ones described in this chapter. Plants and inanimate objects are not intellectual or sentient and therefore tend to be grouped in categories separate from animals (human and otherwise).

There are many examples. One can be found among the Maya who have a few domesticated animals. "Since he [the Maya] shares this 'soul' in a one-to-one manner with his animal spirit, he lives out his entire life-span believing that an essential part of him is permanently attached to a jaguar, coyote, ocelot, opossum, or other wild animal that is somewhere in the domain of Nature" (Vogt 1970:1159). However, and consistent with the proposed

Table 1.1.   Suggested human–nonhuman animal categorization as seen by different societies

Type of society	Animal category 1	Animal category 2	Animal category3
Societies that do not hunt and have domesticated animals	Humans*	Wild animals	Domesticated animals
Societies that regularly hunt and have domesticated animals	Humans* Wild animals*	Domesticated animals	
Societies that regularly hunt and do not have domesticated animals	Humans* Animals*		

* Intellectual entities.

model, Zinacantan Maya with domesticated animals separate humans, animal spirit companions, and wild animals through the concept of domesticating the soul. "But, significantly, Nature, in the symbolic form of the wild animal *chanul* [animal spirit companion], is culturalized by the *chanul* being corralled. Wild animals are not ordinarily found in a corral, but wander quite free in the forest. But in the case of the *chanuletik* they are kept permanently in the series of corrals inside the sacred mountain" (ibid.). These now domesticated wild animals are the ones directly associated with humans as spirit companions, forming the categories of wild animal, domesticated wild animal (or *chanuletik*, the spirit companion), domesticated nonwild animal (chickens, turkeys, etc.), and human. Wild plants are ceremonially significant and it "is worth noting that for all important ritual occasions wild plants . . . are essential for communication with the gods" (ibid. 1161). They thus have a practical purpose – communication with the gods. Unlike animals, domesticated or wild plants are not spirit companions of humans. They are important in Mayan life but are categorically different from animals. There is a fundamental difference between humans, wild animals, domesticated wild animals or spirit companions, domesticated nonwild animals, and plants. This differs from small-scale societies without animal domestication where humans are not differentiated from wild animals but instead form one category of intellectual beings which is subdivided into species – humans, springbok, duiker, and so on – as described above for the Basarwa and other groups. For example, among the Amazonian Eastern Turkanoans who do not have domesticated animals, "Animals play the role of people… they are *like* animals. The animal image is used to describe 'other' people – not only 'other' women but other tribes" (Reichel-Dolmatoff 1985:109; original emphasis).

It is interesting that the same process – delineating self and group boundaries and identities within a society – results in two opposites. In one, nonhuman animals are given humanity, making

them quasi-human in order that the different animal species be usable to delineate between self and others. In the other, where animals have been domesticated and objectified (with some exceptions, most prominent in pluralistic, market economy, segmented, state-level societies as discussed below), animals cannot be given humanity any more than a plant or rock can be. In these societies, humans are distinguished among themselves by cultural strata and other artificial creations. An especially interesting but unfortunate consequence of the extreme dichotomy present in some segmented societies with rigid hierarchies has been the tendency for the exclusion of some humans from the intellectual human category. In these cases, specific humans are stripped of their humanity and seen as only quasi-human animals (e.g. slaves, various minorities, "untouchables").

The cross-cultural importance of hunting and hunters is not a matter of nonhuman animals belonging to an ambiguous category – neither totally human nor totally nonhuman – nor a matter of indistinct or fuzzy human–nonhuman boundaries, *à la* Douglas (1966; 1975). Instead, the demarcation is quite clear – there is no boundary between human and nonhuman animals in small-scale societies without domesticated animals, only between the human species and various other animals species (table 1.1). That is, all animals are put together as a single macro-category – intellectual, sapient, sentient beings – which is divided on the basis of animal species, with some species being inherently more important, intelligent, or useful than others just as some humans have various capabilities. In other words, humans and other species of animals are separated on the basis of species-specific characteristics, just as any other two types of animals are differentiated, but not on the basis of being human–nonhuman. In general, animals (intellectual) are considered to be separate and distinct from plants (nonintellectual) and form two disparate categories – hence the conceptual difference between animals and plants (see note 6).

This is not to deny the importance of using nonhuman animals to define what human animals are, but is to suggest that in these societies humans as a group do not see themselves as more different than they see any other specific group of animals. Humans are obviously not peccaries just as peccaries are obviously not jaguars; but all are animals. Humans often then classify themselves into finer micro-categories than they do other types of animals; nevertheless I am not interested here in how they classify themselves within the group humans (there is a relatively large body of literature on this subject), but in how they classify themselves between the group, human, and other groups, e.g. animal.

From humanity to domestication: animals' new classification in compartmentalized societies

Having described the human–nonhuman or wild animal dichotomy at some length, I will now only briefly mention the human–domesticated nonhuman animal–wild animal relationship in order to complete the discussion (categories 1, 2, and 3 in table 1.1). Once animals become domesticated, they tend no longer to be categorized as animals *per se* – sapient, sentient beings like their wild counterparts. Animals, once domesticated, particularly when they constitute the sole source of meat, are viewed more like plants, in the sense of having no intellect, than like humans, with an intellect. In some societies, such as the Western one, domesticated and nondomesticated or wild animals tend to be classified in categories distinctly separate and different from humans (table 1.1).

In societies that hunt and do not have domesticated animals, humans and nondomesticated, that is wild, animals tend to be in the same macro-group. However, I suggest in societies that regularly hunt and have animal husbandry, domesticated animals tend to be seen as belonging to a separate category while wild animals and humans belong to the same category (table 1.1). It may be that as people became less mobile in the past, some animals also became less mobile as in the case of domesticated animals. In these more complex, sedentary societies, domesticated animals lost the intellect that was attributed to their wild, still free-roaming counterparts. Domesticated animals therefore represent a different category of animal – not human and not wild – that is, a nonintellectual animal.

Evidence for this suggestion can be seen in some Philippine groups. In these groups, humans and wild animals are associated through the good spirits and supernatural aid of the latter in contrast to domesticated animals which are never associated with spirits or anything supernatural (Bacdayan 1985, personal communication). In these cases, there is a sharp distinction between domesticated animals and humans and wild animals. Domesticated animals tend not to portray humans or vice versa in myths. They also tend not to be intellectual or cultural in contrast to wild animals and humans. A good example is discussed by Rosman and Rubel in chapter 3, this volume. The Mafulu of New Guinea maintain domestic pigs and hunt wild pigs which, physically, do not differ at all, *but the wild and domestic pigs are categorically very different*. Only domestic pigs can be used for certain ceremonies, such as the important mortuary ceremony, and they cannot be eaten by their owners, who host the ceremony, but must be given to the guests (chapter 3). In contrast, for the male purificatory rite, only wild pigs can be used and they can be cooked and eaten only by adult males (ibid.). In fact, "Despite the fact that Williamson points out the lack of difference between wild and village pigs, he reports that the Mafulu distinguish between these two kinds of pigs culturally" (ibid.). Moreover, Rosman and Rubel write in chapter 3 that the "same animal, the pig, occupies two clearly separate cognitive categories in the Mafulu mind, representing two diametrically opposed ideas – the wild and the village."

Furthermore, in New Guinea taxonomic differences between other wild and domestic animals have been noted. Bulmer (1967) states that domestic pigs are rarely referenced in the mythology, except in incidental references to being cooked and eaten (ibid.). He also points out that domestic pigs are categorically subhuman or nonhuman in contrast to wild animals which are categorically quasi-human (ibid.). Specific species are, in fact, referred to as sisters and cross-cousins (ibid.). Among Thai rice peasant cultivators with domesticated animals, wild and domesticated animals are categorized separately from each other *and* from humans as well (Tambiah 1969:450). The human–nonhuman dichotomy is additionally quite pronounced as it is in Western culture (Tambiah 1969), which is what would be predicted from the model presented here (table 1.1).

Domesticated animals become socially, ritually, politically, and economically valuable in a way different from wild animals – they become analogous to objects. I suggest that the status of domesticated, in contrast to undomesticated, pigs changes to that of object as they become more important as stores of wealth. For instance, domesticated pigs are seen as objects when used for bridewealth or when Big Men use them to validate their sociopolitical status through feasts and ceremonies. Despite the affection and devotion dedicated, for example, to Navajo sheep or Nuer cattle, I think among many groups domesticated animals become objects – and humans can have great affection for objects. While it is true that many farm children name their animals, note their personality quirks, talk to them, and so on, it is equally true that a number of people also name their cars, note their quirks, and talk to them, and yet cars are still classified as objects! Not all groups display the same attachment to objects any more than all groups, pastoralists or not, have a similar preoccupation with their domestic animals, so variation in both should be expected. In fact, Solway (1986:219) has noted for the Bakgalagadi pastoralists of Botswana that "Clearly the emotional attachment people have to their animals is not based on the animal's having any pet qualities, but in the social and economic benefits deriving from the animals."

I think there is a further distancing between humans and domestic animals that ultimately is generalized to all animals, wild and not wild, in societies where specialists care for, butcher, and sell animals. Market exchange systems emphasize the economic role of animals. This has been documented by Solway for the Bakgalagadi:

> Naming animals and training them to respond to their names is a constant process. An animal that responds to its name is more easily herded, milked, and made to haul a load. The process of naming involves consistent contact and familiarity between animals and humans, and it contributes to the development of a symbiotic relationship between the two. When animals are kept primarily for selling, rather than subsistence, the quantity of interaction between animals and people lessens and the relationship changes qualitatively. Naming then becomes unnecessary; some households name only a portion of their herd, and one Dutlwe herder has totally abandoned naming. (Solway 1986:224)

Conclusions and assessment

Western culture divides human animals, nonhuman wild animals, nonhuman domesticated animals, and plants into separate and mutually exclusive macro-categories. As a result, anthropologists have wondered why the acquisition of nonhuman animals (hunting and meat) and plants (gathering and farming) are seen as different in various cultures since each represents a distinctive but comparable category apart from humans within the Western cognitive framework. Both plants and animals are essential components of human diets, as Sponsel describes in detail in chapter 4, and yet animals, meat, and hunting are cross-culturally deemed more important than plants. I have tried to suggest one cross-cultural reason for why animals and hunting are ascribed more value and status than plants and gathering. Hunter–gatherers and farmers without domesticated animals who hunt have only two separate and mutually exclusive macro-categories – all intellectual animals including humans, and nonintellectual plants. This division into different macro-categories of intellectual and nonintellectual is the reason, I think, why the acquisition of each is seen, *on a cross-cultural level*, as fundamentally different.

Since the value ascribed to meat and hunting is a cross-cultural phenomenon, a cross-cultural understanding is necessary. I have suggested that there is a tendency for animals to be viewed as less intellectual (intelligent and sentient) as groups become more segmented, categories become more exclusive than inclusive, and the human–nonhuman animal interaction is dominated by domesticated, rather than wild, animals. Plants and inanimate objects are not usually seen as intellectual by many groups (although see note 6). Therefore the conception of oppositions between hunting and gathering–farming; meat and vegetable; hunter and gatherer–farmer is fundamentally different. This is the case until domesticated animals become so integrated within a society that animals are no longer hunted and are, in some respects, categorically similar to objects. It is my opinion that, *cross-culturally*, hunting is differentiated from gathering–farming *not* because hunting is seen as fundamentally more dangerous, exciting, socially important, and so on; but because animals are intellectual

beings grouped with humans. This is in contrast to nonintellectual plants that compose a separate and distinct category. It is because of the cross-cultural intellectual status of animals in these societies that they are then perceived on the culture-specific level as more dangerous, exciting, economically, and/or socially important than plants. The dichotomy between human–nonhuman animals is accentuated by animal husbandry where domestic animals are removed from the intellectual beings category of humans and wild animals and put in the object (or no intellect) category.

Culture-specific studies, like many of the chapters that follow, result in culture-specific explanations and understandings, creating diversity out of cross-cultural explanations and understandings. The cross-cultural study presented here attempts to provide context for the following culture-specific studies that cover a range of issues pertaining to farmers as hunters with reduced mobility.

Cross-cultural studies do not in any way validate or invalidate culture-specific ones – they are just different levels of analysis; and the two types are not mutually exclusive, except in the minds of some anthropologists. Together they present the whole picture and provide more complete explanations and deeper understandings. However, they are today rare to nonexistent perhaps because of the strength and conviction of practitioners of one theoretical orientation over those of another. Particularistic views can provide only partial answers and meanings, whereas holistic views sacrifice details and diversity for generalities and universals. I think the complex study of humans must encompass both approaches and hope that this will be the direction of future research. One level of analysis should not totally ignore the other, for the abstract and general is based on the concrete and particular. This chapter is intended to provide the general context for the chapters that follow. Together the chapters form a book that examines farmers as hunters from different levels of analysis – cross-cultural and culture-specific. This permits insights into the role of hunters and hunting in horticulturalist societies.

The reader will discover that many of the authors read and commented on each other's essays, which integrates the book more than is usual in edited volumes. The chapters are grouped according to the abstract nature of their content, beginning with this essay and concluding with the spatial patterning of activity areas at horticulturalist sites. It is in this way that the reader can explore the many fascinating facets of farmers who hunt.

Notes

I would like to sincerely thank Bill Vickers, Mike Lambert, John Speth, Ken Kensinger, Tom Dillehay, Sara Quandt, Ken Hirth, Fekri Hassan, Andy Hofling, Ellen Lewin, and an anonymous reviewer for Cambridge University Press for their thoughtful and insightful comments on various drafts of this paper. Any shortcomings, however, are solely my responsibility.

1 The Basarwa have been called Bushmen and more recently San, although they are referred to as Basarwa in the dominant native official Setswana language, including that used by the government of Botswana (Vierich 1982:213). Particularly since they refer to

themselves as Basarwa in Setswana, Basarwa is used throughout this paper to refer to what others have labeled as Bushmen or San.

2 Among most Inuit groups, "When an individual excelled through his abilities or luck, he would disparage his success or at least not boast of it" (Oswalt 1967:205).

3 The Ihaya Agta described in chapter 6 provide an interesting exception because they sell their meat to non-Agta farmers in exchange for all their plant food. Thus they do not exploit any plant resources for food and obviously as a result do not move in accordance with plant species availability. Even so, these Agta are portrayed as hunting in order to get meat to trade for corn, rice, and roots – in other words, hunting ultimately to acquire plant resources.

4 The role of storage in the development of complexity and other changes among hunter–gatherers has been discussed by a number of scholars including Ingold (1983) and Testart (1982).

5 Unlike some anthropologists, I believe that dogs are inedible in Western European society not because to do so would be cannibalism or because they occupy an ambiguous category between humans and animals (Douglas 1966), but rather because to do so would be to change the nature of the relationship between human and animal from noneconomic to economic. By definition, a pet is not edible (that is, not an economic resource). *Webster's Dictionary* defines pet as "a domesticated animal *kept for pleasure rather than utility*" (Mish 1985:879; emphasis added). Thus pigs in New Guinea, despite being cuddled by humans, are by definition not pets because they are an economic resource. Pets are categorized differently from other domestic animals and are, by the implied definition of a pet, not food.

Pets are seen as companions, friends, and protectors; so, also, in hunting societies that do not practice animal husbandry, are certain wild animals that are *not* classified as pets – and yet the wild animals *are* eaten. It is not that hunting societies are more callous to animals, they just do not categorize the same animals as pets and therefore as not edible. Note that this does not apply to instances where anthropologists have classified people's specific animals as pets and their behavior toward them as that toward pets, since the natives may or may not classify such behavior as that reserved for pets or classify the animals as pets. Naming and caring for specific individual animals does not necessarily confer pet status. For example, in New Guinea pigs are petted in order to be tamed, not because they are considered pets, as is implied by petting in Western society (Rosman and Rubel, this volume, chapter 3). This distinction has been noted among South American horticulturalists:

It seems crucial to me to make a sharp distinction between commensal association per se and those fosterings of creatures which have a marked nonutilitarian character, such as that expressed in our category "pet." Thus, the Bororo indigenously had domesticated dogs . . . Although these animals live in conditions of great intimacy with their masters . . . they are practically never the object of any affectionate regard. [Dogs are used in hunting.]

[In contrast to the dog is the tamed macaw which is treated and is categorized as a pet.] Inquiries into the possibilities of eating domesticated macaws . . . occasioned expressions of intense repugnance whereas the same suggestion concerning dogs was regarded as bizarre but not unconsiderable. (Crocker 1985:32)

It is further pointed out that pet macaws are inherited as property along with ritual paraphernalia (Crocker 1985:32). The domesticated macaws form a subset of the domesticated animal-

object–possession category because they are defined as pets. They are, then, by definition inedible (see Leach 1964:26 and Sahlins 1976:175 for different perspectives). Domestic cattle among the Nuer, New Guinea pigs, and so on, are not classified as pets and therefore, even though embodied with meaning and social, political, and ritual importance, are edible.

6 There are some horticultural groups with domesticated animals in Melanesia among whom wild animals are an inconsequential part of the diet and hunting is very infrequent. Consequently, these groups are not the focus of this chapter. Nonetheless, it was pointed out to me (Kahn 1986, personal communication) that in some of these cultures, people identify themselves with a specific plant, like taro in some groups or yams in others, in contrast to wild animals. In these cases, it may be that the category of intellectual being including humans is shared with taro or yams, rather than with wild animals (note that wild animals do not play a significant role in most of these societies). The similarities of characteristics between wild animals – that are grouped with humans in the same macro-category of intellectual being in some societies – and taro or yams, which I am suggesting are grouped in the same macro-category in these Melanesian groups, warrant further investigation. For example, such plants are given the animal attributes of free movement, intelligence, emotions, and so on. One instance is the common perception that yams move of their own free will. According to a Dobuan islander:

At night they [yams] will come forth from the earth and roam about. For this reason, if we approach a garden at night we tread very quietly. Just as if we startle a man with an abrupt shout . . . he starts back in fear and later is angry – so we approach very quietly at night . . . We wait till the sun has mounted. Then we know they [yams] are back [in the garden]. (Fortune 1963:108)

Yams are thought to be persons. "Like women, they give birth to children" (Fortune 1963:107) and "Yams are persons, with ears" (ibid. 109). Furthermore, yams have human-like emotions such as fear and anger (Fortune 1963:108; 109). Similarly to learning hunting skills in other societies, youngsters play garden. For example, in the Trobriand Islands, "Even small children are often given a toy digging-stick and a miniature axe with which to play at garden work, and they begin to garden seriously at a surprisingly early age" (Malinowski 1935:11).

Also analogous to hunting and meat, taro for the Wamira of Papua New Guinea is the main crop of "social significance, and the taro garden the locus of a man's status and virility" (Kahn 1983:99). It is through the cultivation and exchange of taro that the Wamiran male communicates and manipulates his social status and relationship with others (ibid.). Wamirans classify male and female taro, which are grouped into categories that have the same names as the words for human lineages (Kahn 1986:92). Similar to hunting and wild animals among horticulturalists who hunt, taro is not only associated with males rather than females, but men reproduce themselves through the cultivation of taro in ways that parallel women's reproduction of children (Kahn 1986). In fact, when working in the taro garden, men have to observe the same taboos as women observe when pregnant or lactating (Kahn 1986:118–119). Finally, the "Dobuan will class yams with his own people as personal beings, but he excludes white men. In fact, he has indeed the more friendly feeling for the yams" (Fortune 1963:109). It seems as if plants are endowed with the same attributes as are wild animals in other societies. As with many of the suggestions raised in this chapter, more research is necessary.

Chapter 2

Hunting and male domination in Cashinahua society

Kenneth M. Kensinger

Hunting is the quintessential Cashinahua male socioeconomic activity. It is highly valued because it produces a commodity, meat, which is perceived as scarce, despite an apparent empirical sufficiency. Sex, specifically female sexuality, is also highly valued and perceived as scarce. Furthermore, there is a link between meat and sex in Cashinahua thinking, a link that has been a recurrent theme in the Amazonian literature. Siskind (1973a) has argued that the scarcity of female sexuality is an artificial scarcity created by culture; Murphy (1977:19) has argued that the value of women involves "supervision and control of the sexuality of the female by others, usually men." In this chapter I shall argue that the high value and scarcity of meat parallels the high value and scarcity of female sexuality, and that it is based on male efforts to control women; and furthermore the apparent domination of women by men in Cashinahua society is just as artificial as the scarcity of meat and female sexuality on which it is based.

The Peruvian Cashinahua live in several villages along the banks of the Curanja River (see figure 2.1). (The ethnographic present in this chapter refers to 1955 to 1968.) Each village consists of one or more houses occupied by one or more nuclear or extended families and a total population of between 25 and 100 persons (Kensinger 1977). Hunting and slash-and-burn horticulture, supplemented by gathering and fishing, are the basis of Cashinahua subsistence. Although horticulture provides the bulk of the diet, hunting is viewed by both males and females as the single most important economic activity because meat, the product of the hunt, is the most highly valued component of their diet. The low value given to all other foods, whether produced by women exclusively or by both men and women, corresponds to males' assertions of their natural superiority over women, a superiority based on the fact that men hunt and women do not. Hunting is the only economic activity exclusively pursued by males. Its significance varies with the life cycle of the village. When a new village is established, approximately every five or six years, and before gardens have come into full production, hunting is a more significant source of food than at any other time in the life of the village. This is also the period when hunting is most successful because animals have not yet moved away from the vicinity of human habitation. As a village ages, garden produce becomes more readily available, while game becomes increasingly difficult to find, requiring men to go further afield, and meat becomes more valuable. With more vegetable food available for guests, there is an increase in ceremonial activities during which there is an emphasis on the exchange of meat, requiring special hunts with a concomitant focus on the efforts of males. Decisions to move a village are based on both the reduced availability of game and the lack of sites for new gardens within reasonable proximity of the village.[1]

Only during the rainy season, when men are prevented from hunting by successive days of rain, is there likely to be a day when

Fig. 2.1. The location of the Peruvian Cashinahua

no meat is available. At that time parched maize and/or toasted peanuts are substituted for meat. Following meals that had left me sated, consisting of quantities of maize and plantain gruel, boiled or roasted manioc, toasted peanuts, etc., informants frequently complained that they were hungry, *en bunihaidaki*. Queries regarding the reason for this complaint always elicited the response *en pinsihaidaki, nami yamaki*, "I'm hungry (for meat), there is no meat." Hunger for meat, *pinsi*, contrasts with *buni*, hunger for food, *piti*, which includes both *nami*, meat, and *yunu*, vegetables. Women often attributed children's crying and irritability to their being *pinsi*, and men cited the same cause for their wives' nagging. Even when meat was available, the same complaint could be heard unless the quantity of game brought to the village by hunters exceeded their craving for meat. Most informants insisted that they desired about one kilogram of meat per day, a quantity well above the amount needed for adequate nutrition. My impression is that it is a very rare day when adults consume less than 300–400 grams of animal protein. Although I never collected quantifiable data on food consumption, I did eat most of my meals with the Cashinahua, and I have clear impressions of the quantities of food consumed. I would argue, on the basis of these observations, that the Cashinahua experience no real insufficiency of meat despite their frequent assertions to the contrary. This perceived scarcity of meat in the face of an apparent sufficiency or even abundance has been reported by other researchers in Amazonia (Carneiro 1982; A. Johnson 1982).

I have argued elsewhere (Kensinger 1983) that there are multiple causes for the perceived scarcity and the high value of meat. Meat is highly valued by the Cashinahua because (a) it is part of a cultural tradition – "We eat meat because our fathers and grandfathers ate meat," (b) it is considered good to eat – "Meat tastes good," (c) it is used to create, to maintain and/or facilitate social relationships, and (d) it is the product of the hunt. Hunting serves three important functions for the hunter:

(1)   It is the central feature of male identity. To be a "real man" is to be a successful hunter. The extent of a man's extramarital pursuits and the tranquility of his household are directly related to his success as a hunter.

(2)   It provides a release from the tensions resulting from social life. A man may leave the village "to go hunting" even when there is a good supply of meat. This is particularly true if his relationship with his wife or in-laws is strained. They would complain if he visited his parents' or siblings' households but never do so if he is hunting.

(3)   It gives pleasure. I would submit that some Cashinahua hunters are "addicted" to hunting in the same way that some joggers seem to be addicted to jogging because of the pleasure obtained from the release of endorphins. This argument is, I admit, highly speculative, but I offer for consideration the statement of one old man that "good hunting causes good pain" (Kensinger 1983:129).

To these three motives, I shall now add the argument that the importance of hunting and the high value placed on meat are also related to the apparent domination of females by males. In making such an argument, I must not impose my view of the situation on the Cashinahua. To what extent and in what ways do Cashinahua males actually dominate females? Do Cashinahua females feel that they are dominated by males? To attempt to answer these questions, it is necessary to examine how the Cashinahua view masculinity and femininity, gender roles, and the behaviors associated with them.

Gender: concepts and behaviors[2]

The Cashinahua believe that the difference between males and females is primarily biological. A male has a penis; a woman does not. When a baby is born, the older women assisting with the birth call out either *hinaya*, "It has a penis," or *hinauma*, "It is without a penis." (I have never heard them say in this context *xebiya*, "It has a vagina." The alternate phrasing is *hinauma, xebi hayaki*, "It doesn't have a penis; it has a vagina.") Some informants said that women could not be like men because their penis (i.e., their clitoris) was hidden, *hunu*.[3] When queried about the apparent contradiction in their statements that women do not have penes and their reference to the hidden penis or clitoris, my informants assured me that the clitoris is not a *real* penis. They quickly pointed out that both men and women have breasts but only women have real ones. A real penis gets erect and penetrates vaginas; real breasts enlarge and produce milk. The penis, or the lack thereof, is the central feature around which notions of masculinity and femininity and definitions of gender-specific roles are constructed. The penis (and he who possesses one) is active and assertive, but the vagina (and she who possesses one) is largely passive and restrained. Males are expected to be aggressive and assertive; women, in their dealings with men, are expected to be relatively passive. Men are ambivalent about women who are sexually aggressive, either in the seduction process or in sexual intercourse. They have, say the men, an erect or hot penis (clitoris) which causes them to be aggressive and, like jaguars, they are exciting and dangerous.

Women, unlike men, menstruate, a physiological process which according to the Cashinahua has its origins in a curse placed on women by an incestuous male who had been fatally cursed by his sister before going on a raid. His severed head with the telltale black paint on its face cursed all women as it climbed into the sky to become the moon and each month both men and women are reminded of the consequences of incest.

Menstrual blood is dangerous. At worst, it can cause a man's death through a slow deterioration of his strength and energy. At the very least it results in a loss of his hunting ability by infusing him with a substance, *yupa*, which causes him to miss his shots, makes him inattentive to the dangers of the forest while engaged in sexual fantasies, or gives him a strong odor which drives animals away. The debilitating effects of menstrual blood can be counteracted through a month-long fast which requires abstinence from meat or fish, sweet gruels, any seasoned foods, and from sexual activity, followed by a brief but highly purgative purification ritual.

Menstruating women are not permitted to go into the forest beyond their gardens. To do so would drive the animals deep into the forest. Some informants say that there are spirits that are attracted by the smell of menstrual blood and may kidnap or kill menstruating women who wander into the forest. Others argue that all vaginal fluids have the same potential. In fact, even women who are not menstruating seldom venture into the forest without a male kinsman. Menstruating women are not segregated; they continue to carry out their normal activities, taking care to prevent menstrual blood from getting onto anything with which men might come in contact.

The fact that males have a penis and that females menstruate provides the basis for the division of labor in Cashinahua society. Female tasks are defined as those appropriate for the village and the surrounding region including the gardens, i.e. the area in which menstruating women can move freely without threatening the game supply. Men, however, are free to penetrate the deep forest, the locus of the activity that provides the primary defining ingredient of masculinity, hunting.

Most informants are explicit about the symbolic link between masculinity and hunting; a man's penis is his arrow by which he causes women to die, i.e. to have an orgasm, and his arrow is his penis by which he kills animals. A man who is incapable of having an erection is one whose arrow is broken. Women, having no penis, are incapable of hunting and of protecting themselves. Men, on the other hand, cannot menstruate and therefore are incapable of bearing and nursing children. Notice here the primacy of menstruation rather than childbearing as a defining characteristic of femininity. Because premenarchal and post-menopausal females do not menstruate they are incapable of bearing or nursing children and as a result are not fully female.

Both male and female informants state that the division of labor by gender is to be explained by these biological truths. All tasks are classified as either men's or women's work, and certain tasks are defined as exclusively men's or women's. Men hunt, protect women and children from spiritual and non-spiritual dangers, clear new garden areas from virgin forest, and assure a tranquil village through their political and ritual activities. Women bear and care for children, care for and harvest gardens, cook vegetables and meat, plant and harvest cotton, make hammocks, etc. Fishing and foraging are primarily defined as men's work but women may join in poison fishing expeditions and may forage on their way to or from their gardens. Chopping and carrying firewood and carrying water are primarily defined as women's work but men may assist their wives, mothers, sisters, and mothers-in-law with these tasks without a loss of manliness. The manufacture of all objects is gender-linked (Kensinger 1975).

My female informants provided me with essentially the same reasons as did men when I asked them if women ever hunt, and if not, why not. Women cannot hunt, they said, because they do not know how to hunt. Even if they knew how, they could not go deep into the forest because it is too dangerous for women since spirits might molest them, or because animals would flee from the smell of their vaginas, or because they could not leave their nursing infants alone that long and, if they took them along, their crying would scare the animals away. The only reason cited by men but not by women was that women lack penes.

The identification of men with hunting rather than horticulture reflects, in addition to the symbolic content of hunting, the time and energy expended by men on these activities. Hunting is a year-round activity. Most men spend at least one day in three hunting. Although gardening is also a year-round activity, men's participation in it is seasonal.

No Cashinahua man identifies himself as a horticulturalist although he takes great pride in the gardens he has created. A *man* is a hunter all the time; making gardens is just one of the things a man does as part of the annual routine. To be an indifferent gardener is no reflection on his masculinity, although it makes him less desirable as a husband and son-in-law; to be an indifferent hunter makes him something less than a real man. Surplus garden produce is no substitute for meat as a gift for one's lover. Furthermore, since the products of the garden are a wife's possession, it is she who distributes them.

Although most Cashinahua men complain about the onerousness of making gardens, they never gripe about hunting. Gardening is enervating, hot, and dirty work; hunting is energizing, cool, and cleansing work. Hunting frees a man to pursue his amorous interests; gardening binds him to a wife or wives and her/their mother(s). Hunting is an expression of his manliness; gardening is a responsibility of a married man. The measure of a man is his skill as a hunter, not the size and number of gardens he makes.

Men and hunting

As soon as a boy can walk unassisted, and sometimes before, his father or paternal grandfather gives him a small bow and arrows with which he learns to shoot banana trees, papayas, leaves, insects, lizards, etc. His successes are lauded, his failures are either ignored or gently responded to with instruction. By the time he is five or six he and his peers are shooting at just about anything that moves in the garden surrounding the village, cooking and eating any birds, lizards, and rodents shot during these expeditions. By the time he is ten, he occasionally accompanies his father or another adult on short hunts in the forest where he learns to read animal spoor, to identify animals by sound and smell, and to locate animals as they move through the forest. He also learns how to identify those things, both natural and supernatural, that pose a threat to the hunter and to avoid them or neutralize their potential danger. By thirteen years of age he has learned how to site and build a hunting blind and begins to hunt independently within or just beyond the radius of the village where women are free to move. By fifteen or sixteen he is generally able to hunt like any adult male. Although he has no obligation to provide meat for his family, his catch is widely acknowledged and praised. Women openly talk about what a fine son-in-law he will make and men joke about his desirability as a lover. With the killing of his first tapir, he is recognized as an accomplished hunter and he proudly supervises its butchering. The greater his success as a hunter the wider the swath of his amatory pursuits and the greater his chances of arranging a marriage.

The Cashinahua distinguish three styles of hunting, which I translate here as real, regular, and play hunting.[4]

Real hunting is distinguished largely by its intensity. A man leaves the village at daybreak or shortly thereafter and moves quickly, often at a dogtrot, into the forest. He maintains this pace at least until he is beyond the range at which sounds of the village can be heard; at this point he has reached his hunting territory and is following one of his hunting trails. His eyes constantly scan the forest and his ears are atuned to any signs or sounds of animal movements. A real hunt demands a hunter's full concentration and frequently leaves him exhausted but euphoric. He relentlessly pursues his prey, ignoring the pain from thorns in his feet or insect bites while in the heat of the chase. He pauses only when he has completed his hunt or, after catching an animal that does not satisfy his self-imposed quota, to stash it safely until his return to the village. If he kills a large animal, he returns to the village directly. If not, he hunts until he has reached his quota or become discouraged. He may choose to sit and rest during the heat of the day when there is little animal movement in the forest and chances of scoring a success are minimal, waiting for signs of the resumption of animal movements, or he may forage as he makes his way back to the village.

Following a real hunt, a man generally rests for a day or two, spending most of the time swinging in his hammock or repairing and sharpening his arrows, while recuperating from the physical toll of the hunt. A man rarely returns from a real hunt without having suffered some wound, generally a thorn deeply imbedded in the sole of his foot. Numerous minor to moderately severe injuries occur while hunting and a few days of rest are needed for them to heal before a man can effectively hunt again

(thus explaining some ethnographers' observations that men spend much time just sitting around while their wives work, e.g. Siskind [1973a, b], Murphy and Murphy [1974], Henley [1982]). Real hunting is hard work. But, for a real man, a Cashinahua, it is more pleasurable than any other activity except perhaps sex.

But not all hunting is real hunting and not all hunters are real hunters. All Cashinahua are regular hunters, at least part of the time, and the majority of hunts are regular hunts. Regular hunting shares most of the characteristics of real hunting, differing from it mainly by being less intense, less arduous, and less prey-specific. The pace of the hunt is more leisurely. The hunter may allow his concentration to lapse, thinking about things other than the hunt. When he sights game, however, he will (unless he is not a good hunter) immediately focus his attention on making the kill. A man generally returns from a regular hunt less battered and tired, and, of course, with less game than from a real hunt. Regular hunts are also less pleasurable. Several men compared the difference between real and regular hunts to that between the excitement of sex with a new lover or wife and sex with a wife of many years.

Either a real or regular hunt may be transformed into the other if the mood of the hunter or the circumstances of the hunt change. Some informants said they always leave the village expecting to have a real hunt; that is the way a real hunter is. Others admitted that they were often reluctant to hunt unless there was a shortage of meat or a need to kill enough game to provide for the needs of their wives, with enough extra to make gifts to their lovers. Such men were said to be regular, *kayabi*, hunters rather than *kuin*, real. Such an admission would never be made in public because real men are supposed to be real hunters.

Play hunting contrasts with real and regular hunting primarily in terms of intent or motivation. It is the hunting a man engages in when he wishes to escape from the nagging of his wife, wives, or mother-in-law, or from the whining or crying of his children, or when he wishes to disengage himself from social interaction in the village. He takes his bow and arrows or shotgun and leaves the village. He may make a hunting blind, or use an old one, where he sits and watches for animals to come to eat fruit or nuts in the trees toward which the blind is oriented. Or he may saunter through the forest, pausing frequently to sit down or to bathe in a small stream. This pattern also occurs among the Mehinacu (Gregor 1977:218–219). Such a hunt is rarely transformed into a real or a regular hunt. Should he encounter game, he shoots it, an unexpected bonus, but the object of play hunting is therapeutic. The pace is always leisurely. Play hunting generally takes place in the afternoon, and may occur after a man has hunted in the morning without success. All my male informants agreed that such hunting, even if it does not produce a catch, allows a man to relax without incurring the disapproval of his wife or mother-in-law that he would experience if he stayed in the village doing nothing or visiting with friends.

No man announces his intention to play hunt. If asked, he says that he is going hunting, leaving ambiguous his intention as to the kind of hunting. All are aware that he would have started shortly after daybreak if he were really serious about the hunt. Furthermore, since such hunts are frequently the pretext for meeting a lover at a prearranged location, most onlookers assume that his target is sexual not animal. (This contrasts with marital daytime sexual activity in which husband and wife leave the village together, saying either that they are going to the garden or that they are going to the forest to defecate, a statement that normally elicits understanding smiles and/or ribald comments.)

Cashinahua males, and I suspect this holds true for those of other Amazonian societies, have created a perception of meat as a scarce commodity by defining hunting as an exclusively male activity, by excluding all women with reproductive potential from hunting territories, and by elevating the social and cultural significance of meat while at the same time denigrating, or at least giving a reduced value to, garden products. They have relegated to themselves control over and access to the resources of the forest beyond the gardens.

Scarcity of sex

Like meat, female sexuality is seen by the Cashinahua as a scarce commodity, even though female as well as male members of the society find sex pleasurable. While men are more verbal about the subject, all my female informants who were willing to talk about it indicated that women enjoy sex as much as men do. Both males and females exhibit considerable ambivalence about sex; males fear the pollution of vaginal fluids and menstrual blood and females fear an unwanted pregnancy. Among both sexes there was some disagreement about how much sex is too much. Some of the men, especially older ones, argued that too much sex could be enervating, particularly for youth, citing the debilitating effect of the intensive and frequent copulation of couples "working" at making a baby. The women's arguments focused on the reduced ability of a woman to manipulate men if she made it too obvious that she liked sex.

Both sexes agreed that there is a scarcity of sex. Men spoke of women as sexually insatiable once aroused, but complained that they withhold their sexual favors in order to manipulate men. Most women said that males are assertive and demanding, opportunistic, predatory, promising more than they can deliver, and more concerned with their own satisfaction than with that of their partner. All informants agreed that mutual satisfaction was desirable. Women reward a sensitive lover with bites and scratches, marks that men wear proudly as insignia of their virility. Males who are inattentive to the desires of their lovers soon find their services no longer in demand. Women often complain that a man talks a better game than he can play, whereas the men say that a woman talks a better game than she is willing to play. Moreover, all women fear an unwanted pregnancy, which could result in a painful abortion or in infanticide of the newborn. It is unlikely that any serious scarcity of sex would result from the preceding factors. Other factors, however, like polygyny, female (but not usually male) infanticide, and an incest taboo that excludes, for both marriage and sex, all persons but members of the kin class opposite-sex-cross-cousins, could result in a scarcity not of sex, but of wives.

Scarcity and domination

We return now to the relationship between the high value and perceived scarcity of meat and the apparent male domination of women. The Cashinahua clearly have an objective sufficiency, if not an abundance, of meat (A. Johnson 1982:415). The perceived scarcity is rooted in cultural rather than biological needs and parallels a perceived scarcity of female sexuality.

The link between food and sex in Cashinahua thought is evident in the way they use language. The vocabulary of eating and drinking, of the hunt, of gardening, and of flora and fauna are all sources of blatant and subtle sexual puns. This fact was brought home to me one day after I had spent several hours transcribing song texts recorded at a dance some days earlier. I was sitting with some Cashinahua and absentmindedly began to sing the songs, which were replaying themselves in my mind. The men guffawed, the women giggled embarrassedly, and I was confused, since the words of the songs seemed to be about vegetables and fruits. They were, but these products symbolize sexual organs, as the men quickly informed me after their laughter subsided. My mistake was in singing the songs outside the proper ritual context.

The link between meat and sex has been a recurrent theme in the literature on Amazonian peoples. Holmberg, in his now classic monograph on the Siriono, stated that "food and sex go hand in hand" (1969:126) and that "while the drive of sex is seldom frustrated to any great extent, it is mobilized largely through the drive of hunger" (ibid. 225). Thus, for the Siriono food was the scarce commodity and males gained access to female sexuality through gifts of meat.

More recently, Siskind (1973a) and Murphy (1977) in related papers have discussed the link between sex and meat. Siskind states that "an artificially or culturally produced scarcity of women provides a density-dependent mechanism that functions to disperse groups of hunting-and-gathering or hunting-and-agriculture populations in accordance with the availability of game, where game is the limiting factor" (1973a:226), and that "the exchange of meat for sex is an economic system, a system in which men strive to be good hunters in competition with other men in order to gain access to women" (ibid. 235). A shortage of female sexuality is created by rules of sexual morality, polygyny, and female infanticide (ibid. 235). Siskind further argues that her hypothesis applies "to hunting populations in which women provide the bulk of the food supply and where it can be established that protein resources are the limiting factor and their procurement the responsibility of men" (ibid. 226–227). Thus, according to Siskind both protein, particularly meat protein, and female sexuality are scarce, but the scarcity of female sexuality is artificial, that of meat is not. Although her argument, based as it is on the assumption of protein deficiency, may not stand up, her attempt to link the shortage of female sexuality and the scarcity of meat has considerable validity. It appears that Sharanahua women are competing for what they perceive to be a scarce commodity, meat, while men compete over another item they perceive as scarce, female sexuality.

The ongoing debate between those arguing that there is a protein deficiency in Amazonia (e.g. Gross 1975, 1982, and 1983;

Harris 1974; Divale and Harris 1976; Ross 1978) and those arguing to the contrary (e.g. Berlin and Markell 1977; Lizot 1977; Chagnon 1983; Chagnon and Hames 1979; Hurault 1972; Aspelin 1975; Beckerman 1979; Hames 1980b; Hames and Vickers 1983; Vickers 1978; Johnson and Behrens 1982)[5] has not demonstrated to my satisfaction that there is, for the most part, any real shortage. A. Johnson (1982:414) has argued that "native Amazonian communities typically obtain more than twice as much protein as recommended for minimal health maintenance." He concludes that "despite an objective 'sufficiency' or even an abundance of food, we find that a perceived scarcity exists that influences individual behavior" (ibid. 415). Carneiro (1982:419) states that "among many Amazonian tribes, the physiological need for protein may be satisfied, and yet people clamor for more meat."[6]

In the same paragraph in which Siskind asserts that "the exchange of meat for sex is an economic system" (1973a:235), she adds, "I know of no real evidence that women are naturally or universally less interested in sex or more interested in meat than are men. On the contrary, in terms of the reality of hunting societies a more natural exchange would be hunted game for vegetable produce" (ibid. 234).[7] Are women less interested in sex or more interested in meat than men? Not among the Cashinahua, if one is to believe their statements. Is it possible that the exchange that takes place is not meat for sex but meat for something else?

Murphy, like Siskind, points out that for sexuality "to be used for social purposes, it must have a certain value placed upon it; in short, it must be in scarce supply" (Murphy 1977:19). He also sees this scarcity as artificially created.

> The value placed upon women is in all societies reinforced by a series of norms that may include, with varying emphasis, the ideal of premarital chastity, a sense of personal modesty, the institution of marriage as the approved outlet for sex, the exclusiveness of sexual rights in marriage, *supervision and control of the sexuality of the female by others, usually men*, and the basic injunction that a woman should withhold access of herself except under defined and sanctioned circumstances. (Murphy 1977:19–20, italics added)

He further points out that in contrast to the culturally contrived shortage of female sexuality, "In nature . . . male sexuality is in short supply" (ibid. 21). This cultural inversion of nature has its roots in the masculinization phase of ego development, "which is an escape from early identification with the mother and the assertion of an autonomous ego. Beyond that, it is a denial of passivity and an attempt to assert active dominance over the maternal sex" (ibid. 22). In the process of trying to allay their fears and anxieties – rooted in childhood and reinforced by constant reminders of their potential inadequacy – by establishing their control of, or at least dominance over, women, men have created a scarcity of female sexuality and thus have given a high value to it.

Must we conclude that in the Amazon basin, men dominate women in an attempt to get even with their mothers? Or, are meat and sex kept artificially scarce by males as part of a grand design to subordinate females? Or, are men and women co-conspirators

in an eternal confidence game based on the exchange of two commodities, meat and sex, the values of which are inflated through culturally created shortages?

The psychosocial aspects of male ego development as they relate to the relationship between males and females fall outside the scope of this chapter. (For an excellent discussion of this problem, see Gregor [1985], particularly his chapter 9.) I am less interested here in the psychodynamics of the situation than I am in the shared perceptual myths that foster the ongoing battle of the sexes, a battle that characterizes Cashinahua, and I suspect most Amazonian, male–female relations.

Cashinahua males readily proclaim the superiority of their masculinity and the inferiority of women – "She is only a woman; she doesn't have a penis." Cashinahua females, however, do not seem to feel inferior. One older informant, in response to a man's taunt that she was "without a penis," said "What is he talking about? He has never given birth to a child and he cannot always produce semen." Although they do not agree on the natural superiority of males and inferiority of females, both men and women do agree that meat and sex are scarce and valuable.

Is Siskind correct, then, in arguing for an "economy of sex," wherein men are motivated to hunt in order to gain access to female sexuality and females withhold their sexual favors unless rewarded with meat? I have said elsewhere that "if we limit our attention only to extramarital affairs among the Cashinahua, the answer would be affirmative. Men are expected to reward their extramarital sexual partners with gifts of meat, beads, perfume, etc." (Kensinger 1984). However, extramarital sex in Cashinahua society seems to be less a case of reciprocity, as postulated by Siskind, than a case of market exchange based on the law of supply and demand. While it is true that the best hunters have, or can have, the most extramarital sex partners, the most sexually active females do not seem to have either a larger cache of trinkets or a more reliable supply of meat. Thus, the initiative is with the male since a female who makes herself readily available lowers the value of her sexuality in the extramarital meat market.

If, however, we focus on the relationship between husbands and wives, Siskind's postulated exchange of meat for sex is not sustained among the Cashinahua, even though the wives of successful hunters generally own more luxury goods and preside more regularly over the distribution of large catches of game than those whose husbands are less successful. Both male and female informants agreed that husbands give wives gardens; wives give husbands cooked food. Husbands give wives a house in a peaceful village; wives give husbands a tranquil, orderly household. Husbands give wives meat; wives give husbands sons, a matter of no small importance in a patrilineal system. Husbands give wives sexual pleasure; wives give husbands sexual pleasure.

Wives do, of course, sometimes withhold sexual favors to motivate their husbands to hunt, but they do the same for other reasons. Moreover, men may withhold sex from their wives, may refuse to hunt, or may give their game to a cowife, sister, or mother as a way of showing displeasure with their wives. And men, at least, seem to see a connection between their wives' sexual response and the amount of meat that they had eaten. I have argued, however, that these responses represent not economics, but domestic politics (Kensinger 1984:3). Within marriage, sex is a self-reciprocal, and meat is exchanged for sons. We must now ask whether or not men and women are starting from positions of equal strength or whether the deck is stacked in favor of men. What is the nature of power and authority in Cashinahua society?

Within the context of the village, no individual or group of individuals has the authority or the power to force any other individual to do anything he/she does not wish to do. Those individuals known as headmen, *xaneibu*, have power by virtue of their ability to persuade others to follow their lead. The same holds within the family. Although a man serves as spokesman for his family within the discussions of the men's circle, he may neither make a commitment on behalf of his wife or children nor coerce them to support the position he takes there. Women, who have the greatest responsibility for childcare, are expected to persuade their children to do what they wish them to do. Resort to physical force by anyone, male or female, adult or child, is considered a graver offense than the behavior that precipitated the action. The Cashinahua are uncomfortable with voices raised in anger. Commands (verb forms with an imperative inflection) are best seen as requests or suggestions, and although the speaker expects compliance, there is little he or she can do if the other person chooses to ignore the order. Despite, or perhaps because of, this state of affairs, Cashinahua villages are neither disorderly nor chaotic. Males and females operate in and have responsibility for different spheres of activities and between them they share the responsibilities for a more or less orderly social life.

For the most part, a man does not interfere with his wife's/wives' domestic activities. He may help by chopping or carrying firewood, getting water, butchering game, taking care of a child, etc., if asked or if he thinks that his wife is not feeling well or is over-burdened with work. A husband rarely intervenes in a squabble between cowives; they are left to settle it themselves.

The failure of a wife to fulfill her responsibilities rarely results in comment from her husband unless he is greatly inconvenienced by it, nor is he likely to speak approvingly to her if she does her job well. The way a wife carries out her responsibilities is more likely to elicit comments from others, particularly other women, than from her husband. Only when there are considerable strains on a marriage is a man likely to comment openly about his wife's inadequacies as the manager of the house and gardens. How, when, and how well she carries out her tasks are her problem, not his.

Cashinahua women also control their own sexuality and fertility. A woman is free to have extramarital affairs so long as she is discreet about them and does not refuse her husband sexual access. If he provides her with gardens and game, she is expected to be sexually available to her husband unless sex is interdicted by menstruation, the later stages of pregnancy, birth or other taboos, and during the early infancy of their nursing child. There is disagreement among and between men and women about how often is often enough. Women have a right to expect to have sex with their husbands; wives, often cowives, frequently complain that their husbands are ignoring them sexually. They have the right, of course, to seek sexual satisfaction with other men, and many do. But as they get older and are less attractive to other males, or if they do not want to bother with the problems of arranging and carrying out an extramarital affair, they are likely to take steps to seduce their husbands.

A woman has the responsibility for deciding whether or not to terminate an unwanted pregnancy or to kill the unwanted newborn should she carry the fetus full term. A husband may refuse to accept as his own a newborn child and demand that it be killed, but ultimately the decision is hers. Differences of opinion between husband and wife, particularly when the wife acts in opposition to her husband's wishes, can produce considerable tension between them resulting in alienation and ultimately divorce.

Women have the responsibility for childcare and men rarely intervene in conflicts between mother and child. When tensions develop between a woman and her offspring, other women intervene – frequently the child's maternal grandmother. A man may, but has no obligation to, take care of his child if his wife is busy, sick, or harried, or if it is clear that the mother is exasperated with the child. If there is a disagreement between husband and wife over their child's behavior, her wishes prevail. If he disagrees strongly enough with his wife, he may ask one of his female kinswomen to intervene; he rarely does so himself.

In addition to their economic obligations to provide their wives and immature children with meat and fish and to make the houses, the gardens, all tools used by them and their female kin, and the ceremonial regalia (except for woven objects), men are responsible for maintaining social order within the village, for defending the interests of the village in its relationships with external groups or individuals, and for maintaining harmonious relations with the spirit world.

The men's circle serves as the symbolic, if not the actual, locus for the public phases of these activities, thereby excluding women from participation. It is not, however, the only place where matters of interest to the village are discussed, nor is it the site where most issues are resolved. Rather, it is where matters of interest to the entire community can be and sometimes are discussed. For the most part, conversations in the men's circle are inconsequential, dealing mainly with the weather, hunting, and idle chit-chat about the day's activities.

Most disputes are settled outside the men's circle by the parties themselves, with or without the help of close kin, including women. When they are not settled at this level, there generally is a period during which both sexes use informal methods such as gossip, exhortation, shaming, etc., in order to bring the miscreants into line. Only when the problem is seen to pose a serious threat to the health, safety, and/or tranquillity of the community at large is it discussed in the men's circle. Although formally excluded from the men's circle, women can and frequently do make their views known from their own circle nearby.

Although women control their fertility and are free to enter into extramarital affairs, men are supposed to take the initiative in arranging both marriage and sexual affairs. These matters are not generally discussed in the men's circle unless they result either in an intravillage dispute which the principals and/or their close kin are unable to settle or in intervillage hostilities. For the most part men try to ignore the sexual escapades of other men and even of women unless the behavior becomes so outrageous as to threaten public order. Women play a more significant role than men in social control through gossip,[8] and if that fails to have the desired effect, through public scorning and scolding of the miscreants.

Men are responsible for scheduling the public rituals designed to maintain harmonious relations with the spirits. Men are frequently loath to initiate these rituals because they require large quantities of meat and thus additional, intensive, hunting. Women, therefore, frequently become the instigators by taunting, cajoling, or trying to shame the men into carrying out their responsibilities. But men make the decision to hold the rituals, schedule them, and play the major roles in them. Even the timing of the subsidiary rituals for girls within the initiation rites for which women are responsible, but from which men are excluded as participants but not observers, is determined by the larger ritual process controlled by males.

Although both males and females may interact with spirits and both may become shamans whose power and knowledge is gained largely through dreaming (Kensinger 1974), only males may drink the hallucinogenic beverage *nishi pae* in order to communicate with the spirits on behalf of the community. Women are also not permitted to use tobacco snuff or alcoholic drinks, both of which are viewed as recreational drugs associated with the spirits.

Finally, men are responsible for external relations with other Cashinahua villages, other tribal peoples, and foreigners. Except when other villages are invited to participate in public rituals, at most twice in any year, most contacts between Cashinahua villages are contacts between individuals or families. Contacts with non-Cashinahua are infrequent and are always between small groups of men or less frequently a family when traveling up or down river to hunt or trade.

Cashinahua males clearly dominate the public arena and assert their right to do so based on their superiority over women. However, even in those areas over which they acknowledge male control, women exercise substantial influence on the course of events from behind the scenes. Men frequently discuss important matters with their female kinswomen, particularly their wives and mothers. At the same time, women have virtual autonomy and control over significant areas of their lives. They own and control their houses and gardens. They control their fertility and, within certain limits, are as free as males to engage in extramarital affairs. And, finally, they are responsible for and have control over their young offspring. Thus, it would appear that like the shortage of meat and of female sexuality, male domination in Cashinahua society is a myth, an artifice.

Discussion and conclusions

In this chapter I have been concerned with understanding the importance given to hunting in Cashinahua society and have argued that the key is to be found in the relationship between men and women, specifically in men's attempts to assert their domination over women. Meat, the product of the hunt, is defined as both scarce and valuable. Women are prohibited from hunting and thus dependent on men to provide meat for them. But hunting is hard work and men could adequately provide for nutritional needs simply by planting larger gardens (see A. Johnson 1982 and Johnson and Behrens 1982). Motivation for hunting is provided by linking success at hunting with a highly desirable good, female sexuality, which is also defined as scarce and valuable and made so through rules of exogamy, incest, and female restraint. Furthermore, tasks are divided by sex with men responsible for hunting, politics, and religion, and women responsible for gardening and caring for house and children; childbearing of necessity is a female responsibility.

And therein lies the problem. Although men can define themselves as indispensable as hunters and can attempt to control women through controlling their sexuality, men cannot reproduce themselves. Thus, they substitute the appearance of control for that over which they have no control.

That does not mean that these artifices have no effect on the way the Cashinahua behave and on what they believe. Both men and women believe that meat is scarce and valuable, both accept – at least for others – the regulation of sexuality, and for the most part people behave as they are supposed to. However, there is a price to pay.

Males must hunt. Their sense of identity and worth as men is intimately tied to their success as hunters and hunting is at best a gamble. They have no control over the availability of game or of its movements. And the price of losing is a lack of sons, because in their exchange with women, they give meat for sons.

Women must bear children and are responsible for their care for at least four years. A barren woman has little status and, once she has gone through menopause or has lost her desirability as a sexual partner, she must do the tasks no one else wants to do in exchange for food and a place to hang her hammock. Furthermore, unlike men, women are spatially restricted to the village. They leave the village only in the company of their husbands or other women and cannot visit other villages without a male escort. They are excluded from hunting and from formal decision-making. And finally, although they are free to have sexual affairs, they are supposed to exercise restraint, waiting for the male to be the aggressor. Women who instigate affairs and are brazen about it are beaten by their husbands, fathers, or brothers.

Do Cashinahua women feel dominated? What does it mean when they on occasion refer to their husbands as *xaneibu*, the term used for headman? I suggest that for the most part the term conveys for them what it means when a man refers to another man as headman, namely that he is a person whose judgment one trusts and whose leadership one accepts for the time being. Should circumstances change, one's relationship to the leader may change. When a woman is unsatisfied by her relationship with her husband, she may terminate the relationship by putting his possessions outside their house. She keeps the house and the gardens, and has custody of their children until they are old enough to leave her care. Her husband does not own her. And, should he order her to do something, he has no assurance that she will acquiesce. Theirs is a reciprocal relationship, a relationship between opposites but equals. As her *xaneibu*, he is but the first among equals. Thus, within the context of mutual interdependence characteristic of Cashinahua male–female relationships, the high value given to meat and hunting becomes both the symbol of and the justification for male leadership, but not male domination. And, it is males' attempts to dominate rather than lead that fuels the ongoing battle of the sexes in Cashinahua society.

Notes

When Susan Kent asked me to participate in this volume, I felt that it would be a good opportunity to place on the record some of my data on Cashinahua hunting and to add to previous comments on the importance of meat and hunting in Amazonia (Kensinger 1983). I was interested in resolving an apparent paradox in Cashinahua life that has bothered me for some time, namely why, although they get 55 percent or more of their diet from the gardens, the Cashinahua systematically denigrate garden produce while relishing and highly valuing any scrap of meat. Discussions with and criticisms from Tom Gregor, Lucien Hanks, Rhoda Halperin, Emi Ireland, Susan Kent, Patricia Lyon, Don Pollock, and Sally Sugarman helped to sharpen my argument. I alone am responsible for the inadequacies that remain.

1 What constitutes reasonable proximity of the village depends on the age of children within the family. Mothers of nursing infants complain if it takes them more than two hours to go to their garden, harvest manioc and other vegetables, and return to the village.

2 There is some possible bias in the materials to be discussed in this section. My principal informants were men. Although I got data from most of the women throughout my fieldwork on a wide range of topics, there were several topics about which most of my female informants refused to talk. These topics were what both men and women called "women's knowledge," i.e. birth, menstruation, menopause, female physiological disorders, and to a less limited extent sex. When I broached any of these topics, their usual response was "When you bring a wife with you we will teach her those things. Of course, she won't be able to tell you what we teach her because they are women's secrets." There is no comparable body of men's secret knowledge; male knowledge is public information. Children were a significant source of information; their knowledge, often somewhat limited, was generally very accurate. Although not yet sexually active, they provided graphic and detailed descriptions of adult sexual activity. Their play and discussions of gender roles provided me with both information on how men and women were supposed to act and stories about how specific men and women acted. They often told me about extramarital affairs before I heard of them through the adult gossip network.

3 When discussing the meaning of *hunu*, male informants frequently argued that women are like *hunu bai*, hidden gardens, while men are like *bai kuin*, real gardens. Although both types of garden are cleared in virgin forest, *bai kuin* are *xaba*, i.e. large, bright, open, and largely clear of debris, while *hunu bai* are small and, unlike the larger gardens, are made without burning the vegetation cut to make the garden and thus are hidden, dark, and unclean.

4 These terms mask the distinctions made by the Cashinahua but are used for clarity of exposition. The three classes of hunting are based on the contrasts established by three pairs of binary oppositions, namely between $tsaka\ kuin_1$ and $tsaka\ kuinman_1$, $tsaka\ kuin_2$ and $tsaka\ bemakia_2$, and $tsaka\ kayabi_3$ and $tsaka\ bemakia_3$. (The subscripts indicate the number of the polarity [contrast set].) *Kuin* and *kayabi* can both be translated as real, true, primary, etc. *Kuinman* is the negation of $kuin_1$; *bemakia* is the negation of $kuin_2$ and *kayabi*. Polarity 1 defines a category in idealistic terms and although there is universal or nearly universal agreement on classifications using polarity 1, there is also agreement that, because of its relative inflexibility, it is somewhat impractical for dealing with day-to-day problems of a practical sort. Polarity 2, on the other hand, is idiosyncratic; items or behaviors are classified as $kuin_2$ or $bemakia_2$ largely on the basis of personal motives and goals. Agreements between individuals' classifications based on use of polarity 2 reflect personal friendships and/or political alignments; they change as circumstances change. Polarity 3 reflects social agreement. It is pragmatic and represents the social consensus about what is possible in a less than perfect world. As such, it serves as the mediator between the highly idealistic, sociocentric polarity 1 and the idiosyncratic, almost anarchistic, polarity 2. Hunts which I am calling real in this paper correspond to hunts classified as $kuin_1$. Those I am calling regular correspond to those classified as $kayabi_3$, excluding those that are classified as $kuin_1$. Those called play hunting correspond to those hunts classified as $kuin_2$, excluding those that are classified as $kuin_1$ and $kayabi_2$.

5 Although Ross supports the protein deficiency argument, his data (Ross 1978, as cited in Chagnon 1983:87, table 2.1) show that the Jivaroan Achuara among whom he worked have a daily protein consumption of 84.4 grams per capita and of 116.2 grams per adult.

6 Speth and Spielmann (1983) have argued that the problem may not be an adequacy or inadequacy of protein in the diet but the presence of adequate fat.

7 This is precisely what Pollock (1985) has argued for the Culina.

8 Although both men and women gossip, it is considered by the men to be primarily a female practice. Men who gossip are sometimes called women.

Chapter 3

Stalking the wild pig: hunting and horticulture in Papua New Guinea

Abraham Rosman and Paula G. Rubel

In general, once an animal species is domesticated, hunting of the wild or feral form is rarely a major endeavor. Papua New Guinea provides an illuminating exception to this. Tame pigs were brought into the island of New Guinea by people; the present wild pig population found all over the lowlands and most of the rest of the island is descended from feral pigs. The present-day wild pig freely interbreeds with the domesticated form.

The subsistence base for all New Guinea societies is root crop horticulture. There are no societies in New Guinea which only hunt, forage, and collect; every society is dependent to some extent on horticulture. However, hunting is still an important component in many New Guinea societies. The data from New Guinea, therefore, can shed light on the symbolic relationship between horticulture and hunting, on the cultural meanings attributed to these activities, on the symbolic significance of particular animal species which are hunted, and on the cultural distinctions between the cultivated and wild realms. In these horticultural societies, the role of the hunter is stressed ceremonially, and hunting sometimes plays an important role in male rites of passage.

From the ethnographic picture of people's relationship to pigs, domestication is a matter of degree. Human control over the life cycle of the pig involves three different variables. The first relates to breeding – bringing boars and sows together for the purpose of reproduction. The second variable involves the degree of control over the sow at the point at which she drops her litter. The third variable concerns the feeding of pigs, ranging from foraging in the bush to growing crops to feed the pigs.

The most specialized kind of pig husbandry is found among several societies in the highlands, such as the Chimbu, Enga, and Kapauku (see figure 3.1). Among these societies, most boars are gelded and the ungelded few kept penned up are bred with sows in the settlement itself. Piglets are born in the settlement, or in the bush just outside, from which sow and litter are easily retrieved. Fodder is grown especially for the pigs. The whole process is under the control of humans. More typical of highland societies is the situation among the Maring and Kuma where all boars are castrated and tame sows breed with wild boars. Castrated males and sows forage freely during the day and return to the settlement each night to be fed by women, who give them scraps or culled sweet potatoes. Owners of sows must search them out in the bush after they give birth and bring the litter of piglets back to the settlement.

In the next type of situation, breeding is not controlled at all by humans, but pigs are given food. Away from the broad valleys of the productive central highlands, horticulture is less successful, there are fewer and smaller settlements, and the bush is denser and more widespread. Among societies in these areas, since the birth process of the pig is less controlled by humans, retrieval of the sow and her litter is more chancy. This is the situation which

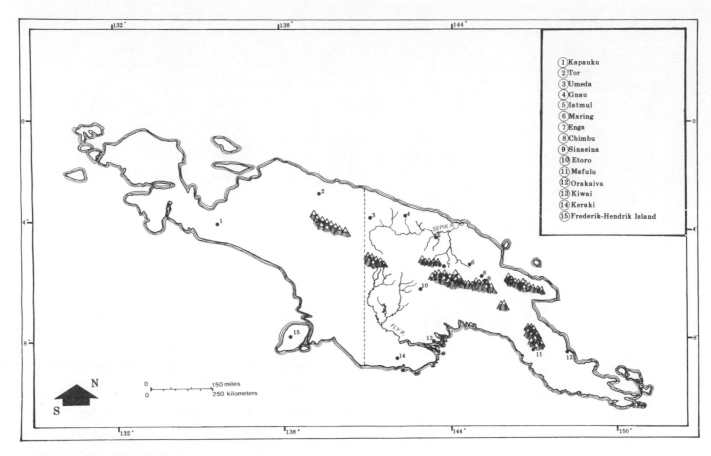

Fig. 3.1. Map of New Guinea

approximates that found among the Iatmul, Orakaiva, and Mafulu. Pigs are fed scraps and, in the case of the Mafulu, tubers from old gardens are fed to the pigs.

At the end of the continuum, humans control neither the breeding nor the birth process, and the pigs subsist solely by foraging. Among societies such as the Keraki, Kiwai, Umeda, and Tor, pigs are reported as present in the village, though not in great numbers. Such pigs are the result of the capture of wild piglets in the bush in the course of hunting. Finally, there are people like those of Frederik-Hendrik Island, from where there are not even reports of the capture and taming of wild piglets. Pigs are only animals which are hunted. In this latter group of societies, hunting of pigs becomes increasingly more important as human control of the breeding and birth process lessens.

To some extent, humans also control another species – cassowaries (*Casuarius casuarius*). Cassowaries are never bred in captivity, but among some societies wild cassowary chicks are captured, tamed, and kept penned up in settlements. Like the pig, the cassowary plays an important role in ceremonial exchange. As will be pointed out in the discussion which follows, the symbolic and ceremonial relationship between humans and pigs, and humans and cassowaries, is significantly different from the relationship between humans and the wide variety of other animal forms (marsupials, birds, and reptiles, etc.) hunted in New Guinea.

A continuum of pig domestication

We have selected for discussion a sample of societies, which exemplify different constellations of the variables relating to pig husbandry presented above.

The Kapauku, in the highlands of Irian Jaya (figure 3.1), are representative of the most elaborate form of pig husbandry. Most male pigs are gelded at the age of two to four months. Only one or two Big Men in a cluster of villages own boars for breeding purposes, and receive fees for the boar's services. If the boar is kept penned in, which means that he must be fed, then the owner is sure that he will receive payments due to him for stud service. The boar may be left to roam freely, but the owner may then be liable for damages caused by his pig and there is no certainty that he will be able to claim payments for his boar's stud service. The owner of the impregnated sow may argue that another boar from elsewhere, or even a wild boar, was responsible. Pospisil observes that "When a sow is expected to give birth to piglets, her movements are carefully watched by her owner so that he can find where she will make a nest for her offspring" (1963a:205). The Kapauku area is densely settled, and virgin forest is found only at quite a distance from the area of settlement. The expectation is that all piglets will be retrieved. Pigs forage for food in the swamp and bush surrounding the village. Sweet potatoes fed to pigs "are classified by the Kapauka as *kidi nota*, 'small root-tubers' unfit for human consumption except in times of starvation" (ibid. 207). After crops have been harvested from the gardens, pigs can enter and eat the remaining forgotten tubers and sweet potato vines. Horticulture among the Kapauku is intensive and produces large surpluses, and this enables them to support a large pig population in relation to the human population. Rearing, caring for, and feeding of the pigs is in the hands of women, while breeding is in the hands of men. Though the Kapauku practice an intensive form of pig husbandry, the number of pigs per capita is low (0.17). However, this low figure was obtained shortly after the village "gave a large pig feast which considerably depleted the local herd. Prior to this feast the herd was about three times as large" (ibid. 217).

Hunting requires long arduous treks away from the areas of settlement, and is not an important economic activity. Pospisil, in fact, notes that hunting for large game such as wild boar, cassowary, marsupials and python "is practiced only as a sport" (1963a:231). However, marsupial meat may be used for the birth ceremony (Pospisil 1963b:65). The meat of wild game is forbidden to women, as are sugar cane and one species of banana, both of which are considered male crops (Pospisil 1963a:110, 127). Cassowaries are of some importance, since cassowary feather headdresses are the required decorations to be worn at dances in the pig feast.

The pig husbandry practices of the Enga are very similar to those of the Kapauku, though the Enga live some distance away in the central highlands of Papua New Guinea (figure 3.1). Waddell (1972) gives a figure of 2.3 pigs per person (which may be slightly higher than average because of delays in the distribution of ceremonial pigs at the time of his census). Most men geld their boars when they are between six to eight weeks old. A few wealthy men keep mature boars for breeding purposes, charging for this service. Breeding boars usually become obstreperous when they reach one and a half or two years at which point they also are gelded. As Meggitt notes, "A boar generally is closely confined at night in or near the owner's men's house" (Meggitt 1958:291). Since boars are allowed to roam freely during the day, and are not therefore deliberately put to the sows when they are in heat, disputes frequently occur as to which boar has sired a litter and thus earned his owner a stud fee. No mention is made of feral pigs growing up in the bush, and indeed little dense bush exists in the neighborhood of settlements, so it would appear that the retrieval rate of piglets from the nests in which they have been born is close to 100 percent. Great care is taken with piglets before they are weaned. Meggitt notes "Women often nurse them and carry them about in net bags when going to the gardens" (1958:291).

In the morning, pigs are fed sweet potato leaves by the women. Pigs are then let out to forage in the abandoned gardens, and in bush and swamp lands. Owing to the intensity of Enga horticulture, "the animals [pigs] are dependent to a very considerable degree on cultivated produce ... Most of the tubers are of inferior quality removed in the later harvesting of the sweet potato mounds, but, as the pig population increases, their owners are obliged to feed them ones of better quality" (Waddell 1972:62). About 80 percent of the pigs are kept in individual stalls in the women's houses at night. A man with more than ten pigs may build a separate small building beside his wife's house to house the excess.

The sexual division of labor operates in pig production. Breeding is the province of men while women deal exclusively with rearing, care, and feeding. Pigs are not given personal names even though women are very close to them, to the point of suckling the piglets. Meggitt attributes the absence of personal names for pigs to the fact that "they change hands too quickly" (1958:287).

Hunting and collecting are of little economic importance. Meggitt characterizes hunting as largely an "ineptly pursued pastime" (1977:8). Waterfowl, pigeons, and cassowaries are hunted for food but only the cassowary is the "prestige meat par excellence" (Meggitt 1958:284). Cassowaries are also captured as chicks and grown to maturity in pens. Wild and caged cassowaries are accorded equal prestige. Since wild cassowaries are not found in the densely populated area of the central Enga, the presence of cassowaries is the result of trade with the more sparsely populated fringe Enga. A cassowary is the equivalent of a large pig in the Te ceremony, the large-scale pig ceremonial of the Enga (Waddell 1972:61).

Though Meggitt characterizes Enga hunters as "inept," game nevertheless is an important part of some Enga rituals. Rituals to placate clan ghosts at times of adversity involve the use of game. When such a ritual is announced, neighboring clansmen, who will be the guests, must hunt in the mountain forests for "tree-kangaroos, possums and smaller game" (Meggitt 1965:116). New gardens may not be started at this time. At the ritual, the hosts provide the guests with pork and vegetable foods; they give game in return. After the guests have left, the men of the host clan, with women and children absent, take cooked pork and black possums to the clan cult house, and perform the placatory ritual to the clan ghosts in which they eat together with their ancestors. In another Enga ceremony in which bachelors periodically rid themselves of the polluting effects of women, the young men seclude themselves in the forest. They may not eat pork, since women have tended the pigs, and may eat only game, tubers harvested at night, and pandanus nuts (Meggitt 1964:219).

The Chimbu who also live in the central highlands, east of the Enga (figure 3.1), are intensive horticulturalists; they too practice a complex form of pig husbandry. The Chimbu pig population, as assessed by Brookfield and Brown (1963), is 1.5 adult pigs per human. Most boars are castrated at the age of a few months. Only a few men keep boars which are handled separately from the rest of the pig population. Fees are charged for the stud services of these boars. Pigs forage during the day in unenclosed garden areas for grass, herbage, and shrubs, and root there for worms. At night they return to the houses of their owners where they are fed sweet potatoes and scraps. Of the harvest of a sweet potato garden in full production, 15–25 percent consists of tubers too small to be fit for human consumption, and the proportion of unfit tubers is even higher in older gardens (Brookfield and Brown 1963:58). These tubers are fed to the pigs. The pigs remain in the women's house at night.

The Chimbu also hunt marsupials. At the Mogena biri, the large-scale vegetable distribution which is held every few years, marsupial meat is included with the large amounts of pandanus nuts, bananas, and sugar cane, which are considered male crops.

The Sinasina are very similar to their Chimbu neighbors

and are members of the same linguistic subfamily. Sinasina pig husbandry is similar to that of the Chimbu (Hide 1980). Most male pigs are castrated between three and six months of age. There is only one boar, who is kept penned up, for every 17–23 sows in the clan pig herd. Fees are paid to the owner of a boar for stud service. When the sow is in heat, both sow and boar are brought together by their owners for breeding purposes. Pregnant pigs make their nests in the bush near the settlements, and their owners keep careful track of where the litters are born. The sow and her litter remain in the nest after the birth and the owner brings food to the nest for several days.

The Local Council has prohibited owners from allowing their pigs to range freely. Pigs return to their stalls at night where they are fed a ration of raw or cooked sweet potatoes and green fodder. Women are charged with the feeding of pigs.

Pig husbandry among the Maring (figure 3.1) is different in a number of important respects from that among the societies discussed above. According to Rappaport (1984), all male pigs are castrated at about three months. Breeding, therefore, is dependent solely on feral boars impregnating domestic sows, a process not controlled by the Maring at all. Since feral boars are usually found below elevations of 3,000 feet, while Maring settlements, the home base of the sows, are usually above elevations of 4,000 feet, the impregnation of sows is unpredictable and highly variable. Rappaport suggests that, in times of settlement dispersal, sow impregnation figures are higher than at times when settlements are nucleated (1984:70, fn. 1). Sows usually farrow in the forest, and piglets are sometimes lost. Rappaport suggests that "Perhaps some of those lost survive in a feral state; if so, they may serve later to impregnate domestic sows or may be recovered through hunting, but most of them probably perish" (1984:71).

Among the Maring, piglets up to the age of 8–12 months literally live with the women. After that point, a stall is built in the woman's house for each pig. During the day, adult pigs forage in the secondary growth and forest, returning to their owners' houses in the evening to be fed substandard sweet potatoes and food leavings. As pigs grow in size, and as the herd increases in number, greater amounts of sweet potatoes, including tubers fit for human consumption, are fed to the pigs. In fact, 82 percent of the manioc harvested was fed to pigs (figures for nine months during Rappaport's fieldwork, 1984:60).

A wide variety of nondomesticated animals is hunted and eaten by the Maring, including wild pigs and cassowaries, marsupials, rats, snakes, lizards, eels, catfish, frogs, birds, bats, grubs, and insects. Rats, frogs, birds, and insects, in small quantities, often form part of the daily diet of women and children. Rappaport reports that, during his year of fieldwork in 1963, the six wild pigs killed provided most of the nondomesticated animal food consumed by the Tsembaga (Maring).

Hunting is important in Maring ritual, particularly in the large-scale Kaiko ceremony. Marsupials must be hunted and preserved by smoking for the Kaiko. The hunters are subjected to the same taboos as in warfare, including abstinence from sex and from eating food prepared by women. Marsupials, which are

hunted in the high ground, are symbolically associated with men, warfare and fire. They are considered to be the "pigs" of the Fight Ancestor Spirits, whose protection is sought by the clan in warfare. At another point in the Kaiko, eels, considered to be the "pigs" of the Ordinary Ancestor Spirits, are trapped and kept alive in cages until they are ceremonially cooked. Eels are associated with water, the cold, and with fertility and subsistence.

What we see among the Maring is an example of pig husbandry where the breeding process is not controlled at all, but where active efforts are exerted to bring piglets back to the settlement. Considerable economic effort is expended in growing food for the pig population, and at certain points in the cycle of pig production for the Kaiko more food is grown for pigs than for humans.

In the next group of societies, we see still less human control over the variables of breeding, retaining piglets, and feeding. By and large, these societies are in the lowlands where sago is a more important crop and sweet potatoes less significant. The exception is provided by the Mafulu who live in the Owen Stanley Mountains, north of Port Moresby (figure 3.1). Being a mountain people, their horticulture is based upon the cultivation of sweet potatoes, yams, and taro. Yams, bananas, and sugar cane are male crops among the Mafulu.

Williamson reports that village pigs are "identical with 'wild' pigs – being, in fact, wild pigs which have been caught alive or their descendants . . . They are bred in the villages by their owners, and by them brought up, fed and tended, the work of feeding and looking after them being the duty of the women" (1912:77). From this quotation, it would appear that breeding is not left to chance; that female pigs are bred and there is some control over their offspring. In fact, Williamson notes that women suckle young pigs. No mention is made of male village pigs being castrated, so the village sows may breed in the bush with feral boars or in the village with village-raised boars. Village pigs may sometimes wander off into the bush and become feral. Williamson further notes that the Mafulu have many more pigs than are to be found among the large coastal Mekeo villages though he does not give an absolute figure for the number of pigs in either Mafulu or Mekeo villages (1912:77).

The houses where families live have stalls with their own apertures occupied by the pigs. Williamson observes that "at every meal in the village the pigs have to be fed also, these sharing the food of the people themselves, or feeding on raw potatoes" (1912:64). Old sweet potato vines in gardens in which banana and sugar cane have been planted are allowed to keep on growing to provide tubers for the pigs. On the question of whether sweet potatoes are grown specifically to feed pigs, Williamson comments that, when pigs are required for a feast, "sweet potatoes must be plentiful for the feeding of these pigs" (1912:126).

The Mafulu are active hunters, pursuing wild pigs, kangaroos, wallabies, large snakes, and cassowaries and other types of birds. Hunting usually takes place in large groups, though parties of two or three may also go out after game. Young boys are taken along as beaters and often bark like dogs while chasing the animals towards the hunters, since the Mafulu have few dogs.

Despite the fact that Williamson points out the lack of difference between wild and village pigs, he reports that the Mafulu distinguish between these two kinds of pigs culturally. At what seems to be a large-scale mortuary ceremony for a chief, to which members of another community are invited as guests, a large number of pigs are required and the bones of the chief whose memory is being commemorated are dipped into the blood of the pigs. At one particular ceremony, 135 pigs were killed (1912:150). These pigs must be village pigs; wild pigs cannot be substituted. The village pigs which are killed on ceremonial occasions may not be eaten by the people of the village but are cut up and given to the guests who take the meat back to their own villages. Not only are the owners of village pigs forbidden to eat their own pigs, but those in other villages who may have been given pigs to fatten are also not allowed to eat the meat of those pigs.

After the mortuary rite at which village pigs are killed, the male hosts must go through a purification rite. They leave the village to go off to the bush to capture wild pig. From one to six are captured and brought back to the village. The pigs are killed on the burial platform of the chief who was the focus of the ceremonial distribution. Then they are cooked and eaten. The meat of the wild pig may never be eaten by young men until after they marry.

Among the Mafulu, a clear ritual separation exists between wild and domesticated pigs, despite the fact that wild piglets may be domesticated and domesticated pigs may become feral. Domesticated pigs may not be eaten, and must be given to guests at the large-scale mortuary ceremonial. Purification rites, which must be held after this ceremony, require the hunting of wild pigs to be eaten by the host community alone. One cannot be substituted for the other.

The Iatmul described by Bateson (1936; see figure 3.1) exemplify the same pattern as the Mafulu. However, in contrast to some other groups, sago is one of the most important parts of the native diet. The number of pigs in relation to the human population is much lower than among the Maring and the other highland groups. In Bateson's description of a Naven ceremony, only eight pigs are killed in comparison to the much larger numbers of pigs killed at the large-scale pig ceremonies of the Mafulu and in the central and western highlands. Bateson refers only once to the breeding of pigs, mentioning an individual "contributing to the bride price which she had got by breeding pigs" (1936:70). In this instance, the reference is probably more to the rearing than to the actual breeding process. Women feed pigs (no indication as to what the food is) and pigs are given names by women (Bateson 1936:52, fn.). Game which is hunted includes wild pig, wallaby, and crown pigeons. The killing by a boy of his first wild pig is noted by Bateson as an occasion for a Naven ceremony.

The Orakaiva are a lowland society (figure 3.1) in which young piglets are captured in the bush to be domesticated and raised in the village. Males are castrated and females are served by wild boars. In order to make a sow fertile, she may be fed the human afterbirth (Williams 1930:94). This would seem to indicate that although the Orakaiva make no attempt to control the breeding of sows, they desire sows to be fecund, implying that they

make some attempt to retrieve the piglets from the bush where they are probably born. These tamed pigs are given personal names, petted and fed every evening in the village. Owners are referred to as "mother" and "father." An owner does not eat the meat from his own pigs (Williams 1930:173). The Orakaiva are active hunters, though Williams reports that "hunting is only a secondary phase of the food quest" (1930:44). Men hunt individually with the aid of dogs but group hunts involving use of nets and fire drives may include up to sixty men. The game hunted includes bush pig, wallabies, rats, birds, lizards, frogs, and snakes. The jaws of wild pigs are hung on a branch of a tree in the village as trophies. Williams comments: "it is said that to throw them away and lose sight of them would have an ill effect on hunting thereafter" (1930:173). Williams notes that social obligations can be fulfilled with either a human corpse or the body of a pig, making them, in this instance, equivalents (1930:203–204). Cassowary chicks are sometimes captured and tamed but when they grow too large to control they are allowed to return to the bush.

The Etoro are located on the Papuan plateau, on the intersection between highland and lowland (figure 3.1). According to Kelly, "Etoro pigs are semidomesticated and spend most of their lives foraging in the bush unattended" (1977:41). The number of pigs per capita for the Etoro ranges between 1.26 and 1.38 (Kelly n.d.:39). Males are castrated, and females are impregnated in the bush by wild boars. When a sow farrows, her owner attempts to track her to her nest. The nest is almost always located, and the piglets are left there until they are partially weaned. Once they have been retrieved, their ears are clipped and they are petted and fed for the following three to six months to tame them. The Etoro do not grow food specifically for pigs. Almost all of the sustenance of village pigs comes from foraging in the bush. Occasionally, when pigs return to their owners, they are fed scraps from the table. If sago is prepared for human consumption, village pigs, who like it, are attracted to the site where the sago is being prepared and are usually given some of it. According to Kelly, "Domestic pigs are killed for brideprice payments, customary exchanges with affines and cross-cousins, [and] at mortuary rites" (1977:42). Pigs are also given in compensation payments and killed for divinatory purposes. Pigs killed on these occasions are usually barren sows, young adult males, and pigs in danger of going feral. The Etoro do not have a large-scale ceremonial pig distribution, like the Te, Bugla Gende, or Kaiko. Instead, pig killing may take place at any time during the year.

Hunting and foraging are important among the Etoro and supply two-thirds of the animal protein consumed, with bush hen eggs the largest single source (Kelly 1977:33). The Etoro environment is optimal for pigs. The oak forests of the intermediate altitudinal zone below their villages offer excellent foraging locations for both wild and village pigs. In fact, the large populations of both types of pigs compete for food in this zone. Wild pigs are hunted actively below the village, on the lower mountain slopes, while other mammals are hunted and trapped in the primary forest of the upper slopes.

Cassowaries are taken with snares, and chicks are taken

alive for exchange with other communities. Marsupials are
trapped and smoked and the meat is given as part of the reciprocal
exchanges between prospective affines (Kelly 1977:38). Kelly
observes that "In Etoro mythology and cosmology lineage spirits
(*sigisatos*) and spirits of the dead (*kesames*) often take the form of
cassowaries, eels, crocodiles, birds and fish – but not pigs. Only
witches are symbolically equated with the latter" (n.d.:17).

The Keraki are a lowland people occupying the region
between the Fly River and the southern coast of Papua New
Guinea (figure 3.1). Yams are the staple, but taro and manioc are
also important crops. Sago, the staple of a neighboring group, is
rare in Keraki territory but since it is highly prized it is planted in
the few swamps available. Though pigs are kept sequestered, they
are not bred. Williams observes that "these natives do not breed
pigs. . . The sow, like the boar, is kept for killing, and the supply is
maintained by the frequent capture of live piglets" (1936:224–
225). Male piglets are castrated after capture. The man who
captures the piglet may either raise it himself or give it to another;
in either case, the man who raises the pig is termed its "owner"
and he will never be the one to kill it. Piglets are named, fondled,
fed by the women and kept penned up in stalls until they have
grown to a very large size when they are slaughtered
and distributed at a ceremony. Williams gives no indication of
what the pigs are fed or whether food is grown particularly for
them.

The Keraki hunt by means of a communal drive carried out
by the men of the village. Wallaby, wild pig, and cassowary are
hunted in this manner. Killers of pig, cassowary, and (in the past)
humans decorated different parts of their bodies in distinctive
ways with mud. In addition, the skulls of the animals killed are
strung on rattan cane to commemorate the event. The only
reference to what is done with the meat of the animals killed is that
hunts took place prior to ceremonies. Cassowaries are hunted for
their meat and for their feathers, which are used for decoration.
Cassowaries are not totemic animals, nor are pigs.

The Kiwai Papuans live in the delta region of the Fly River
and in the surrounding territory, not far from the Keraki (figure
3.1). There is no indication that the Kiwai breed pigs. Landtman
(1927) indicates that they capture piglets, sometimes castrating the
males to make them become docile and grow large. Special
medicine is also used to tame them. The owners are referred to as
the "mother" and "father" of the pig. The sows are given medicine
to encourage pregnancy which implies that the Kiwai attempt to
retrieve the litter. The pig is smeared with a medicine to make it
grow large and also make it return to its owner in the village and
not go feral. Women prepare food (no indication is given as to the
kind of food) for the domesticated pigs.

Hunting techniques are described in detail by Landtman,
and hunting seems to be important (1927:111ff.). The most
important of the animals hunted are pig, cassowary, and wallaby.
The carcass of a wild pig is cut up and distributed in the same
manner as a dugong. If a pig were brought down by a single
hunter, its jaw would be displayed in the men's house. Sexual
abstinence must be practiced before hunting or fishing. The only

indication that Landtman gives of what happens to the products
of the hunt is in his account of the Ceremony of the Fertility Tree.
He notes "Animal food is also required, and the nearer the time of
the festival draws, the more eagerly are fishing of every kind,
hunting, turtling and harpooning of dugong carried on"
(1927:383). The flesh of the wild boar is eaten at a number of
ceremonies, where it is said to be the symbol of strength, health,
and fighting (1927:13, 370). It is unclear how and when the meat of
village pigs is used.

A number of lowland societies dependent on sago as a
staple crop are found north of the central mountain ranges. The
Umeda are located north of the Sepik River, quite close to the
West Irian border (figure 3.1). According to Gell, "A few pigs are
kept (never more than four in Umeda during my stay, and similar
numbers in other villages) but are not bred in captivity: these
domesticated pigs had been captured in the forest when small and
bred up. A boar will be gelded . . . Most meat comes from hunting
wild pig in the forest, an activity which takes up a great deal of the
time of the male members of the community" (1975:17). Hunting
as noted is extremely important among the Umeda. The hunter
cannot eat his own kill. One hind leg of every animal killed must
be given to one's affines (ibid. 109). The bulk of Gell's
ethnography is devoted to the meaning of the Ida Fertility Rite
which should be held annually and for which quantities of meat
are required. Meat caught during much of the year is preserved for
this event by smoking it.

Cassowaries are to be found only in the deep bush and
young cassowaries are never captured and tamed. The cassowary
is the epitome of the wild and is associated with maleness and with
aggressiveness. Its meat and its plumes are both important. The
symbolism of hunting and the hunter are central to the Ida rite.
Masked and decorated actors portray hunters (bowmen) and
cassowaries in the Ida. The Umeda see a relationship between
sexuality and hunting. Gell remarks that: "successful hunting is
the antithesis of sexuality; or rather that hunting is repressed or
sublimated sexuality" (1975:232). The Ida ritual represents the
"reproduction" of society through the efforts of the men. In the
symbolism of the ritual the wild cassowary is transformed into the
hunter which represents culture and to the Umeda the
reproduction of society. After the conclusion of the Ida, the men
of the village hunt game to obtain blood with which they anoint
themselves. This is done to remove "the dirt" of the ritual so that
they may then resume normal life.

The Gnau are found in the same general area as the Umeda
but due east (figure 3.1). Yams, taro, and sago are their important
crops. Lewis (1975) does not discuss pig husbandry among the
Gnau. However, "village pigs" and "rearing pigs" are mentioned.
Wild pig, wallaby, and cassowary are hunted, using a variety of
methods. In a nine-month period 52 wild pigs and 18 cassowaries
were taken. A man is forbidden from eating his own kill.
Furthermore, after a man has proved his skill in hunting, taboos
against eating wild pig and cassowary are imposed on him (Lewis
1975:91–92). If a wife does not obey taboos, her husband will
suffer failure in the hunt. Gnau rituals that require meat obtained

through hunting are: ending mourning taboos and the final mortuary rites; birth and puberty ceremonies; the ceremony of eating the first tubers of the year; exchanges with affinal and matrilateral kin; and building a men's house (Lewis 1975:50). When a sister's son has killed a pig or a cassowary, he gives the pig's skull or the cassowary's breastbone to his mother's brother, along with the meat (since no hunter can eat his own kill), and the latter displays these items with pride. The spirit which is associated with the causes of madness, with ritual bleeding of the penis, and with watching over vegetable foods, is also associated with hunting.

The Tor are found in the northern part of West Irian (figure 3.1). Sago, which grows wild and is never planted, is their staple crop, though bananas are planted. Pigs are never bred; they are caught in the bush as young piglets, brought home, tamed, and raised. These tame pigs forage around the village eating the village's garbage. Very young pigs are fed sago mash and the older animals are fed lumps of unpounded sago by the women. Kinship terms are used by the women in referring to the pigs and they are also given personal names. When the pig is killed in connection with a ritual, the family which has raised it may not eat any of the meat which is distributed to all in the village. Pig meat is given also to affinal relatives to fulfill various social obligations (Oosterwal 1961:72).

Hunting by the men of the group makes only a small contribution to the food supply. Wild boar as well as cassowary are hunted though the latter appear to be very scarce. Marsupials, iguanas, and various kinds of birds also are hunted. The hunter who has killed a wild pig may not eat it. There are rules for the way in which game must be divided up and distributed to various categories of relatives. The lower jaw of the pig is hung as a trophy in the ceremonial house.

The inauguration of a new ceremonial house requires the accumulation of a great deal of food. Women work to prepare sago while men hunt constantly to accumulate enough meat for the large-scale distribution that will take place. The flute feast which is attended only by men and is held in the men's ceremonial house requires the hunting, killing, and cooking of a special "flute" pig which is mixed with sago and ceremonially fed to the flutes.

The people of Frederik-Hendrik Island are located on the south coast of West Irian, near the border with Papua New Guinea (figure 3.1). They cultivate root crops such as yams, taro, sweet potatoes, and cassava on islands in the swamps which they have created with clay, earth, and reeds. Sago palms are also found but they are rare in a number of areas. Serpenti (1977) indicates in his discussion of the Ndambu – a feast of competitive giving – that pigs are looked after by women, pampered, and fattened, and kept in pig sties or in the house in the evening, though they roam freely in the village during the day. There is no information about how young pigs are acquired, nor as to whether males are castrated. The pig is never eaten by its owner but is offered to someone who needs it for a feast. Wild pigs, kangaroos, and, to a certain extent, cassowaries are hunted in communal drives. Kangaroo constitutes most of the game that is caught.

Discussion

We have presented a synchronic picture of the variations in human–pig relations in a number of different Papua New Guinea societies. From this synchronic picture, we deduce a number of hypotheses to be tested concerning the way in which these variations in human–pig relations might have developed. These diachronic hypotheses can then be tested against the archaeological record.

Pigs and dogs were the only placental mammals in Papua New Guinea, aside from humans, until the arrival of Europeans. It seems most likely that humans brought pigs and dogs with them when they came to New Guinea. It is impossible to imagine humans bringing wild pigs with them. Therefore, the pigs introduced into New Guinea were either domesticated (the breeding process being controlled by humans), or at least tamed. Both Allen (1972) and Golson and Hughes (1980) point out that the first pigs that accompanied humans to New Guinea must have been hand-fed with cultivated foods. Thus, all the pigs found in the forests of New Guinea are feral in that they are the descendants of the domesticated or tamed pigs brought to New Guinea by humans.

There are a number of variables which seem to determine the continuum of pig domestication. These variables are interrelated in such a way as to make it impossible to determine which is cause and which is effect. The first variable is the intensity of crop production. There is a significant distinction between highlands and lowlands in New Guinea in terms of type of crop. In the highlands, sweet potatoes are the most important crop. Among the Enga, Chimbu, and Kapauku, crop production is so intensive that extra sweet potato gardens are made just to feed pigs. In the areas peripheral to the central highlands, like the New Guinea plateau and Owen Stanley Mountains, sweet potatoes are not the important crop, and tubers are not grown just to feed pigs. Rather, pigs are allowed to forage in old and abandoned gardens, and are also fed scraps, but gain much of their sustenance foraging in the bush. In the lowlands, where sago production is important, along with that of taro and yams, the pigs forage only in the wild, and are fed the leavings from meals.

The second variable is density of population, human and pig. There is a gradient from high density to low density, which follows the continuum from the highlands to the lowlands. Though human population density is greater in the highlands than in the lowlands, the ratio of pigs to humans is proportionately greater in the highlands than in the lowlands. This demonstrates that the intensity of crop production leads to an even greater increase in the pig population than in the human population. The Etoro are an exception to this in that per capita pig population is high, though there is no intensity of crop production. This is because the Etoro have extensive and excellent foraging resources for their pigs.

In the highlands, intensity of crop and pig production is associated with large-scale ceremonial exchange systems, like the Kaiko of the Maring, Bugla gende of the Chimbu, Moka of the Melpa, and Te of the Enga. These ceremonies require large numbers of pigs since pig distribution is part of the ceremony. In our earlier work (Rubel and Rosman 1978), we analyzed the relationship between the intensity of crop and pig production, structure and scale of exchange ceremonies, and type of social structure. In the lowlands, ceremonial exchange takes the form of exchanges between moieties, and the structure is one of diametric dualism (Lévi-Strauss 1963a). In the highlands, the Maring and Chimbu have a more complex form of ceremonial exchange which we have characterized as having a star-shaped pattern, conforming to the structure of concentric dualism. The Melpa form of situational "chains" or *ropes of Moka* develop from this structure of concentric dualism, and from these emerge the longer and more permanent chains of Te exchange among the Enga. The more complex the exchange structure, the more intensive is the crop and pig production.

In the highlands, large tribal groups are densely settled in the wide valleys. Bushland for hunting is located in the more mountainous areas on the periphery of human settlement. The pattern for the lowlands is of nucleated settlements. Lowland villages are much further apart, and therefore villages are in closer proximity to bushland.

There is an inverse relationship between the intensity of pig production and the economic importance of hunting. In the highlands, where pig production is most developed, hunting contributes little or nothing to subsistence. At the other end of the continuum, among societies like the Umeda and the Gnau, the most important source of protein is derived from hunting, particularly of the wild pig. However, among all these societies, regardless of the importance of domesticated pigs, hunting plays an important role in major rituals.

Among the highland New Guinea societies in our sample, hunting is identified with the wild realm and with maleness. Meat of the hunt is often associated with crops which are designated as male crops, such as bananas, sugar cane, and pandanus nuts. Among the Kapauku, all of these items are taboo to women. Young men in the Enga purificatory rite eat only game, pandanus, and tubers harvested at night. Hunted marsupials are associated with sugar cane, pandanus nuts, and bananas (male crops) which are distributed at the Chimbu Mogena biri ritual. When Maring men hunt marsupials (which they define as the "pigs" of the Fight Ancestor Spirits), sexual intercourse is forbidden them, and they cannot eat food produced by females.

In these same societies, where great emphasis is placed on domesticated pigs for both ceremonial and economic purposes, pigs are symbolically associated with women and are primarily their concern. Young piglets are cared for and fed by women, live with the women in their houses, are sometimes suckled by women, and are often given personal names by their female care-takers. In

spatially symbolic terms, as men are associated with the wild, women are associated with the domestic, with the village. Pigs are identified with women also in another realm, that of exchange. Groups of men create links with other groups of men, by the exchange of women and by the exchange of pigs. As Rappaport notes for the Maring, "they do recognize a special relationship between two clans that have renewed their marriage ties, saying that they form a 'pig–woman road'" (1969:126). Despite the fact that domesticated pigs are symbolically associated with women (or perhaps because of this), it is domesticated pigs which are ceremonially distributed at the large-scale focal rites in these highland societies.

When one moves to the lowlands, maleness also seems to be associated with the hunting of wild pigs and of marsupials, and with cassowaries in general. A number of features related to hunting occur in these societies though no single feature is found in all of them, and any particular society contains only a few of them. These features include: sexual abstinence before hunting (Kiwai Papuans, Umeda); displaying skulls or jaws as trophies (Keraki, Tor, Orakaiva, Kiwai Papuans); a taboo against a hunter eating his own kill (Umeda, Gnau, Tor); a symbolic association of the wild boar with male traits (Kiwai Papuans), and of hunting with male rituals (Gnau, Umeda). In a number of these societies (Keraki, Kiwai Papuans, Umeda, Gnau, and Tor) the meat of the hunt is ceremonially important. In common with the highland societies, men in the lowland groups separate themselves from women by means of sexual abstinence in order to be successful in the hunt, and Gell (1975), in fact, characterizes Umeda hunting as the sublimation of sexuality. Success in the hunt epitomizes masculine traits of bravery and strength, and trophy jaws attest to this. Trophy jaws are retained and displayed also after a Chimbu Bugla gende, but here they represent the wealth of the host clan. As Kent points out in chapter 1 (this volume), this is similar to the Akwe-Shavante association of hunting and virility.

These lowland societies also keep tamed village pigs, though of course they are fewer in number than in the highlands. As in the highlands, it is the women who care for these pigs. They feed them, pamper them, and give them personal names; and these pigs are symbolically associated with women and with the domestic realm. However, in contrast to the highlands where men of a lineage live in the men's house, and women, children, and the pigs reside apart from the men in their own houses, in the lowlands families and their pigs form residential units. Among the Orakaiva and the Kiwai Papuans, both lowland societies, kinship terms like "mother" and "father" are used for the owners of a pig.

The Mafulu seem to be a society at the midpoint of our continuum, and thus they shed light on the processes involved in the continuum. They have sizable numbers of village pigs, and they also hunt wild pigs. Williamson (1912) reports that there is no physical difference between village pigs and wild pigs (as is the case everywhere in New Guinea). However, to the Mafulu these represent two very different cultural categories. Only village pigs may be used for the important mortuary ceremony. These village pigs may not be eaten by their owners, the hosts of the ceremony, but must be given to individuals from other villages who come as guests to the ceremony. For the male purificatory rite, at the close of this ceremony, only wild pigs can be used. These pigs are cooked and eaten by adult males alone. It would appear that since the Mafulu mortuary rite involves the use of domestic pigs which are associated with women, men need to purify themselves from such contact by the exclusively male activity of hunting and eating wild pig. The same animal, the pig, occupies two clearly separate cognitive categories in the Mafulu mind, representing two diametrically opposed ideas – the wild and the village.

We turn now to a diachronic interpretation of the synchronic continuum which we have discussed. We suggested earlier that pigs must have been brought into New Guinea by human beings. They were either tame, or fully domesticated, their breeding controlled by humans. It is almost impossible for the pigs to have been brought in wild. White and O'Connell support this position, arguing that "we think that they [pigs] were transported to New Guinea by people. This could have happened to young wild pigs, in the same way as cuscus, cassowary and other wild animals are transported between other islands today and were so in prehistoric times. Alternatively, the transported animals could have been tame (serving as pets and food) or domesticated ... On the whole, it seems most likely that pigs arrived in New Guinea tame, and with human assistance" (1982:187–188). White and O'Connell use the tame cuscus and cassowary as possible analogues for the pigs transported to New Guinea. Why was the pig the only placental mammal brought to New Guinea of the hundreds of possible tamed animal forms that could have been brought as pets (monkeys, for example)? It seems likely that the pig was further on the road to domestication than merely being tamed. Whenever this transport of pigs to New Guinea occurred, domesticated pigs would already have had to be present in southeast Asia.

The earliest remains of pigs found in New Guinea all occur in the highlands and go back to more than nine thousand years ago. Bulmer (1975) has reported a pig incisor in the faunal material from the highlands rock shelter of Kiowa, in a level dating to about 10 000 years B.P. Another fragment of pig bone is reported from the Yuku site from about the same time. The presence of pig wallows in 9000-year-old levels at the Kuk site has also been tentatively proposed (White and Allen 1980:731). White and Allen argue that, if these early dates are correct, Australia should also have evidence of pigs prior to European contact, since there was a land bridge between New Guinea and Australia at this time, but feral pigs are absent from northern Australia in prehistoric times (White and Allen 1980:731; see also White and O'Connell 1982:188–189). Golson turns this argument on its head, and uses the "indirect and controversial evidence for pigs in montane New Guinea 10 000 years ago" to argue for the existence of horticulture in the highlands of New Guinea at this early date (Golson 1981:56). White and O'Connell suggest yet another possibility – that montane New Guinea was the site of independent development of horticulture, based upon local forms of taro, sugar cane, and banana. This development of horticulture

based upon "a gradually developing expertise in plant exploitation" would have been independent of pig husbandry (White and O'Connell 1982:184).

The archaeological evidence clearly indicates the presence of pigs in the central highlands by 6000 to 5000 years ago (Golson and Hughes 1980:300). In half a dozen sites, these pig remains are in association with evidence for the firm establishment of horticulturally based economies (Christensen 1975; White and O'Connell 1982:189). Wurm (1983) points out that his linguistic evidence for the entry of Austronesian speakers into the New Guinea area coincides with this dating of 5000 to 6000 years ago. It thus seems likely that the Austronesian speakers who entered New Guinea at this time were horticulturalists who brought pigs with them. Wurm also notes that "the widespread presence of an Austronesian loanword for 'pig' in Papuan languages does indicate that the actual spreading of the pig through much of the New Guinea area post-dates the arrival of the Austronesians" (1983:28).

There is, however, clear evidence of a much earlier population of hunters and gatherers in New Guinea dating back to 26 000 years ago (White and Allen 1980:728). When domesticated (or possibly tamed) pigs were brought to New Guinea by humans, the hunters and gatherers already there no doubt began to hunt the feral descendants of those pigs and also eventually became horticulturalists, since there are no societies in New Guinea today which depend solely on hunting and foraging.

Golson's analysis of the Kuk site in the Wahgi area of the highlands describes the complete transformation of this environment as a consequence of horticulture over a 9000-year period. Beginning at 2500 B.P., the process accelerated. Golson sees the decline of forest resources and the concomitant development of grasslands as resulting in the reduction of wild fauna, a limitation on the ability of domestic pigs to forage for themselves, a greater reliance on garden produce, and an increasing need for the intensive management of pigs, whose upkeep becomes a charge on agricultural production (Golson 1982:115–125). It should be noted that Golson's hypothesis depends entirely upon his interpretation of the archaeological remains of the evolution of the agricultural system at Kuk, since no pig bones have been found there. Golson also uses a comparative analysis of three "montane" societies by Morren to support his interpretation (Morren 1977).

Morren's material also has implications for our own discussion. Morren presents a three-point continuum consisting of Miyanmin, Tsembaga Maring, and Raiapu Enga societies. These represent "points in a developmental continuum, [of] the expansion and intensification of controlling activities bearing on the pig chain in montane New Guinea" (Morren 1977:311). The Tsembaga Maring and Raiapu Enga are among the groups discussed in this chapter; the Miyanmin, a fringe highland group studied by Morren, are not considered here. Some of the variables discussed by Morren, such as whether "wild or domesticated" pork is consumed, whether piglets are captured or sows are bred, whether or not boars are castrated, and whether or not part of garden production is for pig feeding, are also dealt with in this chapter. Though both this chapter and Morren's paper present hypothesized developmental sequences, in other respects the analyses diverge. Morren's main focus is on the flow of energetics. He is concerned with the caloric output of hunting, whereas we are concerned with its continued symbolic significance, even among societies with the most intensive pig husbandry.

The archaeological record reveals a significant expansion in the pig population in more recent times, associated with the introduction of the sweet potato to New Guinea. White and O'Connell, basing their argument on the pig bone evidence, suggest that this increase in numbers of pigs occurred as early as a thousand years ago. They argue that since the sweet potato is present in Polynesia and Micronesia 600 to 1000 years ago, "the arrival of this plant in the New Guinea Highlands as much as 1200 years ago is not impossible" (White and O'Connell 1982:183). They suggest that the archaeological evidence supports a "slow revolution." This contrasts with Watson's view of this process as a rapid transformation occurring with the introduction of the sweet potato within the last 300 years (Watson 1977).

The intensification of pig husbandry was accompanied by a transformation in the form of society. At the beginning of this "slow revolution" societies in the highlands had particular social structures with a number of common characteristics. The nature of the transformation which took place was dependent upon the structural potential of those structures. In our earlier work (1978) we hypothesized that a prototypic form of social structure existed in the highlands before the introduction of sweet potatoes and the expansion of the pig population and that it evolved into the two kinds of social structures which are present in the highlands – the star-shaped pattern of concentric dualism and the more elaborate chains of exchange of the Melpa and Enga (see Rubel and Rosman 1978, chapter 18). This prototypic form of social structure has the potential to expand the exchange system based upon pigs and other valuables into larger and more stable exchange networks. Direct exchange gives way to delayed exchange which may occur years later. This development of delayed exchange occurs when the potential for the intensification of pig husbandry is present, as in the introduction of sweet potatoes.

We have noted that even in the highland New Guinea societies which are predominantly horticultural, hunting, though it may contribute little economically, continues to carry important ritual meaning. One possible explanation for this is that the pigs were introduced by Austronesian speakers into a population of Papuan speakers who were either protohorticulturalists or hunters and gatherers. We are suggesting that because these people had previously been hunters and gatherers, the ritual significance of hunting continues, despite the fact that their political economy is based on intensive pig husbandry and gardening. In the lowlands, where intensive pig husbandry was not possible, hunting – especially of the pig in its feral form – is both ritually and economically central.

Our analysis of this body of information raises certain questions. Is the ease with which feral piglets are tamed and controlled after capture due to earlier species domestication, implying that the pigs first brought to New Guinea were domesticated? Is the area-wide association of women with the care and raising of pigs due to universal features of division of labor in which women care for and feed animals when this activity takes place in close proximity to the house, or is it a distinctive cultural feature of this area? These questions can be answered only by still wider cross-cultural research.

Chapter 4

Farming and foraging: a necessary complementarity in Amazonia?

Leslie E. Sponsel

Introduction

In the majority of ecologically oriented anthropological studies on indigenous societies in Amazonia, cultural ecology serves as a means to the ends of the cultural evolutionists. Their principal end is to document and explain the processes through which cultural complexity and related phenomena develop over time. Within this conceptual framework, foraging societies in Amazonia are considered to be either survivors of a lower and simpler stage of cultural evolution antecedent to farming societies, or the end product of devolution from farming to foraging through competitive exclusion from the richer floodplains into the poorer interior forest. While this perspective has generated a great deal of useful thought and data collection, it harbors a number of serious limitations, not the least of which are various ethnocentric biases. In the first part of this chapter cultural evolutionism is critically analyzed in historical perspective through a concise review of those theories on Amazonia which most directly address the central theme of this book – the relationship between foraging, farming, and mobility.

The second part of this essay is an initial effort toward the development of another framework, one which considers cultural ecology as a means to the end of documenting and explaining human adaptation. This framework pays much more attention to biological ecology. For example, adaptation, rather than cultural

complexity, is the focus. Adaptation is defined as the phenomena and processes which promote the survival, maintenance, and reproduction of a population within the carrying capacity of its ecosystem. This framework is also more holistic. For example, it seeks to integrate a diversity of relevant variables ranging from population, health, nutrition, and economy to social organization, political organization, and religion. Moreover, it gives priority to cultural change (acculturation), something which, ironically, is usually excluded from the considerations of cultural evolutionists.

In the context of Amazonia this second framework offers a whole new perspective on the central theme of this book. Foraging and farming are considered to be overlapping, interdependent, contemporaneous, coequal and complementary domains in this region. Moreover, it is argued that in Amazonia foraging and farming are necessarily complementary for the overwhelming majority of indigenous societies, largely because of the limited protein available from wild and domestic plants and the limited carbohydrates available from wild plants. Traditional indigenes achieve this complementarity within a society either by combining hunting and/or fishing with farming, or through a mutualistic exchange between symbiotic societies in which one focuses on hunting and/or fishing and the other on farming. This complementarity permeates all levels of the cultural system.

Cultural evolutionism

Limiting factors

Although the foundations of the study of the cultural ecology of Amazonia extend back to the great naturalist explorers like Humboldt, Darwin, Bates, and Wallace, for present purposes it is sufficient to start in the modern era with the Berkeley geographer Carl Sauer. In several essays, such as his classic "Man in the Ecology of Tropical America" of 1957 (reprinted in 1963), Sauer delimited some of the central and perennial problems and issues of cultural ecology in the neotropics including the Amazon. One of these was the question of what factor or factors limit the size, distribution, and permanence of human populations in tropical forest ecosystems. Sauer (1963:186) identified soil fertility and aquatic resources of the riverine zone as the principal limiting factors:

> The riparian habitat, I wish to submit, has been favorable to progress, since its environment is diversified as to plant and animal life both of land and waters. Riparian folk are likely to live sociably in groups clustered at sites advantageous for getting a living and protected from flood hazard, and affording easy communication with other groups. The economic of such folk is to be read from the productivity of the kinds of stretches of water and their bordering lands, from what military jargon now calls "trafficability," and from the attractions of the sites selected for habitation. Here human ecology must begin with limnology as known and used by primitive man ... The water's edge is especially rewarding to hunting ... Of animal sources for the sustenance of man, there is no lack in quantity or diversity adjacent to and in the water bodies.

Here is one of the most basic and enduring distinctions in the ecology of Amazonia, that between the riverine and interior forest. Correlated with this distinction is the notion that, in comparison to the interior, the riverine zone has a higher biological diversity, productivity, and carrying capacity.

Ecology as evolutionism

Julian Steward, a student of Sauer as well as of anthropologists Alfred Kroeber and Robert Lowie, was of seminal importance in the early development of cultural ecology from the 1930s through the 1950s (Hanc n.d.; Speth 1972). For Steward cultural ecology was merely the means to the end of understanding the processes of cultural evolution (1955:3, 5; 1977:43). In other words, his multilinear variety of cultural evolutionism subordinates cultural ecology as a methodological tool. This Stewardian framework inevitably persists, even though it is usually only implicit, in the work of subsequent scholars including Betty Meggers, Robert Carneiro, Donald Lathrap, Daniel Gross, Marvin Harris, and Emilio Moran. Although each of these scholars developed their own variation on Steward's basic theme, they share a tenet of cultural evolutionism – the carrying capacity of the environment restricts cultural evolution by limiting the size, distribution, and permanence of the human population in the different environ-

mental zones of Amazonia. This is considered to be the explanation for the higher population density and correlated greater level of sociocultural complexity of floodplain societies in Amazonia prior to their decimation through European contact. The assumption is that the correlation reflects causality in the direction from environment to population to culture.

Agricultural potential

Some of the implications of the above were developed explicitly and concisely in two classic essays by Meggers:

> the level to which a culture can develop is dependent upon the agricultural potentiality of the environment it occupies. As this potential is improved, culture will advance. If it cannot be improved, the culture will become established at a level compatible with the food resources. (1954:814)

Later Meggers suggests that shifting cultivation requires mobility, but of a different kind and degree from foraging (1957:82).

In Meggers' view (1954:814), cultural evolution in the Amazon is limited by agricultural potential which is mainly a matter of soil fertility. Although many floodplains are annually rejuvenated during the wet season by the deposition of nutrient-rich sediments from the floods, still the environment has limited cultural evolution to pre-state levels. Estimates of the extent of these floodplains range from one to ten percent of Amazonia. The impression of the poverty of most soils led Meggers (1971, 1973, 1974) to label the Amazon a "counterfeit paradise."

Carneiro (1956:230–232) was one of the first to critically assess the cultural evolutionist ideas of Meggers. Moreover, he went beyond theorizing to test Meggers' hypothesis with quantitative field data. He studied an indigenous riverine village of 145 Kuikuru in the Upper Xingú of Brazil. The village remained in the same location for about 90 years with its gardens in a radius of less than five miles. He calculated that it would take the Kuikuru 400 years to use all of the arable land in the vicinity of their village, by which time they could then return to their first gardens which would have recovered through secondary succession. Furthermore, he asserts that 500 Kuikuru could remain completely sedentary by using only seven percent of their arable land. In contrast, Carneiro noted that most Amazonian villages average only 50–150 residents, and concludes that some factor other than agricultural potential must limit their populations.

In search of the other factor Carneiro (1968b) compared his field data on the fluvial Kuikuru and interfluvial Amahuaca. In the case of the Amahuaca of the Peruvian montaña, Carneiro (1970a:332) argued that in the interior forest hunting provides most of the protein because the small streams are poor in fish resources. That is, the body size, population size, and productivity of fish are all poor in the aquatic ecosystems of the interior forest. Then he anticipates the protein hypothesis:

> In habitats of this type it is hunting, not fishing, which must be relied on for the bulk of the protein in the diet. This fact

is of special significance for settlement patterns, since *a heavy reliance on hunting is incompatible with sedentary village life*. Even communities as small as 15, which are characteristic of the Amahuaca, severely deplete the game in their vicinity in a year or two. After that, a village may need to be moved several miles away if the supply of meat is to continue to be met without an inordinate amount of walking time being required. The result is that a horticultural-and-hunting society living in a habitat with only small streams will be *unable to take full advantage of the potentialities of agriculture* for settlement size and permanence. (Carneiro 1968b:245, emphasis added)

Here is the proposition that foraging and farming are incompatible because of their different kinds and degrees of mobility. Its correlate is that progress in cultural evolution will be retarded for sylvan societies with a high dependence on hunting for protein.

Competitive exclusion and devolution

Cultural devolution of societies through competitive exclusion from the fluvial zone was added to the aforementioned concepts of cultural evolutionism by Lathrap (1968). The floodplain zone is very limited. After the initial occupation in pre-Columbian times, Lathrap believes that a natural increase in the human population on the floodplains eventually led to resource competition resulting in warfare. Weaker groups were expelled from the fluvial zone and took refuge in the deep interior of the forest (1968:24–25, 28–29). In this poorer habitat they were reduced to scattered, small, and mobile bands of hunter–gatherers. Consequently their horticulture was rudimentary, inefficient, and unproductive. These societies reverted to a much lower level of cultural complexity.

Lathrap's argument is very enlightening and convincing in its broad outlines, but there are several problems. Foremost, in my opinion, is its normative character. Lathrap (1968:25, 29) characterizes interior cultures using ethnocentric terms such as devolution, degradation, and wreckage of former agricultural societies.

Secondly, from the perspective of biological evolution and ecology (rather than cultural evolutionism) these sylvan foragers merely made a shift in their adaptive strategy after exclusion by more politically powerful and aggressive riparian societies. From this perspective, survival, maintenance, and reproduction of a population are the most significant parameters of adaptation, whereas increasing population density, sedentariness, and sociocultural complexity are relevant only to the degree that they affect these parameters, however important they might be to the cultural evolutionist. Similarly, Bennett (1976:147) suggests that such shifts have a double meaning. From a cultural and historical view they imply a social breakdown, but from an ecological view they imply restoration of equilibrium.

There are other problems with Lathrap's study (for details see Sponsel 1981:296–303). For instance, agriculture along the floodplain is limited to short-cycle crops which are subject to the hazards of the irregularities in the timing and intensity of flooding (cf. Roosevelt 1980). In the supposedly rich fluvial zone, large expanses of forest are flooded during the wet season; fish and game therefore disperse widely and are not readily accessible.

Even in riverine zones the wet season may be a period of hardship and hunger, in comparison to the glut during portions of the dry season. In addition, insects are more abundant in riverine areas, not only as pests, but also as vectors of diseases such as malaria. Higher human population densities provide a reservoir for some diseases and in other ways enhance the transmission of diseases. Riparian societies were also more vulnerable to the multiple-level disruptions from European contact, in comparison to the scattered, mobile, and small sylvan societies deep in the interior and headwaters (cf. Bunker 1984).

In spite of these and other problems with Lathrap's cultural evolutionist argument, he raises the very important question of whether or not sylvan foraging societies are survivors of a pre-agricultural period, or the result of cultural devolution from farming to foraging through competitive exclusion from the riparian to the sylvan zones (1968:29). As a biological and cultural ecologist, I prefer to consider such sylvan foraging societies as refugees who shifted their adaptive strategy.

Cultural evolutionist ideas such as those of Lathrap tend to disparage hunting in Amazonia. However, ultimately it does not matter whether the hunter is a traditional or acculturated indigenous forager and/or farmer, descendant of Afro-American refugees from slavery (see e.g. Butts 1977), *caboclo*, Latin American or European colonist (see e.g. Smith 1976, 1978). For all of these people hunting in sylvan zones and fishing in riparian zones usually provide the most important source of quality protein in the diet. In these cases probably much of the ecology of the forest, river, prey, and predator remains the same. In this regard foraging is not contaminated by farming, or vice versa. Adaptation is the ecological issue, although "purity" may be one for the cultural evolutionist. (This is not to exclude the possibility that simultaneously there may also be important cultural and ecological differences between the foraging behavior of societies as diverse as the aforementioned.)

Protein hypothesis

Gross (1975) most clearly formulated the hypothesis that animal protein is the limiting factor on the size, distribution, and permanence of indigenous populations in Amazonia. His hypothesis is that the staple plant foods of traditional societies in Amazonia provide only low quantity and quality of protein. The cultigens are mainly root crops, and manioc is by far the most important one. It has only a low concentration of protein, that lacks the full complement of necessary amino acids. Animals were not domesticated as an alternative or supplemental source of protein. Fishing is poor at best in the small streams of the interior forest. Hunting, the only remaining source of protein, is difficult everywhere, but especially so in the interior forests. The populations of prey species are low in density and patchy in distribution, while most are arboreal and nocturnal (1975:527–529).

From the ethnographic literature Gross (1975:530–532) found 35 g/capita/day to be the mean protein yield from hunting and fishing for a sample of nine indigenous societies. This he contrasted with 63 g/capita/day as the standard recommended by most nutritionists. Finally, from the literature he found that indigenes express a concern for meat scarcity through their use of special words for meat hunger, the prestige of a successful hunter, and sexual favors women give to a good hunter.

Chagnon (1983:81–88), Chagnon and Hames (1979), and Lizot (1977) attempt to refute the animal protein hypothesis by demonstrating that the Yanomama actually consume surplus protein. However, the design, data, and interpretations of their research have been questioned (Gross 1982; Harris 1984a, b; Ross and Ross 1980; Sponsel 1981:308–317, 1983). Perhaps more importantly, these critics of the protein hypothesis miss the whole point. A nutritional investigation will never prove or disprove the hypothesis. Regardless of whether there is a deficiency, adequacy, or surplus of quality protein in the diet, faunal resources may still be problematic. The critics confuse faunal resources as a limiting factor on the hunter population in its local ecosystem with protein as a component of the diet of these populations. Available faunal biomass is one thing, its acquisition, consumption, and assimilation are quite different things. The first refers to the environment of the human organism, the second to the organism itself. (Ross 1979:544 and Ross and Ross 1980 also note this confusion.) Thus, as an adaptive challenge to the foraging society, game may still influence its population dynamics and culture, regardless of its nutritional status. The critical factor is the cost/benefit ratio in protein procurement (Harris 1984a, b).

Another critic, Beckerman (1979), contends that Gross underestimates the quantity and variety of protein available from sources other than hunting and fishing, namely gardening and gathering (wild plants and animals). However, there are difficulties with the alternative protein resources he suggests. Many of the additional aquatic resources (fish, manatee, caiman, turtle, and eggs, etc.) are either concentrated in, or limited to, the fluvial zone, and so they are mostly if not completely irrelevant to the interfluves. Insects are rich in many nutrients including protein, but most are ephemeral and of limited quantity (cf. Taylor 1975).

Most wild plant resources, like the animals, have a high species diversity, low population density, and patchy distribution in space. In addition, fruits and many other wild plant foods are irregular in time, their availability depending on the plant's phenology. During my fieldwork with Sanemá (northern Yanomama), Ye'kuana, Curripaco, and Yeral indigenes in Amazonia, I was impressed by the fact that in general most plant foods in the forest provide little more than a snack. Harvesting wild plant foods demands an adaptive strategy geared to mobility (for searching) and scheduling (precise empirical knowledge of botany and phenology). As a reflection of the relatively low accessibility of most wild plant resources in the interior forest, Milton (1984) identifies carbohydrates as a limiting factor for the Maku foragers in northwestern Amazonia. Werner (1983:234) argues that one of the richest plant resources for protein, the Brazil nut, is less economical in terms of the time and energy invested in harvesting it than is wild game.

The great majority of wild plant foods have a low quantity and quality of protein. The low protein concentration can be partially circumvented by consuming large amounts of the food such as in palm drinks. However, this is no solution for children with small stomachs who also have special protein requirements during the critical period of growth and development.

Chronic mobility

The most recent and explicit treatment of mobility in relation to foraging and farming as an issue in the cultural evolution and cultural ecology of Amazonia is found in studies by Moran (1980, 1983). He argues that mobility is not necessarily a purely positive response that enhances human adaptability to environments in Amazonia (1983:118). He cautions that not all human behavior is adaptive, and mere persistence is not a sufficient basis for considering something to be adaptive. Also he emphasizes that the ecology of Amazonia is far from homogeneous. For example, not all soils are poor, but the richer ones are patchy in distribution (ibid. 123). Moran further asserts that four to ten years are required for the people in a community to acquire site-specific ethnoagronomic knowledge about the microvariability of the soils and their fertility in the vicinity (ibid. 131).

In striking contrast to Conklin's (1957) Hanunóo swiddeners in the Philippines, Moran believes that Amazonians lack such detailed and sophisticated ethnoagronomic knowledge. He blames this on hunting. Since sylvan societies depend on hunting rather than fishing and gardening as their primary source of protein, they are forced to be mobile rather than sedentary. Hence Moran's hypothesis: "chronic mobility prevents the development of site-specific ethnoagronomic knowledge necessary to develop complex and stable agricultural systems" (1983:129). In other words, agriculture in the Amazon is limited, not because of poor soils, but because of the indigenes' poor knowledge about soils (ibid. 125). They emphasize species-specific rather than site-specific environmental information because of the nutritional importance of hunting and the mobility it requires.

According to Moran, while mobility has a positive function in foraging, it has a negative function in farming. This fundamental dialectical dilemma is

> a consequence of the systemic interactions between chronic mobility, dependence on hunting, subsistence reliance on protein-poor manioc due to its trustworthiness in yield regardless of soil conditions, and inadequate ethnoagronomic criteria for soil selection. (1983:129)

In the end all of this also has consequences for cultural evolution:

> Such a system lacks the potential to increase production per unit of time per unit of labor, and therefore it lacks the potential for population growth and for increase in social complexity within a sustainable production system. (1983:134)

Moran qualifies this model by stating that it refers to areas other than the floodplains and major clear-water tributaries (ibid.).

Moran's earlier model (1981) is based largely on his field experience with agricultural colonists along the TransAmazon Highway in Brazil. He never explains the rationale for extending the model from colonists to indigenes. If he had as much first-hand experience with indigenes perhaps he would not be so quick to extrapolate. The complexity of indigenous knowledge about wild animals and plants as well as about other aspects of hunting and gathering may just reflect the etic and emic importance of foraging as the primary source of concentrated quality protein for sylvan societies. The ethnographic literature from fieldwork with indigenes is replete with numerous observations and comments on the greater cultural interest and value placed on hunting and meat in sharp contrast to gardening and crops. Again Moran may have a problem with extrapolation. Although the Hanunóo in the Philippines are swiddeners, in many respects their situation is very different from that of most indigenes in Amazonia.

Mobility is not necessarily antithetical to the exploration of the environment and acquisition of detailed knowledge about it. Moran fails to recognize Binford's (1980) distinction between residential and logistic mobility. Residential mobility refers to movements of all members of the community from one location to another. Logistic mobility refers to the movement of individuals or subgroups on foraging or other forays who eventually return to the residence, usually after a period of hours, days, or weeks. As Kelly notes (1983:299), logistic mobility functions as "remote sensors" for a group to acquire important information about resources. This may include soils, contrary to Moran's opinion. For example, Butts writes: "When hunting or travelling, Akawaio carefully note any useful resources for future exploitation – good soils, fruit trees, even a shoal of fish or the presence of an animal" (1977:9). This distinction points to the ethnographic fact that sylvan societies have developed land use and settlement patterns which provide residential stability for adequate farming (if nutrition and health are any measure) for periods as long as or longer than Moran's four to ten years, his critical period for site-specific knowledge of soils in the vicinity. At the same time these patterns allow logistic mobility for species-specific knowledge and other factors which contribute to efficient foraging.

Assessment

The preceding survey reveals that cultural evolutionism stimulates a great deal of useful thought and data collection on the cultural ecology of Amazonia including the relationship between foraging, farming, and mobility. The survey also reveals some of the limitations, including ethnocentric biases, of this approach.

Cultural evolutionists usually identify only the fluvial and interfluvial zones as giving rise to the major ecological contrast in Amazonia. This contrast provides the foundation for explaining cultural differences and evolution in the region. The focus is on causally correlated patterns of increased population density,

sedentariness, and sociocultural complexity. Either soil infertility or protein scarcity is identified as the single limiting factor on the size, distribution, and permanence of indigenous populations. Warfare is proposed as a negative feedback mechanism regulating population dynamics including mobility in relation to animal resources for protein.

Foraging and farming are often viewed as almost incompatible, and the former is usually devalued. Foraging societies are considered to be at a lower and simpler stage of cultural evolution, or the product of devolution from farming societies through competitive exclusion from the richer floodplains into the forest interior. In one way or another mobility is thought to be positive for foraging and negative for farming. The consequence is a dialectic between foraging and farming within any society dependent on a mixed subsistence economy. The ultimate conclusion is that foraging retards cultural evolution and progress.

For the cultural evolutionist, adaptation is a synonym for increasing sociocultural complexity built on increasing population density and sedentariness. Implicit in this is the concept of progress. In recent years an increasing number and diversity of scholars are questioning and rethinking human evolution, adaptation, and progress. For example, on the basis of energetics and other cultural ecological considerations, Bodley (1981, 1985) sees the evolution of social stratification and the state as maladaptive in the long term, and "tribal" society as the only proven adaptive system. (See also L. Brown 1985; Eckholm 1976; Rifkin 1980; Watt, *et al.* 1977.)

The concepts of both evolution and adaptation as formulated by the cultural evolutionists are not only independent of, but also alien to, the concepts of the biological evolutionist and ecologist (see Bargatzky 1984; Brandon 1984). For the biologist, adaptation is more likely to be considered as the phenomena and processes which promote survival, maintenance, and reproduction of a population, including its nutrition and health, within the carrying capacity of a specific ecosystem and without degrading the latter. The biologist focuses on adaptation regardless of the relative richness of the environment or the complexity of the behavior of the organism.

The framework and procedure which the cultural evolutionist employs in the study of adaptation is quite different. The cultural evolutionist in Amazonia must rely mostly on ethnographic evidence to provide insights into the prehistoric past and cultural evolution, because of the sparsity of archaeological research and evidence. For the purposes of salvage ethnography and the reconstruction of culture history, the cultural evolutionist either ignores or filters out the dynamic changes in most indigenous environmental, demographic, and cultural systems stimulated directly and/or indirectly by centuries of Western contact. As a consequence, ironically, the past cultural adaptations studied by the cultural evolutionist have limited relevance for the ongoing and future adaptations of the indigenous societies.

Cultural evolutionism, however, is relevant to recent indigenous adaptations from another point of view. Fabian (1983) and Pandian (1985), among others, assert that cultural evolutionism is part of a political ideology which contributes to the cultural dominance over and exploitation of indigenous societies by Western civilization by treating a study group as if it exists in a pristine state of some prior evolutionary time. Thus the anthropologist's view of the relationship between foraging and farming may extend far beyond merely academic concerns to take on political significance. Furthermore, the introduction of Old World diseases created a demographic disaster which challenges any view of the past based on ethnographic analogs in Amazonia (Beckerman 1979:553). According to Colchester (1984:311), even the remote Yanomama have experienced continuous change over several generations and therefore cannot be treated as static adaptations to their environment. He states:

> it is time that we started examining Amazonian societies in terms of the recent radical transformations that have occurred and that are occurring in their technological, demographic, and economic bases, and must begin to consider what effects these changes might have had on other aspects of their social organization and systems of thought. (1984:311)

With its roots penetrating centuries into the history of anthropology, it is unlikely that cultural evolutionism will ever be completely abandoned (Carneiro 1973; Harris 1968). More importantly, it has proven validity and utility, despite its limitations (Levinson and Malone 1980). Nevertheless, merely revising this orientation is not sufficient for many anthropologists. They and even indigenes are calling for the development of additional approaches which are more responsive to recent and future problems of adaptation in Amazonia. The remainder of this essay turns toward an initial attempt to develop another approach with material from the Amazon and to apply it to the central theme of this book – the relationship between foraging, farming, and mobility.

Cultural ecology
Foundation
In this approach cultural ecology is one means to the end of documenting and explaining human adaptation. A biological concept of adaptation is applied, as previously defined. In contrast to the use of cultural ecology by the cultural evolutionists, this approach is more ecological, holistic, dynamic, contemporary, and applied.

Analysis begins with a focus on the network of interactions between the ecosystem, infrastructure (including aspects of demographic, economic, nutritional, and medical anthropology), and cultural change (including aspects of economic, social, and political anthropology). The interactions of primary concern are the flow of energy, matter, and information.

The indigenous culture is viewed not as a pristine isolate, but as an integral part of a larger system, extending progressively outward from neighboring indigenous societies to the national and international levels. Cultural change through contact with other societies, and especially with Western civilization, is not ignored, filtered out, or relegated to an epilogue. Instead the dynamics of cultural and environmental change through contact are an initial step in the study of recent and ongoing adaptation. This necessitates a diachronic perspective. However, past adaptation, including the prehistory and history of the region, is of importance only in so far as it enlightens understanding of present and future adaptations.

Concern for adaptation also directs attention to the level of superstructure. In particular, ethnoscience (including indigenous knowledge of the ecosystem and its application), indigenous religion (including cosmology, myths, symbols, values, and beliefs which affect adaptation), and politics (including internal and external power relationships) are all critical for understanding indigenous adaptation. The emphasis on ethnoscience contrasts with the cultural evolutionist's neglect of indigenous knowledge which follows from the view of the indigene as being in a lower and simpler stage of evolutionary development.

This approach recognizes the problems of colonialism, inequality, the denial of coevalness, and related matters as it seeks to place relevant cultural ecological knowledge in the hands of the indigenous culture for application to their own purposes. Simultaneously, this approach recognizes that one of the products of the dialectics between Westerner and indigene, outsider and insider, observer and observed, etc., will be a feedback of the field research into academic anthropology to render it more objective, universal, and humanistic. Such considerations presuppose some fundamental changes in the values of the professional anthropologist (Sponsel 1985).

While this approach is geared toward the analysis of a particular culture in a local ecosystem, to some extent it may be usefully applied to a more general level such as the central issue of this book. Its utility is demonstrated in the fact that not only does it provide new answers to old questions, but it also raises new questions. The remainder of this essay discusses in succession Amazonian archaeology, forest ecology, and human nutrition as these apply to the question of the relationship between foraging, farming, and mobility.

Prehistoric adaptations
Archaeologically South America is probably the least known continent in the world, and the situation for the Amazon portion is even worse. Nevertheless, some tentative statements may be made about the human prehistory of the region which may provide clues for a better understanding of the relationship between foraging and farming.

There is substantial evidence that the continent of South America was colonized by Paleo-indians more than 12,000 years B.P. Indeed, the earliest evidence, although still very limited, points to a human antiquity of more than 20,000 years (Meggers 1982:485 and others). In the Amazonian subregion, however, the earliest human occupation appears to date from only about 4000–6000 B.P. (Lathrap 1970; Sanford, *et al.* 1985). Moreover, there is no direct evidence for a preceramic period in these forests

(Meggers 1982:485). The earliest societies seem to have practiced some farming as well as gathering, hunting, and fishing. Lynch (1978:109) believes that Paleo-indians never occupied Amazonian forests because the savannas were more attractive and hospitable. While Lynch does not pursue this idea in detail, some leads may be extracted from several recent studies on the biological ecology of the tropical forest ecosystem.

Ecology and nutrition

Foley (1982:398) argues that, in the subsistence economy of foragers in the tropics, hunting tends to be more important in the savannas than in the forests:

> Areas with between 500 and 1500 mm of rainfall per annum . . . are characterized by grass-dominated plant communities, unsuitable for direct human consumption, and a high large mammal biomass. Above 1500 mm per annum a wooded and forested environment reduces the resource base of the large herbivores, thus simultaneously increasing edible plant biomass and decreasing large mammal biomass. It may be predicted on this basis that below 500 mm and above 1500 mm rainfall per annum gathering-based economies will be more viable, but in between these limits hunting is likely to be of greater importance.

The human digestive system cannot assimilate the grasses which predominate in the plant communities of savannas. However, humans can exploit the energy and nutrients in the grasses by using herbivores as intermediaries to transform them into edible tissue. Hunting wild herbivores or herding domestic ones are alternatives to accomplish this.

Similar views are expressed by Kelly (1983:287) who also points out that even though primary productivity of forests may be greater than that of savannas, in the latter biome the secondary productivity is more readily available to humans. It is also noteworthy here that, in comparison, the neotropics are impoverished in species diversity and size (Herskovitz 1972:372). Accordingly, Kelly (1983:286) goes so far as to assert that primary and secondary productivity are inversely correlated with the accessibility of plant and animal resources. That is, the greater the plant biomass, the lower the proportion of it which is available for herbivore consumption, and in turn, the lower the animal biomass.

In the Amazonian forest biome there are a number of factors which reduce the availability of faunal resources in particular, including the low proportion of edible plant biomass (Fittkau, *et al.* 1975). As previously discussed, others were recognized by Gross – prey population dynamics (high species diversity, low population density, and patchy distribution) and behavior (emphasis on arboreal habitat and nocturnal habit). Even if prey were relatively abundant, they would not necessarily be readily available, given their behavioral and ecological characteristics. My survey of 41 common mammalian prey species in Amazonia reveals that 39.4 percent are small in body size (5 kg or less), 53.6 percent solitary, 73.2 percent nocturnal, and 43.9 percent arboreal. (See Sponsel 1981:319–321 for a detailed analysis.)

The one outstanding exception to these generalizations on mammalian prey availability is the wild pig (*Tayassu pecari*). It is large in body size (up to 30 kg), social (herds of 50–100 or more individuals), diurnal, and terrestrial. The reproductive capacity of the peccary is remarkable. Females have a gestation period of about 148 days and produce up to four young in each litter (Walker 1975:1365–1366). In some ecosystems where their natural predators are absent wild pig populations increase to the point that they overgraze and degrade the habitat (Bratton 1975; Diong 1973:133; Mueller-Dombois 1981:309–346). Accordingly, it is no surprise that peccary rank first by number and weight in the predation records of many Amazonian societies (Vickers 1984:370). Peccary composed 74 percent of the biomass of mammalian prey taken during four months in one Sanemá (northern Yanomama) village on the Erebato River of Venezuela (Sponsel 1981:185). Ross calls peccary "a moveable feast" (1979:545; see also Sowls 1984).

Peccary do have some disadvantages. Herds are relatively rare and their appearance in a particular area is sporadic, infrequent, and short-lived (Kiltie 1980:542). According to my Ye'cuana informants in the Cunucunuma River of Venezuela, the home range of a peccary herd is so large that it would take about two weeks to walk its diameter, and it may overlap the hunting range of several villages. Nevertheless, peccary are the most important prey for many Amazonians. Without them, sylvan indigenes would have much more difficulty satisfying their protein needs, and the animal protein hypothesis of Gross would be much stronger.

There are other complications regarding prey availability in the Amazonian forest. The human predator has no monopoly on secondary productivity since many other predator species are competitors. Also, compared to other predator species such as the jaguar (*Panthera onca*), the human predator is distinct in its combination of large body size and large group size (forest villages of 50–100 or more individuals).

Even large aquatic ecosystems do not always supply an abundance of fish and other protein resources. Wet-season innundation of floodplain forests stimulates widespread dispersal of fish and game which lowers their accessibility for the human predator. Thus even in the relatively rich fluvial zone, societies may experience seasonal protein scarcity. I observed this among the Curripaco and Yeral in the Río Negro region of Venezuela (Sponsel 1986). Milton (1984:19) reports this problem for another northwestern Amazon group, the Tucanoans. Moreover, the blackwater–white sands ecosystems of this region are oligotrophic – relatively poor in productivity, biomass, and species diversity (see e.g. Fittkau, *et al.* 1975). For instance, Smith (1982:130) found that the mean annual biomass of the whitewater várzea lakes was 15–19 times greater than that of the blackwater lakes.

Hunting and fishing are not the only sources of protein and other nutrients for indigenes in Amazonia, as previously noted. Perhaps the role of gathering is greatly underestimated, but there are no comprehensive and detailed analyses of this component in the subsistence economy of Amazonian societies. There are reasons to be cautious. For example, Milton (1984:19) notes that "A population meeting much of its energetic as well as protein needs from animal food will require considerably more meat each day to sustain itself than will a population meeting energy needs from plant foods and using animal foods only to meet protein requirements." Consequently, a society is likely to take advantage of the resources offered by both hunting and gathering.

Gathering wild plant foods presents many difficulties. Some of these can be appreciated from a primate field study on Barro Colorado Island in central Panama. Milton (1981:538) found the average home range size of spider monkeys (*Ateles geoffroyi*) to be about 25 times as large as that of howlers (*Alouatta palliata*). This difference relates to diet. Spider monkeys are mainly frugivores whereas howlers are mainly folivores. Generally humans only occasionally consume small quantities of leaves from wild plants. The consumption of fruits and most other non-leaf portions of plants as human food would require mobility over a wide home range.

The ecological and nutritional considerations outlined so far provide some rationale for Lynch's assertion that savannas were probably more hospitable and attractive than forests to the earliest human colonizers of South America. These considerations also point to the importance of agriculture in exploiting the Amazon forest ecosystem. While farming may not have been a prerequisite for dispersal into this biome, it most probably facilitated the process. Not only does this view fit the available archaeological record, but it is also supported by the ethnographic record in which mixed subsistence economies (including farming, gathering, hunting, and/or fishing) overwhelmingly predominate. In particular, gardens provide a concentrated, steady, and reliable supply of plants for food and other purposes (firewood, medicines, crafts, etc.). They allow the population to be more sedentary than otherwise.

The chief problem for agriculture in the Amazon is the relatively poor fertility of most soils. The only major exception to this generalization is the floodplain or várzea. However, the várzea is largely confined to the lower and middle Amazon and its major tributaries up to the first rapids. Estimates of its aerial extent vary from one percent to ten percent of Amazonia (Sponsel 1981:128).

In contrast, the unflooded hinterland or terra firma is a disproportionately vast region, which forms the environment for the adaptations of the great majority of indigenous societies in Amazonia. Generally the soils of the terra firma are much less fertile than those of the várzea (Schubart and Salati 1982:217). This is the reason why Meggers (1971, 1973:311) characterized Amazonia as a "counterfeit paradise." Such considerations led Schwabe (1968:121, 127) to coin the term "demineralization" to refer to the impoverishment of the very ancient soils of long quiescent land masses where climate and time have allowed extensive leaching of minerals.

Against such obstacles where many cultigens fail, one excels and thus provides salvation – cassava or manioc (*Manihot esculenta*). This perennial cultigen grows in a wide range of tropical climates from the lowlands to elevations above 1800 m where the average annual rainfall is greater than 500 mm. Manioc is drought-tolerant. It is adaptable also to a wide range of cropping systems and soils (Norman, *et al.* 1984:230). Manioc thrives in infertile acid oxisols, ultisols, alfisols, and histosols (ibid. 235), conditions which inhibit most other cultivars. Finally, Roosevelt (1980:139) points out that "It fosters the achievement of sustained-yield agricultural systems in the forest by its protection of the soil, recapture of nutrients from deep soil horizons, and contribution to forest regeneration." Moreover, manioc contains hydrocyanic acid which may deter pests and predators, as do its underground storage organs (Norman, *et al.* 1984:227).

Manioc is one of the most efficient producers of carbohydrates under poor agricultural conditions (Cock 1982:761). It yields more calories per hectare than most other crops. Also it requires very little labor input, although after harvesting three to four times as much labor is invested in the arduous task of processing as is required for planting and weeding (Moran 1976:187).

Manioc's nutritional value is exceptional in providing natural storage of starch in underground roots for up to two years without deterioration. By providing a reliable and continual supply of energy, it eliminates any problems of seasonal scarcity of calories from other sources (Roosevelt 1980:129). (However, Frechione [1982] mentions periods of famine among Ye'kuana as a result of failure in their manioc crop.) Manioc is a remarkable source of fairly inexpensive energy which frees people from much farm labor to pursue other activities including gathering, hunting, and fishing (Coursey and Booth 1977:81; Moran 1976:186).

The multiple advantages of manioc explain its widespread use and dominance in terra firma swiddens. For example, Boster (1983:50) found that manioc composes over 80 percent of the crops in the gardens of Jívaro in Ecuador. Furthermore, he discovered that the number of manioc varieties is far greater than that of all other crop species combined (ibid. 47).

Manioc also has disadvantages. Firstly, dependence on this cultigen as a dietary staple requires people to search elsewhere for foods which supply adequate protein. It actually produces a large amount of protein per hectare because of its high yield. However, the concentration of protein in the roots is very low, only about 1.6 percent. Thus enormous quantities of manioc would have to be consumed to accumulate a sufficient amount of protein (Roosevelt 1980:126; Terra 1964:98). To some degree this is accomplished by adults who consume large amounts of bread, beer, and other preparations made from manioc. However, this does not help children with their special nutritional needs for growth and development. They cannot consume large amounts because of the small size of their stomachs.

Secondly, manioc does not provide quality protein. It is rich in vitamin C and calcium, and gives significant amounts of thiamine, riboflavin, and niacin (Moran 1973:34). However, it is deficient in amino acids such as methionine and tryptophan. Nor does the composition of manioc allow amino acid complementation by consuming a mixture of manioc and legumes or corn. For example, both manioc and corn are deficient in tryptophan (Roosevelt 1980:128).

Thirdly, manioc is toxic. The latex contains cyanogenic glucoside which begins to break down into prussic acid, acetone, and glucose when harvested. Cyanogenic glucoside is highly soluble in water and decomposes when heated to 150 °C (Moran 1976:184). While proper processing and cooking eliminate most of the toxicity, a small residue remains which is released on digestion. A daily intake of quality protein with methionine is necessary to buffer the toxic residue to avoid small increments of permanent damage to the nervous system (Spath 1981).

In summary, while manioc has great benefits, it also has great costs. As an incomplete food, low in quantity and quality protein, and because it demands protein to counter toxicity, manioc as a dietary staple requires that adequate protein be secured from other sources. These may include other crops, wild plants from gathering, and meat from hunting and/or fishing. Thus, in terra firma forests, farming based largely on manioc actually magnifies the importance of foraging rather than reducing it.

Conclusion

The above considerations lead to the conclusion that for indigenous societies in the interior forests of Amazonia, foraging and farming are overlapping, interdependent, contemporaneous, coequal, and complementary. This situation is not limited to traditional indigenes. It applies to anyone who lives from a subsistence economy where manioc is the dietary staple, and where livestock and/or canned foods are either unavailable or too expensive to provide a regular source of adequate protein. In fact Smith (1976, 1978) documented extensive reliance on hunting by colonists along the TransAmazon highway.

In spite of these ecological and nutritional dilemmas, the nutritional and health status of most traditional indigenous populations appears to be fairly good (see e.g. Bamberger 1968; Berlin and Markell 1977; Black, *et al.* 1977; Holmes 1984). One of the more important ecological questions then becomes not whether there is sufficient protein in the diet, but what adaptive strategies have indigenous societies developed to maintain good nutrition and health?

When cultural ecology is subordinated to cultural evolutionism as a means to its ends, a very limited view of foraging, farming, and mobility in Amazonia results. Foraging societies are considered to be a lower and simpler stage of cultural evolution antecedent to farming, or products of devolution through competitive exclusion from the richer floodplains to the forest interior. The focus of cultural evolutionists on cultural complexity excludes many important considerations of ecology and adaptation.

On the other hand, when cultural ecology is liberated from cultural evolutionism and developed as an alternative approach on its own merits, a broader and deeper view of the relationship between foraging, farming, and mobility in Amazonia emerges. Foraging and farming are revealed as overlapping, interdependent, contemporaneous, coequal, and complementary domains. The validity and utility of this second approach has been demonstrated through ecological, nutritional, archaeological, and ethnographic considerations which raise new questions and answers as well as new answers to old questions.

Chapter 5

Patterns of foraging and gardening in a semi-sedentary Amazonian community

William T. Vickers

Introduction

At times anthropological theories and concepts can be misconstrued and even used to perpetuate stereotypes about certain categories of people or societies. One example is the notion that hunters and gatherers are "nomadic" and cultivators "sedentary." Neither characterization is entirely appropriate or satisfactory. Rather, they represent overgeneralizations that are derived from a more complex body of ethnography and cultural evolutionary theory.

To be realistic, we should recognize that "hunting and gathering" is a broad label for human foraging adaptations that may be temporally and spatially organized in various ways (i.e., it is not simply a "nomadic" subsistence activity). Likewise, "horticulture" and "agriculture" are broad categories for cultivation practices that may be temporally and spatially organized in many different patterns (i.e., they are not simply "sedentary" subsistence activities).

Such a perspective allows the consideration of various propositions concerning spatial and temporal organization. One such proposition is, "Under certain conditions foraging is most efficiently practiced from a central location" (this is a prediction from optimal foraging theory and will be discussed in more detail later). Another proposition is, "Some forms of cultivation do not require a sedentary population." The first proposition suggests that even a sedentary community may practice foraging in an ef-

ficient manner, and counters the assumption that cultivation-induced sedentism *per se* has a negative effect on foraging. The second proposition suggests that there are patterns of cultivation that do not impose sedentism. Such statements do not imply that variable forms of settlement and organization should be random or chaotic; rather, the assumption is that people select specific patterns for pragmatic reasons.

The objective of this chapter is to illustrate such processes via an analysis of the subsistence ecology and spatial organization of the Siona–Secoya Indians of northeastern Ecuador. This is an Amazonian society whose members get most of their food through the cultivation of plants, but who also add vital components to their diet via hunting and other foraging activities. The Siona–Secoya fit neither the "sedentary cultivator" nor the "mobile hunter" stereotypes, so the nature and significance of their semi-sedentary settlement dynamics will be analyzed in detail.

Theoretical perspectives

Studies of the costs and benefits of foraging in animals give little support to the notion that a predator should move in a fully "nomadic" manner. Rather, movement is an activity that entails certain energetic costs and environmental risks, and therefore it is best employed when these costs and risks are offset by potential advantages to the predator. A benefit of movement is that it often increases the ability of an animal to acquire food or other necess-

Table 5.1. *Horn's (1968) model of optimal predator spatial organization as amended by Heffley (1981)*

Resource availability	Observed spatial organization
1 a Evenly distributed and stable (Horn)	Territorial spacing of bird nests
b Evenly spaced and stable (Heffley after Horn)	Small and dispersed Athapaskan family units
2 a Moving food dsitribution; highly clumped and transient (Horn)	Colonial nesting of Brewer's Blackbird nests in a central location
b Clumped, mobile, and unpredictable (Heffley after Horn)	Large Athapaskan settlements in a central location
3 Clumped and predictable, naturally occurring in environment or as cached food stores (Heffley)	Large and semi-permanent Athapaskan aggregations

Table 5.2. *Strategies of predator movement and resource use as presented by Kiester and Slatkin (1974)*

Resource availability	Predator strategy
1 Unpredictable environment; speed of predator response is significantly slower than speed of changes in resource availabilities	"Random search"; predator's movements are independent of the spatial and temporal distribution of the resource
2 Spatial and temporal variations are relatively predictable with large and permanent regions of high and low resource abundance	"Hill climbing"; predator searches and then attempts to follow an increasing gradient in the abundance of a resource
3 Resource is highly clumped with individual clumps being widely dispersed and stable over a long period of time	"Trap lining"; predator moves a long distance each day, stopping at certain locations to check resources
4 Temporal variability of the resource at a specific location is so small that a predator does not have to wait long periods without it becoming available	"Sit and wait"; predator does not move, but waits for the prey to come to it
5 Environment with temporal variations of large magnitude in the availability of resources	"Conspecific cuing"; predator observes the movements, density, and activity of conspecific individuals in addition to observing food resources and uses these to organize its movements

ary resources. Movement may also be an important aspect of securing a mate, establishing and maintaining a territory, exploring a habitat, or escaping danger. If movement offers no such incremental benefits to the animal, it wastes energy and incurs unnecessary risks to the animal's well-being and survival.

Optimal foraging theorists have attempted to identify specific conditions under which differing forms of predator organization will occur. One of the best known efforts of this type is a study by Horn (1968) of the spatial organization of the Brewer's Blackbird. Horn's analysis focuses on the resource conditions that influence nesting patterns among Brewer's Blackbirds. These birds display a "colonial" pattern in which many nests are located in close proximity; this is in contrast with another common pattern of some bird species in which the nests are widely dispersed over the landscape. Horn proposes that these divergent patterns are related to the temporal and spatial availabilities of food in the environment. Colonial nesting occurs when the resources are clumped and moving, so that their appearance at any given location is transient. More dispersed and territorial nesting is associated with more evenly distributed and temporally stable resources. Horn's explanation for these nesting patterns is that each minimizes the average distance of foraging flights (i.e., when resources are clumped and mobile the mean distance of flights is minimized by departing from a central location, and when resources are dispersed and stable the mean distance of flights is minimized when they originate from dispersed locations). Hence appropriate nesting patterns can improve the "efficiency" (food yield relative to effort) of bird foraging.

Recently, Horn's model of predator spatial organization has been taken one step further by Heffley (1981), who analyzes the spatial organization of three Northern Athapaskan Indian populations. She finds that Horn's "central" and "dispersed" cat-egories can be applied to certain Athapaskan settlements, but proposes two resource conditions not discussed by Horn: (1) when detailed information about resource locations is being actively shared; and (2) when clumped but predictable resources (including stored food) are used. Heffley furthermore (1981:146) suggests that Horn's categories of resource availabilities should be expanded to include a third type in which resources are "clumped and predictable." Among certain Northern Athapaskan groups such clumped and predictable resources included seasonal fish runs in the rivers and also cached food supplies. Both of these conditions supported large and semi-permanent Athapaskan settlements. Table 5.1 presents a summary of the basic predator–resource relationships proposed by Horn, and the additional pattern suggested by Heffley.

Another framework for the analysis of forager behavior has been proposed by Kiester and Slatkin (1974). They discuss a series of predator strategies that are deemed appropriate for five situations with differing resource characteristics. These situations and

Table 5.3. *Comparison of resource availability patterns as described by Kiester and Slatkin (1974), Horn (1968), and Heffley (1981)*

Kiester and Slatkin	Horn; Heffley
1 Unpredictable environment	Not discussed
2 Large and permanent regions of high and low resource abundance	Not discussed
3 Resource is highly clumped, with clumps widely dispersed and stable for long periods	Not discussed
4 Resources come to specific location predictably	Most like Heffley's type 3, "clumped and predictable"
5 Temporal variations of large magnitude	Most like Horn's type 2, "moving food distribution; highly clumped and transient"
6 Not discussed	Horn's type 1, "evenly distributed and stable"

strategies are summarized in table 5.2. Kiester and Slatkin do not focus specifically on settlement or nesting patterns, but are more concerned with patterns of predator movement. Nevertheless, the various resource conditions that they propose can be compared to those described by Horn (1968) and Heffley (1981). Table 5.3 presents such a comparison of the various proposals initially outlined in tables 5.1 and 5.2. As table 5.3 indicates, the schema share some similarities, but also a number of differences. For example, Kiester's and Slatkin's situation in which there are "temporal variations of large magnitude" is similar to Horn's "moving food distribution that is highly clumped and transient." But Kiester's and Slatkin's basically "unpredictable" resource situation is not fully compatible with any of the types proposed by either Horn or Heffley, although Heffley does use the adjective "unpredictable" to describe Horn's "moving food distribution that is highly clumped and transient." Also, Kiester and Slatkin do not appear to anticipate Horn's condition of resources that are "evenly distributed and stable."

What these comparisons suggest is that the various resource availability conditions discussed were derived from analyses of specific field situations, and that the situations encountered by Horn, Heffley, and Kiester and Slatkin varied along certain dimensions. If we combine all of the dimensions that these scholars predict will affect game availabilities and hunting strategies we have the following:

1. spatial patterning
2. temporal duration
3. mobility
4. predictability
5. density

It is obvious that some of these parameters are interrelated. For example, "mobility" involves both the spatial and temporal dimensions, and "predictability" may involve space, time, mobility, and density. Nevertheless, concepts such as "mobility" and "predictability" do provide a convenient terminology for the expression of qualities that may subsume a combination of more fundamental elements (e.g., "mobile" is easier to express than "spatial variation through time," and "predictability" may be grounded in the consideration of a complex series of factors concerning both the prey and the environment). Later, I will examine the utility of these formulations in assessing Siona–Secoya foraging and settlement patterns.

The Siona–Secoya

The Siona and Secoya Indians of northeastern Ecuador are representative of the "tropical forest" culture type as defined by Steward (1948). That is, they live in relatively small and semi-permanent settlements and cultivate tropical crops, and their social organization is based on kinship and the local residential group with an absence of tribal organization and chiefs. Hunting, fishing, and the collection of wild plant products are integral components of their overall subsistence system, even though the bulk of their food comes from gardening. Hence they represent a good case for the consideration of the impact of cultivation on hunting.

"Siona" is a term that generally is applied to the Western Tukanoan-speaking peoples inhabiting the upper portions of the Putumayo and Aguarico Rivers in Colombia and Ecuador. One gloss for Siona is "to the garden" as in /siona sayï/ ("I go to the garden"). How this term came to be applied as a cultural designation, or whether the "to the garden" gloss is of any particular significance in the matter, is uncertain. The term "Secoya" has a clearer origin. It comes from /sekoya/, which is the name of a small tributary of the Santa María River in Peru (which is in turn an affluent of the Napo River).

As of 1980 the population of Western Tukanoans in Ecuador was approximately 347 people who were living along the Aguarico River and its tributaries, the Eno and Cuyabeno (figure 5.1). Within this larger cultural and linguistic grouping were people who self-identified themselves to outsiders as Siona and Secoya, a small number of Kofán who had married Siona or Secoya spouses, and an even smaller number who identified themselves as "Angotero" or "Makaguaje" (both of the latter terms indicate Western Tukanoan identity). Those people who consider themselves to be "Siona" generally trace their roots to historical communities on the Aguarico River while the "Secoya" consider their homeland to be the Santa María River.

In sections that follow below I will discuss the basic parameters of Siona–Secoya cultivation, foraging, and settlement. These are central to the "farmers as hunters" theme of this volume, as well as to the spatial predictions of optimal foraging theory already discussed. It will be shown that the Siona–Secoya base much of their subsistence economy on the cultivation of plants, and that their system of shifting cultivation is both produc-

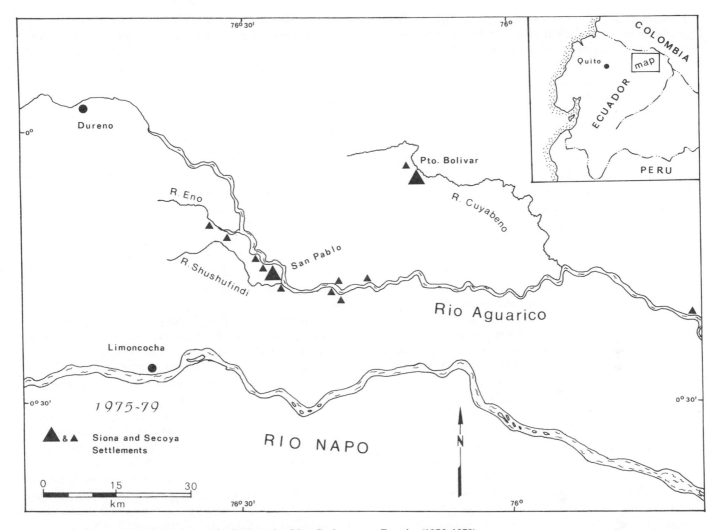

Fig. 5.1. Siona and Secoya settlements in the Aguarico River Basin, eastern Ecuador (1975–1979)

tive and reliable. Further, it requires quite low investments of labor and does not impose true sedentism or any rigid form of spatial organization.

Hunting and fishing are also integral components of the overall economy since they provide most of the essential dietary proteins and fats. Indeed, Siona–Secoya hunting is quite comparable to the hunting activities of many purely foraging peoples, especially with regard to the level of technology and hunting strategies employed. The demands of shifting cultivation appear to impose few, if any, artificial limitations on the range or extent of Siona–Secoya hunting (see Griffin's chapter 6 in this volume for similar findings among the Agta).

Finally, the settlement dynamics of the Siona–Secoya are fluid in that all settlements are composed of households that may cluster or separate at any time. In comparative terms, Siona–Secoya settlements may be less flexible than the camps of many hunting and gathering peoples, but only marginally so.

Cultivation

The Siona–Secoya practice gardening of a type that is va-

riously referred to as "slash-and-burn," "shifting," or "swidden" cultivation. Gardens are made in both primary and secondary growth, and the debris in most gardens is burned (unless rains catch the cultivator unawares). An estimated 95 percent of gardens are polycropped, with the bulk of the harvesting occurring over a two- to three-year period (certain palms and tree crops are exploited for a much longer period). Old gardens are generally fallowed for a period of years, but fallow periods may be relatively short in certain locations owing to a scarcity of well-drained land (e.g. in the Cuyabeno River Basin).

The major crops of the Siona–Secoya include fifteen varieties of manioc (*Manihot esculenta*), fifteen of plantains (*Musa × paradisiaca*), and nine of maize (*Zea mays*). Various tubers (*Ipomoea batatas*, *Xanthosoma*, *Dioscorea* spp.) and fruits (e.g., *Carica papaya*, *Inga* spp., *Pourouma cecropiifolia*, *Matisia cordata*, and many Solanaceae) are also cultivated (Vickers and Plowman 1984).

Siona–Secoya gardens are divided into three basic types based on the degree of their diversity; such types include high-diversity intercropping or "kitchen gardens," low-diversity intercropping, and the relatively rare monocropping (Vickers 1983a). High diversity in kitchen gardens is due to the fact that they contain a variety of condiments, and many medicinal, fruiting, and ornamental plants. The gardens located farther from the houses have a somewhat lower diversity and are primarily composed of the starchy staples (manioc, plantains, and maize), plus a few fruits, condiments, and medicinals. Monocropped gardens consist entirely of manioc, maize, or plantains and appear to be a comparatively recent phenomenon in Siona–Secoya culture, and are usually associated with production destined for marketing in the frontier town of Lago Agrio.

The Siona–Secoya prefer to locate their various gardens near their houses, but this is constrained by several factors. If a single household is established at a new site along the river and there is ample land of suitable quality, the first gardens will be adjacent to the dwelling. These will be extended outward in succeeding years. In some areas (e.g. the Cuyabeno River Basin) well-drained land may be scarce and the gardens will be situated at scattered locations where suitable conditions prevail.

When a number of households come together to form a new village a perimeter of gardens forms within two years. People extend this perimeter as they make new gardens, or select riverine sites that are farther away from the village (but can be reached by canoe). The preference for having gardens nearby is primarily based on the desire to minimize travel time and the work of carrying heavy loads of manioc and plantains to the house.

Most households make a new garden during the dry season of each year (December–January). Since gardens have a primary life cycle of about three years, each household has several gardens in production at any given time (plus older "abandoned" gardens that still yield some tree crops, especially the fruits of the *Bactris gasipaes* (palm)). Two aspects of Siona–Secoya cultivation deserve emphasis. The first is that their gardens require quite low investments of time and labor. Secondly, most of these investments are concentrated into relatively brief periods. Hence the Siona–Secoya enjoy a great deal of freedom in carrying out their foraging activities.

I studied one household's garden labor for a two-year period (1973–1974), and found a total investment of 1210 man-hours in four gardens totaling one hectare in size (67.5 hours in clearing, 185.8 in planting, 202.6 in weeding, 72.2 in walking, 622.6 in harvesting, and 58.9 in transporting crops). Hence the average annual time investment in gardens was 605 man-hours, with the actual labor being shared by Esteban, a 36-year-old man, Clementina, his 30-year-old wife, and Zoila, the eldest of his two daughters (age 12). I estimate that Esteban performed about 196 hours of this annual work, Clementina 278, and Zoila 132 (much of the women's time reflects the cultivation and harvesting of manioc).

If we were to compute artificial weekly means for this gardening work, Esteban gardened an average of 3.8 hours per week, and Clementina and Zoila 5.3 and 2.5 hours, respectively. In reality, a good deal of the work comes in spurts, such as in December and January when gardens are initially cleared and

planted, or at other times when they are weeded. The gardens do not require the constant attention of their owners. Many gardens are located several kilometers from their owners' households and are visited infrequently for the harvesting of crops or an occasional weeding. An isolated garden may go for weeks and even months without human intervention (as the household harvests from other gardens or goes off on expedition hunts). Hence Siona–Secoya gardens require low and sporadic investments of time.

Despite these low labor inputs, the gardens are quite productive. The estimated gross yield from Esteban's four gardens was 12,300 kg of foodstuffs per year, with an edible portion of nearly 8,400 kg, or 8.8 million calories (Vickers 1976:87). If these foods were completely utilized, they would meet the annual calorie requirements of eleven people. In fact, some of the garden produce spoils, some is given away, and some is simply not harvested because it is not needed. Such "excess" production is functional in that it provides a buffer against environmental uncertainties and risks.

Tables 5.4 and 5.5 provide information on the average individual dietary intake of the Siona–Secoya at San Pablo during 1973–1974. They are based on dietary surveys and the weighing of foods consumed in actual meals (Vickers 1976). Table 5.4 indicates the number of calories and grams of macro-nutrients that various classes of cultivated and wild foods provide to the diet. In table 5.5 the percentage contributions of these foods are presented. It shows that domesticated plant foods provided 72 percent of the dietary calories, 14.8 percent of the proteins, 22.2 percent of the fats, and 90.9 percent of the carbohydrates.

Domesticated animals made no significant contribution to the diet. Recently, a few households have attempted to raise small numbers of chickens, pigs, and cattle, but without notable success. One of the major difficulties is that the mobility of the Siona–Secoya prevents their attending to the needs of household stock. The few domesticated animals that survive to maturity are not eaten, but are sold to river traders or pioneer settlers.

Foraging activities

Among the Siona–Secoya foraging consists of exploiting wild animal and plant resources via hunting, fishing, and collecting. The relative significance of each of these activities is variable through time and space. For example, wild plant foods usually make a relatively small contribution to the overall diet (about five percent of the total calories as indicated in table 5.5). However, they may assume seasonal importance (e.g. during the fruiting of *Mauritia flexuosa* palms in the months of January and February), or when people do not have immediate access to productive gardens (e.g. during migrations or hunting trips away from settlements). Collected plant products do make indispensable contributions to the material culture of the Siona–Secoya as craft and construction materials, medicines, toilet items, etc. (Vickers and Plowman 1984).

Hunting and fishing are of great nutritional significance because they provide all of the meat in the diet, and an estimated

Table 5.4. *Mean nutritional intake per individual per day at San Pablo, 1973–1974*[a]

Foods	Grams	Calories	Animal protein (g)	Plant protein (g)	Total protein (g)	Fat (g)	Carbohydrate (g)
Domesticated plants	1,092	1,594	–	12	12	8	402
Wild plants	81	82	–	2	2	–	21
Domesticated animals	–	–	–	–	–	–	–
Hunted animals	314	413	58	–	58	27	–
Fish	45	45	8	–	8	1	–
Purchased foods[b]	22	81	–	1	1	–	19
Total	1,554	2,215	66	15	81	36	442

[a] Annualized mean for all age and sex groups.
[b] Primarily rice and sugar.

81.5 percent of the proteins, 77.8 percent of the fats, and 20.6 percent of the calories (table 5.5). Hunting and fishing are practiced by all Siona–Secoya households, but the relative significance of hunting versus fishing varies according to season and/or local habitat conditions. For example, people living on the Cuyabeno River (figure 5.1) derive more meat from fishing than from hunting. The reason is that this small river provides a habitat in which a variety of fishes can be found in virtually any season. Furthermore, the swampy conditions in the Cuyabeno Basin make terrestrial hunting rather difficult during most of the year.

In contrast, at San Pablo hunting produced far more food than did fishing (on an annual basis). Fishing in the Aguarico River is highly seasonal, with the best catches coming during the drier months of December through February. During this period impressive catches of large migratory catfish (*Pimelodidae*) are made, but throughout much of the year the turbidity and swift current of this large white-water river make fishing difficult. During the wetter months the people of San Pablo did engage in some fishing in smaller streams and creeks, but the yields were relatively minor. Overall, the gross production of hunting at San Pablo surpassed fishing by a factor of more than nine to one.

In summary, it seems best to consider hunting and fishing as complementary foraging activities that provide dietary meat. The emphasis given to one or the other at various places and times reflects specific environmental conditions. This chapter will focus somewhat more on hunting because of its relatively greater significance at the San Pablo study site, and because of the special concerns of this volume.

Hunting
Siona–Secoya hunting is almost exclusively the domain of young to middle-aged men. Exceptions to this sexual division of

Table 5.5. *Relative contributions of various foods to Siona–Secoya diet at San Pablo, 1973–1974*[a]

Foods	Grams (%)	Calories (%)	Animal protein (%)	Plant protein (%)	Total protein (%)	Fat (%)	Carbohydrate (%)
Domesticated plants	70.3	72.0	–	80.0	14.8	22.2	90.9
Wild plants	5.2	3.7	–	13.3	2.5	trace	4.8
Domesticated animals	–	–	–	–	–	–	–
Hunted animals	20.2	18.6	87.9	–	71.6	75.0	–
Fish	2.9	2.0	12.1	–	9.9	2.8	–
Purchased foods[b]	1.4	3.7	–	6.7	1.2	trace	4.3
Total	100.0	100.0	100.0	100.0	100.0	100.0	100.0

[a] Based on data in table 5.4.
[b] Primarily rice and sugar.

labor occasionally occur, such as when women assist in the collection of turtle eggs, encounter a tortoise along a path, or are forced to hunt for themselves owing to an absence of adult males in their household. Such female hunting is very limited in its frequency, scope, and yields. Women take no shame in stating their view that "Hunting is for men," or "The forest is the place of the men, and our place is around the village." (Kensinger, in chapter 2 of this volume, discusses similar gender distinctions among the Cashinahua.)

Boys learn about hunting by listening to the accounts of their elders, and by playing hunting games around the village and in gardens (such as practicing with blowguns and spears, and building small traps for rodents and birds). As they enter adolescence they may sometimes accompany their fathers on hunting forays, but rarely engage in serious hunting before the age of 16. There is no precise age at which men retire from hunting, but individuals in their 50s and 60s tend to hunt less frequently and intensively than do younger men. Men of this age usually have sons or sons-in-law who provide the bulk of the household's meat. Men seem to enjoy pole fishing until quite advanced ages. This is a far less strenuous activity than deep forest hunting.

Hunting technology

The traditional hunting technology of the Siona–Secoya includes such weapons as the blowgun and spear, plus various types of traps and deadfalls. Clubs are also employed to subdue animals. At times smaller animals are simply captured by hand. These methods are similar to those employed by purely hunting and gathering peoples.

Prior to the 1950s, the blowgun (with its poisoned darts) was the weapon of choice for birds, monkeys, and other small mammals (e.g. agoutis and squirrels). The blowgun is especially effective in taking arboreal game because of its accuracy, range, quiet operation, and the muscle-relaxing qualities of the curare dart poison (Yost and Kelley 1983). The spear was the weapon of choice for killing larger animals like peccaries and tapir. Among the Siona–Secoya, this classic weapon is beautifully crafted and based on an ingenious and functional design. The point is made from a section of bamboo and is semicircular at its base, but tapers to a finely-sharpened point. It is attached to the spear shaft both by beeswax that has been placed in the semicircular cavity of its base and a binding of twine made from the fibers of the *Astrocaryum* palm. The shaft is approximately two meters in length, and is made from the dense wood of the *Iriartea* palm.

In the late 1950s missionaries who lived among the Siona–Secoya began to supply them with crude muzzle-loading shotguns. By the early 1970s, most men had acquired more modern breech-loading designs of Canadian, American, or Brazilian manufacture (usually a basic single-barrel model in 16 gauge). While shotgun shells are expensive in this remote frontier region, all men can afford to buy a few shells at a time and then use less expensive components to reload the shell casings (i.e. primers, powder and shot). These are actively traded and supplied through itinerant river merchants, stores at frontier outposts, and missionaries.

The hunting "technology" of the Siona–Secoya also includes the dog. While some have questioned the utility of dogs in Amazonian hunting (e.g. Ross 1978), there is no doubt that the Siona–Secoya benefit from the dog's abilities in the sensing, tracking, chasing, and cornering of animals, and even in the killing of smaller game. Siona–Secoya men give considerable attention to the selection, training, and doctoring of their dogs, and those that prove to be good hunters are among a man's most valued possessions. These beasts are scrawny, flea bitten, and mistreated (by our own ethnocentric standards), but when hunting they are active searchers and pursuers, and can be ferocious and even valiant in their attacks on larger animals. Dogs are of greatest utility in the tracking and taking of animals like tapir, white-lipped and collared peccaries, capybara, paca, agouti, armadillos, and coatimundis. These dogs receive most of their food as spoils from hunting kills; those that prove to be incompetent hunters often starve.

While there are ritual and supernatural dimensions to hunting, the Siona–Secoya insist that the essential purpose of hunting is to provide meat for consumption by household members. Hunters do "optimize" in that they attempt to hunt effectively and successfully; indeed the key to hunting behavior is that it is almost entirely directed towards efforts to encounter, kill (or capture), and carry game to one's home. Kills are often shared with those beyond the immediate household, but only after the household has been provisioned. Such "giving away" of meat is sensible in that it allows for full utilization of a perishable product (the Siona–Secoya have no adequate means of preserving large amounts of meat for a long time). It also establishes reciprocal relationships whereby meat is received from other hunters who make large kills.

Seasons, hunt types, and strategies

Hunting is practiced on a year-round basis. Seasonality influences certain aspects of hunting, but it does not cause the people to switch from one exclusive hunting pattern to another. The most common form of hunting is the "day hunt" in which a single hunter or a small group of hunters depart the settlement early in the morning, hunt opportunistically along forest trails, and return in the afternoon. Such day hunts are practiced in all seasons and can be viewed as the background against which more seasonal and specialized hunts take place. (Kensinger, in chapter 2 of this volume, presents a different classification of hunt types for the Cashinahua.)

The spatial attributes of day hunts are displayed in figures 5.2 and 5.3. Figure 5.2 indicates the routes taken in three day hunts. The first involved two hunters who followed a trail to the southwest of San Pablo and then branched to another trail that led to the northwest. This hunt covered a total of 9 km, took 8.1 hours to complete, and resulted in the kill of two white-lipped peccaries (*Tayassu pecari*), one Spix's guan (*Penelope jacquacu*), one piping guan (*Pipile pipile*), one trumpeter (*Psophia crepitans*), and the capture of a tortoise (*Geochelone denticulata*). The total meat yield of this hunt was 76.7 kg. It took place on January 10, 1974, or during the "dry" season.

The second hunt followed the same southwestern trail as the

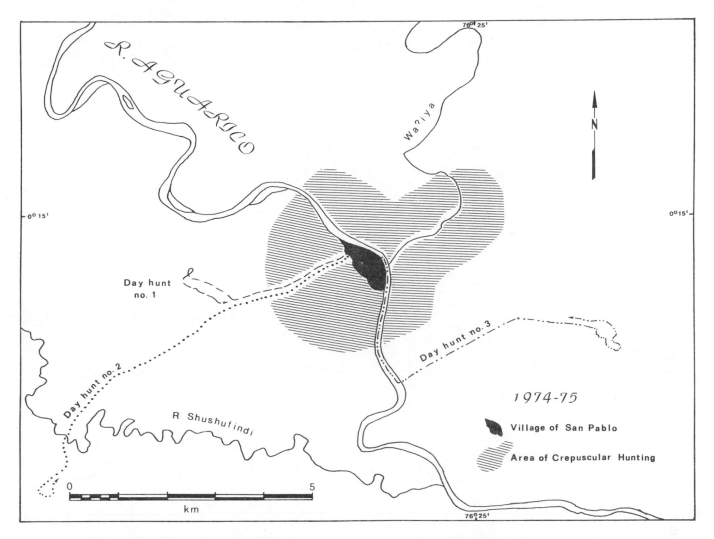

Fig. 5.2. Routes taken in three day hunts and area of crepuscular hunting around San Pablo, Ecuador

first, but continued on to a location on the south bank of the Shushufindi River. It involved one hunter who covered a total of 19 km in nine hours, and who bagged a total of 19.7 kg of meat consisting of one woolly monkey (*Lagothrix lagotricha*), an agouti (*Dasyprocta* sp.), two piping guans, and a tortoise. It took place on May 31, 1974, or during the "rainy" season.

Four men took part in the third hunt, which occurred on May 18, 1974 (also the "rainy" season). They traveled 2.5 km down the Aguarico River by canoe and then took overland trails to the northeast and then the east. Overall, this hunt covered 17.5 km, had a duration of 7.8 hours, and resulted in a yield of 35.4 kg of meat, consisting of one collared peccary (*Tayassu tajacu*), four woolly monkeys (*Lagothrix lagotricha*), and two curassows (*Mitu salvini*).

The mean yield per hunter per day on these three hunts was 18.8 kg of butchered meat, or nearly the 21.4 kg average obtained in a study of 283 hunts during 1973–1974 (Vickers 1980:13). Hence the days described are representative of this genre of hunting. Day hunts such as these proceed along known hunting trails that

radiate in all directions from the village (Vickers 1983b:458). The hatched area in figure 5.3 indicates the usual limits of day hunting as conducted from San Pablo.

Specialized forms of day hunting include the communal hunting of white-lipped peccary herds, and the waiting at salt licks for game to appear. The former takes place spontaneously when someone brings word to the village that a peccary herd or its tracks have been spotted. The latter is limited to a few special locations in the Aguarico and Cuyabeno drainages, none of which are located in the immediate vicinity of San Pablo.

Men also engage in less frequent crepuscular, or "morning" and "evening," hunts. These hunts typically last for about one to three hours and take place near the village in gardens, at the edge of the forest, or along streambanks. (Chapters 7, by Speth and Scott, and 8, by Szuter and Bayham, in this volume, discuss the significance of such hunts in North American Indian archaeology.) The hatched area in figure 5.2 indicates the limited areal extent of crepuscular hunting from San Pablo. The most typical game killed in these hunts are smaller species such as

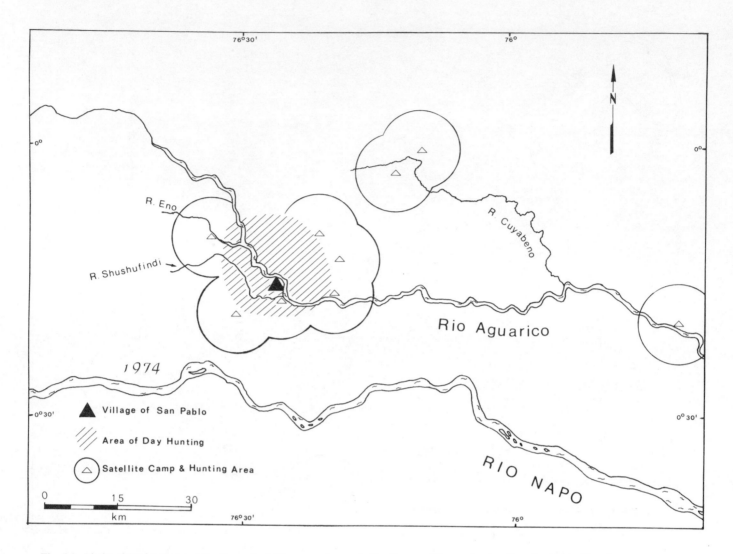

Fig. 5.3. Limits of day hunting and locations of satellite camps frequented by Siona and Secoya hunters from San Pablo, Ecuador

agouti, paca (*Agouti paca*), coatimundis (*Nasua* sp.), squirrels (*Sciurus igniventris*, and *Microsciurus* sp. or *Sciurillus* sp.), and various birds. Such hunts provide meat for a household meal or two, and are viewed as a stopgap measure to fill an empty pot and not as a substitute for day hunting (i.e. they are analogous to urban man's going to a convenience store to get a few necessary items, when he really needs to do his weekly shopping at the supermarket!).

Another form of Siona–Secoya foraging is what I term "expedition hunting." When engaging in an expedition the hunter is away from the settlement for at least one night, and sometimes for periods of up to three or four weeks. Hunts of a few days may involve a single hunter, small groups of hunters (two or three being most common), or a hunter and his wife and children. The longer expeditions usually consist of the hunter and family combination making a canoe trip to a hunting camp at a known location. These hunting camps fit the "satellite camp" definition of Jochim (1976:61). In essence they allow the Siona–Secoya to expand the radius of their foraging activities beyond the area that

can be reached by day-foraging from their primary settlements, and allow them to stay afield longer. Figure 5.3 shows the locations of nine satellite camps that were used by people from San Pablo during 1974.

Some hunting camps may be reached with only a half-day's travel, while getting to others may take two or three days. Members of the group carry provisions (e.g. manioc cakes or flour, plantains, smoked meat), and, if the trip is a long one, they may be given food and lodging by kin or acquaintances whose houses they pass. Otherwise, they will make temporary shelters on river beaches.

The hunting camps themselves are occupied for days or weeks and often have small but well made thatched structures that are maintained and reused. If no such shelter exists, one can be constructed in times ranging from an hour to several days (depending on the anticipated length of occupation and the amount of interior space, and degree of weather tightness and comfort desired). Life in the hunting camps consists of a variety of activities. The men often go out on day hunts and return in the evening. Women involve themselves with childcare, cooking, and foraging for plant materials. Men, women, and children may all participate in fishing, and collecting turtles and their eggs. And sometimes men construct heavy traps for ocelots (*Felis pardalis*) and margays (*Felis wiedii*), whose pelts provide a useful, if illicit, source of income.

Most hunters engage in at least four or five expedition hunts per year, and at least one of these will be of fairly long duration (i.e. ten days or more). Expedition hunts of shorter duration can take place in any season, while the longer ones tend to be associated with seasonal abundances of particular game in specific locations, such as the November/December turtling season on the Cuyabeno River and lower Aguarico River.

Specialized "dry season" foraging activities including fishing for large migratory catfish in the deep holes of the large rivers, using piscicides in small streams and oxbow lakes, and harpooning paiche (*Arapaima gigas*) that are trapped in the same lakes (the heart of the dry season falls in December and January). April and May are the period that the Siona–Secoya call "woolly-monkey-is-fat season" /nąsówiyape tïkáwï/. The fattened condition of the monkeys at this time is due to the fruiting of certain forest trees. According to Yost and Kelley (1983:218), this is also the birthing season of the woolly monkeys, and troop sizes are at their maximum (both to exploit the fruiting trees and to provide defense for the young). The Siona–Secoya give emphasis to hunting woolly monkeys at this time, but take them also at other times in the year (usually when encountered during the routine day hunting).

The absolute frequency of generalized day hunting may decline as these specialized seasonal hunts are engaged in, but the former are never entirely abandoned. As can be seen, most of the animals that become the foci of specialized seasonal foraging live in aquatic habitats. When such aquatic resources become available people can reduce their forest hunting to an extent, but do not give it up completely. Indeed, the period of November through January (when many aquatic resources are most easily exploited) is also a good time for forest hunting because this is the season of lowest rainfall and the relative lack of standing water makes it easier to traverse forest trails.

Some Amazonian scholars have characterized the "dry" and "wet" seasons as periods of "abundance" and "scarcity." This is based on the observation that both fishing and hunting conditions are easier during the dry season. In observing Siona–Secoya hunting, fishing, and foraging yields and consumption patterns I found less seasonal variance than such descriptions would suggest. The "woolly monkey season" is a case in point, for 58.5 percent of the recorded woolly monkeys killed at San Pablo during 1973–1975 were taken in months other than April and May. And when it is not "fishing season" on the Aguarico, people still do some hook and line fishing in the smaller streams and tributaries. While the Siona–Secoya may find forest hunting somewhat more tedious during the rainier months, they continue to engage in it on a regular basis, and with good results. Data from 1973–1975 indicate that the mean yields for "wet

season" hunts were as good as or better than the averages for the entire year (Vickers 1980).

While this finding might seem to contradict conventional wisdom, it should not be overly surprising if one considers the nature of the habitat. The Great Basin Shoshone (Steward 1938), the Northern Athapaskans (Heffley 1981), and the Inuit (Smith 1981), who all display marked seasonal shifts, are from the highly seasonal temperate, sub-Arctic, or Arctic zones. And the seasonal changes in !Kung organization and activities are linked to rather drastic variations in water availability (Lee 1984). In contrast, tropical rainforests constitute one of the most seasonally stable biomes known to science. Temperatures are remarkably consistent year-round, with significant rainfall in all months. In the Amazon "dry season" simply means a period when there is somewhat less precipitation than in other months, and the rivers are lower. Furthermore, in the western portion of the Amazon Basin the distinction between "wet" and "dry" seasons is far less pronounced than it is in eastern Amazonia (Salati, Marques, and Molion 1978). Since the Siona–Secoya reside within such a remarkably stable environment it is logical that most of their hunting strategies can be applied throughout the year.

The complexity of the multiple game resources that the Siona–Secoya hunt is evidenced in the fact that they employ all of the predator strategies discussed by Kiester and Slatkin (table 5.2), and sometimes employ two or more of these strategies in a single day. Day hunts often begin as a "random search" in which the hunter has no idea which specific game he will encounter. The strategy of "hill climbing" is employed if a hunter locates clusters of game such as a white-lipped peccary herd or a troop of woolly monkeys (i.e. the hunter makes an initial contact at the periphery of the cluster and then attempts to penetrate toward the center where abundances are higher). "Trap lining" is not very common, but the Siona–Secoya do employ a similar strategy when they set dispersed traps for ocelots and margays, and also when they dig earthen pits to capture tortoises (all of these traps and pits are baited with meat). Finally, "conspecific cuing" is extremely common as hunters share information on sightings of game and their spoor, or otherwise observe the activities of their neighbors.

Settlement patterns

Siona–Secoya settlement patterns are complex in that they are quite variable, although movements have traditionally occurred within recognizable territories estimated to average about 1150 square kilometers in size (Vickers 1983b). In order to understand Siona–Secoya patterns, we must first look at the fundamental units of social organization. The most basic unit is the household, which is also the most important unit of economic production and consumption. The simplest form of the household consists of the conjugal–nuclear family (i.e. a husband and wife, and their children) inhabiting a single thatched house or /wïɁé/. A somewhat more complex and traditional form of the household is the extended type that consists of a man, his wife, and married offspring and their spouses and children residing in a "big house" or /hai wïɁé/ (virilocality is the modal pattern in such households, but a few uxorilocal examples do exist). A modern variant of the extended household is the "household cluster" in which the married offspring and their children reside in separate dwellings that are located adjacent to the parents' dwelling (again, virilocality is the modal, but not exclusive, pattern). Such extended households and household clusters also form units of production and consumption in subsistence activities such as gardening and foraging.

The only settlement type beyond the household types described above is the /dadipï/ or "village." As defined here, the village is any Siona–Secoya settlement that contains multiple households that function as separate economic units in most day-to-day activities (i.e. the village is an aggregation of households, with the households representing any of the three forms discussed).

In terms of kinship, the "separate" households in a village may be unrelated, or may have linkages that are more distant than those found within the extended households. The population of a village can range from a low of about 50 individuals to a high of approximately 200, but a single figure is not a completely adequate indicator for people flow in and out frequently.

An analogy that can help us to conceptualize Siona–Secoya settlement is that of several dozen beads on a long string. While there are quite a few beads, they take up but a small portion of the string's length. The string represents a major river system such as the Aguarico. The beads represent Siona–Secoya households. Each of the beads (households) can occupy a solitary position on the string (river), or can be grouped with other beads. As time passes the beads can be shifted along the string in varying configurations, sometimes forming large aggregations, sometimes smaller groupings, and sometimes separated by greater or lesser distances. The beads can also jump over one another such that it is possible for them to vary their original linear order along the string, and new beads can be added from other strings (river systems).

This bead and string analogy illustrates some of the properties of Siona–Secoya settlement. Just as the beads are located

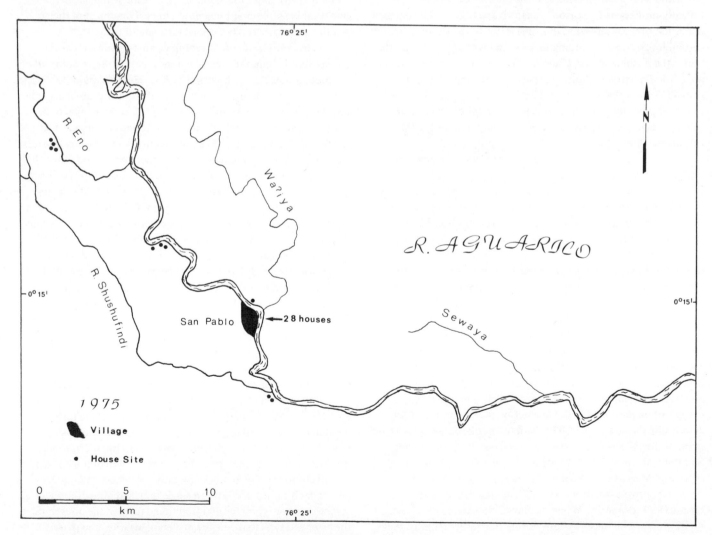

Fig. 5.4. Details of Siona and Secoya settlement along the middle Aguarico River in 1975. The house immediately opposite San Pablo (north bank of the Aguarico) is included in the count of 28 houses for the village

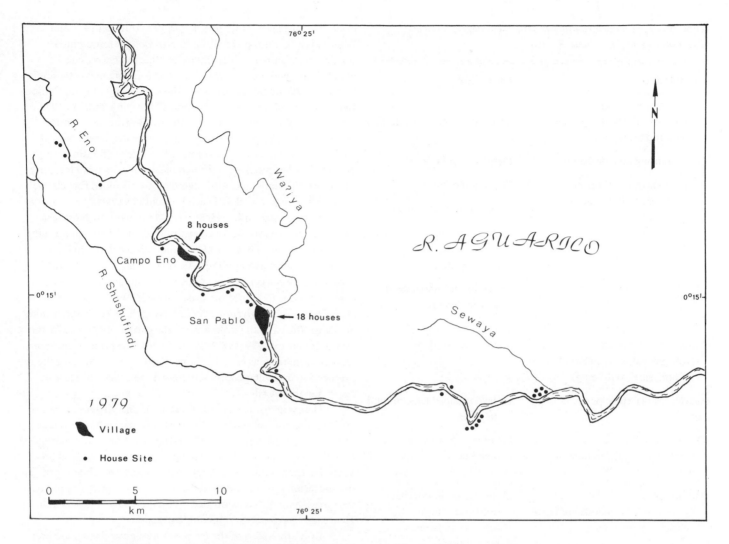

Fig. 5.5. Details of Siona and Secoya settlement along the middle Aguarico River in 1979

along the string, the relationship of households to the river system is a close one. And just as the beads can form a wide variety of patterns or configurations on the string, so can Siona–Secoya settlements on the river.

During 1973 the village at San Pablo was being formed as households migrated from the Cuyabeno River to a site on the Aguarico. The most frequent reason given for this migration was that the scarce garden lands along the Cuyabeno had been exhausted, whereas the San Pablo area was blessed with ample and well-drained lands. In 1974 the village continued to grow as more households arrived from the Angusilla River in Peru. These people had been invited to the new village by a kinsman who stressed that it had advantages such as a school and the presence of a missionary. By early 1975 San Pablo was a sort of "maximal" village with 28 houses, and nine other houses were located within a 16 km radius (figure 5.4). These settlements included conjugal–nuclear, extended, and extended cluster household types. More distant settlements (see figure 5.1) were located at Caño Negro on the Aguarico (about 90 km downriver from San Pablo), and Puerto Bolívar on

the Cuyabeno River (about 40 km northeast of San Pablo by air, or 100 km by the more circuitous river route). The Caño Negro settlement was an extended household, and Puerto Bolívar was a small village consisting of an extended household and several unrelated conjugal–nuclear households.

When I returned to Ecuador in 1979 it was evident that a number of changes had occurred in the settlements. In 1978 seven households had left the village of San Pablo and constructed dwellings adjacent to an extended household at Campo Eno, thereby turning that settlement into a small village (figure 5.5). Several households from San Pablo had also established new houses and gardens at Sewaya (a small tributary of the Aguarico whose mouth is about 25 km downstream from San Pablo). The extended household from Caño Negro had moved upriver to Remolino (a site on the Aguarico 8 km upriver from Sewaya). Both the Río Eno and Puerto Bolívar settlements had remained relatively stable during this period, although some houses had been moved a short distance.

To summarize, in 1974–1975 San Pablo was a maximal

Table 5.6. *Factors contributing to settlement aggregation and dispersion among the Siona–Secoya*

Aggregation	Dispersion
Physical environment	
Conditions suitable for gardens (soils and drainage)	Exhaustion of nearby garden sites
Good hunting and/or fishing	Depletion of fauna
Abundance of floral resources (for construction, crafts)	Depletion of flora
	Deterioration of house
	Increase of household and garden pests (insects, rodents, etc.)
	Incidence of human disease and epidemics
Social environment	
Influence of a shaman (who provides for spiritual and physical well-being)	Sorcery accusations
Search for marriage partners	Everyday social tensions and disputes
Defensive alliances (under aboriginal system of warfare)	Death of a household member
Missionaries (who provide religious guidance, schools, medical care)	Desire to avoid external influences and/or oppression (whites, labor bosses, missionaries)

village (with a population of 132 or 50 percent of the total Siona–Secoya population in Ecuador at that time), and coexisting with it at that time were a smaller village at Puerto Bolívar with eight households (48 people, or 18 percent of the Siona–Secoya population), and extended households or household clusters at Eno, Campo Eno, and Caño Negro. In 1979–1980 San Pablo was reduced in size, but still relatively large, and coexisted with smaller villages at Campo Eno and Puerto Bolívar, and extended households or household clusters at Eno, Remolino, and Sewaya. Finally, María Cipolletti, an Argentine anthropologist who lived among the Siona–Secoya in 1983–1984, reports (1985, personal communication) that San Pablo has been reduced to but a handful of households, with many of the people having moved downriver to Remolino. Hence Remolino appears to be emerging as the new primary village.

Discussion

This description of Siona–Secoya settlements reveals some of the difficulties in classifying these people as either "central

place" or "dispersed" foragers. From 1973 through 1978 San Pablo was a "central place," and Puerto Bolívar represented a smaller, but legitimate, "central place" (i.e. these were communities composed of several distinctive foraging units at a single location). During the same period, the households at Eno, Campo Eno, and Caño Negro were "dispersed" foraging units. In 1979–1980 San Pablo, Campo Eno, and Puerto Bolívar were central places and Eno, Sewaya, and Remolino were dispersed. Now Remolino appears to be a central place. The satellite hunting camps discussed earlier provide additional means of dispersing foraging effort over the landscape, although they are occupied for relatively brief periods (a few weeks of each household's year).

As discussed earlier, Heffley (1981) shows how Northern Athapaskans changed between centralized and dispersed foraging camps on a *seasonal* basis, and that this corresponded to fluctuations in resource availabilities. Among the Siona–Secoya the variation between centralized settlements and dispersed households is not due to such short seasonal cycles, but rather is associated with longer *multiyear* cycles involving the waxing and waning of villages (just as San Pablo grew in the period of 1973–1975 and was in decline by 1979–1982). Table 5.6 lists the principal ecological and social reasons cited by Siona–Secoya informants for their aggregation into village-level settlements, and their subsequent dispersion to new sites.

The cycles for relocating households and villages are multiyear ones because of the labor investments and resources in gardens. Once people have made the initial investments in a garden or two, the amount of food that will be available over the next few years determines that they should not be carelessly abandoned. To use the terminology of optimal foraging theory, gardens provide resources that are "concentrated," "predictable," and "reliable." Hence they have a certain binding attraction.

In contrast, few of the tropical forest animals that are hunted by the Siona–Secoya appear in clumps or concentrations, nor are most of them predictable. Exceptions include white-lipped peccaries, which form large herds (but are unpredictable in time and space), woolly monkeys which congregate around fruiting trees in April and May, and turtles which lay eggs on river beaches in November and December. The vast majority of the animals that the Siona–Secoya hunt are dispersed and unpredictable in occurrence, so they do not reward large aggregations of hunters. However, Siona–Secoya gardens do not require constant attention, so the people are free to engage in a wide variety of individual and small group foraging activities that take them far beyond their houses and garden sites.

In summary, the Siona–Secoya demonstrate settlement dynamics that are intermediate between those of most hunter–gatherers and agriculturalists. Ultimately, the Siona–Secoya pattern reflects their reliance on a mixed economy of both feral and domesticated resources that present a complex variety of availability parameters (i.e. density, patterning, duration, mobility, and predictability). While settlements (at either the village or household levels) do endure for a period of several years in response to the availability of domesticated plant foods, the people retain a high degree of mobility and flexibility in their overall adaptation.

In terms of hunting, fishing, and collecting, they act as central-place foragers when they live in villages, and as dispersed foragers when they operate from dispersed households and satellite hunting camps.

Conclusions

In assessing the Siona–Secoya data relative to the "farmers as hunters" theme of this volume, several key points stand out. Firstly, cultivated plant foods have far more dietary significance than wild plant foods, yet animal domesticates have made no impact on subsistence. Siona–Secoya hunting and fishing patterns are very analogous to those of many hunting and gathering groups (in terms of the division of labor, strategies, technology, and dietary significance). While the form of cultivation practiced does require the people's presence at times, its demands are far less than those of most forms of agriculture. Hence it does not prevent their hunting over a large territory, engaging in expedition hunts, or establishing satellite hunting camps. In effect, the village or household settlements function as semi-permanent base camps from which other activities originate.

If we try to relate this ethnographic information to cultural evolutionary theories, we might view a group such as the Siona–Secoya as being intermediate between foraging and agricultural societies. Based on the Siona–Secoya evidence alone, one is tempted to conclude that plant domestication is of greater initial significance to the economy than is the domestication of animals. Among these people gardening has essentially replaced foraging as the primary means of providing the vegetable foods in the diet, yet hunting continues unabated. An interesting comparison with the !Kung San foragers of Botswana demonstrates this point. Lee (1984:54) estimates that hunting provides 230 grams of meat per day to the average !Kung individual. Among the Siona–Secoya the estimate is 314 grams per day (table 5.4). In both cases, the hunting of wild animals is the essential means of providing dietary meat. The !Kung, however, get 69 percent of their overall diet (weight in grams) from wild plant foods. The Siona–Secoya get only about 5 percent of their total dietary grams from such feral plants, but derive 70 percent from their garden plants. Hence the !Kung and the Siona–Secoya are somewhat comparable as hunters, but differ greatly in how they acquire plant foods.

In cultural evolutionary terms, the ultimate decline of such a "cultivator–hunter" way of life can be predicted as a consequence of human demographic growth and modification of the habitat. The suggested scenario is the following:

1   As the cultivator–hunter population increases people occupy more land, causing the hunting territories of local groups to shrink, and increasing the rates of habitat modification and predation on animal populations.
2   The populations of many game species decline, while a few may benefit from human intervention in the environment (e.g. intentional or unintentional provision of foods from gardens and other human-modified habitats). A degree of animal domestication occurs at this point, but most of the meat in the diet is still derived from hunting.

3   With the continuing transformation of the environment, wild animal populations become greatly reduced and make hunting a relatively minor economic activity; animal domesticates provide most of the meat.
4   Hunting becomes a highly regulated "sport" and status activity affirming "male" values of "the thrill of the chase," "camaraderie," "getting back to nature," etc. (consider for example the hunting of boars by the European landed elite, African safaris, the American who uses a $1,500 "presentation-quality" shotgun to shoot tame quail on a private reserve, etc., with only lower-class "poachers" continuing to hunt on a subsistence basis).

While this scenario may seem logical enough, several caveats are in order. The first is that the "Neolithic" process has had a variety of expressions owing to differences in local plant and animal resources and other habitat conditions. It is not necessary to demand that domestication everywhere followed the same precise sequence of events. As I argued earlier, rigid typological formulations and evolutionary sequences distort the range of variation in human adaptations. The relative lack of success with animal domestication in Amazonia (and the New World generally) has been attributed to a paucity of suitable candidate species. Since manioc cultivation has few spatial and temporal constraints, Amazonians have been able to retain a good degree of mobility in their adaptations. The same conditions probably do not apply to Eurasian grain farming.

Finally, the archaeological evidence for the Middle Eastern Neolithic appears to indicate a more or less simultaneous domestication of plants and animals (Braidwood and Howe 1962). For this situation I hypothesize that those who were initially domesticating both plants and animals would still have been getting most of their meat supply from the hunting of wild individuals (in order to conserve their domestic stock) until such feral populations were greatly reduced, at which time meat from domesticates would have become predominant.

Note

Various periods of my research among the Siona–Secoya in Ecuador from 1973 through 1980 have been supported by the Henry L. and Grace Doherty Charitable Foundation, the National Institute of Mental Health, the Florida International University Foundation, Inc., Cultural Survival, Inc., and the Latin American and Caribbean Center and College of Arts and Sciences of Florida International University. Affiliations with Ecuadorian institutions were provided by the Instituto Nacional de Antropología e Historia and the Instituto Nacional de Colonización de la Región Amazónica Ecuatoriana. The time for the writing of this chapter has been supported by the School of American Research, Santa Fe, New Mexico and a Resident Scholar Fellowship from the National Endowment for the Humanities. I thank Susan Kent for her comments on the manuscript. Edite Vickers, Mary Vickers, William E. Carter, Charles Wagley, Norman E. Whitten, Jr., Hernán Crespo Toral, Timothy Plowman, Raymond B. Hames, Theodore Macdonald, Mark B. Rosenberg, James A. Mau, Jorge Uquillas, James A. Yost, Orville and Mary Johnson, Marianne Schmink, and Jonathan Haas are among the many people who have provided me with assistance and encouragement through the years. I thank both the named and the unnamed. Most of all, I thank the Siona and Secoya people.

Chapter 6

Hunting, farming, and sedentism in a rain forest foraging society

P. Bion Griffin

Introduction

The Agta are diversified foragers found scattered throughout northeastern Luzon, the Philippines. In this chapter I examine data collected among two groups of Agta, those of Nanadukan on the coast of southeast Cagayan Province, and those of Ihaya, in the mountains of southern Isabela Province.

Agta foragers build their subsistence strategies around the dynamic complexities of a humid tropics natural environment and a diverse social environment. Hunting and other forms of protein procurement dominate the Agta world, as farming dominates the various non-Agta peoples of Luzon's eastern mountains, rivers, and coastline. The Agta fit horticulture activities into the broader mesh of their subsistence cycles, while farmers only rarely stray from fields to the forest. Agta hunting, farming, and mobility are best understood by considering both forest game and the demands of non-Agta neighbors.

The Agta are, when seen from both emic and etic stances, foragers who manipulate several subsistence tactics within a larger hunting strategy of daily and yearly food procurement (Estioko-Griffin 1984; Griffin 1984). In addition, they are economically and politically dominated by farming-based non-Agta societies (Griffin 1985, 1981; Headland 1986; Rai 1982). All Agta fit somewhere in a set of relations with swiddeners or fixed field farmers, or both, and adjust their own hunting and farming activities to the demands of their dominant neighbors. Much of the daily starch is

gained through attention to these people (Headland 1986, 1984, 1978; Peterson 1978). Hunting is, however, at the heart of the Agta culture (Estioko-Griffin and Griffin 1981b).

Subsistence and settlement are obviously intertwined. As Agta subsistence activities vary within their environmental matrices, the permanence and location of residences change, and the composition of the residential groups fluctuates. With abundance of food comes stability; minor adjustments in housing placement come from extraneous influences such as the need to leave unsanitary surroundings. As social and natural resources are depleted, and as weather permits, settlement in other locations may be necessary. Ongoing experimentation in subsistence tactics may influence the amount of sedentism (this is to be discussed in detail later), although the experiments in mobility reduction are always intruded upon by the adjacent dominant society. All Agta are somewhat knowledgeable about cultivation, and most claim swidden plots (Estioko-Griffin and Griffin 1981a). A general conclusion of this chapter is that, as horticultural efforts are increased, hunting activities are diminished, and semi-sedentary residences are more often found.

Throughout the subsistence and climatic cycle, the Agta adjust their emphases around both the demands of the environment and their concern for ensuring a minimally adequate supply of protein and starch. Horticulture, as practiced by the Nanadukan Agta, discussed below, fits the strengths of the growing seasons and the weakness of the game cycles. Every month entails both hunting and gardening, yet each allows attention to be given to the other. Neither is adequate by itself, as the strategy now works.

Agta settlement is first and foremost based on identification with traditionally used foraging ranges, membership in family units, and location of collectible foodstuffs. Given these, the consideration of seasonality is paramount. Rainy-season residence placement combines safety factors (above floods and beyond landslides and falling trees), a consolidation of kinspeople earlier dispersed in smaller units, and proximity to arable land. The Agta are required to plan their residence months ahead, since they cut swiddens for the next season while they are in the process of moving out of the last season's homes. In fact, since 1980 Nanadukan Agta have each year reported eight to ten months ahead where they would reside in the following rainy season. As will be seen, such predictability and sedentism are unheard of among the less horticulturally oriented Agta in Isabela Province.

Agta hunting, farming, and sedentism

Humid tropics foragers today usually have economic and social relations with farmers, with the possible exceptions of the Andamanese and Tasaday.[1] In the distant past – at least during the late Pleistocene in the Philippines – such was not the case. Clearly the Philippines foragers either were "pure" hunter–gatherers or had developed a minimal horticulture, because their presence is known in northeastern Luzon since the early Holocene (Griffin 1985; Theil 1980). Models of the origins of plant domestication are well known (Harris 1977, 1972), but data are inadequate. The ability of the rain forest to provide sufficient plant and animal foods for human consumption is arguable,[2] but some data from northeastern Luzon suggest that animal protein is abundant (Griffin 1984). The strategy of the hunting of abundant game and the gathering of less abundant plant starches may begin in a combination of limited movement over foraging ranges and in the caching of plant foods through "tending."

All Agta today have regions over which they secure the food and maintenance materials of daily living. No bounded territories exist, either cognitively or behaviorally.[3] River drainages, however, comprise the aquatic and terrestrial domain of extended family residential clusters. Movement up- and downriver is the rule, with residence often on the coastal beaches on the eastern side of the Sierra Madre or in the upriver sections of the mountains' western watercourses (figure 6.1). Residence and subsistence on the western side of the Sierra Madre are limited by the concentration of permanent farmers found along the tributaries flowing into the Cagayan River. Encampments are found in the forest interior; their occupants seldom travel to the ocean or to municipal settlements so easily accessible to less remote Agta. The more remote Agta may make swiddens (and have done so more especially in recent years), and their horticultural practices provide the best insights into the early relationships of hunting and farming.

These Agta of the mountain interior shift their residences along the rivers that are the focus of their social and economic identities. They place their homes close by good hunting and fishing locales. Since non-Agta trade partners are always some distance away, they are less relevant in settlement decisions. Horticulture, with its delayed returns, is a minor pursuit. To argue that minor means unimportant, however, would be untenable. Since all Agta do engage in some planting, lessons may be learned from the two styles of crop cultivation that are commonly observed.

Firstly, as Agta in the forest interior anticipate the rainy season, small swidden clearings are cut and burned, sometimes near the probable location of the houses. Sweet potato and cassava cuttings are planted, as may be more minor plants. The swiddens seldom measure, in our experience, more than 50 m to a side. They are neither weeded nor tended unless hunters walk through at night, establishing their scent in order to discourage wild pigs from entering. Roots are dug in emergencies late in the rainy season, when the food stores of non-Agta farming trade partners are low.

The second style of horticulture is even more an emergency food tactic, and more crude in technique. The main thrust of the style is the planting of a "swidden" plot of as few as three or four cuttings, generally in a damp yet sheltered spot. Thomas Headland pointed out to me, while we were examining such a plot in the interior Casiguran area, its seemingly useless nature, but wondered if it might not be a single meal tucked away for future use. Subsequent research indicates that these "caches" are indeed scattered about up- and down-river. A single pineapple, a cluster of cassava, or, especially, a dozen or so sweet potato plants may survive animals and other humans, and be remembered by the passing forager–planter. As with the fruit trees of the forest, each cache is known as to condition and location by the planter.

The caching of cultigens may have developed out of a practice still found today – the replanting of wild tuber stem bases. Some kinds of wild yams are replanted after digging up the corm, and again harvested when mature. At least some Agta know the location of many of the individual wild yams growing within their foraging range.

Caching of modern root crops is especially advantageous since they are easily planted, mature rapidly and are much more readily eaten than are wild varieties. In addition, securing cuttings is quickly done during visits to farmers' fields. The result of caching is the existence of scattered emergency foods, usually within a short walking distance of campsites. Hunting and fishing trips need not be curtailed, since an extra day or two may be gained by harvesting the caches. Only as problems are encountered in obtaining adequate returns from hunting does horticulture expand into larger-scale swiddening.

Nanadukan Agta

The Eastern Cagayan Agta are found along the coast of northeastern Luzon from the municipality of Maconacon north to the tip of the island (figure 6.1). Family residential clusters are situated throughout much of the year along the many rivers flowing easterly out of the mountains. Some of the families prefer rivermouth and beach-front locations, with ready accessibility to fresh and marine water resources, a variety of forest zones, and contact

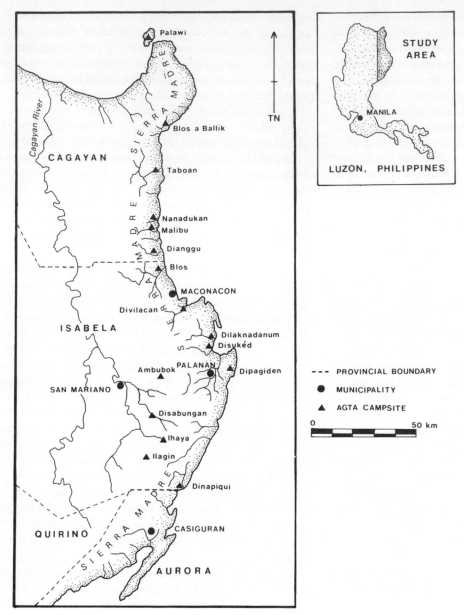

Fig. 6.1. The location of the Agta

with traders. The Nanadukan River Agta are such a group (Estioko-Griffin 1984).

Nanadukan is a relatively small, isolated, yet typical river, fronted by the Pacific Ocean and backed by the 3000 m high Sierra Madre. The mountains in southern Cagayan Province are especially rugged and steep and cut by innumerable streams and rivers. Dipterocarp forest covers much of this broken terrain, although the coastal jungle and the stunted mountain-top growth are also parts of the Nanadukan environment.

Rivers, forests, and mountain terrain are best understood in their seasonal contexts. Nanadukan experiences an annual cycle of variation in rainfall, air temperature, wind velocities, and storm frequencies that defies easy classification, but is of critical importance to the human, floral, and faunal components of the ecosys-

tem. Called non-seasonal by the Philippine Weather Bureau (Pagasa) and Flores and Balagot (1969), and "two-seasonal" by myself (Griffin 1984), the climate is divided into four seasons by the Agta. Beginning shortly after the start of the new year, late January or early February, *kattikel* sees the coldest temperatures exacerbated by the last weeks of the northeast monsoon winds. While the rains are diminishing in quantity and intensity, nearly daily cold, driving showers keep the rivers high and the forest floors soggy. The season is simply cold and miserable. *Kattikel* fades into *kasinag*, or a semi-dry season that may begin in March and last until September. May, June, and July average about twenty days per month without rain. Sunlight is intense; the forest floor dries and rivers fall to a fraction of their earlier levels. Mountain streams often completely disappear and the ocean calms with the lack of wind. This dry, or less wet, season receives some of its moisture through afternoon showers, but most derives from occasional tropical storms.

Beginning as early as a rare May typhoon, these storms are most likely in August, September, and October. The storms may be just rainy depressions or full-fledged cyclones which drop great amounts of water in a few hours and then pass beyond the area. While the forest is drenched and rivers flood, run-off is rapid and a return to dry conditions usually ensues. *Katbigew* briefly follows the dry months. This season is a transition to the full rainy season so noticeable to human residents. During *Katbigew* there is a deterioration in pleasant weather and an increase in wind and rain brought by the appearance of the northeast monsoon. Annual storms are certain in this major Philippine typhoon belt. *Ahidid* completes a single cycle as now reconstructed. *Ahidid* is the period of the northeast monsoon, with about 25 days per month of rain, plus rough seas, strong winds, and overcast skies. The season becomes progressively colder through November and December, although the rainfall lessens as *kattikel* appears.

Animals, plants, and humans live according to this cycle; the flowering and fruiting of the dipterocarps and other trees follow, in part, the rainfall patterns. Wild pig, deer, and monkey thrive or fail as the fruit and other floral foods are found. Human subsistence in turn is a reflection of the condition of game and of plant productivity. Agta foragers are most tightly keyed to game animals dependent on wild roots and fruits. Non-Agta farmers, while less directly influenced by the environment's wild fauna, are additionally affected by the climate. Their growing cycle and the success of crops depend on relatively predictable rains appearing and disappearing each year, and on the behavior each year of the major storms. The abundance of harvest is largely determined by rain and wind characteristics, and the consumption of the ripe rice by insects and birds. Since the number of game animals is ultimately a function of the same weather conditions, the Agta also live according to climate.

Agta hunting is a year-round activity that dominates the subsistence system, the attentions of the people, and relations with non-Agta (for an in-depth treatment see Estioko-Griffin 1984). Agta are bow and arrow hunters, sometimes driving game with dogs, sometimes stalking by day or night, singly or in teams. Both men and women may hunt, especially among the Eastern Cagayan groups and those resident at Nanadukan. Hunting does have its variation in tactical patterns, differing by season and weather, by local forest and game conditions, and by human inclination.

The rainy season is considered by the Agta to be the best for hunting. Wild pig (*Sus barbatus*), deer (*Cervus philippinensis*), and monkey (*Macaca philippinensis*) are the game animals actively sought, although smaller animals are shot on sight. The animals are generally healthiest and fattest after the dry season and its abundance of fruits. Animals may remain fat until the end of the wet season. The young of wild pigs, born in the dry season, will either have died, been killed by the Agta, or survived to near adulthood. Deer, which bear young over twelve months, are nearly as desirable as the pigs, being only somewhat less fat.

Fat animals are most valuable, since Agta and farmer alike need and want fat to consume during the cold months. Game is most easily approached and killed at this time, as most animals should be "overweight, cold, wet, and sluggish." Hunters often stalk in the wet, silent forest to within easy arrow shot. Animals also may be at lower elevations and hence more readily reached in spite of travel made difficult by flooding.

The dry days and months favor diversification of subsistence activities, while hunting tactics shift to include an Agta favorite, driving game with dogs. Lone males are more likely to spend the day slowly walking the deep forest. Teams of men and women may take both short and long trips with all available dogs, chasing game up and down the mountainsides. The success rate of drives is high, although the animals shot are smaller than on the typical stalk.

Spearfishing in both rivers and littoral waters is a frequent dry season activity. Rivers are relatively low and slow, and the ocean may be entered close to shore and reefs. Fish are most easily speared during *kasinag,* when waters are clear and swimmable, having lost the sediments of flooding and the debilitating coldness of *kattikel.* Both Agta and non-Agta also desire the change from meat to fish. Ease of procurement, climatic conditions, and cultural preferences together conspire to lessen dependence on hunting in favor of fishing. In addition, because less time is spent on both the short game drives and brief fishing forays, an increase in horticultural activities is made possible. The Agta of Nanadukan reflect this advantage in their commitment to swiddening, as will be described in detail below.

The organization of residence and of task groups is based on the maximally efficient extended family, the integration of food resources within the subsistence cycle, and the seasonal cycle itself.[4] Daily work within a group may take many specific forms; one person alone may hunt, fish, gather, cultivate, and trade. Little gender-based division of labor is found outside of a few maintenance tasks, and men and women may hunt, fish, and farm. Men do, however, tend to cut the larger trees, or hire non-Agta labor, while women and girls dig the bulk of the root crops. All Agta value hunting highly in the sense that it dominates their thoughts, pleasures, and activities. However, hunters are not valued over non-hunters, and all food collection activities seem to be found enjoyable. Both animal protein and starch are desired with meals, although lack of the latter is considered a real hardship. The participation of both sexes of a wide range of ages in most subsistence pursuits is typical of most Agta (Estioko-Griffin and Griffin 1981b; Griffin, *et al.* n.d.a). The residential pattern closely reflects the personnel demands and potentialities of subsistence. Each extended family cluster locates itself in a traditional, well known campsite. This unit tends to be the single occupant of a small river, but will share the larger rivers with one or two other clusters, all related by kinship, with five kilometers or more separating most clusters from each other. Each extended family is divided into two to six nuclear families, each with its own dwelling structure. The result is a campsite of several small houses closely spaced and situated in a location adjacent to flowing drinking

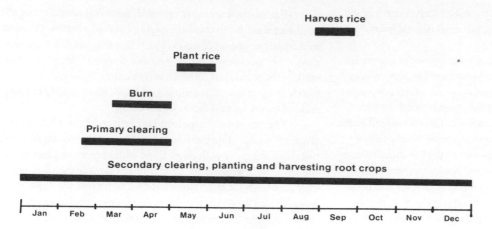

Fig. 6.2. The horticultural cycle among the Nanadukan Agta

water. In a rainy-season site, the houses are located well beyond the reach of floods, landslides, and storm-blown trees, with the main swidden fields nearby.

The Nanadukan Agta, like nearly all the Agta of northeastern Luzon, adhere to a seasonal pattern of residence location, size, mobility, and relationship with subsistence activities. Rainy-season base camps are constructed just before the rains start – about October. Some people build houses in September, others wait until late October. The specific details vary from year to year and family to family, but usually about three months are passed in the small pole and thatch houses. The Agta such as those in southern Isabela Province seldom use rainy-season houses for more than two months, depending on the weather in a given year.

Dry-season habitations are very temporary units. The classic form is the lean-to shade, a rectangular thatched shield held up by a single pole and readily adjusted for changes in rainfall, sunlight, and wind. A lean-to may last through one dry season, although repairs may make an old one suffice for overnight use during trips away from home. The simplest lean-to is good for only a few nights in good weather, but the large, well thatched ones, when placed face to face, will survive days of typhoons. Since a light lean-to may be built in less than one hour, their use is favored in special-activity camps.

During the rainy season, all horticultural activities are undertaken from the houses near the swiddens. Field houses are uncommon. An abandoned house might be used to store seed rice or to sleep in if game is anticipated in an old swidden.

Dry-season and special-activity camps are less carefully located than are the more permanent rainy-season homes. By early January, the Agta are eager to get out of their by now insect-infested pole houses and into less substantial lean-to structures placed on sand beaches or rocky riverbeds. These dwellings may be only a few meters away from the abandoned houses or may be several kilometers removed. They are often nearly as mobile as their owners, being carried whole or dismantled to new locations, or they may be "stacked" and left for eventual reuse. The ideal locations for these dry-season homes are

at traditional sites that are adjacent to old but still bearing gardens, good hunting and fishing spots, and special resource collection areas.

Dry-season residence among the Nanadukan Agta tends to be a "central place" pattern near the rainy-season houses, accompanied by ready movement into the scattered houses placed upriver, along the coast, and on nearby streams. The base camp is seldom completely abandoned by all families, but some are frequently absent on food-getting activities or visits to relatives. The Nanadukan Agta are reluctant to leave the locations of their swidden since even a few days' absence can lead to land theft by non-Agta.

Subsistence seasonal cycle

The Agta settlement and subsistence patterns are highly interdependent, as can be seen in the description of the latter. The Nanadukan Agta horticultural cycle begins with the clearing of new swidden for planting the food that will be eaten in the subsequent rainy season (figure 6.2). The cutting of swidden fields from secondary and primary forest growth is not a complex affair. People work in a haphazard manner, some cutting early, some late. Other tasks take priority, and may in cases preclude getting the year's swiddening done at all. A few Agta men and women are industrious, carefully planning and completing cutting, burning, and planting. Others get by with token plots.

Cutting trees and brush may be done in rainy weather, but a dry period is necessary for proper burning. Occasionally no dry weeks appear through the early months of the year; and then most Agta swidden are poor indeed. Generally burning is possible in March and April, with planting immediately following. Given luck and the presence of mild days with occasional showers, the swidden grows well with a minimum of attention throughout the dry season. Once the crops are planted, no further work, such as weeding, is done, except sporadic replanting of sweet potatoes and cassava (a year-round task).

Maize may be harvested as early as June or July, but the tendency for the Agta to plant late (by non-Agta standards) means the task often extends into September. Upland rice, the more

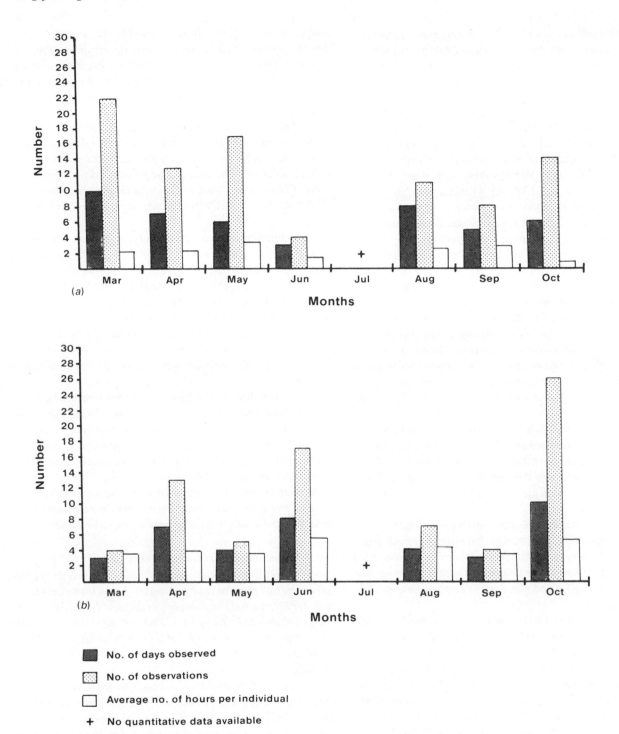

Fig. 6.3. (a) Horticultural and (b) hunting labor investment by Nanadukan Agta in 1981. Fifteen days per month were sampled. Number of days indicated are counts of days actually observed for a specific activity. Number of observations is irrespective of daily count

frequent Nanadukan crop, may be harvested in September. Unlike settled farmers, who plant and harvest large fields at one time, the Agta harvest as the rice ripens. Since plots are planted days apart, the staggering of harvesting allows easy scheduling of labor as well as the freeing of people for other pursuits. Harvested rice bundles are stored within floored pole houses that have been newly built for rainy-season habitation and for storage. The need for storage facilities and the availability of a food supply increase the demand for longer sedentary periods during the rainy season.

Data on hunting and horticulture among the Nanadukan Agta (figure 6.3) demonstrate the relationships between the two activities over the relevant portion of the seasonal cycle as observed during fieldwork in 1981.[5] February is a cold and wet month, yet has a markedly decreased rainfall, compared with January. In February people have moved at least partially out of their rainy-season homes and may have begun sporadic clearing of new swiddens.

March brings more sunny days and investment of labor in clearing fields and in fishing. Stores of rice have long since been exhausted, and the only crops left to harvest are sweet potato and cassava. Of 15 days sampled in March, ten saw horticultural activities. Roots were dug on six days, replanting occurred on four, and weeding only once. Clearing (11 events) and burning (one event) took the bulk of the time invested in horticulture, since digging roots and replanting are brief episodes. April contained only two root-digging events during the seven days that horticultural activities took place. Clearing continued, but burning began in earnest, with four events.

May continued the trend. Horticulture was a dominant activity, but occurred on only six of 15 days. Clearing was finished; burning proceeded seven times, or more than once daily. Planting of rice started in this month and eight planting events were totaled. In June attention to horticulture disappeared. During the month's 15 days of observations only five horticultural events occurred on three days: one rice-planting event and four root-harvesting events. Duration of activity per person hit a low of 1.3 hours.

August found a shift in horticultural activities to increased harvesting, including rice and roots. Roots were dug twice, rice was cut twice and bananas cut once. Interestingly, clearing of secondary growth was observed six times. This clearing was for root-crop planting; the Agta plant only one crop of upland rice per year.

In September the rice aspect of Agta horticulture at Nanadukan was emphasized. The Agta harvested rice five times while processing it once (processing includes drying bundles in the sun before storage). Roots were dug twice. October was primarily taken up with clearing for and planting of sweet potato and cassava.

As horticulture fluctuates, hunting follows a nearly opposite level of intensity. February, 1981 followed a decidedly poor hunting season (Griffin 1984). By mid-January, rice was gone, root crops were depleted, non-Agta farmers were low on goods, and the game continued to elude hunters. In March, fishing permitted more trading with loggers and, as seen above, labor was invested in clearing new swidden fields. Three days of the 15 recorded saw hunting. April was a better month. On only seven days did hunting occur, but two forays per day were averaged. Hunting declined in May again; work in the swiddens increased owing to the good clearing and burning weather. Fishing, seldom demanding the time that hunting does, contributed the needed protein. Hunting in May continued with two trips per day, but on only a few days. These hunts were mainly brief (average 3.4 hours per person) team drives with dogs.

June combined minimal horticulture with frequent hunting. About two hunting trips per day continued on eight days. The dry forest allowed successful use of dogs and encouraged teams of men and women to hunt. June, we should note, is a month for diverse activities, frequent visits to relatives in other camps, journeys to the homes of non-Agta, and reinforcement of many social ties. From year to year either hunting or fishing may take up much of one's time, depending largely on abundance of resources and demand by others.

The importance of hunting diminished during August and September, although horticultural work did not dominate. The Agta's own rice harvest was coming in, hence little need was felt to hunt for saleable meat. Much of the game killed was consumed at home. Fishing was still good. The Agta did not work especially hard, but relaxed, rebuilt their houses, and planned for the rainy season.

October began a very successful rainy-season hunting period. The previous months had seen the flowering and fruiting of the dipterocarp trees (which come on a four- to six-year cycle), large and well fed pig litters, and healthy game. The Agta hunted on one out of three days of the month, averaging nearly three trips per camp per day. Dogs were especially useful in running both deer and pigs. Hunts lasted longer (5.15 hours per person) and ranged further afield. With ready access to rice, only planting of root crops needed to be done to ensure food at the end of the next rainy season.

At Nanadukan a traditional hunting system has been modified to accommodate the differences now found in increased dependence on cultivation of swiddens. Hunting has decreased and, as I state below, dependence on the crops of non-Agta or on wild plant foods has been diminished. Concurrently, greater sedentism is necessary, since the more farming there is, the less residential mobility. Hunting is still easy, given the general proximity of game-rich forests, but becomes less productive as sedentism eventually leads to depletion of nearby game.

Settlement pattern change and continuity

The settlement system has adjusted to fit a greater attention to horticulture now seen at Nanadukan. At the time of my first visit in 1972, the Agta were much less sedentary, traveled far to trade, and consumed more meat. They appeared to be not unlike the remote forest interior Agta of Isabela Province, and indeed farms and logging operations were at a much greater distance than are found today.

Since 1979 Nanadukan has been a major focus of residence, in spite of a recent (and predictable) temporary evacuation because of the death of an important camp member. A semi-sedentary status might characterize the Agta today, in that they have tended to place their rainy-season house clusters close to the mouth of the Nanadukan River every year. The houses are built and occupied by September or October, and are immediately adjacent to the largest and newest swiddens. These floored pole homes each house a nuclear family; from two to seven units are found in a settlement.

Shifts by single families are by far the most common residential moves, but these are independent of the general subsistence cycle. Young couples irregularly move between in-laws, staying in one place longer than two years only in special circumstances. The larger extended family group tends to move in a predictable fashion and to locate itself near the same rainy-season site with some regularity.

The Nanadukan Agta built their rainy-season houses at the north end of their bay in 1979 and 1980. In 1981 they shifted south a few hundred meters and close by the river. In 1982 the group divided, but a core extended family stayed at Nanadukan. In 1983 this group moved, for the first time since mid-1979, away from their "central place" near the Nanadukan River (the move was related to the death mentioned above). In terms of rainy-season residences, therefore, the Agta utilized a single general location, spread over about 400 meters, for four consecutive years.

By early 1983 a logging road had reached the large Malibu River just south of Nanadukan. The lure of available trade partners and plentiful fish in the river, plus social dissonance among themselves, encouraged the move to Malibu (where former swidden fields were in fallow and the people's traditional campsites and hunting grounds were present). The sudden and traumatic death of an older man, however, led to abandonment of both Malibu and Nanadukan. The two widows claimed in July 1985 that they would be psychologically able to resume residence and planting at Nanadukan in 1986.

The base camp at Nanadukan between 1979 and 1982 has been replicated at new base camps in the north. In 1984, 1985, and 1986 these were still the focus of horticultural activities and were located beside the swiddens planted with upland rice, sweet potatoes, cassava, pineapples, and squash. Only in the dry season of 1987 were several families clearing and planting at Nanadukan, with actual residence planned from full establishment by the beginning of the rainy season, about September or October.

As before, settlement, hunting, and horticulture were interlocked. Dry-season habitations are, for Nanadukan people, usually situated close to the rainy-season structures, but on the beach instead of behind the dune and the vegetation line. Either lean-tos or small, roofed pole houses may be seen, but they serve only as base camps in which belongings may be left and on which others may keep a protective eye.

Hunting parties may live in rough shelters while on two- to four-night trips into unoccupied forest. The simple lean-to structures are used throughout the year, during such hunting trips, being made more rainproof in the wet months. During the dry season, however, they tend to be used by nuclear families while hunting and fishing, instead of by parties of male hunters. Fishing trips well upriver are the usual reason for special camps, although rattan collection houses have been seen. Families may spend a week or two away, before returning to the base camp and the larger extended family. In any case, these forays are not the base camp shifts found in Isabela but are for subsistence activities.

Comparisons with other Agta groups

Nanadukan Agta are not representative of all Agta in northeastern Luzon. Based on our own work and on that of Rai, we are able to provide a general view of the more traditional and mobile Ihaya Agta. Their subsistence–settlement system has been described, although in less quantitative terms than for the

Table 6.1. *Percentage of work time per activity*

Gender	Average daily hours	Hunt	Gather	Fish	Trade	Swidden	Other
Male	7.73	74.5	0.6	2.5	15.4	0.2	6.8
Female	4.15	8.5	24.6	6.0	33.0	1.3	26.5

Based on Rai 1982:232.

Nanadukan Agta (Estioko and Griffin 1975; Estioko-Griffin and Griffin 1981b; Rai 1982). I use the term Ihaya Agta somewhat loosely, since the Ihaya area south of Palanan and San Mariano, Isabela, is ill-defined by most Agta. The Ihaya Agta reside on both sides of the mountain divide and north of the Casiguran Agta south of Isabela. The Ihaya Agta consider cultivation, as described early in this paper, merely supplemental. No serious rice or corn production is attempted; they are perhaps best seen as "commercial hunters" (Headland 1986). These Agta are dependent on non-Agta for nearly all their plant staples, i.e. rice, maize, and roots. Ihaya Agta must get their daily starch from others unless an infrequent collection of wild roots is made, the sago-like palm *Caryota cumingii* is processed, or palm hearts are cut. No Agta intend to go without daily starch, nor do they enjoy digging wild roots or collecting other forest plant foods as staples.

The hunting cycle follows the patterns of abundance and desirability of the game by Agta and non-Agta. Demand for fat pig is greatest between November and February, especially by the poor, remote non-Agta farming peasants of the region. With no access to cooking oil, sweets, and pork, they trade with Agta to an extent that the majority of other non-Agta find unacceptable. In addition, the Agta are absolutely dependent on the food stores of these same subsistence farmers. The incidence of Agta resorting to forest foods is directly correlated with the success of the peasants' permanent fields and swiddens. A poor crop means either eating wild foods, or making residential shifts to be in proximity with other peasant farmers who have food stores, or relying on loggers when they are available. They seldom are in the rainy season.

Rai (1982:105) recorded 20 base camp movements by the Ihaya Agta extended family he lived with through one annual cycle. The shortest stay in one place was less than a week, while the rainy-season camp was occupied for two months. These moves were explicitly for the purposes of proximity to good hunting and fishing. Rai (ibid. 107) notes that "the mean distance traveled in such a move is 5.3 kilometers. The total annual circuit distance covered in residential movements is one hundred and seven kilometers."

The Ihaya Agta are properly described as hunters by using summary statistics on the overall work schedule, although with seasonality ignored (see table 6.10). The Ihaya Agta families studied in 1975 (Estioko and Griffin 1975; Estioko-Griffin and Griffin 1981b) follow the pattern summarized in table 6.1. Their base camps for the 1974 rainy season broke up in early January 1975. By the first of January the pole houses were abandoned and lean-tos were built on the river bed. Owing to disagreements, the group completely divided. Only an elderly couple and two nuclear families (a brother–brother bond) remained together until joined by a third family traveling with the anthropologists.

To our knowledge, years passed before the families who had spent the rainy season of 1974 together were reunited. Several divisions and recombinations occurred throughout the drier months. The group first divided into two groups in March and moved about three and five kilometers up separate river forks. New families joined from locations both downriver and on the western side of the mountains. This process continued in the same fashion as Rai found in his group, through the construction of rainy-season camps and the settling in from late October until January.

Compared with the example of the Nanadukan Agta, and those of southeastern Cagayan in general, the Ihaya Agta are unpredictable in their location of rainy-season base camps and are minimally sedentary. The constant in their lives is the need to reside near the river of their "social identity" or that of their spouses. Along such a river, many acceptable and named, well known camp sites may be found. Selection of a specific rainy-season encampment depends on game characteristics of the moment, on relations with non-Agta, and on interpersonal relations among the Agta themselves. Whatever the case, these same demands and the desire to get back into lean-tos early in January translate into brief periods of stable residence in thatched pole houses. The Nanadukan Agta's propensity of residence near one location is unknown and unwanted.

The reason for this semi-nomadism, or movement through the seasons over a limited but well understood subsistence range, is found in the emphasis on hunting as a means of procuring most plant food. The exchange of meat and fish for rice, maize, roots, and other items is central to the residential mobility. Hunters must constantly shift residences in order to locate near to good game and fish stocks. These Agta have a two-fold relationship with horticulture. They find the sale of meat as favorable as the production of crops by their own efforts, and they also find that non-Agta will seldom permit them to cultivate substantial swiddens. As is discussed below, their social environment is the source of much of their food, provides the impetus to remain hunters, and is the force against farming.

With Ihaya Agta, horticulture remains constant through their moves; the small early-rainy-season swiddens and the scattered caches of root crops are an insurance system that may be only sporadically tapped. Hunting remains a year-round pursuit, varied only as fishing and game conditions change. The provisioning of non-Agta with animal protein in exchange for plant foods is the central relationship. The nature of this relationship, then, is in need of further discussion.

Agta–non-Agta-farmer relations

The issue of humid tropics foragers and their dependence, or the lack thereof, on farming societies remains unclear. The classic theme is whether foragers such as the Pygmies of Central Africa are or are not dependent on farming villagers for a part of their sustenance in the form of cultivated plant foods (Turnbull 1965; Bailey and Peacock in press). Turnbull has long argued an independence view, but more recent work is tending to weaken his position (Harako, personal communication; see Bailey and Peacock in press). The debate is spilling into the humid tropics of other parts of the Old and New Worlds, including southeast Asia.

The Agta–farmer relationship in the Philippines has been characterized as a symbiotic one in which Agta are the controllers of exchange. The Agta are characterized as having an advantage in access to the most desired and abundant commodity, meat. Farmers, in an expansionist mode as they cut the forest and make new swiddens, are thought to be working to the advantage of the Agta. The swiddens reputedly have game-rich ecotones between the forest and the cropland in which the Agta hunt; they then trade the meat for starches and thereby reap the benefits (Peterson 1978, 1981, 1982).

None of these assertions, however, furnishes an accurate portrayal of the nature of Agta hunting and non-Agta farming (Griffin 1984; Rai 1982). In brief, the Agta do not have a surplus of meat, nor do they enjoy the ability to provision the bulk of the farming population. Their usual purpose in hunting is to get meat to trade for corn, rice, and roots. Even the Nanadukan Agta seldom have enough starch stores to ignore a chance to sell meat. The Ihaya Agta are absolutely dependent on keeping a clientele that will give them rice in exchange for meat, *or on credit*. Much of the social interaction between the groups and the structure of the debt relationships is based on maintaining the exchange ties. Most of the 10 000 farmers of Palanan are not major consumers of food procured by the Agta. Paranan (non-Agta natives of Palanan) have fished throughout this century, and occasionally slaughter and eat water buffalo. Some do supplement their own animal resources, including eggs, with Agta foods, but most either live far from the Agta, or have inadequate stores for exchange, or go without meat or fish. Many poor farmers, in our experience, often eat no animal protein of any derivation with most of their meals. Lastly, game-rich ecotones do not exist and game does not tend to congregate near cultivated areas. The Agta do not, by and large, hunt near fields but travel into forested areas where they say the best hunting is always found (Griffin 1984; Griffin, *et al.* n.d.a; Rai 1982).

Of all Agta, the Nanadukan Agta may be the least dependent on non-Agta farmers. Their ability to grow their own food is at present limited to rice that lasts as long as two months and roots that are supplemental for the rest of the year. They have diminished dependence upon non-Agta farmers, but must exchange whenever possible. The Ihaya Agta are nearly totally dependent on non-Agta for daily rice or other carbohydrates. Table 6.1 verifies this assertion; men spend only 0.2 percent of their time at swiddening and women 1.3 percent of theirs. Males' hunting is the productive activity and a full 74.5 percent of the work day is spent hunting.

Clearly, the Agta must hunt to get enough protein for trading to make up for lack of their own plant foods. Equally certain is the relationship between residential mobility, emphasis on hunting, and the need to exchange animal protein for cultivated plant foods. The subordinate social status of all Agta, and their use to non-Agta as providers of meat, restricts their options in adjusting hunting and farming. The contrast between the Nanadukan Agta and the Ihaya Agta is one of relative emphasis of cultivation and hunting. The Nanadukan people, during our observation period, have been able to enlarge their swiddens, and they have selectively diminished their dry-season hunting and seen an advantage in decreased residential mobility. The Ihaya Agta find that they can obtain a regular amount of cultivated food by emphasizing hunting and by regularly and immediately exchanging their meat to non-Agta. They thereby choose not to engage in, and are denied the option of, serious swidden cultivation.

Discussion and concluding remarks

The main conclusions may be summarized as follows. Among the Agta of northeastern Luzon, hunting is a dominant subsistence strategy. As horticulture is undertaken, hunting is initially completely compatible and undiminished. As horticulture increases in emphasis, hunting is seasonally diminished, although fishing may remain important for protein acquisition. Greater sedentism throughout the seasonal cycle goes with an enlarged dependence on domesticated plant foods. Within a subsistence system which depends solely on hunting providing the basis for exchange, residential mobility is very high.

An increase in horticultural efforts may be the result of several pressures. Firstly, Agta may have engaged in some exchange of meat for plant food for many years – perhaps for centuries. In addition, some Agta have had a knowledge of, and perhaps involvement in, small-scale swiddening for just as long (Headland 1986). The basic system has been possible as long as non-Agta have resided in the Sierra Madre range (Griffin 1985). Assuming that hunting and gathering sufficed to provide the bulk of the diet, "caching" of plants in tiny, scattered plots may have been the only involvement with cultivated plants.[6] Modest growth in Agta populations and in those of non-Agta neighbors may have favored a small increase both in swidden size and in the exchange of meat for plant food. Certainly the knowledge of cultivation would have been universal. Unless the Agta realized a food gain by growing roots or rice, however, field holdings would have been minimal.

The rapid growth of the non-Agta population since World War II may have been the impetus for substantial change. This farming population became a better resource in itself – more farmers meant that more food could be secured by trade. De-emphasis of wild plant foods occurred; however, depletion of game resources seems to have resulted in areas near population growth centers. The difficulty of acquiring enough game for trading is a worsening problem, and it has been a major stimulus for increased swiddening and sedentism among the Agta. Troubles, however, have been attendant.

As game has become somewhat less plentiful in recent years, demand has increased and pressure on Agta land has become severe. The Agta choose to make swiddens, they say, because they need the supplemental food when they cannot trade, and because they foresee that non-Agta will seize all arable land unless the most strenuous efforts are made to retain it. Sedentism and active cultivation are the only possible mechanisms to keep the land. In addition, farming initially diminishes the strain on the wild game, since people are taken up with clearing, planting, and harvesting, and because they hunt less for meat to trade. Long-term residential stability may cause depletion of nearby game, but the Agta may still undertake long-distance hunting trips into the mountain interior.

The initial investment in horticulture means expenditure of labor in both hunting and swiddening. During the early months of the dry season, when clearing and planting occur, hunting proceeds at a pace sufficient to gain meat for trade, or reliance on wild plants is maintained. Only after a swiddening system is in place and productive may dry-season hunting be diminished, as is the case at Nanadukan.

The Agta are today constantly experimenting with different emphases in food procurement. Variation is known both temporally and locationally. Individuals, families, and groups all differ from year to year and place to place. The more industrious and capable adults tend to be heavily involved in whatever activities will ensure the acquisition of food. Innovations in emphasis begin with the perceptions and acts of these same people. In addition, the abundance of forest, riverine, and marine resources is not constant. Game populations fluctuate according to season and with longer environmental cycles. Specific events may diminish the providence of a resource; storms may lead to additional root crop planting because of anticipated grain and game shortages. The Agta respond to any crisis or opportunity by favoring the short-term resource and holding the long-term one in abeyance. Hunting gains food quickly; horticulture is advantageous only if it can be integrated with other demands.

Sedentism is one demand that may be difficult to meet. While sedentism may be important for the retention of land, exchange relationships favor mobility, both in food procurement and in access to trade partners. The example of the Nanadukan Agta shows that sedentism is possible, with concomitant adjustment of hunting and farming. More time is spent residing near swidden fields and therefore at the rainy-season base camp area. Dry-season foraging trips involve temporary campsites scattered upriver and in forest locations, instead of the frequent movement of the whole camp through a series of base camps. The Ihaya Agta avoid sedentism and farming by constant shifts of their camps to good hunting and fishing spots and to proximity to trade partners. Hunting is not seasonally diminished since it is the basis of obtaining nearly all plant food. The Ihaya Agta move their families to the game; the Nanadukan Agta send out parties of hunters who return to a base camp through much of the seasonal cycle. The former have not integrated farming into their hunting and mobility systems. The latter demonstrate a foraging people's integration of cultivation into a successful hunting adaptation. As horticulture displaces hunting, Agta favor greater stability in their residences.

Notes

Agnes Estioko-Griffin and the Agta of Isabela and Cagayan Provinces are thanked for their help. Discussions of hunting, farming, and residence mobility profited especially from the detailed comments of the Taginod family of Nanadukan, of Navin K. Rai of Tribhuvan University, Kathmandu, Nepal, and of Thomas Headland of the Summer Institute of Linguistics, Dallas, Texas.

The many years of interest, assistance and friendship of Alfonso Lim, Jr., and of the management of Acme Plywood and Veneer, Inc., are noted and thanks extended. Nick Cerra and Pat Jackson of Goodwood Management Corporation, Ltd., are thanked for their ever-present aid.

The research was funded by the National Science Foundation (grant nos. SOC73-09083-A01 and BNS80-14308), the National Endowment for the Humanities (grant no. RO-000168-80-0123), the Wenner–Gren Foundation, and the University of Hawaii.

1 Both the Tasaday of Mindanao (Yen 1976) and the Andamanese of India (Pandit 1976) are so poorly known that serious questions remain unanswered concerning the basis of their adaptation. Data from these groups should not be used (for example, as in Hayden 1981) until they are of a sufficient quality and quantity.

2 The humid tropics rain forests are poorly understood by ecologists. Questions have been raised (Bailey and Peacock in press; Bahuchet 1978; Hutterer 1982; Griffin 1984) concerning their viability for foragers without some access to domesticated plant foods or metal. The questions remain incompletely resolved.

3 Peterson (1985, 1978) states otherwise, but researchers fluent in the Agta language (T. Headland, A. Estioko-Griffin, P.B. Griffin, N. Rai) have been unable to locate any Agta groups with such characteristics. See Headland (1978) and Rai (1982) for discussions; the problem is of great importance to questions of Agta subsistence strategies and residential mobility.

4 Agta residential groups may *not* include Agta who are neither consanguineal or affinal kinspeople. Contrary to Peterson (1985:128–129), "other families" and "orphans" cannot join a group (her "core cooperative group") since Agta groups are necessarily extended families. In-depth questioning always reveals the kinship connection tying group members together.

5 One of Griffin or Estioko-Griffin has worked among the Agta, albeit at times briefly, every year from 1972 through 1987, excepting 1977 and 1986. Between June 1974 and June 1976 16 months of field time were totaled, the bulk in late 1974 and throughout 1975. This work occurred primarily among forest-interior-dwelling Agta in central Isabela. Between October 1980 and June 1982 the Griffins conducted fieldwork on the coast of southern Cagayan, when 15 months' work among the Agta was achieved. From November 1980 through November 1981, February and July 1981 excepted, a formal recording of subsistence data on a survey instrument was undertaken. Approximately 50 percent of each month's days were sampled following a randomizing procedure. On each chosen day, all subsistence activities were recorded as to activity, actors, duration, distance, location, result, related tasks, and disposition of food acquired. Data used in this chapter are drawn from this subsistence file.

6 Alternatives to a simple caching system of swiddening are possible (Griffin 1984). A greater dependence on swiddening, with minimal or no trade with other ethnic groups, is possible, although purely speculative. Archaeological research will eventually decide the past subsistence strategies of the Agta:

Chapter 7

Horticulture and large-mammal hunting: the role of resource depletion and the constraints of time and labor

John D. Speth and Susan L. Scott

Introduction

Archaeologists interested in the hunting strategies of prehistoric horticulturalists commonly make two assumptions concerning the impact of farming communities on their wild animal resources. Firstly, they often argue that gardening, by disturbing primary vegetation, creates new habitats or "edge zones" which support higher local densities of game, especially of smaller species. As a consequence, horticulturalists focus a considerable part of their hunting effort on small mammals which are easily taken in and around their gardens (e.g. Emslie 1981; Neusius 1984). This is the familiar "garden-hunting hypothesis," first clearly articulated by Linares (1976).

Secondly, archaeologists often argue that horticulturalists, by virtue of the relative stability of their villages, deplete their preferred large game resources and are forced to take both a broader range of species and a greater proportion of small, less desirable forms (e.g. Nelson and Cordell 1982).[1] This view derives from classic diet breadth models in optimal foraging theory, which suggest that as search costs increase the optimal diet expands to include lower ranked species (see Winterhalder and Smith 1981, and references therein).

Both of these arguments together have led archaeologists to the view that, as evolving horticultural systems become more heavily dependent on cultivated foods and more residentially stable, they increasingly focus their hunting on small mammals. A closer look, however, at both the archaeological and ethnographic record of hunting by horticulturalists reveals a more complex and often quite different picture; while this is by no means universal, the literature documents many cases in which the ratio of large to small species actually increases rather than decreases as communities become more stable and more heavily committed to horticulture. This chapter explores the hunting strategies of both prehistoric and contemporary horticulturalists, and attempts to provide a more comprehensive and realistic framework for understanding the changes in hunting patterns that accompany increases in sedentism and horticultural dependence.[2]

We begin by briefly examining faunal assemblages from a variety of prehistoric horticultural village sequences in the American Southwest. We focus on the Southwest purely as a matter of convenience and personal familiarity with the data; though details differ from context to context, similar trends involving increasing ratios of large to small mammals are common in the archaeological records of many other regions of North America and the Old World (e.g. during the Plains Woodland to Plains Village transition [Wedel 1983; Lehmer 1971; Dallman 1983:60]; during the Middle to Late Woodland transition in the upper Great Lakes region and perhaps elsewhere in eastern North America at approximately the same time [Cleland 1966:97, 1976; but see Robison 1982 for a contrasting view]; and during the Early Neolithic of the Near East [Cauvin 1978:74]).

Following this brief archaeological overview, we turn to ethnographic literature on contemporary horticultural societies to identify the principal socioeconomic factors that underlie this shift in hunting strategies. These studies demonstrate a close relationship between hunting patterns, village permanence, and level of dependence on starchy cultivated crops. We examine these interrelationships and conclude by identifying a number of strategies available to horticulturalists to assure them of an adequate intake of high-quality protein (and calories) as their villages become larger and more permanent, and their diet more heavily dependent on cultivated carbohydrate-rich plants.

Horticulture and large-mammal hunting in the American Southwest

The faunal literature of the American Southwest is replete with examples of increases in reliance on large mammals as horticultural communities become larger, less mobile, and more heavily dependent on cultivated plants. For example, Speth and Scott (1985) have documented increases in the proportion of large mammals such as deer, mountain sheep, antelope, and bison relative to small mammals such as lagomorphs (rabbits and jackrabbits), and perhaps rodents, taken by horticulturalists in the Sacramento Mountain area of southeastern New Mexico between approximately A.D. 1100 and 1300–1400. This change in faunal resources accompanies shifts throughout the uplands toward increasing dependence on maize cultivation, and changes in settlement patterns from small pithouse villages to large, aggregated pueblos such as Gran Quivira (cf. Kelley 1966, 1984; Caperton 1981). The striking increase in bison hunting by horticulturalists in the Pecos Valley lowlands of New Mexico (Jelinek 1967; Collins 1971; Rocek and Speth 1986) and by Panhandle Aspect farmers in the Canadian Valley of northwest Texas (Wedel 1983; Collins 1971; Duffield 1970; Dillehay 1974) is usually accounted for in terms of climatic or environmental changes, though it may actually reflect a similar trend.

In southern Arizona, Bayham (1982; see also Szuter and Bayham, this volume, chapter 8) documents a gradual and progressive trend throughout the 4500-year Archaic and Hohokam sequence at Ventana Cave toward decreasing emphasis on lagomorphs and greater specialization in deer. This shift is accompanied by changes in the ratio of projectile points to ground stone and in other artifactual indicators, all of which point to a change in the function of Ventana Cave from a hunter–gatherer base camp during the Archaic to a more specialized large-mammal hunting station during the Hohokam.

Haury (1976:114) observes that large ungulates, especially bighorn sheep, increase relative to lagomorphs at Snaketown and elsewhere in the Hohokam area during the Sedentary and Classic periods (i.e. after about A.D. 900–1100). This faunal change coincides, according to Haury (1976:356), with peak population levels and agricultural activity in the Hohokam area.

More recently, Szuter (1984a:163–165) has recognized a similar trend toward increasing reliance on artiodactyls in a large series of Hohokam sites excavated as part of the Salt–Gila Aque-

duct Project. According to Szuter (1984a:163), the ratio of large to small mammals is low from Santa Cruz through Sacaton times (i.e. before *ca.* A.D. 900), and then rises in subsequent phases. The trend is unaffected by site location or site function (see Szuter and Bayham, this volume, chapter 8, for a broader look at Hohokam hunting patterns).

A small faunal sample from the Point of Pines area in east-central Arizona shows the same general trend (Stein 1962). Between A.D. 1 and A.D. 900 (Circle Prairie, Stove Canyon, and Dry Lake Phases), the proportion of large mammals (deer, antelope, mountain sheep, bison) relative to lagomorphs is about 30 percent. Between A.D. 1000 and A.D. 1400 (Reserve, Tularosa, Pinedale, and Canyon Creek Phases), large mammals increase to nearly 60 percent. During the Point of Pines Phase (A.D. 1400–1450), large mammals exceed 70 percent. Heavy utilization of deer at about the same time has been noted by Olsen (1980) at Grasshopper Pueblo, also located in east-central Arizona.

Using coprolite data, Stiger (1979) documents an increase in the importance of deer in the diet of the inhabitants of Mesa Verde between Basketmaker III (*ca.* A.D. 470) and Pueblo III (A.D. 1250). Turkeys also become increasingly important in later sites. According to Stiger, this faunal shift parallels an increase in reliance by local populations on horticulture.

Binford, *et al.* (1982) observe a sharp increase in the relative importance of deer and a decline in lagomorphs in the McKinley Mine area of northwestern New Mexico between A.D. 900 and A.D. 1100–1200. The occupational sequence is interpreted as one of increasing local aggregation of population (Nelson and Cordell 1982) and greater horticultural commitment (Toll and Donaldson 1982).

Another interesting case is provided by the faunal studies of Arroyo Hondo, a large pueblo located near Santa Fe in north-central New Mexico (Lang and Harris 1984:128–131). Deer are a major focus of hunting when the village is first occupied *ca.* A.D. 1275. As population expands toward its maximum in the second and third decades of the 14th century, deer decline as a major resource and communally procured grassland forms, especially bison, become the principal focus. It is not clear to what extent these grassland animals were hunted by the villagers themselves or instead were acquired through exchange from other groups. Turkey raising is intensified during this stage.

Perhaps the best documented case in the Southwest comes from Chaco Canyon in northwestern New Mexico. Here, large mammals, first antelope and then deer, increase steadily in relative importance from A.D. 600 until about A.D. 1100–1150, while economically important small mammals such as lagomorphs and rodents decline (Akins 1982a:28, 1984). These faunal trends are paralleled by steadily increasing human population levels and horticultural activity in the canyon. In the 12th century, population begins to fall off, and artiodactyls once more decline in relative importance. At this same time, small mammals become proportionately more common again, and turkeys, probably domestic, become important for the first time in Chacoan faunal assemblages.

In addition, faunal data from Pueblo Alto, one of the larger masonry structures in Chaco, suggest, at least tentatively, that as communities in the canyon were becoming larger and more horticulturally committed, meat had to be procured (either by hunting or by exchange) from progressively greater and greater distances. At Pueblo Alto, the proportion of large mammal vertebrae drops from 51 percent in deposits dating between A.D. 920 and A.D. 1050 to less than 11 percent in trash dating between A.D. 1050 and A.D. 1150, whereas limb elements increase from nearly 16 percent to over 40 percent (Akins 1982b:47). After A.D. 1150, vertebrae increase again to almost 37 percent and limb elements drop slightly to about 33 percent. The sharp decline in low-utility axial elements between A.D. 920 and A.D. 1150 may reflect increasing selectivity as meat is transported to the canyon from more distant sources.

An alternative and equally plausible scenario for the Pueblo Alto patterning, of course, is that the change in body-part representation reflects not increasing transport costs but greater economic and/or political differentiation among communities within the canyon or its immediate surroundings. A similar argument has been put forward recently by Bayham and Hatch (1984, cited in Szuter 1984a) and Szuter (1984a:167) regarding element frequencies in Hohokam sites. They have noted that anatomical parts of high utility tend to be found primarily in larger communities, while less valuable parts are more common in smaller, more peripheral settlements. More faunal data from the full range of settlement types in Chaco are needed before the two alternative interpretations can be properly evaluated. Obviously, data on body-part frequencies from other regions of the Southwest where shifts in the ratio of large to small mammals have been observed would also be useful.

The role of climatic, technological, demographic, and socioeconomic factors

The few cases mentioned here are sufficient to indicate that shifts toward increasing reliance on larger mammals are common, though by no means universal, in the prehistoric Southwest (we will return later to the issue of why the ratio of large to small mammals increases in some sequences and apparently not in others).[3] Interestingly, the timing of the onset of these faunal shifts, and the rate at which they occur, are different in different parts of the Southwest. For example, in Chaco the large to small mammal ratio begins to change as early as A.D. 600 and continues to change over a period of nearly five centuries; in southeastern New Mexico, on the other hand, the faunal shift does not become apparent until after A.D. 1100 or 1200 and the changes that occur in the ratio of large to small mammals are complete within, at most, only two or three centuries.

Moreover, as both Bayham (1982) and Speth and Scott (1985) have argued, these faunal shifts often appear to be largely independent of climatic and environmental factors (although the particular large mammal species selected in each area is clearly affected by environmental conditions and availability within the local catchment; see Driver 1984, 1985). Thus, for example, the

lowland parts of southeastern New Mexico in the 13th to 15th century see a marked increase in bison hunting which, while beginning during a period of more favorable climatic conditions, persists and probably actually intensifies during a subsequent prolonged period of drought (Speth 1983; Speth and Scott 1985; Hall 1984; Rocek and Speth 1986). Similarly, at the same time that bison hunting becomes more important to lowland communities, the inhabitants of the highland portions of southeastern New Mexico increase their reliance on deer, antelope, and mountain sheep hunting, a trend which also persists through the same extended period of unfavorable climate (see data and discussions in Speth and Scott 1985; Driver 1984, 1985; and McKusick 1981).

Not only do these widespread shifts in the ratio of large to small mammals appear to be unlinked to environmental and climatic conditions, but they also are not driven, at least in any direct sense, by changes in the absolute numbers of people in a region that might affect the abundance and distribution of prey species. As cogently argued by Bayham (1982) in his reevaluation of the Ventana Cave fauna, human population levels in the Hohokam area were increasing over the several-thousand-year period represented by the site's archaeological deposits. According to Bayham, who relies heavily in his discussion on arguments from optimal diet theory, such population changes would have led to reductions in overall densities of preferred, larger species, which in turn would have given rise to less rather than greater selectivity on the part of the hunters. Population growth in the Chaco region (Akins 1982a) and in southeastern New Mexico (Speth and Scott 1985; Caperton 1981; Kelley 1966:80, 1984; Jelinek 1967; Collins 1971; Leslie 1979) points to similar conclusions for these areas.

Finally, the changing ratios of large to small mammals seen in many parts of the Southwest are unlikely to be explained by reference to technological innovations, such as the introduction of the bow and arrow, that might lower procurement costs of larger species (see discussion in Speth and Scott 1985 and Bayham 1982). In the Ventana case, the faunal change is gradual and commences well before the introduction of the bow. In southeastern New Mexico, the faunal change occurs long after the appearance of the bow (cf. Jelinek 1967; Kelley 1966; Willey and Hughes 1978).

While communal procurement techniques might also lead to greater emphasis on larger species, there is no convincing evidence at present to suggest that such techniques were unknown to the inhabitants of the various areas of the Southwest prior to the advent of the faunal shift in these areas. Therefore, any increase in large game that might be attributable to communal hunting techniques is not likely to be the result of the sudden discovery of such techniques, but rather the result of increased reliance on communal hunting brought about by other factors. We will return to this issue later.

In sum, the widespread shifts in the Southwest toward progressively greater reliance on large mammals, especially deer, antelope, mountain sheep, and bison, do not seem to be direct responses to altered climatic or environmental conditions, changes in the absolute size of regional populations, or technological innovations. Instead, the faunal shifts appear to reflect fundamental changes in the socioeconomic sphere. More specifically, the shifts in hunting selectivity appear to be linked to increases in community size, residential stability, and degree of horticultural commitment; but why?

The ethnographic data

An obvious point of departure for exploring this interesting question is an examination of the ethnographic literature that deals explicitly with hunting strategies of horticulturalists. As might be expected, this literature is spotty, often anecdotal, and concerned for the most part with groups in tropical forest habitats. Moreover, ethnographic studies deal almost entirely with short time spans, generally of the order of a few months or at most a few years, whereas the changes with which we are concerned prehistorically may span decades or even centuries. Finally, most of the ethnographic literature with quantitative data on hunting yields derives from Amazonian groups that depend on cultivated crops for more than 70 percent to 80 percent of their total calorie intake (e.g. Hames 1980a:35; Vickers 1983b:455; Hames and Vickers 1983, and references therein). Data relating hunting patterns to differing degrees of horticultural commitment unfortunately are almost non-existent (for an interesting exception, see Griffin, this volume, chapter 6). Despite the obvious limitations of these studies, they nevertheless will help identify some of the key parameters that influence prey selection by cultivators.

High-quality protein needs

Perhaps the most obvious aspect of tropical horticultural systems, such as those found in Amazonia and southeast Asia, is the need for an efficient source of high-quality protein to supplement diets based heavily on cultivated carbohydrates. For example, manioc and plantains, two of the most important crops in the Neotropics, are extremely low in protein (1–2 percent; Gross 1975:527). Groups such as those in Amazonia that obtain most of their calories from these starchy plants rely heavily for protein on fish and/or hunted foods. Protein is also obtained from other vegetable sources, but these sources are often inadequate and they generally are less efficient than meat or fish (but see discussion in Beckerman 1979 and Lizot 1977). Maize is higher in total protein than manioc or plantains, but maize protein is low in quality, being deficient in two essential amino acids and niacin (Gross 1975:527, 534, and references therein; Reidhead 1976:308–309). Thus, heavy reliance on maize cultivation probably also increases, at least seasonally, the need for an efficient source of high-quality protein.

Garden hunting and resource depletion

Gardening disturbs existing habitats and creates new ones that support higher densities of small mammals than are found in surrounding undisturbed areas (Linares 1976; Hames and Vickers 1982; Fagerstone, Lavoie, and Griffith 1980; Emslie 1981; Neusius 1984). Thus, one consequence of increased horticultural activity may be an increase in the abundance of small mammals available to the local community (i.e., "garden hunting" as described by Linares 1976).

The impact of gardening on the abundance of larger species of game is less clear. Gardens clearly attract larger animals, at least at certain stages in the growth of the crops. This is amply attested to in the literature by frequent reference to crop damage caused by deer, wild pigs, monkeys, and other large species (Eder 1978:60; Carneiro 1968a:133, 1983:83–85; Freeman 1955:58–60; Parker, *et al.* 1983:171; Berlin and Berlin 1983:316). These animals are often taken in the gardens, especially at night by hunters with flashlights (Hames and Vickers 1983).

There are few quantitative data, however, which demonstrate that garden hunting significantly increases overall hunting success of larger mammals or that large-game biomass is greater in areas with gardens (Peterson 1981; Linares 1976). In fact, most studies suggest the opposite (see, for example, Eder 1978:68; Griffin 1984:111; Hart 1978:336; Milton 1984:14–15; Abruzzi 1979; Hames and Vickers 1982; Hill and Hawkes 1983:165; Yost and Kelley 1983:216; Carneiro 1968b:245). Peterson's (1981) study of Agta hunting in the Philippines, therefore, is unusual in this regard. She argues that edge zones along the boundaries between gardens and forest support a higher biomass of large game than does surrounding primary forest. Peterson concludes that expansion of horticulturalists into Agta territory has been beneficial to Agta hunter–gatherers by increasing the overall abundance of larger prey species.

A more recent study of the Agta by Rai (1982:184–188) disagrees with Peterson's conclusions. Rai argues instead that large game rarely concentrate near garden boundaries, and that in the long run horticultural activity is degrading Agta habitat and causing widespread resource depletion (see also Estioko-Griffin and Griffin 1981a; Griffin 1984:111; and Griffin, this volume, chapter 6).

Several studies from Amazonia support the conclusions reached by Rai, and provide valuable quantitative evidence that the level of game depletion around horticultural communities, especially of larger species, is positively correlated with settlement age and size (e.g. Baksh 1985; Paolisso and Sackett 1985). For example, Vickers (1980; see also Hames and Vickers 1982, 1983; but see Vickers 1988 for a shift in position) studied hunting yields between 1973 and 1975 in the newly founded Siona–Secoya village of San Pablo in tropical northeastern Ecuador (see also Vickers, this volume, chapter 5). Vickers found that when the village was first established hunting yields were high (on average *ca.* 25 kg butchered meat per hunt) and hunters focused on areas close to the village. Large species contributed the highest percentage of total kills and provided most of the total meat yield by weight. During the first two years of occupation, however, hunting yields dropped precipitously (to an average of *ca.* 15 kg per hunt) and hunters began to take smaller species close to home, and travel greater distances and spend more time hunting to take larger mammals. Despite the sharp decline in hunting returns during the first two years the village was occupied, large species nevertheless still contributed over 98 percent by weight of the total meat yield and over 93 percent of the total kills.

Vickers returned to San Pablo six years later in 1979 and found that hunting yields had declined further (to an average of *ca.* 12 kg per hunt), though the rate of decline was less steep. His data show that, after six years, returns (by weight) had dropped to about 56 percent of what they had been during the first two years the village was occupied. He also found that time invested in hunting had increased by nearly 12 percent and average travel distance to productive hunting areas had increased by about 18 percent (from 17 km to 20 km). Large game continued to be the principal focus of hunting and still contributed most of the kills (71 percent) and total meat yield (93 percent).

Cuyabeno, another Siona–Secoya settlement which had been occupied continuously for more than 30 years, had even lower returns (average *ca.* 6 kg butchered meat per hunt) than the 1979 levels at San Pablo, but the per annum rate of decline in hunting yields had leveled off. On the basis of these data, Vickers (1980) and Hames (1980a) suggest that hunting returns asymptotically approach an equilibrium level in older settlements, provided that available hunting territory is large, populations remain more or less stable, distant hunting zones are periodically rotated, and villages are periodically relocated.

Once large game close to the village of San Pablo had been depleted, the Siona–Secoya exploited nearby areas primarily for short morning or evening hunts when time constraints due to other activities such as garden clearing prevented them from engaging in long-distance hunting. Animals taken on these hunts generally were less-preferred smaller species which comprised a comparatively small proportion of the village's total hunting returns (Vickers 1980).

Hames (1980a; Hames and Vickers 1982, 1983; see also Good 1982; Baksh 1982; and Harris 1984a) studied hunting by Ye'kwana and Yanomamo villagers in southern Venezuela. His data also clearly show the effects of game depletion in the vicinity of villages. Ye'kwana and Yanomamo hunters took a greater range of prey types, including less-preferred, smaller varieties close to the village. At greater distances from the village, the range of prey types taken was narrower and larger species contributed a much greater proportion, both in terms of number of kills and in terms of weight. Like the Siona–Secoya, Ye'kwana and Yanomamo hunters exploited depleted areas near the village primarily at times when critical gardening activities prevented them from traveling to distant, more productive hunting areas.

Similar trends were observed by Saffirio and Scaglion (1982) in a study of hunting by Yanomamo groups in northern Brazil (see also Saffirio and Hames 1983). They compared the strategies of hunters in traditional forest villages with those of hunters in two rapidly acculturating villages which had recently relocated themselves permanently along a newly built highway. Increased residential stability and proximity to the highway has led to greater environmental degradation and resource depletion around the highway villages than around the less permanent forest villages. As a consequence, hunters in the highway villages hunt almost three times as often as those in the traditional villages, devote substantially more time per day to hunting (1.5 times more), and travel greater distances into the forest to obtain adequate yields. They also take a narrower range of species than hunters in the forest villages, focusing particularly on two species,

one relatively large, the peccary, the other of moderate size, the spider monkey.

Communal hunting

The highway Yanomamo have also altered their techniques of hunting in response to resource depletion, increasing their reliance on communal methods (Saffirio and Scaglion 1982). Communal techniques are less efficient, in terms of kilograms of meat per hour of hunting (0.66 kg/hour), than are solitary methods (0.97 kg/hour), but provide larger total yields. Hunters in the traditional forest villages employ communal hunting techniques on infrequent occasions (in less than 2 percent of their hunts) when they need large quantities of meat for inter-village feasting.[4] In contrast, the highway Yanomamo have begun to use collective hunting for routine subsistence (more than 17 percent of their hunts).[5]

The adoption of communal hunting techniques in response to resource depletion is not unique to Amazonia. For example, according to Abruzzi (1979:185), the use of communal net-hunting techniques by various Pygmy groups in Zaire represents a similar response to resource depletion. He states that

> The larger camps and the cooperative hunting technique employed by the net-hunters, unique among contemporary hunters, may be seen to represent predictable responses to the subsistence pressures that accrue from continued population growth within a fixed, or declining, resource base.

Others working with the Pygmies have reached comparable conclusions. For example, Hart and Hart (1986) and Bailey and Peacock (in press) have suggested that the Pygmies probably could not have existed as discrete entities in the heart of the Ituri prior to the advent of horticulturalists into the forest. They argue that the principal reliable sources of carbohydrate for the Pygmies were the cultivated crops produced by the farmers; these crops were obtained by the Pygmies in exchange for meat (and labor). To meet the demands of these exchanges, the Pygmies probably turned increasingly toward communal techniques, taking prey at levels well above their immediate subsistence needs.

Bahuchet and Guillaume (1982) convincingly show that for centuries many Pygmy groups have been involved not just in local exchanges with farmers, but also in extensive, non-local commercial exchanges of meat, hides, and ivory with Portuguese, French, and other European colonial powers. According to Bahuchet and Guillaume, these commercial enterprises may have played a significant role in augmenting the Pygmies' use of net-hunting and other communal forms of animal procurement.

In a perceptive cross-cultural synthesis of communal hunting practices, Hayden (1981:371) reaches conclusions very similar to those cited above:

> It seems that communal hunting is most practical when obtaining a given amount of meat per day is more crucial than the increased work effort associated with communal hunting (i.e., under resource-poor or commercial hunting conditions).

Shifting from the occasional use of communal procurement techniques, conducted largely within a ritual or ceremonial context, to the routine use of such techniques in day-to-day subsistence activities presupposes basic changes in the social and organizational realms. These changes stem from "scalar communication stresses" and diminished decision-making performance that arise when larger numbers of people must interact and coordinate their activities on a regular basis (see G. Johnson 1982). Thus, for example, most Southwestern archaeologists would explain a shift in the focus of prehistoric hunting strategies from cottontails to jackrabbits, or from deer to antelope or bison, as a response to changes in species abundance that in turn reflect climatically caused alterations in the physical environment. However, such shifts toward communally hunted species may instead reflect fundamental organizational and socioeconomic changes in the community that are set in motion by culturally induced game depletion, altered time and labor constraints arising from the horticultural sector, amplified actual or potential hostilities as long-distance hunting increasingly takes place in inter-community buffer zones (Ross 1980:54), and other factors related to increasing sedentism and horticultural commitment. These clearly are issues in urgent need of further consideration.

Degree of dependence on cultivation and large-mammal hunting

Up to this point, we have focused entirely on the hunting strategies of horticulturalists who obtain over 70 percent to 80 percent of their total calories from starchy cultivated crops. Among these groups, especially those for whom fish are unavailable as a major resource, large mammals comprise the bulk, by weight and number of kills, of their hunted food. While "garden hunting" obviously provides an important supplementary source of protein and calories, the considerable time and energy invested by these horticulturalists in traveling to distant hunting zones to obtain larger species reflect the inadequacy of small-mammal kills made close to the village.

Ideally, we would like to be able to compare the hunting patterns of a series of horticultural groups, each with a different degree of residential stability and dependence on cultivated crops. Based on the discussion above, our expectation would be that the percentage contribution to hunting yields of large species would increase among those groups that are more sedentary and rely more heavily on horticulture (additional factors that affect hunting selectivity, such as time and labor constraints arising from horticultural activities, will be discussed below).

Unfortunately, comparative data of this sort are almost nonexistent. There are data, however, for two groups of Neotropical hunters and gatherers, the Aché of eastern Paraguay (Hill and Hawkes 1983) and the Maku of northwestern Brazil and southeastern Colombia (Milton 1984). Although the Aché live for much of the year in relatively permanent settlements near missions and obtain a fair amount of their calories from cultivated plants, they nevertheless spend extended periods in the forest where they are highly mobile and subsist almost entirely off the products of the hunt. It is their hunting patterns on these trips that are of particular interest to us here.

The Aché take almost the same range of animals as those exploited by the Yanomamo and other Amazonian horticulturalists (e.g., two species of peccary, deer, monkey, various birds, and so forth). Traditional Aché hunters, using only bows and arrows, killed mostly small and moderate-size prey (i.e. paca, coati, armadillo, capuchin monkey, birds, and snakes). Less than 25 percent by weight of the total meat yield came from large species (peccary and deer; Hill and Hawkes 1983:164). This contrasts strikingly with the meat yield (by weight) of Yanomamo bow-hunters, more than 80 percent of which came from large or moderate-size species (especially tapir, peccary, and giant anteater; Hames and Vickers 1982:366). Only when the Aché employed shotguns did their take of large animals approach the levels achieved by Yanomamo bow-hunters (Hill and Hawkes 1983:164).

The Maku are semi-nomadic hunters and gatherers who cultivate an unknown but relatively small and variable amount of manioc (Milton 1984), obtaining additional carbohydrates through exchange with riverine horticulturalists. Maku hunting is done mostly with blowguns and bows and arrows, although on occasion they hunt with shotguns. Data provided by Milton (1984) indicate that only about 45 percent by weight of the meat (excluding insects) taken by Maku hunters is from large and moderate-size species (peccary, deer, and woolly monkey). The contribution of larger animals might be reduced further if the kills made with shotguns were excluded.

While far from conclusive, the Aché–Maku–Yanomamo comparisons reinforce the suggestion that horticulturalists who live in relatively stable settlements and obtain most of their calories from a restricted range of protein-poor starchy crops rely more heavily on large animal species than do groups in broadly similar habitats who are more mobile and are less dependent on cultivated crops.[6]

Time and labor constraints

The time and labor constraints that arise from horticultural activities also play an important role in determining the size of prey sought by hunters. As pointed out earlier, Ye'kwana, Yanomamo, and Siona–Secoya hunters rapidly deplete larger species of game close to their villages. They must therefore travel further and invest more time in order to reach productive hunting zones. However, the competing demands of garden work and other activities around the village restrict the amount of time hunters can devote to long-distance hunting (see discussions in Beckerman 1983 and Hames 1983a). Thus, when hunters do engage in long-distance hunting, they focus heavily on species with the highest returns in order to make the trip energetically worthwhile. This is well illustrated by Hames and Vickers (1982) who show that larger species comprise only about 35 percent by weight of Yanomamo kills within 4 km of a village. Between 5 km and 9 km of the village, the contribution of larger species rises to about 80 percent by weight. In hunting zones more than 9 km from the village, where most hunting time is spent, larger game comprises more than 88 percent by weight of the kills.

The observations of Hames and Vickers (1982) fit comfortably with predictions from central place foraging theory (Orians and Pearson 1979). As observed by Pulliam (1981:67):

> People should be food generalists when hunting and gathering near home (a central place) and become progressively more selective about foods they choose to bring home when they forage farther afield.

Flowers (1983:358) makes the interesting observation that the time budgets of Amazonian groups who depend on root crops such as manioc are less constrained than the time budgets of those who depend more heavily on seasonal grains such as maize. This suggests that groups who rely on manioc are able to engage in long-distance hunting more often and more regularly than those who rely on maize. The seasonal constraints of maize cultivation would certainly appear to be a factor among ethnographically documented Southwestern pueblos who restrict much of their deer hunting to the winter following the harvest (see, for example, Ford 1968).

Other factors also place time and labor constraints on the hunting activities of tropical horticulturalists. Among these are the cropping patterns employed in the gardens (e.g., polycropping produces greater yields per unit area than monocropping, but requires greater labor inputs for weeding; see discussion in Beckerman 1983 and Hames 1983b); the level of game depletion in the area; seasonal characteristics of the environment that affect the abundance, distribution, and accessibility of hunted animals (Hames and Vickers 1983); the size and distribution of other competing groups, as well as the overall social and political climate in the region (Chagnon 1968a; Hames and Vickers 1983, and references therein).

Risk

Finally, we should note that the increased emphasis on large species among groups who obtain a substantial proportion of their total calories from cultivated plants may be a response not just to depletion of animal resources close to home and time and labor constraints imposed by gardening activities, but also to the greater predictability of their horticultural food base (presumably coupled with an effective storage technology), which may allow hunters to indulge in higher-risk procurement strategies.[7]

Alternative strategies for obtaining protein

The ethnographic literature from Amazonia documents a wide range of strategies available to horticulturalists to assure them of access to an adequate intake of animal protein and calories. We have already discussed a few of these: increasing the amount of time devoted to hunting; increasing the travel distance to productive hunting areas; focusing on larger, higher-yield species; and adopting communal hunting techniques. Other well-documented strategies include extended seasonal trips (trekking) by entire villages to productive hunting areas (Werner 1983, and

references therein); periodically relocating villages to gain access to new hunting areas (Gross 1975; Hames and Vickers 1983, and references therein); maintaining "buffer zones" between adjacent communities through intergroup conflict (Hames and Vickers 1983; E. Ross 1978; J. Ross 1980; DeBoer 1981; Harris 1984a; Gross 1975; Durham 1976; Moore 1981; Hickerson 1965); "detabooing" species previously considered inedible (Hames and Vickers 1982; Ross 1978; Yost and Kelley 1983:205; Berlin and Berlin 1983:318); and exchanging carbohydrates and animal protein between groups (Milton 1984). In addition, protein may be acquired by shifting crop complexes to include plants that provide more and higher-quality protein (Flowers 1983:389; Hames and Vickers 1982:375; Johnson 1977); increasing reliance, where feasible, on fish and other aquatic resources (Hames and Vickers 1983; Hames 1983a:395–396; Carneiro 1968b:245); using domestic animals such as pigs, chickens, cattle, turkeys, and even dogs (Johnson 1977; Berlin and Berlin 1983:318; Rosman and Rubel, this volume, chapter 3; Bozell 1985); and increasing involvement in external market economies (Flowers 1983:384; Gross, *et al.* 1979).

This list is certainly not exhaustive, but it identifies a number of the most important strategies used by horticulturalists to maintain adequate protein and calorie intakes. Clearly, some of these options are viable only when groups have relatively unrestricted mobility. When residential mobility is reduced, for whatever reason, habitat degradation and resource depletion may increase to the point where groups are forced to adopt other strategies. Most important among these are fishing, intergroup exchange of animal protein and carbohydrate, use of domesticated animals, and greater involvement in external market economies.

It is clear that in many situations fish may offer an important source of high-quality protein, the availability of which can significantly reduce or eliminate the pressure on horticulturalists to travel long distances in search of large game. However, the mere availability of fish does not automatically guarantee that they will be used to any significant degree. As pointed out in an interesting paper by Colchester (1984), horticulturalists whose dependence on cultivated starchy plants is low rely heavily on hunting and gathering to provide calories. Many species of fish (and molluscs) are low in fat and are therefore inefficient sources of calories. As a consequence, they may be ignored, at least seasonally, even if they are available (see discussion in Speth and Spielmann 1983). As the proportion (and reliability) of calories in the diet provided by cultivated plants increases, hunting may become less important as a source of calories and more critical as a source of high-quality protein. At this point, fish (and molluscs) may be incorporated into the diet and provide an important supplement or alternative to long-distance hunting of mammalian prey.[8]

The diversity of options outlined above makes it clear that horticulturalists need not all pass through the same ordered sequence of steps in response to increasing resource depletion or greater time and labor constraints. While we are convinced that the decisions made by horticulturalists are far from haphazard or random, there nevertheless may be considerable latitude in their choices depending upon a wide range of impinging factors. As indicated earlier, these include such things as the nature, productivity, and reliability of alternative subsistence resources, local and regional demographic, economic, and political conditions, and a host of other factors. Thus, the decision to focus more and more heavily on large mammals may be a common, but certainly not an inevitable, response to increasing residential stability and horticultural intensification. Turning toward fish and other aquatic resources, altering crop mixes, incorporating domestic animals, and engaging in intergroup exchange appear to be four of the more common and widespread supplements or alternatives to large-mammal hunting. (For the archaeologist, the absence of evidence for an increasing focus on large game in an evolving prehistoric horticultural system may, in fact, be one of the best clues that other strategies for acquiring protein were being employed.)

Moreover, even if different horticultural communities select similar responses to problems stemming from resource depletion, the rates at which these choices are adopted need not be comparable. Thus, for example, two communities may both move toward greater reliance on large mammals but one may deplete its available game much more rapidly than the other, or find its mobility options curtailed, forcing it to shift quickly toward other options. These variable rates complicate matters for the prehistorian, because an option whose tenure is short-lived (e.g. lasting only a few years) is unlikely to be as visible archaeologically as one that is employed for decades or centuries. Certain options may also have lower visibility archaeologically than others because they involve materials which preserve poorly (e.g. plant remains indicative of changing crop mixes), or which are small and hence less likely to be recovered (e.g. fish bones).

Returning to the Southwestern cases

What do these ethnographic observations suggest about the shifts toward larger species of game that we have noted in the American Southwest and elsewhere? We very tentatively offer the following reconstruction. We see the shifts primarily as socio-economic responses which accompany the aggregation of populations into more residentially stable and more horticulturally based communities.[9] Greater horticultural commitment increases, at least seasonally, the need for efficient sources of high-quality protein; it also introduces time and labor constraints that necessitate the rescheduling of hunting activities to more restricted periods of the year. Larger and more stable communities also degrade their immediate environs and deplete locally available game, forcing hunters to travel greater distances to more productive hunting areas. At the same time, greater reliance on horticulture may improve the predictability of the principal calorie sources, permitting hunters to indulge in higher-risk procurement strategies such as large-mammal hunting. Where fish are not a viable alternative, these factors together, at least initially, favor the taking of selectively greater proportions of larger, higher-yield prey. Resource depletion may also favor increased reliance on communal techniques of hunting both small and large species, such as jackrabbits, antelope, bison, and perhaps deer and mountain sheep. So long as population densities remain relatively low and groups relocate

their settlements relatively frequently, or so long as competition among adjacent groups maintains buffer zones in which larger prey species are subject to reduced predation pressure, emphasis on large species may persist.

At some as yet unknown threshold of resource depletion, brought about by reduced community mobility, or by increased horticultural activity, or by a change in the political or demographic environment, other strategies may be favored for maintaining adequate protein intakes. One option is to alter one's crop complexes to include plants with higher protein yields. This option, for example, may be reflected by the great diversity of plants, including several varieties of beans, cultivated by the Hohokam (Ford 1981, and references therein). Another option is to shift to greater dependence on domesticated sources of animal protein. In many parts of the Southwest, the turkey may have become such a resource (see discussion and references in McKusick 1980). Another strategy is to increase one's reliance on fish. Documenting the role of fish in the prehistoric Southwest is severely hampered by the tendency for fish bones to preserve poorly, and by the inadequate recovery techniques used in many Southwestern excavations prior to the advent of flotation. Isotopic approaches may one day clarify the dietary importance of fish. Still another strategy is to engage in exchange for meat with other populations that have greater access to large game. In the Southwest the emergence of Plains/Pueblo exchange for bison meat along the eastern frontier provides a classic example of this option (Spielmann 1982; Ford 1983). Intergroup exchange for deer meat, though difficult to demonstrate archaeologically, may also have been important (Ford 1983). Another option which may have occurred periodically in the Southwest is a reduction in the commitment to horticulture, with an increase in mobility and shift to a more generalized pattern of hunting and gathering (cf. Upham 1984). This option, which at times may have involved entire communities and at other times only segments of communities, presupposes of course the existence of relatively unpopulated hinterlands to which groups could retreat.

An interesting implication of the line of reasoning outlined in this chapter is that the increasing importance of bison in late prehistoric Pecos Valley and Panhandle Aspect subsistence systems may reflect a greater commitment on the part of the inhabitants of these areas of the southern Plains to a village-based horticultural economy, much like the transition from Plains Woodland to Plains Village economies in the central Plains (cf. Wedel 1983; Lehmer 1971; Dallman 1983:60), rather than a transitional stage of a group en route to becoming nomadic bison hunters (cf. Jelinek 1967). Following this line of reasoning a little further, increasing reliance by local villagers on large ungulates may have "preadapted" them to the mutualistic food exchanges that characterized Plains/Pueblo interaction at the time of European contact (cf. Spielmann 1982; Speth and Spielmann 1983).

Concluding remarks

The scenario outlined here is by no means the only plausible one to account for the faunal trends that we have observed among horticulturalists in the Southwest. Unfortunately, we lack at present the archaeological data necessary to identify more precisely the changes that were actually taking place. More importantly, we still lack adequate quantitative studies of the relationships between horticultural intensification and hunting strategies in living societies. These relationships must be worked out far more explicitly and precisely before the present reconstruction can be evaluated.

We have tried to squeeze a great deal, perhaps too much, from a small sample of archaeological and ethnographic cases. In our defense, we hope that this discussion will encourage others to explore what we feel is potentially a highly productive research direction. It is clear that much remains to be learned about the adaptations of small-scale horticulturalists, both past and present-day; the research potential of these fascinating middle-range societies remains largely untapped.

Notes

We are grateful to Jonathan Driver, Richard Ford, Karl Hutterer, Michael Jochim, Susan Kent, John O'Shea, Thomas Rocek, Bruce Smith, David Snow, Katherine Spielmann, Bruce Winterhalder, John Yellen, and Lisa Young for helpful comments and suggestions on various drafts of the manuscript. Responsibility for the final product, whatever its faults or merits, rests with us. Funding for various portions of the research was provided by the Museum of Anthropology and the Horace H. Rackham School of Graduate Studies of the University of Michigan.

This paper is a revised, expanded, and reorganized version of a paper originally presented at the 17th Annual Meeting of the Canadian Archaeological Association, Victoria, B.C., Canada (April 18–21, 1984), and subsequently published by the Archaeological Survey of Alberta (Speth and Scott 1985). In the present endeavor, we pursue several interesting issues that we did not deal with previously, and we have also attempted to clarify and expand areas that were not adequately addressed before.

1 Throughout this chapter, the terms "large" and "small" game refer respectively to the upper and lower ends of the range of prey sizes available in a given region, rather than to fixed, arbitrary size classes.

2 While the present chapter focuses on groups whose carbohydrates derive primarily from cultivation, similar arguments may be extended to hunter–gatherer systems that become increasingly sedentary and rely heavily on starchy wild seeds and nuts (cf. Jackson 1986).

3 For an example of a well-documented prehistoric horticultural sequence which shows no obvious trend toward increasing reliance on large mammals, see Anyon and LeBlanc's (1984) discussion of the fauna from Mimbres sites in southwestern New Mexico.

4 For a comparable example in Australia of communal hunting largely for ritual purposes, see Altman (1984:188); see also Fawcett (1985) for similar suggestions concerning the primary social importance of communal bison hunting during the pre-horse period in the North American Plains.

5 Hunting with shotguns by Yanomamo and other Amazonian groups has also been cited as a consequence of, not just a cause of, resource depletion (Hames 1979; Hames and Vickers 1982:375).

6 Jones (1984), in a detailed review of the hunting strategies of several ethnographically documented, non-Arctic hunter–gatherers (e.g. !Kung and G/wi San), argues that small game animals normally predominate in the diet of such groups.

7 We are grateful to Michael Jochim, Bruce Winterhalder, and John O'Shea for bringing this important factor to our attention.

8 The rather sudden increase in the importance of molluscs in the Middle to Late Archaic of eastern North America may, at least in part, reflect the emergence of a comparatively stable calorie base, provided by increasing use of starchy wild seeds and nuts. Similar arguments might also be used to account for the rapid increase in the use of marine shellfish during the Mesolithic in Europe and of landsnails during the Epipaleolithic in the Near East and North Africa. Likewise, the disappearance of fish from the diet of Tasmanian hunter–gatherers might reflect a decline in the security of the carbohydrate base rather than a shift in food preferences.

9 The reasons for increasing sedentism and horticultural intensification are themselves issues of considerable interest, but are beyond the scope of this chapter. Numerous studies have examined the causes of increasing sedentism, and the factors which may encourage, or force, hunters and gatherers to cultivate plants (for recent discussions of these issues, see Rafferty 1984, and references therein).

Chapter 8

Sedentism and prehistoric animal procurement among desert horticulturalists of the North American Southwest

Christine R. Szuter and Frank E. Bayham

Introduction

... the Bushmen of the Dobe area eat as much vegetable food as they need, and as much meat as they can. (Lee 1968:41)

In the arid deserts of Africa, Richard Lee observed an almost paradoxical significance attached to meat by the Dobe !Kung. The actual diet of these Dobe hunter–gatherers was dominated by vegetal foods, but Lee documented their palate for meat. Perhaps the very scarcity of meat protein enhanced its desirability. This situation is probably not unique (see chapter 1), and may have a parallel in the subsistence regime of populations who occupied the arid deserts of the North American Southwest.

Prehistoric populations have occupied the desert regions of south-central Arizona from Paleo-Indian times until the Spanish conquest. From 2500 B.C. to A.D. 1350 two cultural traditions, the Archaic and the Hohokam, dominated the archaeological record. Although the actual temporal placement and nature of the transition are topics of debate (Doyel and Plog 1980; Haury 1976; Schiffer 1982), most researchers acknowledge that a group of prehistoric horticulturalists known as the Hohokam supplanted the hunter–gatherers of the Late Archaic Period. The later Hohokam flourished from around A.D. 500 to A.D. 1350, and were characterized by a relatively high degree of sedentism in comparison to the earlier hunter–gatherers. The Hohokam, like

the Dobe !Kung, extracted the major portion of their "daily bread" from vegetal foods, yet animal motifs adorn their pottery and shell, and dominate the figurine complex (Haury 1976). Perhaps even more revealing is the substantial quantity of animal bone that has been recovered from numerous Hohokam sites – a physical testament to the importance of animals in the prehistoric Hohokam diet. The continuous occupation from the Archaic through the Hohokam Period and the quality of the archaeofaunal record afford the opportunity to examine the effects of sedentism and of the adoption of horticulture on the patterns of animal utilization in the arid deserts of the Southwest.

The Archaic people are traditionally classified as hunters and gatherers, but evidence of corn cultivation and of some degree of sedentism has been established during the latter part of the Archaic occupation (Dart 1985; Huckell 1986). Despite this evidence, during most of the Middle and Late Archaic people were more mobile and relied more extensively on the gathering and hunting of wild plants and animals than did the Hohokam.

The Hohokam sequence is divided into the Pioneer, Colonial, Sedentary, and Classic periods.[1] During the Pioneer period, settlements were small and located along rivers where farmers utilized canals to irrigate various domestic plants including corn, beans, and cotton. The Colonial period, by contrast, was marked by geographic expansion. Previously unoccupied areas were inhabited, and sites grew larger and exhibited such architectural features as platform mounds and ballcourts. Within the arts and crafts industry, stone was sculpted into many animal forms such as snakes, toads, and birds. During the Sedentary period, the Hohokam territory contracted with some decline in the overall craftsmanship of items. Houses continued to be brush and mud structures that were often arranged in village communities. The Classic period, on the other hand, exhibited a novel suite of characteristics. New architectural forms such as surface structures, compounds, and multi-story houses flourished. Contact with areas to the north and south expanded and influenced the Hohokam. Canal irrigation, which was employed throughout the Hohokam sequence, was even more extensive and is primarily responsible for the Hohokam being known today as the "desert farmers."

Despite their well-deserved reputation for horticulture the Hohokam never relied solely on domesticated plants for their sustenance. Not surprisingly, they gathered wild plants and hunted both small and large game as well. Animal resources in particular were needed both for the protein and for the variety that they supplied to the diet.

The convenient labels of hunter–gatherer or farmer do not hold for the Hohokam, and are of minimal value even for heuristic purposes. These distinctions tend to mask the overlap in subsistence activities that often occurs. Farmers are often hunters; far from being mutually exclusive, the two activities are actually complementary. (See Speth and Scott, chapter 7, and Sponsel, chapter 4, in this volume.)

Animal utilization in the desert environs of the Southwest has traditionally been viewed as an economic pursuit subsidiary to the exploitation of plant resources. Faunal studies undertaken in the desert Southwest from the 1940s through the 1960s documented that most Archaic as well as Hohokam faunal assemblages were dominated by various species of lagomorph, with other desert-dwelling species showing up consistently but in lesser proportions (e.g. Haury 1950; Sayles and Antevs 1941). Furthermore, hunting was thought to have declined in importance from the Archaic to the Hohokam Periods. As a consequence, little emphasis was placed on evaluating the role of hunting among the Hohokam.

Within the past decade, however, several major archaeofaunal studies in south-central Arizona have revealed an unanticipated degree of temporal and spatial variability in the proportionate representation of various taxa. In this chapter, we synthesize and present some of the recent archaeofaunal data which has accumulated for the Hohokam as well as for their hunter–gatherer predecessors. Emphasis is placed on the utilization of lagomorphs and artiodactyls; these two orders of mammals account for approximately 70 percent of the number of identified specimens from the majority of Archaic and Hohokam sites in the Southwest. We then examine the temporal and spatial distribution of these taxa in order to make a comparative evaluation of the factors influencing changes and variability in

animal exploitation among populations of the desert Southwest. Of particular interest is the archaeologically demonstrable effect of sedentism, firstly, on the proportionate use of large and small game, and secondly, on the use of different species of lagomorph.

The data base

Information from a considerable number of faunal studies is mentioned throughout this chapter. Most of the excavations upon which these analyses are based have resulted from cultural resource management work; consequently they often consist of a group of sites that were excavated as part of a larger project. The sites from any given project may span a long period of time, or represent functionally different components. In order to minimize confusion in subsequent discussions, we have organized and consolidated the relevant archaeological information by project or site in table 8.1. The temporal component(s) and elevation given for each project or site are derived from the site reports. One problem we encountered in determining the temporal component for a particular site is that the faunal remains from multicomponent sites are often reported without a breakdown by time period (e.g. Sparling 1978). In these instances, we either omitted the site from analysis or approximated its chronological position in the cultural historical framework of south-central Arizona. Habitat and annual precipitation were derived from a standard Southwestern habitat classification scheme (Jordon 1981).

The primary data referenced in this chapter represent, to the best of our knowledge, all the published and much of the unpublished Archaic and Hohokam faunal data for south-central Arizona.[2] These data are presented in table 8.2. We have focused on taxa known to be of economic value, i.e. lagomorphs and artiodactyls, in an effort to minimize bias introduced via divergent analytical and quantification procedures, and taphonomic problems. In order to minimize the effect of small samples in assessing the proportionate representation of different species, sites with an NISP (number of identified specimens) less than 12 were excluded from this analysis. Ultimately, 70 temporally distinct components were included in our sample.

The quantification of faunal remains is a major topic of concern in any analysis. Many means of measurement exist, each with their own advantages and disadvantages. The NISP, the number of identified specimens, is the most direct measure of taxonomic abundance and is used in this presentation. Although criticism has been leveled against the use of the NISP, researchers have argued that none of the objections to the NISP approach is strong enough for its use to be abandoned (Chaplin 1971; Grayson 1984; Klein and Cruz-Uribe 1984).[3] Since the goal of most faunal analyses is a comparison of the "*relative* taxonomic abundances across time or through space" (emphasis in original; Grayson 1984:25), the use of the NISP provides an estimate of proportionate representation requiring minimal extrapolation from the recovered information. In addition, archaeological sites frequently contain only small quantities of bone that do not lend themselves to more sophisticated forms of measurement. Rather than focus-

Table 8.1 Description of the project or site setting of Archaic and Hohokam sites discussed in the text.

Project or site name	Temporal component	Project setting	Elevation (feet)	AAP (inches)	Faunal reference
Ventana Cave	Middle Archaic–Classic Hohokam	Upper Sonoran Desert shrub	2,500	8–12	Haury 1950, Bayham 1982
Picacho Reservoir Project	Middle Archaic	Phoenix Desert shrub	1,500–1,600	7–10	Bayham 1986
La Paloma Site	Middle–Late Archaic	Upper Sonoran Desert shrub	2,620–2,630	8–12	Szuter 1985b
Harquahala Valley Project	Late Archaic	Lower Sonoran Desert shrub	900–1,200	2–7	Bostwick and Hatch 1987
Gu Achi Site	Sedentary Hohokam	Upper Sonoran Desert shrub	1,920	8–12	Johnson 1980
Quijotoa Valley Project	Sedentary–Classic Hohokam	Upper Sonoran Desert shrub	2,000	8–12	White 1978
Snaketown	Pioneer–Sedentary Hohokam	Phoenix Desert shrub	1,175	7–10	Greene and Mathews 1976
Escalante Ruin Group	Sedentary–Classic Hohokam	Phoenix Desert shrub	1,400	7–10	Sparling 1974
Salt–Gila Aqueduct Project	Sedentary–Classic Hohokam	Phoenix Desert shrub	1,500–1,600	7–10	Szuter 1984a
New River Project	Sedentary–Classic Hohokam	Phoenix Desert shrub	1,500	7–10	Bayham and Hatch 1985a
West Branch Site	Sedentary Hohokam	Upper Sonoran Desert shrub	2,450–2,500	8–12	Szuter 1986
Valencia Road Site	Sedentary Hohokam	Upper Sonoran Desert shrub	2,450–2,480	8–12	Szuter 1985a
Miami Wash Project	Sedentary Hohokam–Salado	Upper Sonoran Desert shrub	3,200–3,300	8–12	Sparling 1978
Ash Creek Project	Sedentary Hohokam–Salado	Upper Sonoran Desert shrub	2,200–2,500	8–12	Bayham and Hatch 1985b
ANAMAX–Rosemont Project	Colonial–Sedentary Hohokam	Chihauhan semi-desert grassland	4,600–5,000	12–16	Glass 1984

Project setting and AAP adapted from Jordon (1981).

AAP = Average annual precipitation.

ing only on species lists, an analysis using the NISP is one means of understanding patterns among small samples of faunal remains (Szuter 1984b).

The MNI, minimum number of individuals, is probably the second most common method of quantifying faunal remains. Whereas NISP is a simple and straightforward count of bone, the MNI attempts to derive a more realistic estimate of the number of animals represented. MNI determinations have been fraught with problems ranging from differences in basic quantification to their relationship with the NISP. Grayson (1978) has pointed out that MNIs should be used only when the MNI/NISP ratio is less than 0.15 in order to correct for small sample sizes. The published MNIs, particularly for artiodactyls, rarely meet this criterion for the sites used in this analysis. In addition, the method used for calculating the MNI varies among different sites or projects, with the result that the MNI estimates are not comparable.

For these reasons, we have opted to use NISPs rather than MNIs in the calculation of taxonomic ratios for this Archaic and Hohokam faunal analysis. However, in a few instances, we have used MNI as the basis of calculation rather than NISP, and these are duly noted. NISP is defined as the quantity of bone identifiable below the level of class, excluding any domestic animal remains. This would include bone identified to the level of order, family, genus, or species. The NISP has been adjusted in cases where one bone was obviously broken into numerous fragments. This adjustment was primarily made for artiodactyls where an antler tine or other bone was heavily fragmented, and only when specific provenience information was given.

Two taxonomic ratios based on the NISP are calculated for each site in table 8.2. The lagomorph index compares the relative proportion of cottontails (*Sylvilagus*) to jackrabbits (*Lepus*). It is derived from a similar index presented in Bayham and Hatch (1985a). Lagomorphs include the antelope jackrabbit (*Lepus alleni*), the black-tailed jackrabbit (*Lepus californicus*), and cottontails (*Sylvilagus*) as well as those faunal remains only identified to family or genera. Both cottontails and jackrabbits are abundant at most sites, but in different proportions. The artiodactyl index compares the relative abundance of artiodactyls to lagomorphs. This index is derived from Bayham's (1982) work at Ventana Cave. Artiodactyls include mule deer (*Odocoileus hemionus*), white-tailed deer (*Odocoileus virginianus*), pronghorn antelope (*Antilocapra americana*), and bighorn sheep (*Ovis canadensis*) as well as those faunal remains that could be identified only to order or genera. While lagomorphs occur in large numbers at all sites, the presence of artiodactyl remains is more variable. This artiodactyl index is a ratio of large to small game. The factors that can influence these indices are discussed in the following sections.

Long-term patterns of animal use

Archaeofaunal research in the desert Southwest has documented a general pattern of emphasis on smaller species extending minimally from the Middle Archaic (*ca.* 2500 B.C.) to the end of the Hohokam Period (A.D. 1350). Hunting as a contribution to

the subsistence economy during this period was thought to have gradually decreased in importance (Haury 1950:544). Among the canal-building Hohokam at Snaketown, Haury observed that animal bone constituted a "surprisingly small fraction" of the trash deposit and further concluded that the preponderance of small taxa suggested that the Snaketown inhabitants, driven by a protein-deficient diet, ate anything that would fill the void (1976:114–119).

This perspective on animal utilization was consistent with the idea that adoption of a sedentary lifestyle in the desert Southwest would over-extend the already meager faunal resources. Dramatic seasonal temperature fluctuations coupled with unpredictable and low rainfall limited the potential productivity and reliability of animals as a stable source of protein. It was, and remains, perfectly logical to think that regional increases in population density would intensify the use of less preferred (using energetic or nutritional criteria) animal resources such as rabbits, rodents, and lizards. This perspective was also consistent with the fact that most Hohokam sites, situated in the alluvial basins of south-central Arizona, were dominated by rabbits. The generality and geographic uniformity of this view, however, required some clarification with the discovery at Ventana Cave of a long-term diachronic trend toward an increased use of artiodactyls (Bayham 1982). Results of the Ventana Cave analysis provide a foundation for the regional examination of variation in patterns of animal use, and are briefly reviewed.

Diachronic patterns of animal use at Ventana Cave

Ventana Cave is located in the Upper Sonoran Desert shrub habitat of south-central Arizona at an elevation of 2460 feet (figure 8.1). The cave, perhaps more precisely termed a rockshelter, is situated in one of a number of low-altitude mountain ranges overlooking the broad alluvial basins which typify this area. Emil Haury (1950) excavated Ventana Cave in 1941–1942 and established that the occupational sequence at the site spanned a 10,000-year period. The Paleo-Indian horizons contained a Pleistocene fauna associated with stone tools, and were separated from the Holocene midden deposits by a geologic unconformity. The upper portion of the midden deposits (level 1 through the middle of level 3) was associated with the Hohokam Period which dates roughly from A.D. 500 to about A.D. 1350. The lower levels of the midden (from the middle of level 3 to level 8) were assigned to the Middle and Late Archaic Period by Haury (1950:522–525) who estimated this occupation to span the period from 2500 B.C. to the beginning of the Hohokam Period.

Analysis of a large quantity of unworked animal bone from Ventana Cave in 1980–1981 indicated that some variation existed in the proportionate representation of taxa through time (Bayham 1982). Vertebrate remains from the Archaic Period horizons were dominated by jackrabbits and deer, but a wide variety of species were recovered. Other taxa of economic significance included the pronghorn antelope, bighorn sheep, coyote (*Canis latrans*), and some ground squirrels (e.g. *Spermophilus* spp., *Ammospermophilus* sp.). The Middle/Late Archaic levels (levels 8 through 4) docu-

Table 8.2. *The number of identified specimens (NISP) for each taxonomic group of lagomorphs and artiodactyls from temporally distinct sites discussed in the text. The artiodactyl index, (A/(A + L)), is the artiodactyl NISP divided by the sum of the artiodactyl and the lagomorph NISPs. The lagomorph index, (S/L), is the cottontail (Sylvilagus) NISP divided by the total lagomorph NISP. The total site NISP and the percentage of the site NISP comprised of artiodactyls and lagomorphs are given.*

	Lagomorpha (L)						Artiodactyla (A)	
	Leporidae	Lepus sp.	Lepus alleni	Lepus californicus	Sylvilagus sp.(s)	Subtotal	Artiodactyla	Odocoileus sp.
Archaic Period sites								
Ventana Cave, Level 4	0	0	11	224	29	264	43	40
Ventana Cave, level 5	0	0	19	114	12	145	13	15
Ventana Cave, level 6	0	0	1	167	9	177	22	14
Ventana Cave, level 7	0	0	2	108	8	118	10	6
Ventana Cave, level 8	0	0	2	42	4	48	3	2
Picacho Reservoir, Arroyo Site	2	4	5	36	8	55	2	1
Picacho Reservoir, Gate Site	1	23	2	55	23	104	0	0
La Paloma, early phase	1	8	0	3	2	14	0	0
La Paloma, late phase	0	1	0	6	5	12	0	0
Harquahala Valley, AZ S:7:30	1	18	0	39	3	61	1	0
Hohokam Period sites								
Ventana Cave, level 1	0	6	46	107	20	179	56	77
Ventana Cave, level 2	0	0	55	184	20	259	96	67
Ventana Cave, level 3	0	0	28	81	16	125	17	16
Gu Achi	0	16	7	18	11	52	26	0
Quijotoa Valley, AZ Z:11:5	65	0	3	0	1	69	0	0
Quijotoa Valley, AZ Z:14:21	114	0	39	8	9	170	4	4
Quijotoa Valley, AZ Z:11:30	6	0	6	7	0	19	0	0
Quijotoa Valley, AZ Z:11:33	23	0	6	8	3	40	1	5
Snaketown, Vahki–Snaketown	0	0	54	326	36	416	4	0
Snaketown, Gila Butte–SC	0	0	30	389	79	498	8	1
Snaketown, Sacaton	0	0	7	47	5	59	1	0
Escalante, AZ U:15:22	0	3	0	0	7	10	38	0
Escalante, AZ U:15:27	0	136	0	0	63	199	3	0
Escalante, AZ U:15:32	53	436	0	0	174	663	14	0
Escalante, AZ U:15:3	0	86	0	0	64	150	3	0
SGA, AZ U:10:06 Santa Cruz	76	201	20	294	134	725	11	10
SGA, AZ U:15:61 Santa Cruz	27	127	35	270	109	568	4	0
SGA, AZ U:15:77 Santa Cruz	0	13	0	8	2	23	1	2
SGA, AZ U:15:97A Santa Cruz	1	4	0	13	2	20	0	0
SGA, AZ U:15:61 SC/Sac	2	3	1	22	4	32	0	0
SGA, AZ U:15:83 SC/Sac	2	18	1	41	36	98	0	0
SGA, AZ U:10:06 Sacaton	19	21	2	22	12	76	1	1
SGA, AZ U:15:57 Sacaton	17	41	0	5	1	64	0	0
SGA, AZ U:15:61 Sacaton	26	117	6	239	55	443	5	1
SGA, AZ U:15:62 Sacaton	2	3	0	10	29	44	0	0
SGA, AZ U:15:99 Sacaton	0	0	0	12	0	12	0	1
SGA, AZ U:15:48 Sacaton	13	5	0	14	146	178	2	0
SGA, AZ U:14:73A Sac/Soho	0	5	0	9	2	16	2	0
SGA, AZ U:15:77 Sac/Soho	4	5	0	8	13	30	8	1
SGA, AZ U:15:76 Soho	5	15	1	64	121	206	3	5
SGA, AZ U:15:87 Soho	8	12	1	174	76	271	1	1
SGA, AZ U:15:83 Soho/Civano	1	2	0	6	9	18	0	0
SGA, AZ U:15:59 Civano	71	94	10	255	24	454	3	4
SGA, AZ U:15:19 Civano	73	90	5	348	219	735	66	92
SGA, AZ U:15:83 Civano	8	8	2	26	9	53	2	4
New River, AZ T:8:18	0	0	0	477	45	522	69	9
New River, AZ T:8:17	0	0	14	1,092	101	1,207	182	5
New River, AZ T:4:12	0	0	0	57	23	80	6	1
New River, AZ T:4:16	0	0	4	301	52	357	17	7
New River, AZ T:8:16	0	0	2	418	38	458	0	0
West Branch Site, Early Rincon	2	8	10	21	11	52	2	0
West Branch Site, Middle Rincon	2	82	22	74	12	192	20	1
West Branch Site, E/M Rincon	0	8	5	12	2	27	0	3
Valencia Road Site, Early Rincon	0	5	4	7	18	34	0	0
Valencia Road Site, Late Rincon	0	10	3	15	11	39	0	0
Miami Wash, AZ V:9:57	15	52	0	0	78	145	117	167
Miami Wash, AZ V:9:55	1	0	0	14	14	29	0	7
Miami Wash, AZ V:9:56	6	0	0	15	24	45	13	0
Miami Wash, AZ V:9:60	0	0	0	11	3	14	5	0
Miami Wash, AZ V:9:62	23	0	0	149	48	220	78	0
Ash Creek, AZ U:3:51	1	0	0	5	13	19	4	0
Ash Creek, AZ U:3:46	0	0	0	14	40	54	10	6
Ash Creek, AZ U:3:49 (Salado)	0	8	0	12	22	42	20	2
Ash Creek, AZ U:3:50 (Salado)	0	2	0	11	3	16	3	14
Ash Creek, AZ U:3:86 (Salado)	0	1	0	35	3	39	2	0
ANAMAX, AZ EE:2:113	38	0	7	373	105	523	144	69
ANAMAX, AZ EE:2:105	24	0	18	343	149	534	200	117
ANAMAX, AZ EE:2:76	3	0	4	31	13	51	26	5
ANAMAX, AZ EE:2:129	0	0	0	3	1	4	6	5
ANAMAX, AZ EE:2:77	0	0	0	10	5	15	7	1
Totals	736	1,697	500	7,309	2,448	12,690	1,405	789

E/M = Early/Middle; Sac = Sacaton; SC = Santa Cruz; SGA = Salt–Gila Aqueduct.

Odocoileus hemionus	Odocoileus virginianus	Antilocapra americana	Ovis canadensis	Subtotal	Total (A + L)	Ratio (A/(A + L))	Ratio (S/L)	Total site NISP	Percentage ((A + L)/NISP) for site
18	14	31	9	155	419	0.370	0.110	604	69.4
9	11	13	1	62	207	0.300	0.083	295	70.2
1	3	10	1	51	228	0.224	0.051	321	71.0
1	0	4	0	21	139	0.151	0.068	191	72.8
1	1	1	2	10	58	0.172	0.083	82	70.7
0	0	0	1	4	59	0.068	0.145	71	83.1
0	0	0	0	0	104	0.000	0.221	123	84.6
0	0	0	1	1	15	0.067	0.143	26	57.7
0	0	0	0	0	12	0.000	0.417	26	46.2
0	0	0	0	1	62	0.016	0.049	70	88.6
94	17	35	42	321	500	0.642	0.112	811	61.7
84	20	45	59	371	630	0.589	0.077	870	72.4
22	3	14	19	91	216	0.421	0.128	314	68.8
4	0	0	12	42	94	0.447	0.212	108	87.0
0	0	0	0	0	69	0.000	0.014	112	61.6
0	0	0	0	8	178	0.045	0.053	222	80.2
0	0	0	0	0	19	0.000	0.000	19	100.0
0	0	0	0	6	46	0.130	0.075	165	27.9
83	0	0	9	96	512	0.188	0.087	555	92.3
209	0	1	12	231	729	0.317	0.159	752	96.9
12	0	0	4	17	76	0.224	0.085	79	96.2
25	0	0	0	63	73	0.863	0.700	75	97.3
153	0	0	0	156	355	0.439	0.317	416	85.3
21	4	0	0	39	702	0.056	0.262	760	92.4
8	1	0	0	12	162	0.074	0.427	287	56.4
3	0	0	0	24	749	0.032	0.185	1,025	73.1
1	0	0	0	5	573	0.009	0.192	661	86.7
0	0	0	0	3	26	0.115	0.087	55	47.3
0	0	0	0	0	20	0.000	0.100	25	80.0
0	0	0	0	0	32	0.000	0.125	38	84.2
0	0	0	0	0	98	0.000	0.367	103	95.1
0	0	0	0	2	78	0.026	0.158	95	82.1
0	1	0	0	1	65	0.015	0.016	262	24.8
1	0	1	0	8	451	0.018	0.124	511	88.3
0	0	0	0	0	44	0.000	0.659	47	93.6
0	0	0	0	1	13	0.077	0.000	13	100.0
0	0	0	0	2	180	0.011	0.820	317	56.8
0	0	1	0	3	19	0.158	0.125	46	41.3
0	2	0	0	11	41	0.268	0.433	44	93.2
1	0	0	0	9	215	0.042	0.587	370	58.1
0	1	0	0	3	274	0.011	0.280	347	79.0
0	0	0	0	0	18	0.000	0.500	20	90.0
3	0	1	0	11	465	0.024	0.053	607	76.6
10	0	1	0	169	904	0.187	0.298	1,391	65.0
0	0	0	0	6	59	0.102	0.170	131	45.0
1	0	0	13	92	614	0.150	0.086	660	93.0
0	0	0	0	187	1,394	0.134	0.084	1,512	92.2
1	0	2	0	10	90	0.111	0.288	92	97.8
0	0	0	3	27	384	0.070	0.146	436	88.1
0	0	0	0	0	458	0.000	0.083	476	96.2
0	0	0	0	2	54	0.037	0.212	80	67.5
1	0	0	0	22	214	0.103	0.063	217	98.6
0	0	0	0	3	30	0.100	0.074	31	96.8
0	0	0	0	0	34	0.000	0.529	93	36.6
0	0	0	0	0	39	0.000	0.282	39	100.0
0	0	1	0	285	430	0.663	0.538	488	88.1
0	0	0	0	7	36	0.194	0.483	42	85.7
7	0	0	0	20	65	0.308	0.533	79	82.3
0	0	0	0	5	19	0.263	0.214	29	65.5
99	0	2	0	179	399	0.449	0.218	413	96.6
3	0	0	0	7	26	0.269	0.684	37	70.3
2	0	0	0	18	72	0.250	0.741	82	87.8
3	0	0	0	25	67	0.373	0.524	104	64.4
1	0	0	0	18	34	0.529	0.188	47	72.3
0	0	0	0	2	41	0.049	0.077	45	91.1
13	19	35	1	281	804	0.350	0.201	868	92.6
8	37	43	3	408	942	0.433	0.279	1,060	88.9
4	6	3	5	49	100	0.490	0.255	113	88.5
1	0	0	0	12	16	0.750	0.250	168	9.5
5	5	0	0	18	33	0.545	0.333	33	100.0
913	145	244	197	3,693	16,383	0.225	0.193	20,706	

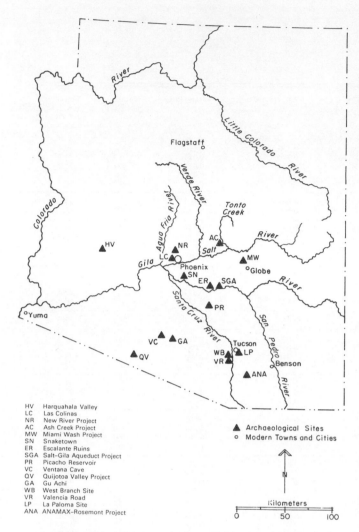

HV   Harquahala Valley
LC   Las Colinas
NR   New River Project
AC   Ash Creek Project
MW   Miami Wash Project
SN   Snaketown
ER   Escalante Ruins
SGA   Salt-Gila Aqueduct Project
PR   Picacho Reservoir
VC   Ventana Cave
QV   Quijotoa Valley Project
GA   Gu Achi
WB   West Branch Site
VR   Valencia Road
LP   La Paloma Site
ANA   ANAMAX–Rosemont Project

▲ Archaeological Sites
○ Modern Towns and Cities

Fig. 8.1. Map of Arizona showing the location of Archaic and Hohokam archaeological sites

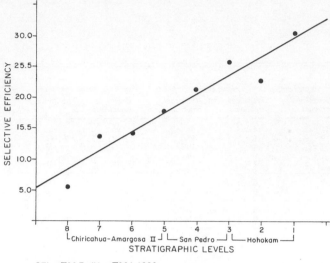

$$SEI = \Sigma M_i E_i /(1 + \Sigma M_i)\ 1000$$

Where E_i = Caloric value per individual prey item i

M_i = Estimate of the relative abundance for individual prey item i

Fig. 8.2. Change in the selective efficiency index over time at Ventana Cave illustrating increasing specialization on larger game from the Middle to the Late Archaic Period ($y = 3.02x + 5.46$; $r^2 = 0.909$; Bayham 1982: 243)

ment a much stronger utilization of rabbits, particularly the black-tailed jackrabbit and to a lesser degree the desert cottontail (*Sylvilagus audubonii*), in comparison to the artiodactyls. The later Hohokam levels provide evidence of much greater exploitation of deer and other endemic artiodactyls.

The energetic constituent of this diachronic faunal trend was evaluated by comparatively weighing the relative contribution of different-sized prey items in the diet. Larger prey items, such as artiodactyls, provide more energy per individual and are likely to be taken in preference to small game when they are available. This proposition is different from the frequently employed assumption that species are taken in proportion to their natural abundance. This latter assumption has proven to be incorrect in a number of situations using either simple measures of numerical abundance or biomass values (Munson, Parmalee, and Yarnell 1971; Smith 1975). Considerations of the effect of prey body size on the process of selection incorporates one variable which is uniformly deemed significant by researchers (see Bayham 1979 and Styles 1981:84–96 for discussions on importance of body size). If we presume that

large game are systematically selected for utilitarian purposes when they are available, then the proportion of small game in the diet may be an indirect index to the availability of large game. The selective efficiency index (SEI) was developed to measure the relative energetic contribution of different-sized prey animals in a given assemblage (Bayham 1982:241):

$$SEI = \Sigma M_i E_i /(1 + \Sigma M_i)1000$$

where M_i is an estimate of the relative abundance for individual prey items i and E_i is the caloric value per individual prey item i. This value may be construed as an aggregate output/input efficiency estimate over some specified time interval.[4]

Selective efficiency index or SEI values were determined for each level from the Middle Archaic through the Hohokam Periods at Ventana Cave (see Bayham 1982:241–249). When plotted over time, the SEI produced a strong linear trend toward the utilization of larger game items throughout the sequence. This translates to an increase in the selective efficiency of animal utilization in the vicinity of the cave accounting for 91 percent of the variation over time in the faunal assemblage (figure 8.2; $r^2 = 0.91$; $p < 0.001$).

This dramatic shift over time in animal use is antithetical to the predicted and presumed pattern of subsistence change during the Archaic–Hohokam transition in southern Arizona. Several problems come into focus. Firstly, it does not support the conventional view that gathering activities increased in importance from the early Archaic through the later Archaic Periods culminating in horticulture, and that hunting decreased to a level of lesser importance (Haury 1950:544; Schiffer and McGuire 1982:235). Why this pattern exists and how it relates to the changing function of

Ventana Cave are dealt with in the following section. Secondly, this gross change in proportionate use is rather unexpected since no animals in the Sonoran Desert are excessively abundant. Lastly, the strength of the linear trend over time, in probabilistic terms, is far less than would be expected by chance, implicating causal processes that were not precipitous, but sequentially gradual or punctuated over intervals not detectable in the archaeological record.

Patterning in animal utilization similar to that at Ventana Cave has been explained with reference to changes in the environment (cf. McMillan 1976). If, for instance, environmental changes increased the abundance of artiodactyls over time, the pattern could be accounted for. This, however, does not appear to be the case. Packrat midden studies document a trend in effective moisture that is declining over time: from a woodland in the early Holocene, to a wet summer desert scrub, to the drier arid regime of today (Van Devender 1977; Van Devender and Spaulding 1979). While fluctuations no doubt occurred since 2500 B.C., no evidence suggests an environmental transformation which would have increased the relative or absolute availability of mule or white-tail deer, bighorn sheep, or pronghorn antelope through time.

Natural changes in the local environment around Ventana Cave cannot by themselves account for the diachronic trend in animal procurement. Also, no technological innovations in the hunting repertoire appear to have been developed which would have increased the ability to capture larger prey items in preference to smaller ones. One hypothesis which can effectively account for the pattern focuses on the ecological and economic consequences of increased sedentism.

Socioeconomic consequences of increased sedentism

Irwin-Williams and Haynes (1970) have suggested that south-central Arizona was depopulated during the height of the proposed Altithermal. Their contention is supported by the fact that the proportion of sites dating to the Altithermal (5500–3000 B.C.) bridging the Early and Middle Archaic Periods are surprisingly rare in this area. At some point around or after 3000 B.C., the frequency of sites assignable to the Middle Archaic appears to increase (Irwin-Williams 1979). Although perhaps not uniform, a net trend toward population increase seems to characterize the Late Archaic and Hohokam Periods. No doubt, increasing population size would have altered the arrangement of human–environmental interactions.

It is possible that the gradual trend toward specialization in animal exploitation at Ventana Cave is related to regional population increase, but not in a direct fashion. Regional population increases would reduce the per capita availability of meat protein and, in general, should result in the increased use of less preferred game. But the data from Ventana Cave indicate that this did not occur. It is likely that the directional change at Ventana was affected by an organizational shift in the socioeconomic system. Specifically, the costs of hunting at Ventana Cave may have been changed owing to reduced residential mobility, or increased sedentism. The occupation of Ventana Cave is known to have

spanned the Middle Archaic through the Hohokam Period; during this period in the Southwest, sedentary villages first appear in the lowland, alluvial basins.

During the Middle Archaic, Ventana Cave may have operated as a base camp like many other localities in the regional procurement system. Decisions concerning which resources to exploit were made from the cave itself, functioning as a base camp. As plant and animal resources in the vicinity of the cave declined, the local band would have moved on. Foraging theorists suggest that groups should move on when the energetic return rate at a specific location falls below the average return rate for that habitat (Charnov 1976; Winterhalder 1981).[5]

Population increases, even at an extremely slow rate, could have altered the basis of an effective, stable socioeconomic system. An increase in population density exacerbates the problem of survival during the unproductive winter months. Avoidance of the late winter/early spring starvation period necessitates the implementation of storage strategies to assure adequate provisioning (Binford 1980). One likely consequence of regional population increase (or in-migration) during the Middle/Late Archaic may have been an increase in the need for storage facilities and a decrease in residential mobility. It is likely that during the Late Archaic, and continuing into the Hohokam Period, the major alluvial basins of south-central Arizona were occupied for longer periods of time in the annual cycle. Rather than moving base camps to upland localities, such as may have been done at Ventana Cave in the Middle Archaic, it probably became more efficient to engineer expeditions from base camps to acquire those resources not immediately available (see idealized diagram in figure 8.3).

Resource depression and central place foraging

The very existence of a human population in an area for an extended length of time may create non-natural changes in prey density and distribution. One important consequence of decreased residential mobility, or increased sedentism, is resource depression. Resource depression refers to an actual or perceived reduction in the availability of prey species due either to shifts in their natural distribution, or to learned avoidance responses. Animal ecologists have observed this patterned response among animals such as ants or various nesting species which forage from a stable location for a period of time. Human ecologists studying patterns of animal use among sedentary horticulturalists have also documented prey responses to both environmental modification (Linares 1976) and hunting pressure (Vickers 1980). It has been suggested that these prey responses should evolve to relocate prey items where predators find it more difficult to encounter and capture them (Charnov, Orians, and Hyatt 1976:248).

Hamilton and Watt (1970) have explored how populations may modify the spatial relationships of non-domesticated resources. They define several broadly overlapping zones which surround a core area (figure 8.4). Whether the central habitation area is seasonally occupied or permanent, the core is generally devoid of resources during the period of occupation. They also note that as the intensity of occupation – measured in the amount of dis-

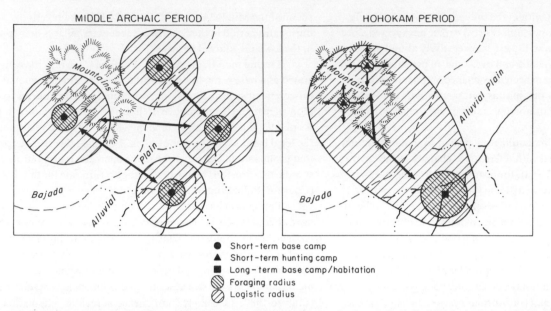

Fig. 8.3. Schematic representation of hypothetical regional socioeconomic changes from the Middle Archaic to the Hohokam Period in south-central Arizona

turbed space – increases, the distance from the core area to the beginning of resource-producing areas should also increase. The biodeterioration zone is one of low availability owing to the habitually intensive use of resources within that zone. Beyond this zone lies the main resource-acquisition zone where prey species have mostly been unaffected by human occupation; this zone may or may not blend gradually into the other zones. Binford (1982) has discussed an analogous economic zonation pattern among the Nunamuit which concurs with this scheme.

Another factor that may alter prey selection at an outlying locality is the increased cost of traveling to and returning from a resource patch. Models dealing with this general problem are structured around the concept of central-place foraging. These models assume that prey are not consumed where they are captured, but are returned to some fixing locality where they are eaten, stored, or distributed. In general, as the distance and hence traveling time from a central place to a foraging locality are increased, selection should proceed in favor of those items providing more energy per load (Orians and Pearson 1979:161; Killeen, Smith, and Hanson 1981).

The interaction of these two related, but independently acting, processes may account for the observable change through time in the faunal assemblage at Ventana Cave. An idealized representation of these interacting processes is depicted in figure 8.4. Firstly, increased transport and travel costs associated with the expedition hunts in the uplands would have shifted selection toward large game. Put simply, it would not have been efficient to travel a great distance to upland localities, and settle for a mere cottontail (although this certainly may have occurred). Secondly, unintentional habitat destruction in the vicinity of more permanent base camps would have created unnatural, mosaic distributions in the availability of certain resources, necessitating the increased travel

to productive hunting areas. Both of these factors would engender greater amounts of selectivity and specialization at upland localities, even if the same basic constellation of resources was being utilized.[6]

Animal use in the Archaic and Hohokam Periods

The model outlined above suggests that sedentism and decreased mobility may have altered the logistics of animal utiliz-

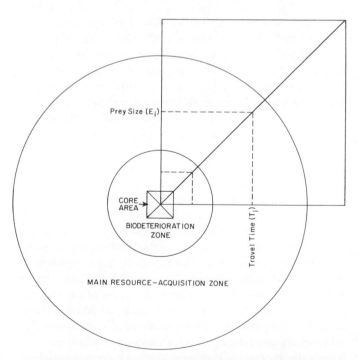

Fig. 8.4. Idealized representation of the interacting effects of resource depression and the costs of increased travel from a central place on the energetics of animal exploitation

ation from the Archaic through the Hohokam Periods. The plausibility of this explanation can be more fully evaluated in the context of a broader comparative data base. Elsewhere, it was demonstrated that the relative frequency of hunting equipment such as projectile points, bifaces, and flake knives increases through time at Ventana Cave, while those of vegetal-processing tools, such as manos and metates, proportionately decline (Bayham 1982:265–276). This pattern supports the main thesis that Ventana changed from a base camp to a hunting locality, and implies a reorientation in the function of the cave from the Archaic through the Hohokam Periods. The representation of artiodactyl body parts through time at Ventana Cave was also examined for the purpose of assessing the effect of potential increased transport costs associated with sedentism. This analysis yielded inconclusive results. Carnivores had impacted the faunal assemblage at Ventana to the extent that no clear human behavioral use pattern could be recognized (Bayham 1982:289–340).

If the hypothesized explanation for long-term change at Ventana Cave is true, regional patterns of animal food consumption should give rise to two predictions: firstly, that the pattern of change from the Middle Archaic through the Hohokam Period is different from that represented at Ventana Cave; secondly, that this change should be marked by increasing variability among sites in selective efficiency related to both the degree of sedentism and the position of the site in the regional procurement system (see Bayham 1982:341–359 for extended discussion of difficulties associated with testing this prediction). In order to evaluate these predictions the proportionate representation of artiodactyls relative to the lagomorph–artiodactyl total was determined for all available Middle Archaic, Late Archaic, and Hohokam sites situated in the lower elevation alluvial basins of south-central Arizona as a basis of comparison with each level at Ventana Cave. This value, referred to as the artiodactyl index, summarizes the contribution of high-ranking artiodactyls in an assemblage and is analogous to the previously described index of selective efficiency. Low values of the artiodactyl index indicate intensive utilization of smaller species, such as jackrabbits, which provide less return per item; higher values of the artiodactyl index indicate greater proportional utilization of larger species (figure 8.5).

The results of this comparison are interesting and tend to support the major hypothesis of regional socioeconomic reorganization. Firstly, the chronological sequence of stratigraphic levels from Ventana Cave (V8 through V1) indicates essentially the same basic trend as was noted earlier (figure 8.2) using a slightly different index which incorporated all represented taxa: from the Middle Archaic continuing to the Hohokam Period, the sequence shows an increasing dependence through time on larger game in what presumably typifies upland habitat utilization. The artiodactyl index at lower elevation Archaic and Hohokam sites, in contrast to the temporal trend at Ventana Cave, indicates a strong emphasis over time on species of lagomorph with an apparent increase in variability during the later periods. Each of the Middle Archaic lowland open sites (Gate Site; Arroyo Site; La Paloma, early), contemporaneous with the Middle Archaic strata

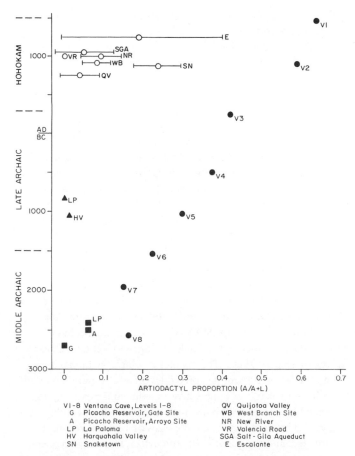

Fig. 8.5. Comparison of the artiodactyl index for Middle Archaic sites (■), Late Archaic sites (▲), and Hohokam sites (○) with Ventana Cave, levels 1–8 (●)

at Ventana Cave (levels 8–6), are dominated by the smaller, low-ranking lagomorph species. Artiodactyl representation ranges from zero to only a few element fragments. The Middle Archaic strata at Ventana Cave, located in a mountainous upland habitat, contain proportionately more artiodactyls than do these contemporaneous lowland sites. Why might this difference exist?

The frequency of residential moves of hunter–gatherers during the Middle Archaic was arguably determined by human population densities, overall habitat productivity, diminishing returns on resources, and "incongruities" in seasonal resource production (Binford 1980; Kelly 1983; Winterhalder 1981). If a greater amount of residential mobility characterized the Middle Archaic, the smaller artiodactyl index from the lower elevation campsites may simply reflect the lower availability of potential large game in the lowlands in comparison to the uplands. The generally greater abundance of large game in upland habitats may account for their prevalence in the Middle Archaic levels at Ventana Cave. In the two lowland basin sites attributable to the Late Archaic Period (La Paloma, late; Harquahala Valley), lagomorph species continue to dominate the faunal assemblages. An increasing disparity in the utilization of artiodactyls between lowland and upland habitats is highlighted by a comparison with levels 4 and 5 from Ventana Cave.

The artiodactyl index for a substantial number of Hohokam sites distributed across the desert environs of south-central Arizona is summarized by site or project in terms of the mean and standard deviation in the upper left portion of figure 8.5. Most of these later Hohokam habitation sites show a similarity to the lowland Archaic sites in the proportion of artiodactyls represented, although greater variation in this pattern characterizes several sites along the Gila River (Snaketown and Escalante). The comparability of these two sites to the other sites is questionable in terms of both sampling and faunal analytical techniques, and they may, in fact, be less anomalous than they appear. The Hohokam levels at Ventana Cave (levels 1 and 2) produced a much greater proportion of artiodactyls in comparison to any of the lowland sites. Additionally, the high proportion of artiodactyls in the upper levels at Ventana Cave culminates a trend which began in the Middle Archaic.

Sites in the mountain ranges punctuating the alluvial basins of the Sonoran Desert similar to Ventana Cave are rare. A late prehistoric hunting camp, MAV-37, located in the Mohawk Mountains may provide the single analogue to Ventana Cave in the region (Doelle 1980). The manner in which the faunal data from MAV-37 are quantified precludes direct comparability with the other data sets, but a subjective assessment is possible. Data presented by Fritz (1980) indicate that this faunal assemblage is dominated by artiodactyls. On the basis of a specialized lithic assemblage, and the quantity of "mule deer, bighorn sheep, and, to a much lesser degree, rabbits or other small mammals," Doelle (1980:215) concluded that this site was a specialized hunting camp. The position of MAV-37 is estimated to be near level 1 of Ventana Cave in figure 8.5. This lone example supports the dichotomous pattern between lowland and upland habitats during the late prehistoric occupation of the region.

The increasing disparity over time between upland and lowland habitat utilization is a predicted outcome of decreased residential mobility and an increase in the use of Ventana Cave as an outlying hunting camp. The overall similarity among lowland valley residence sites in terms of their low degree of selective efficiency is explicable by the proposed diachronic model of increased resource depression in the vicinity of sedentary villages in the lowlands. A reduction in hunter–gatherer mobility over time would encourage intensification on the locally available resources resulting in a continued low degree of selective efficiency in the alluvial basins. In no documented lowland residence site prior to the Hohokam Period does the proportion of artiodactyls relative to the lagomorph–artiodactyl total exceed 0.10. It does appear, however, that even from the Middle Archaic the degree of selective efficiency at residence camps is sufficiently low that intensification on the animal resource base through time was either not feasible or imperceptible using only the species selected for this index.

The emphasis on lagomorphs at sedentary sites continues into the Hohokam Period, but variability appears to increase.

Increase in the complexity of social organization into the Hohokam Period may well have influenced activity specialization and the variability of site types, as well as the logistics of animal procurement. Also, variation in the spatial arrangements of sites in relation to animal procurement areas may well have affected the travel and transport costs of hunting expeditions and the subsequent distribution of meat. These issues are discussed in the following section. Yet, the results of this diachronic comparison imply that a change in the regional settlement system from a more mobile hunter–gatherer regime to a sedentary system based on horticulture effected a concomitant change in the logistical decisions associated with the acquisition of animal foods. These changes, in turn, have affected the degree of heterogeneity in Southwestern archaeofaunal assemblages.

Variability in animal use among the Hohokam
Artiodactyl exploitation among the Hohokam

While lagomorphs continue to dominate the faunal assemblage in the Hohokam period, the variability expressed in the artiodactyl index, that is the ratio of artiodactyl NISP to the sum of artiodactyl NISP plus lagomorph NISP, needs to be investigated. The artiodactyl index is generally less than 0.10 at lowland Hohokam sites but quite variable when all Hohokam sites, regardless of environment, are examined. The preceding discussion focused on the diachronic changes in this index among the Archaic and Hohokam peoples. This section discusses the broad range of environmental and organizational factors that contribute to the variability in both access to and use of artiodactyls by the Hohokam.

The Hohokam inhabited an area of great environmental contrasts. The occupation of these different ecological zones meant that the Hohokam had access to a wide array of resources. Moreover, while horticulture was practiced at all of these sites, differences in the degree of commitment to horticulture existed. The Salt–Gila River Hohokam practiced extensive canal irrigation while evidence of canal irrigation by the Tucson Basin inhabitants has only more recently been uncovered (Bernard-Shaw 1987). The Papagueria Hohokam lived in a more xeric environment with less ground cover. By contrast, Hohokam in the more upland areas may have exploited wild resources to a greater extent as well as being constrained by a shorter growing season. All of these factors undoubtedly influenced artiodactyl exploitation.

Figure 8.6 plots the artiodactyl index for each of the sites by environmental area. Sites are located in upland areas (ANAMAX, Miami Wash, Ventana Cave, Ash Creek), in the Papagueria (Gu Achi, Quijotoa Valley), in the Tucson Basin (West Branch site, Valencia Road), and in the Salt–Gila Basin (Snaketown, Escalante Ruins, Salt–Gila Aqueduct Project, New River). With the exception of a few Salt–Gila Basin sites, all of the lowland sites have artiodactyl indices between 0 and 0.16. In other words, artiodactyl exploitation appears to be minimal among the lowland Hohokam. The lowland sites that do exceed this range – two sites from Escalante, the three temporal components at Snaketown, and two Salt–Gila Aqueduct Project sites – are all situated along the Gila

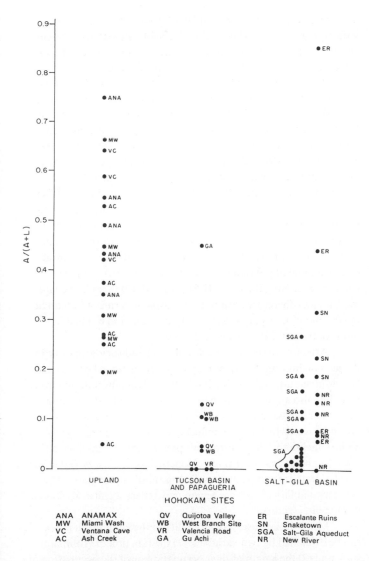

Fig. 8.6. Artiodactyl index (A/(A + L)) plotted for upland, Tucson Basin and Papagueria, and Salt–Gila Basin sites

the uplands owing to habitat preference, the exploitation of these animals was also influenced by socioeconomic factors relating to demography and site function.

While a few village sites exist in the Santa Rita Mountains, the majority of upland sites are small farmsteads, hamlets, field-houses, or seasonal occupations. They are all relatively small, indicating an overall smaller population, even though exact estimates have not been made for most of these sites. Smaller upland populations and smaller sites suggest that the upland Hohokam altered their natural environment to a lesser extent than did the lowland Hohokam. In all probability, then, resource depletion was less of a problem around upland as opposed to lowland sites.

Another likely factor is a difference in the intensity of horticulture. While the upland Hohokam did farm, their reliance upon agriculture was not as great as that among their lowland counterparts. The only domesticated crop recovered through either pollen or macrobotanical analysis is corn (Fish, Gasser, and Swarthout 1985; Hall 1978; Lytle-Webb 1978; Miksicek n.d.). Furthermore, there is no evidence of canal irrigation at these sites; the upland Hokokam relied entirely upon dry farming techniques. Finally, only one growing season was possible because of the constraints of elevation, thus further limiting a commitment to horticulture. Some of these sites, including Ventana Cave, have even been classified as non-agricultural seasonal occupations utilized primarily as hunting camps (Bayham 1982). The upland Hohokam therefore placed more of an emphasis upon hunting, including the hunting of locally available large game.

Lowland subsistence practices, on the other hand, contrasted sharply with the upland pattern. The lowland sites, all below 2500 feet, are located in the Salt–Gila Basin, the Tucson Basin, and the Papagueria. They differ both in size and function from the upland sites. First of all, the degree of horticultural commitment among the lowland Hohokam was clearly greater. Recovered domesticated plant remains are far more diverse at the lowland sites than at the upland sites. They include not only corn but beans, squash, cotton, and occasionally tobacco as well. In addition, all lowland sites occur at elevations that allow for the cultivation of two crops a season. Moreover, extensive prehistoric canals are found in the Salt–Gila Basin at Las Colinas, Snaketown, and at the Salt–Gila Aqueduct Project sites and more recently at Tucson Basin sites (Bernard-Shaw 1987). A reliance on irrigation at these sites means a greater reliability in crop yield. All of these characteristics help explain why so much more acreage was under cultivation in the lowlands than in the uplands.

Secondly, many of the lowland sites are large village sites. These villages must have supported greater populations which had a greater impact on the environment, including the depletion of certain wild resources. And if large game, especially artiodactyls, were indeed scarce around these villages, then more time, effort, and organization would have to be expended in their pursuit. Sophisticated desert farmers might have had little such time available for the extended hunting expeditions necessary to kill, process, and transport deer, antelope, or bighorn sheep back to their villages. Consequently Hohokam living in lowland villages

River. The possible significance of their riverine location is discussed later in the chapter.

The majority of upland sites, on the other hand, have artiodactyl indices ranging between 0.19 and 0.75. These upland sites include the Hohokam occupation of Ventana Cave, the sites in the Santa Rita Mountains (ANAMAX in table 8.2), and those along Ash Creek and Miami Wash, all with elevations between 2200 and 5000 feet. Consequently artiodactyl exploitation among the upland Hohokam was certainly greater and more variable than among those living in the lowlands.

This observed difference between upland and lowland artiodactyl use may be related to resource availability, site function, or site size. However, the range of variation suggests that factors other than resource availability may be at work. As previously mentioned, animals are not hunted in direct proportion to their natural abundance. While more artiodactyls may have resided in probably devoted less attention to the hunting of large game than did their upland neighbors.

Not surprisingly, then, all of the lowland sites, with the exception of Snaketown, two of the Escalante sites, two of the Salt–Gila Aqueduct Project sites, and Gu Achi, have an artiodactyl index of less than 0.16.[7] Interestingly enough, five of these sites are located along the Gila River. While not all sites along the Gila have high artiodactyl indexes, the five that do suggest that the Gila River may have offered better hunting than did other lowland areas. During prehistoric times, the Gila was a permanently flowing stream that provided a lush riparian environment for all types of wildlife (Rea 1983). Early explorers' reports note the abundance of animals, including artiodactyls, along the river course (Davis 1982). It is therefore possible that the lowland Hohokam communities along the Gila secured more big game than did lowland settlements in more xeric environments.

In summary, differences in the artiodactyl index appear to be influenced by a number of factors. While lagomorphs provided an abundant and constant source of food supply throughout the Hohokam occupation, the availability of artiodactyls may have been more concentrated in the uplands. The occupants of these sites were less committed to horticulture than were their lowland neighbors and also lived in smaller settlements with less impact on the natural environment. The lowland Hohokam, on the other hand, relied upon farming to a much greater extent. Consequently the hunting of large game with its greater expenditures of time and more elaborate logistical arrangements was less frequent because of the scheduling constraints imposed by intensive lowland horticulture with its irrigation, its double-cropping, its wider array of cultigens, and its much greater acreage. Under such constraints, small-game hunting became a more practical endeavor, i.e. one that required less time and energy to meet specific protein requirements. Therefore, the following sections examine the effects of increased sedentism on the hunting of cottontails and jackrabbits, the most important small-game species among the Hohokam.

Jackrabbit and cottontail exploitation among the Hohokam
The presence of jackrabbits (*Lepus* spp.) and cottontails (*Sylvilagus* spp.) is ubiquitous at most sites in south-central Arizona. While these two genera are generally lumped together in discussions of subsistence practices, the behavior and habitat preference of the two animals are quite different. Since these differences affected how they were hunted and utilized prehistorically, it is necessary to understand them in order to interpret Hohokam faunal assemblages in a comprehensive and sophisticated manner.

Jackrabbits and cottontails are found throughout the Southwest, and they often share the same desert environment. Nonetheless, their habitat preferences and their relative abundance within these areas vary considerably (Madsen 1974). Cottontails are more likely to be found along water and in areas of thicker vegetation, while jackrabbits, specifically *L. californicus*, are located in barren fields and less densely vegetated areas. Arch-

aeological studies (Bayham and Hatch 1985b:204–206) have demonstrated a greater relative abundance of cottontails at heavily vegetated upland sites and relatively more jackrabbits at sites located in the sparsely vegetated lower alluvial plains.

At first glance, then, it appears that both ecological studies and the archaeological record suggest that the lagomorph index, the ratio of cottontail NISP to the sum of lagomorph NISP, can be used as an index of the ground cover in a particular environment. When studying the remains from archaeological sites, however, it must be stressed that these environments are not pristine. On the contrary, we are discussing environments modified by human occupation (Fish 1984; Fish, Miksicek, and Szuter 1984). The distinction is a critical one because there is no simple one-to-one relationship between the faunal assemblage from a site and the proportion of those animal species in the natural environment. Humans transformed the ground cover around sites, thereby affecting animal populations as well. Furthermore, they made choices concerning the animals they hunted. Changes in the lagomorph index therefore need to be discussed in terms of human behavior and its interplay with the environment, and not just in terms of the natural environment alone.

Attempts to separate environmental and socioeconomic influences on hunting behavior may very well be futile because the two domains are inextricably interrelated. Humans not only transform but also adjust to their natural environment. At the same time, their behavior affects environmental conditions such as ground cover, which in turn influences plant and animal availability. Jackrabbits and cottontails prefer different habitats, so their numbers vary accordingly. Nonetheless, it must be reiterated that habitats are culturally as well as naturally determined. The relative availability of the two genera may reflect social as well as environmental factors.

Much of the observed variability in the lagomorph index can be explained by two variables: (1) the function of Hohokam sites, and (2) the length of their occupation or of the occupation of the surrounding geographical area. The ecological and archaeological evidence indicates that cottontails are more likely to be found in more densely vegetated areas than are jackrabbits. This fact suggests that the lagomorph index will be high if a site was small or occupied for a short period of time and will decrease if population densities were greater and occupation spans longer.

Intensity of occupation refers to the function of the site and its length of occupation. Hohokam sites have been classified as village-hamlets, farmsteads, fieldhouses, and plant- or lithic-processing sites (Crown 1984). Generally, few faunal remains have been recovered from either the processing sites or fieldhouses. Instead, farmsteads and village-hamlet sites provide most Hohokam animal bone. Village-hamlets are large, permanent settlements occupied by numerous families over many generations. The large size of these sites contrasts with that of the smaller farmsteads. Although also occupied on a permanent basis, farmsteads are smaller with fewer houses and may have been occupied by extended families. These two site types differ primarily in terms of size. Both types have houses, pits, hearths, and other domestic features,

Table 8.3. *Hohokam sites or project areas that demonstrate a decrease in the lagomorph index through time*

Site or project area	Temporal component	Lagomorph index
Valencia Road site	Early Rincon	0.53
	Middle Rincon	0.28
West Branch site	Early Rincon	0.21
	Middle Rincon	0.06
Miami Wash project	Sedentary through Salado	0.54
		0.48
		0.53
		0.21
		0.22
Escalante Ruins	Sedentary through Classic	0.70
		0.32
		0.26
		0.43
Salt–Gila Aqueduct AZ U:10:6	Santa Cruz	0.19
	Sacaton	0.16
Salt–Gila Aqueduct AZ U:15:61	Santa Cruz	0.19
	Sacaton	0.12

yet villages often have ballcourts, reservoirs, or irrigation canals as well. Village-hamlets with their larger populations therefore had a greater impact on the vegetative cover than did the smaller farmsteads.

Differences of size and, to a lesser degree, of function are reflected in the lagomorph index. The lagomorph index at farmsteads is higher and somewhat more variable than at village sites with an average of 0.36 and a standard deviation of 0.23. Village sites, on the other hand, have a mean lagomorph index of 0.19 and standard deviation of 0.11. These contrasting means suggest differences in the interplay between human behavior and animal ecology at village-hamlets and farmsteads as well.

With their larger, more aggregated populations, village-hamlets would be more likely to engage in communal hunting than would smaller farmsteads inhabited by single households. Cottontails are more easily captured by solitary hunters who stalk them individually. Jackrabbits are more often taken in hunting drives in which communal parties sweep through an area and force the jackrabbits into nets or restricted killing grounds. The smaller population sizes at farmsteads made communal hunting less feasible, while individual hunting may have been practiced more. In addition, the overall larger size of villages creates a more favorable environment for jackrabbits by reducing the vegetative cover of an area. By contrast, the smaller size of the farmsteads probably meant less alteration of the natural environment. Not as much ground cover would have been destroyed, thereby preserving a habitat preferred by cottontails. Thus, through a combination of factors including hunting behavior, lagomorph habitat preferences, and the cultural modification of the environment, village-hamlet sites and farmsteads manifest significantly different lagomorph indices.

In addition to site size and function, length of occupation also affects the lagomorph index. Sites or geographical areas occupied for longer lengths of time show a decrease in the ratio of cottontails to jackrabbits (table 8.3). In other words, the longer a site was occupied, the more ground cover was destroyed, making the environment more favorable to jackrabbits than to cottontails. This pattern, along with the one associated with site function, strongly suggests that more intensely occupied sites are associated with a degradation of the surrounding environment and a corresponding shift in the densities of the two lagomorph genera. Again, the interplay between human and animal populations is readily apparent.

Table 8.3 presents the series of sites or geographical areas that follow this trend. While the temporal components vary for each site/area, the earlier occupation always has a higher lagomorph index. This trend can be observed regardless of geographical location.[8] In short, intensity of occupation, ground cover, lagomorph densities, and hunting behavior all seem to be interrelated variables that changed through time in clearly patterned ways. When population densities were low or areas were occupied seasonally or for short periods of time, the proportion of cottontails in the Hohokam diet increased. With increased sedentism, however, that ratio declines. The procurement of jackrabbits, always greater than that of cottontails, became even more important as the environment deteriorated under the impact of denser populations and longer occupations.

Conclusion

The focus of this chapter has been on exploring the effects of increased sedentism on hunting practices among the prehistoric horticultural inhabitants of southern Arizona. One of the major findings was that as human populations occupy an area their presence creates changes in the environment that alter subsistence practices. In particular, greater numbers and longer occupations of fragile desert areas lead to a decrease in the vegetative ground cover and a subsequent shift in the densities of economically important animal species. That shift, coupled with the organizational transformations involved in sedentism and intensive horticulture, significantly influence hunting behavior and the amount of energy and time devoted to different types of wild game.

The increasing exploitation of artiodactyls through time at Ventana Cave suggests a change in the function of the cave determined in large measure by increased sedentism in the lowlands. Ventana Cave appears to have changed from a residential base camp during the Archaic Period to a more specialized hunting camp during the Hohokam Period. This reorientation was linked to changes in the broader regional economic system. The increased difference between upland and lowland sites in the proportionate representation of artiodactyls during the Hohokam Period implies a degree of interrelatedness in site use that was not apparent during the Archaic Period.

The more sedentary of the Hohokam occupations exhibited variability in terms of both artiodactyl and lagomorph procurement. Lowland Hohokam sites with their greater commitment to horticulture relied less heavily on artiodactyls than did their upland neighbors. The lowland sites cultivated a wide variety of domesticated plants; this was made possible by elaborate canal irrigation systems as well as a climate that permitted two growing seasons. The upland sites, on the other hand, devoted more attention to the hunting of artiodactyls, because: (1) their horticulture was less intensive, and (2) artiodactyls themselves may have been more available owing to natural abundance and because the environment itself was less degraded because of lower population densities and shorter occupancies of upland sites.

The variability expressed in the artiodactyl index among the Hohokam sites is also apparent in the lagomorph index. Site function and length of occupation affected the relative abundance of jackrabbits and cottontails. The larger village sites had lower ratios of cottontails to jackrabbits compared to the smaller farmsteads because their larger, more aggregated populations altered the environment to a greater extent and led to a decrease in the vegetative ground cover. This decrease created a more favorable environment for jackrabbits, which the inhabitants of village-hamlets could also hunt more effectively in communal drives because of their larger populations. The converse was true at farmsteads, where smaller populations destroyed less of the surrounding habitat and therefore did not trigger a major shift in the densities of cottontails and jackrabbits. In addition, the small size of the farmsteads probably implied more individual than communal hunting techniques – techniques better suited to the procurement of cottontails than of jackrabbits. The lagomorph index also appears to be sensitive to the length of occupation of a site. In other words, the longer a site was occupied, the more jackrabbits were exploited relative to cottontails.

What all of these patterns point to is that increased sedentism among the horticultural Hohokam of south-central Arizona affected their use of animals. The dietary importance of large game, as evidenced by the proportionate representation of artiodactyls, increased through time in upland, peripheral areas and decreased in lowland, alluvial habitats. Over time, the lowland Hohokam became increasingly reliant upon small-game species, especially jackrabbits, that thrived in disturbed environments. As they modified the lowland environment for horticulture, so too did they transform it, albeit unconsciously or indirectly, for hunting as well. Consequently any attempt to establish a simple correlation between animal utilization and the environment is inadequate because it fails to account for human modification of the environment in all its subtle and complex manifestations, particularly in relation to horticulture and sedentism.

Notes

This chapter represents a cooperative effort between the authors. Frank Bayham's portion of this chapter on Ventana Cave is based on his dissertation. He would like to thank all those who contributed to that endeavor. Conversations with his fine colleagues, including Neal Ackerly, Glen Rice, and Steve Shackley, were important in helping to complete this chapter. Christine Szuter's portion of this chapter is partially based on work for her dissertation. She is appreciative of the institutional support she has received from the University of Arizona, the Arizona State Museum, and the Institute for American Research. Professor Stanley J. Olsen, as mentor to both authors, has been instrumental in their faunal training. We thank him for his support throughout the years.

John Speth commented on the numerous drafts of this chapter. We have incorporated many of his thoughtful comments into it. Susan Kent's attention and energy expended in coordinating the production and editing of this chapter was most welcome. We would also like to thank Thomas Sheridan for his expertise and time devoted to editing the original draft. We would particularly like to acknowledge our families for their continual support. In addition, we thank the editors and staff of Cambridge University Press for their comments.

Charles Sternberg skillfully drafted all the figures. Carmen Villa Prezelski, John Kohl, and Lee Fratt helped immensely in producing the final draft of this chapter. We thank them all. As with any endeavor, we alone are responsible for the final content of this chapter.

1 While some agreement exists on this basic sequence, the calendrical dates associated with each period are much debated (Plog 1980; Schiffer 1982; Wilcox and Shenk 1977) with the focus being on whether the chronology should be shortened from that originally proposed by Haury (1976) and Gladwin, *et al.* (1938). Using Haury's scheme (1976:338) the Pioneer extends from 300 B.C. to A.D. 550, the Colonial from A.D. 550 to A.D. 900, the Sedentary from A.D. 900 to A.D. 1100, and the Classic from A.D. 1100 to A.D. 1450. The revised short chronologies do not begin until anywhere from A.D. 100 to A.D. 500. We rely on absolute dates when they are available. When those dates are not available we base our assessment on period or phase assignments.

2 The original draft of this chapter was completed in October, 1985. The data base, therefore, reflects works published and analyzed prior to this date. Additional Hohokam faunal assemblages have been analyzed since the original completion of this chapter but these data have not been incorporated into this analysis.

3 Not all animals have the same quantity of bones; therefore, differences in NISP from different taxa may be a result of skeletal variation. Fragments of bone are interdependent and may be from the same animal. Excavation techniques, along with differential

breakage or preservation rates, or butchering methods, will affect the number of fragments per taxon differently. These criticisms are only a brief review of problems involving NISP.

4 This index assumes that whole animals were used at some point after procurement.

5 Martin (1983) notes that the actual determination of the "average return rate" for a habitat is impossible to carry out, but posits no objection to the theoretical existence of variable return rates.

6 This model is idealized and is not meant to imply that resource availability or selection are simple linear functions of distance measured in travel time.

7 Sampling methods for the faunal remains analyzed from Snaketown and the Escalante Ruins are not reported. Therefore, possible sampling biases may exist in how the faunal remains were selected for identification.

8 This same trend, a decrease in the lagomorph index during continuous occupation of a site, has more recently been demonstrated at the Tanque Verde Wash site (Szuter and Brown 1986).

Chapter 9

The myth of ecological determinism – anticipated mobility and site spatial organization

Susan Kent and Helga Vierich

Intrasite spatial organization has been analyzed within a framework of ethnicity by a few anthropologists (e.g. Hodder 1982, 1987). More tend to view spatial organization within an ecological perspective, emphasizing environmental factors such as climate, vegetation, and predators (Gould and Yellen 1987; O'Connell 1987). Anthropologists have studied spatial patterning from an economic framework also (e.g. Binford 1978a; Layne 1987; and others). Some anthropologists have emphasized the relationship between site structure and mobility patterns (e.g. Binford 1981; Brooks and Yellen 1987; Kent 1984, 1987; Hitchcock 1982, 1987). Although all are ultimately related at one level, each approach has been examined as the primary, or sometimes only, factor influential in the organization of space and site structure. The distribution of activity areas at sites has been attributed to the activities themselves, usually viewed within an overall subsistence mode, such as hunter–gatherers' activities versus farmers' activities (for example, in the case of storage). Site activity area patterning has been attributed also to ethnicity: different ethnic groups exhibit different activity distributions based on ethnic identification and/or ethnic-specific symbolism and behavior (for example, the distribution of ash areas, Hodder 1987).

In this chapter we attempt to address all the major approaches in viewing the causes and meaning of spatial

patterning on the intrasite level, the intersite level being beyond the scope of the chapter. Specifically investigated is the question of what structures a site's spatial organization. Is spatial patterning dictated by the habitation of farmers as hunters at a site – a subsistence orientation – or by the habitation of farmers as members of a particular ethnic group? Alternatively, is spatial patterning determined by farmers living in a particular geographical locale or is it determined by the mobility of the farmers within the locale – i.e., a question of sedentism versus nomadism – regardless of ecological setting, subsistence orientation, and ethnic affiliation?

Ecology is probably the most common explanation for site structure and use of space (e.g., Gould and Yellen 1987; O'Connell 1987). Our analysis reveals a deficiency in explanations that focus primarily on ecology, ethnicity, or on mobility *per se* and finds that another variable, anticipation of mobility, is consistently more influential in most aspects of the organization of site space. This leads to a number of interesting and provocative relationships, or lack of them.

Basarwa (also known in the literature as San or Bushmen)[1] and Bakgalagadi or Bantu sites from the Kalahari of Botswana are examined from these different approaches. Basarwa and Bakgalagadi mobility and subsistence strategies sometimes overlap within the same ecological setting (Vierich 1982). This permits the comparison of sites occupied by people with similar and different types of mobility, ethnicity, and subsistence strategies, while holding constant the environment.

The current prevalence of ecological deterministic thinking has resulted in mobility being conceived of primarily in terms of ecology. However, as mentioned in chapter 1 (this volume), mobility is not necessarily ecologically determined, and the roles played by social, and ritual factors in determining mobility can be as important as, or in some cases more important than, those played by ecology. It is for this reason that ecology, economics, ethnicity, and other factors that influence mobility patterns are examined in this chapter separately from mobility. In all cases, the ecology was kept constant, although the subsistence strategies were allowed to vary. Bivariate regression analysis shows that anticipated mobility actually accounts for more variance than does subsistence orientation. This in and of itself indicates that ecology, of which subsistence strategies are a part, does not necessarily determine site structure (Kent n.d.b). There are cases when knowing a group's anticipated mobility strategy actually explains more than, for instance, knowing their economic orientation. An example from the preliminary analysis of recent fieldwork by Kent conducted among Basarwa and Bakgalagadi shows that, in the majority of cases, households moved to their present camps for social (to be close to or away from kin and friends) and political reasons (57.4 percent). Only 19.2 percent moved solely for ecological/subsistence motives. The rest moved for a combination of reasons or for indeterminate reasons (19.2 percent and 3.9 percent respectively; Kent 1987; field notes).[2]

In this chapter we do not look at ecology as a causal agent for the different types of spatial organization discussed because all sites are located in the same environmental setting. Thus, the environment, at least in these cases, is inconsequential in creating the variation in site patterning explored here. As a result, the variation in the patterns observed cannot be attributed to environmental factors. By holding ecology constant we can investigate other variables. That variation should still occur in spatial patterning despite holding constant ecological factors, such as the environment, indicates that nonecological variables are responsible for the observed variability. These observations are not to imply that ecology has no influence on mobility patterns, only that, in this study, the ecological setting was held constant and variation still existed. As a result ecology cannot explain the variation recorded in this data base.

This chapter, perhaps more than the others in the book, attempts to evaluate the subtitle of *Farmers as hunters: the implications of sedentism*. The following represents a preliminary study of how sedentary people organize space and what the role of hunting and gathering or farming is in the organization of space.

Ethnic diversity

The Kalahari desert of Botswana is ethnically more diverse than many realize (figure 9.1). The current interaction between groups appears to be of considerable antiquity but is sometimes

Fig. 9.1. Map of Botswana and of groups referred to in the text

underemphasized in the literature. Although Herero, Batswana, and Europeans are recent immigrants to the Kalahari (see for example Vivelo 1976; Schapera 1930), other groups have a much longer history and prehistory (Gordon 1984; Parkington 1984; Tlou and Campbell 1984). Basarwa have been in the area for at least 5,000 years (Clark 1970) and hunter–gatherer sites approximately 80,000 years old have been identified in the northern Kalahari (Brooks and Yellen 1987). Iron Age peoples have occupied parts of the Kalahari for at least 2,000 years. "The patterns we see in the Kalahari today, taking away the trappings of industrial society, are perhaps not too different from what they were 2,000 years ago, with pastoral and agricultural populations coming into increasing contact with hunter–gatherers" (Hitchcock 1978:94; see also Wilmsen 1978). This interaction has a long prehistory (Denbow 1984). "Finds of Late Stone Age tools in the midden deposits of many stone-walled ruins . . . suggest that at least some Khoisan people were incorporated in the social hierarchy of the kingdoms based on Zimbabwe and Khami, actively participating in these systems rather than being isolated from them" (Denbow 1986:24).

Many Bantu ethnic groups are relatively recent arrivals to the Kalahari or live on the periphery and exploit primarily the margins with only some penetration of the region. The Bakgalagadi, in contrast, have occupied and adapted to the Kalahari for a long time, for at least 800 years in the eastern Kalahari and probably much longer (Vierich 1981). The Basarwa and Bakgalagadi are the focus of this chapter.

Basarwa

The Basarwa traditionally depended on hunting and gathering for their subsistence, although since more recent times some are engaged in farming, pastoralism, and employment, including work as hired laborers, as is discussed in a following section. They have a band level of sociopolitical organization. Their small group size, egalitarian relationships, and fluid residence pattern and group composition are characteristic of this level of organization.

Basarwa settlement patterns represent a continuum of mobility from nomadism to sedentism.[3] Their interaction with more sedentary, horticultural, and/or pastoral ethnic groups also varies. Some interaction, however, is present in most groups studied thus far. The Basarwa sites studied in this chapter are occupied by Kūa, !xo, G/wi, and eastern ≠hūa from the southern Kalahari, and the non-Basarwa sites are occupied by Bakgalagadi living in the same area.

Bakgalagadi

The Bakgalagadi are Bantu speakers who practice mixed farming and pastoralism. They grow primarily millet, sorghum, maize, and melons, and raise sheep, goats, and cattle. These subsistence activities are supplemented by wage work, hunting, and gathering. The emphasis varies regionally (Solway 1979; Cashdan 1984; Vierich 1981). Bakgalagadi tend to live in sedentary dispersed settlements. These settlements are organized around a chief with limited political power (Kuper 1970; Solway 1986). Some Bakgalagadi have two compounds, one located near agricultural fields, while other Bakgalagadi have only one compound (Hitchcock and Campbell 1982). As a consequence of this and other regional differences, there is much variation between Bakgalagadi settlement patterns and ways of life in general. There is unequal access to wealth which is equated with cattle: some wealthier families own many hundred cattle, while poor families own few to none. Bakgalagadi often interact with neighboring Basarwa in a number of ways. For example, Bakgalagadi sometimes act as mediators in Basarwa disputes and hire Basarwa to do various subsistence-related tasks.

Basarwa–Bakgalagadi interaction

The relationship between Basarwa and other ethnic groups has both political and economic components (Vierich 1981; Tagart 1933). Batswana and Bakgalagadi are politically dominant[4] and their relations with the Basarwa have ranged from overt and coercive serfdom (Joyce 1938) to more benign patron–client and employer–employee relations (Silberbauer and Kuper 1966; Vierich 1981). More recently there has been social interaction between Basarwa and Bakgalagadi resulting in a number of children of mixed parentage.

The long history of contact and interaction between Basarwa and Bakgalagadi has led to more than just genetic exchanges.

For example, the name of one group in the central Kalahari, G//annakwe, translates as "mixed people" and they are thought to be the product of G/wikwe and Bakgalagadi intermarriage (Jeffers and Childers 1976:2). The G//ana today are semi-sedentary and supplement their hunting and gathering subsistence with small-scale farming and goat husbandry (Cashdan 1980). A particularly poignant picture of Basarwa–Herero acculturation at Dobe is painted by Yellen (1985).

Settlements in the Kalahari tend to be ethnically mixed. At /ai/ai in northwestern Botswana, there is one Herero to five !Kung and their interaction is visible in the fact that 25 percent of the latter subsist "almost exclusively on traditional bush food, 25 percent largely on domestic foods (mainly cultured milk and maize meal), [and] 50 percent employ a mixed strategy" (Wilmsen 1978:66). A similar finding is reported among !xo, Kūa, and ≠hūa in the southwestern Kalahari where the various Basarwa groups also share their settlements with Bakgalagadi (Vierich-Esche 1977). Chobokwane is a dispersed community of about 100 Khoi speakers which looks physically like a Bantu settlement, depending on agriculture, pastoralism, and migrant labor, and only marginally on hunting and gathering (Mayane 1979). The fluidity of economic organization among the ethnic groups is explored in the following section.

Economic diversity

There are a number of different subsistence options available in the Kalahari. These include hunting and gathering, farming, employment, herding, and a combination of each. Both Basarwa and Bakgalagadi tend to use a variety of these different options in conjunction with a dominant strategy. Depending on the area, the dominant strategy for most Basarwa is hunting and gathering, while it is mixed farming for the Bakgalagadi.

These strategies, however, overlap seasonally in some areas. Towards the end of the dry winter a proportion of Bakgalagadi in the more remote areas rely heavily on gathering and hunting. In the southeastern Kalahari, the Kūa engage in agricultural employment with the Bakgalagadi during the late rainy season when there are jobs available, such as scaring birds from fields, and harvesting. As seasonal pools dry up in the more remote areas, Kūa tend to move near Bakgalagadi communities to take advantage of job opportunities and of the permanent water present at the settlements (although subsistence is not the only factor influencing moves to these communities). Their diet is often supplemented with wild foods. Other Kūa remain permanently at Bakgalagadi settlements where they are sometimes employed as herders.

The spectrum of subsistence strategies used by both the Basarwa and Bakgalagadi is adaptive in an area with great climatic, faunal, and floral variations and current animal and human population pressures. The poorest of the Bakgalagadi do *majako* (seasonal agricultural work), domestic labor, and odd jobs, and hunt and gather just as some Basarwa farm on their own and herd livestock. The sites examined below represent examples of each ethnic group participating in a range of subsistence strategies.

Mobility patterns

Earlier chapters in this volume have shown that the time-honored assumption that hunter–gatherers are nomadic and farmers are sedentary is not cross-culturally valid (e.g. Kent, chapter 1, and Vickers, chapter 5). There is considerable variation in mobility among both the Basarwa and Bakgalagadi. Some Basarwa groups are more sedentary as a direct result of the Botswana government's forced settlement of the country's border areas (Lee 1979); others are sedentary in order to be near friends, medical clinics, jails, and so on. Among the Basarwa, Nata River residents tend to be more sedentary than many !Kung and many !Kung are more sedentary than central Kūa. Many Basarwa are more nomadic during one season than the other. In the south-central Kalahari, other groups like the G//ana and Bakgalagadi follow a more semi-sedentary transhumant pattern of mobility (also see Cashdan 1984). Mobility patterns are not simply due to subsistence or environment. This is not to imply that economics or the environment have no influence on mobility strategies, but is to imply that other factors are equally important. Mobility patterns, then, need to be viewed as a separate variable from economic patterns.

The analysis below indicates that short-term camps tend to be smaller per capita and more limited in dwelling types than long-term camps. House durability fluctuates with degree of mobility (see below). More substantial mud brick houses are associated with the more sedentary Batswana, the less substantial huts made from grass and woven branches with thatched roofs are associated with the less sedentary Bakgalagadi, and the least substantial small grass-thatch huts are associated with the least sedentary Basarwa (figure 9.2). All three groups build windbreaks but storage cribs are restricted to sedentary sites (figure 9.3). As described below, anticipated mobility appears to be more influential in determining the organization of space than do the particular number of occupants at a site, their current economic activities, or their ethnic affiliation. Because mobility is patterned and activity-related, it can be anticipated. It is when anticipation fails to meet reality that the role of mobility in the organization of site space becomes clear.

Description of Basarwa and Bakgalagadi camps

The 31 Basarwa and Bakgalagadi sites used in this study were mapped and inventoried by Vierich as part of a demographic study during 1976 and 1978. Five sites were occupied by Bakgalagadi, 25 by Basarwa, and one by a mixed Basarwa–Bakgalagadi group (table 9.1). Data were gathered at a variety of habitations. Some were hunting and gathering camps, others were employment-based camps, farming camps, or a mixture of each. Sites 1–5, 7, 8, 11–13, 26, and 31 are illustrated in figures 9.4–9.15. These, and tables 9.1–9.12, show the various permutations of site structure and spatial organization by ethnic group, subsistence pursuit, anticipated mobility, and actual length of occupation at the time of the camp's mapping.

As is demonstrated in table 9.1, the mobility strategy originally planned when a site was established – that is, an anticipated short, medium, or long stay – did not always conform to the actual length of occupation at the time of mapping the site or never actually occurred, for a variety of reasons. Our somewhat arbitrary but functional classification of mobility strategies, which range from what might be termed nomadic to sedentary, consists of short (a stay of less than 2.9 months), medium (between 3 and 6 months), and long stays (over 6 months); the longest recorded stay was of a number of years. We define "anticipated mobility" as the length of time informants anticipated staying at a camp when the site was first occupied and "actual mobility" as the length of time a site had been occupied at the time when it was mapped. Anticipation of mobility was ascertained by Vierich by asking informants how long they had inhabited a site and how much longer they planned to continue occupying it; the circumstances of the initial habitation (their occupation plans at that time, etc.); and the purpose of their habitation at that locale. Not all anticipated or actual long-term sites are farming camps (e.g. sites 8, 26, and others) any more than all anticipated short-term sites are hunting–gathering camps (e.g. site 23) or all farming camps are anticipated long-term sites (for example, site 7 is an anticipated short-term farming and gathering camp). There is no direct correlation between subsistence strategy and mobility strategy, although there is a tendency for anticipated short-term sites and hunting–gathering pursuits to be associated.

The camps used in this study are all domestic habitations (rather than special-purpose sites, with the possible exception of site 7) that were occupied by at least one conjugal unit. The smallest was site 6, inhabited by an old couple without children. This relatively unusual situation – that an old man and woman would be living completely by themselves without any relatives – produced unusual figures in the various measurements computed (for example, see table 9.2) and represents one incidence of variability and "noise" common to some extent in most situations.

Most Kūa camps consist of two to five conjugal units and their dependents. The particular families who live together in the same group change over time, as has been reported for the !Kung. In most cases, new camps are founded by two or more families who move to a location together and anticipate a similar length of stay, although they may not necessarily leave together.[5] The camps are generally formed on the basis of pre-existing agreements about living arrangements made between the member families in advance of the actual settlement of a camp. Short-term visitors are not generally considered members of the camp for the purposes of our analysis and they usually were not present when a site was built or during its major habitation. People who arrive in an area for the first time and plan more than just a casual stay were observed by Vierich to create their own site some distance from the camps of already pre-existing residences.

Although site composition varies with length of anticipated mobility, all sites have habitation hut(s), hearth(s), and windbreak(s). Three basic types of huts are used: (1) grass "Basarwa-style" which are less substantial structures in terms of construction, (2) grass and woven branches "Bakgalagadi-style" huts which are more substantial, and (3) mud brick "Batswana-style"

Fig. 9.2. Hut styles found in the research area; (a) Basarwa-style grass rainy-season hut; (b) Basarwa-style dry-season hut; (c) Bakgalagadi-style grass hut; (d) grass and woven branches hut; (e) Batswana-style mud brick hut

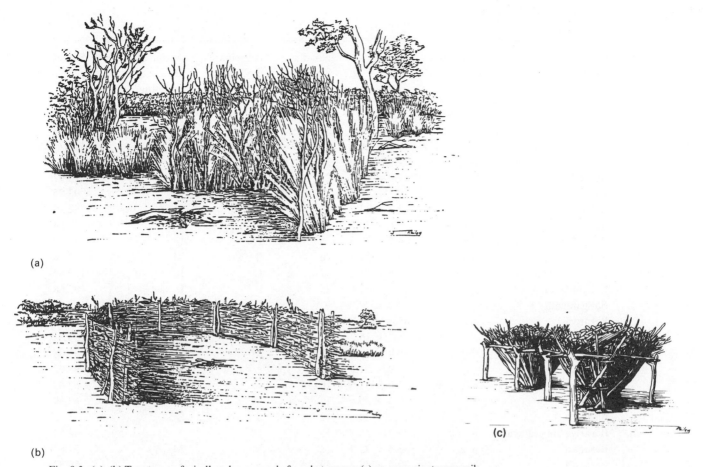

Fig. 9.3. (a), (b) Two types of windbreak commonly found at camps; (c) an open air storage crib

huts, the most substantial type of dwelling (figure 9.2). Windbreak styles are much more similar in material and form, although they can also vary in the amount of construction time required (figure 9.3). Informal storage areas, including wood piles, and formal storage areas such as specialized storage platforms, huts, and open air grain cribs, are common at a number of the sites (figure 9.3).[6]

Because we are not interested in the more conventional measure of population density – or people per unit area – but in site investment, we calculated a square meters per person value.[7] This was done to evaluate the hypothesis that anticipated longer occupations result in more complex sites requiring greater area per person. We thought that, at least in non-nucleated (or non-aggregated) sites, such as those in this study, people would build larger sites when they anticipated a longer stay. This, we thought, would then be linked to the proposition that a greater number and diversity of activities would use more space per person. The value was formulated based on the assumption that an increase in space would be necessary for an increase in activities and facilities, a common supposition in archaeology, particularly concerning base or habitation and/or sedentary sites.

The results of comparing this value for different sites are both startling and provocative. The ethnic affiliation and current subsistence pursuit of inhabitants are not as reliable predictors of

the square meter per person value as is anticipated mobility (tables 9.2, 9.5, 9.6, and 9.10). Camps where the occupation was anticipated to be long-term, whether they were hunting–gathering or employment camps, all have square meters per person values of over 66. With only one exception, anticipated medium-term camps have values of 33 to 65.9 m²/person and, also with just one exception, anticipated short-term camps have values of under 32.9 m²/person. These values do not correlate as strongly with the ethnic group inhabiting the site nor with the subsistence pursuits of the occupants (see discussion of statistical analyses presented below).

The economic pursuits of the inhabitants do not determine the area per person or, in most cases, how a site is internally organized. Typically people are able to anticipate their length of occupation prior to building a camp, partially because if, to give one example, they move for employment, they usually know the approximate duration of a job before they start. This is true of other endeavors such as hunting–gathering and of other reasons for moving, such as social visits. Because things do not always work out as planned we are able to obtain insights into what structures intrasite spatial organization. Our analysis indicates that an anticipated short-term employment camp resembles another short-term hunting–gathering camp more than it does a long-term employ-

Table 9.1. *Description of sites*

Site no.	Figure no.	Group affiliation	Economic mode(s)[a]	Site size (m)	No. of occupants	Anticipated mobility[b]	Actual mobility at time of mapping[c]	Square meters per person
1	9.4	Basarwa	h–g	20.0 × 12.2	8	S	S	30.50
2	9.5	Basarwa	h–g	24.4 × 22.9	31	S	L	18.02
3	9.10	Basarwa	e	16.8 × 29.7	4	L	M	124.74
4	9.11	Basarwa	h–g; e	27.4 × 34.3	22	M	L	42.72
5	9.12	Basarwa	h–g; e	32.0 × 28.2	21	M	S	42.97
6		Basarwa	h–g; e	13.7 × 13.7	2	M	M	93.85[d]
7	9.6	Bakgalagadi	f; g	22.9 × 13.7	6	S[e]	S	52.29
8	9.8	Basarwa	h–g	36.6 × 33.5	14	L	S	87.58
9		Bakgalagadi	f; e	36.6 × 29.0	5	L	L	212.28
10		Basarwa	h–g	51.8 × 21.3	40	S	M	27.58
11	9.13	Bakgalagadi	f	30.5 × 28.2	7	L	L	122.87
12	9.9	Bakgalagadi	f	48.8 × 52.6	25	L	L	102.68
13	9.7	Bakgalagadi	f	27.4 × 29.7	7	L	L	116.25
14		Basarwa	e	45.0 × 29.7	6	L	L	222.75
15		Basarwa	e	15.2 × 15.2	7	M	S	33.01
16		Basarwa	h–g; e	30.8 × 30.8	28	M	S	33.88
17		Basarwa	f; e	21.9 × 21.9	5	L	L	95.92
18		Basarwa	h–g; e; f	32.0 × 33.5	16	L	L	67.00
19		Basarwa	e	29.7 × 30.5	15	M	L	60.39
20		Basarwa	h–g	19.1 × 30.5	12[f]	S	S	?
21		Basarwa/Bakgalagadi	h–g; e	26.7 × 26.7	16	M	?	44.56
22		Basarwa	h–g; e	33.5 × 22.9	22	M	M	34.87
23		Basarwa	e	30.5 × 34.3	39	S	S	26.82
24		Basarwa	e	41.9 × 50.3	17	L	L	123.97
25		Basarwa	e	46.0 × 46.0	23	L	L	92.00
26	9.14	Basarwa	e	53.3 × 30.5	20	L	L	81.28
27		Basarwa	e	49.5 × 38.1	20	L	L	94.30
28		Basarwa	e	36.6 × 27.4	13	L	L	77.14
29		Basarwa	e	15.2 × 25.2	3	L	L	127.68
30		Basarwa	e	53.3 × 22.9	15	L	L	81.37
31		Basarwa	e	35.7 × 35.7	17	L	S	74.97

[a] h–g = hunting–gathering; e = employment (including herding, *majako*, odd jobs, domestic work, mine wage work, etc.); f = farming.
[b] S = short anticipated stay (less than 2.9 months); M = medium anticipated stay (between 3 and 5.9 months); L = long anticipated stay (over 6 months).
[c] S = short actual stay at time of mapping (less than 2.9 months); M = medium actual stay (between 3 and 5.9 months); L = long actual stay (over 6 months).
[d] Old couple residing by themselves without children, which affects the m²/person value.
[e] Planned reoccupation results in a longer anticipated site habitation.
[f] People missing (number unknown); hence the unknown m²/person value.

ment camp (e.g. sites 1, 23, 26). This can be seen by comparing the square meters per person value with the subsistence pursuits of the inhabitants. For example, site 23, occupied by people with an employment orientation who anticipated a short-term habitation, has a m²/person value of 26.82. This value closely resembles the m²/person value for site 1, a camp inhabited by hunter–gatherers who also anticipated a short stay (the m²/person value for site 1 is 30.50). However, the m²/person value for site 23 does not resemble that of site 26, another employment-orientated camp but whose inhabitants anticipated long-term occupation, which has a value of 81.28 m²/person (see table 9.1). A hunting–gathering camp (#8) where a long-term occupation was anticipated has a

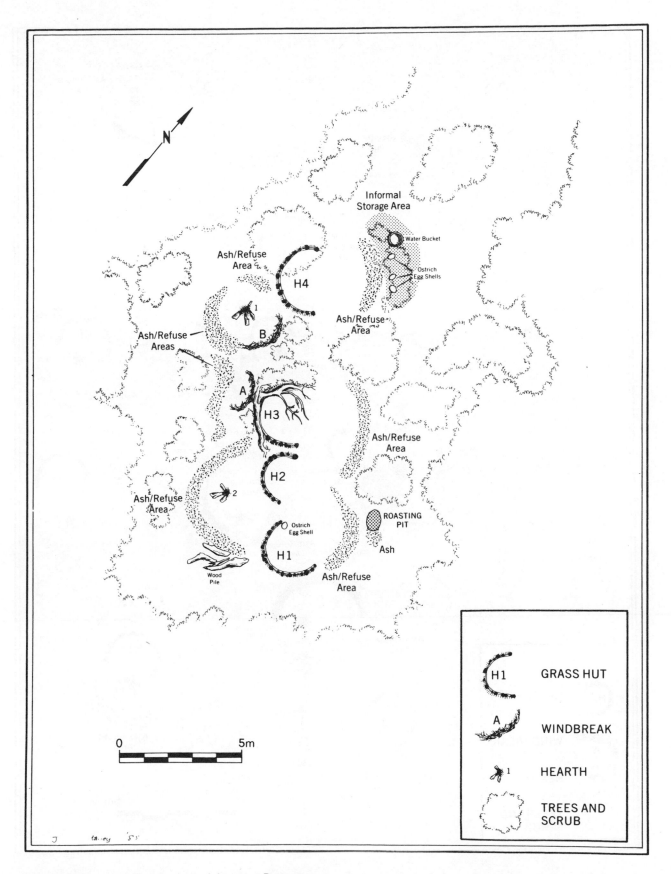

Fig. 9.4. Site 1, an anticipated and actual short-term Basarwa camp

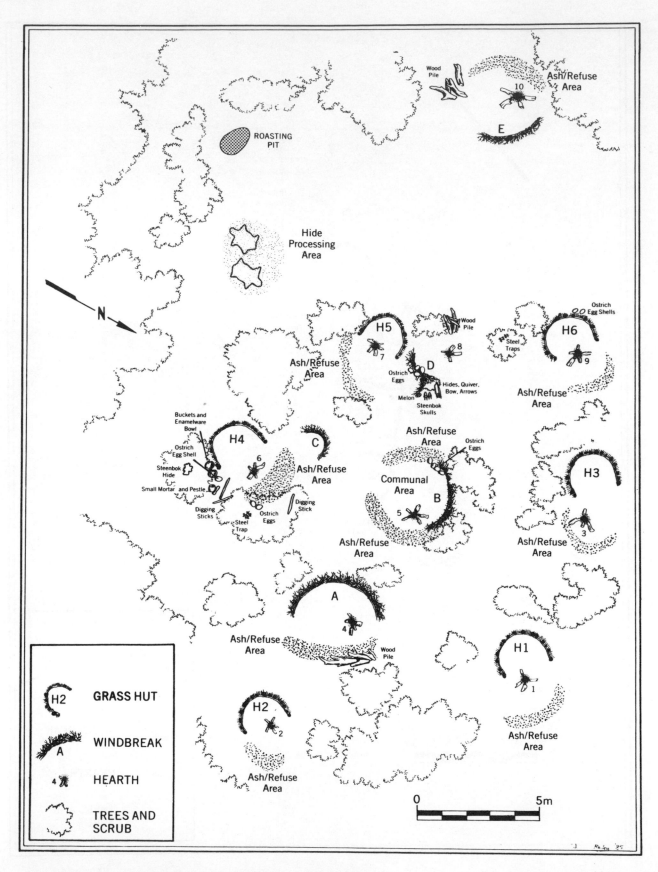

Fig. 9.5. Site 2, an anticipated short-term but actual long-term Basarwa camp

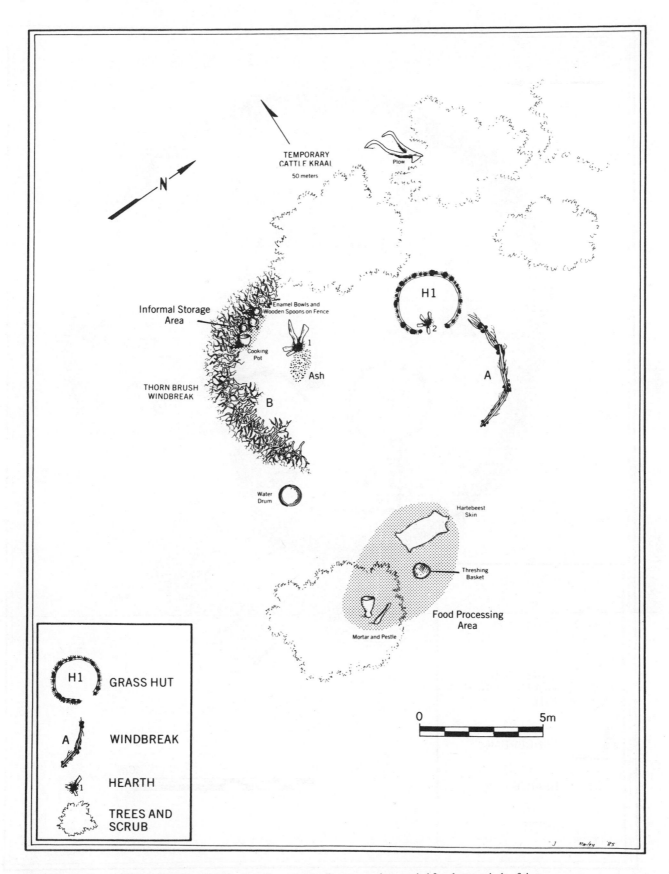

Fig. 9.6. Site 7, an anticipated short-term Bakgalagadi camp actually recurrently occupied for short periods of time

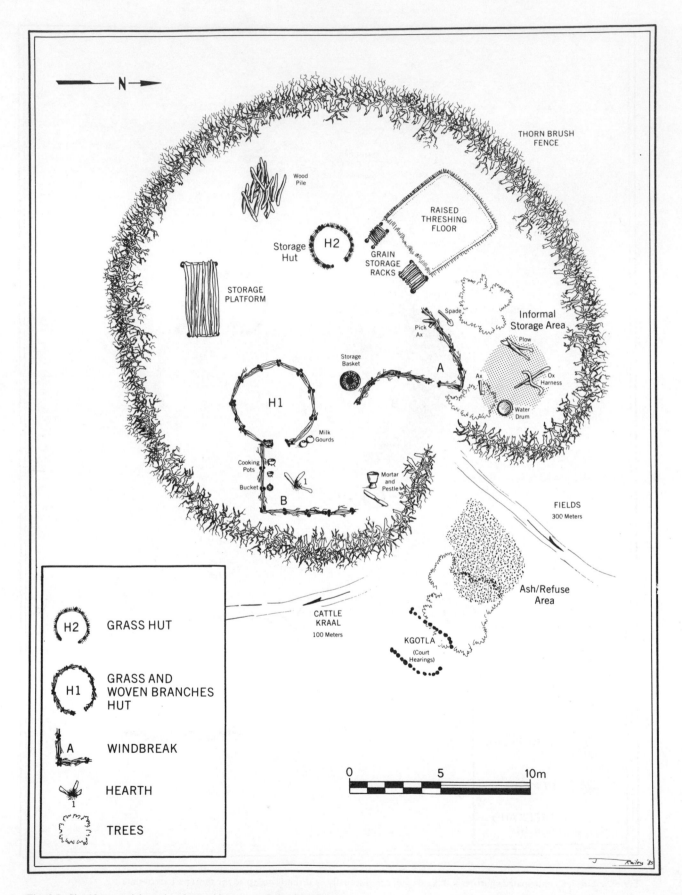

Fig. 9.7. Site 13, an anticipated and actual long-term Bakgalagadi camp

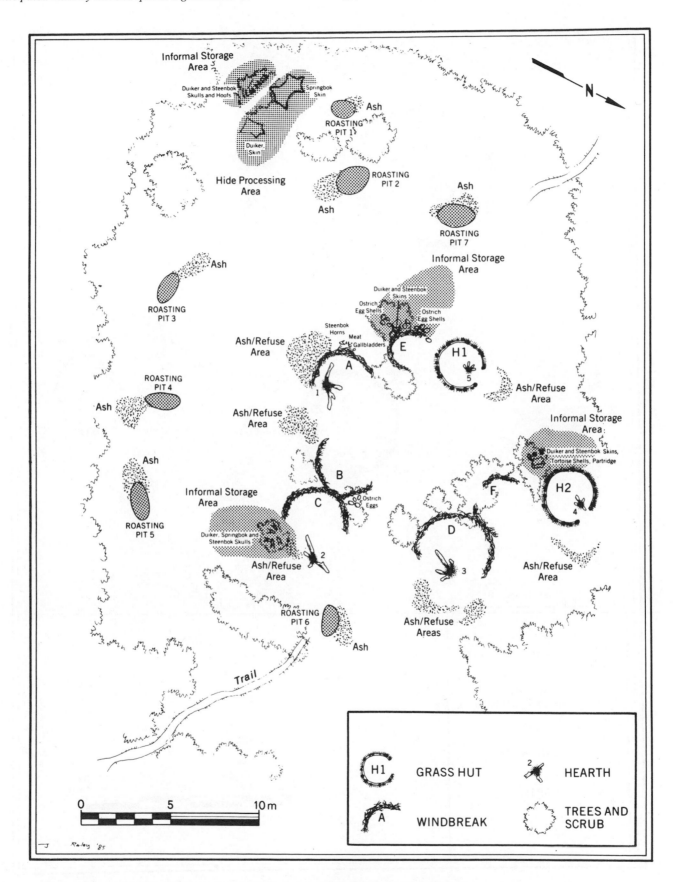

Fig. 9.8. Site 8, an anticipated long-term but actual short-term (at time of mapping) Basarwa camp

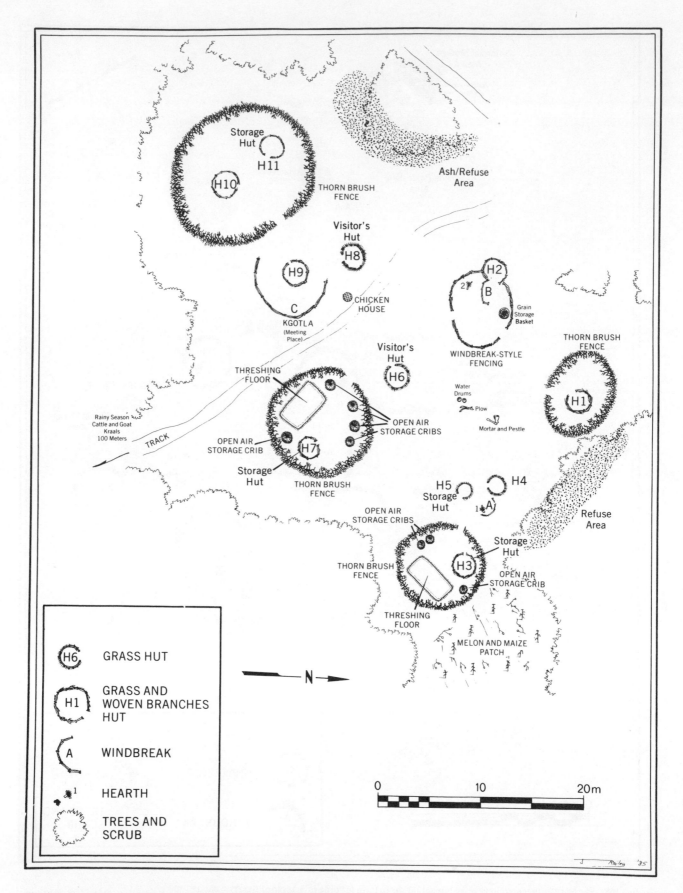

Fig. 9.9. Site 12, an anticipated and actual long-term Bakgalagadi camp

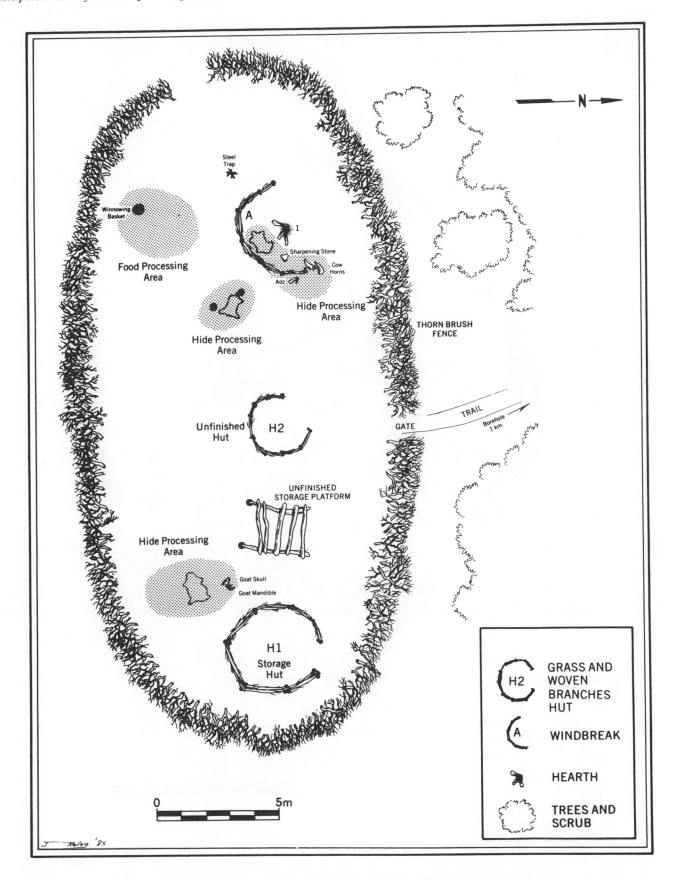

Fig. 9.10. Site 3, an anticipated long-term but actual medium-term (at time of mapping) Basarwa camp

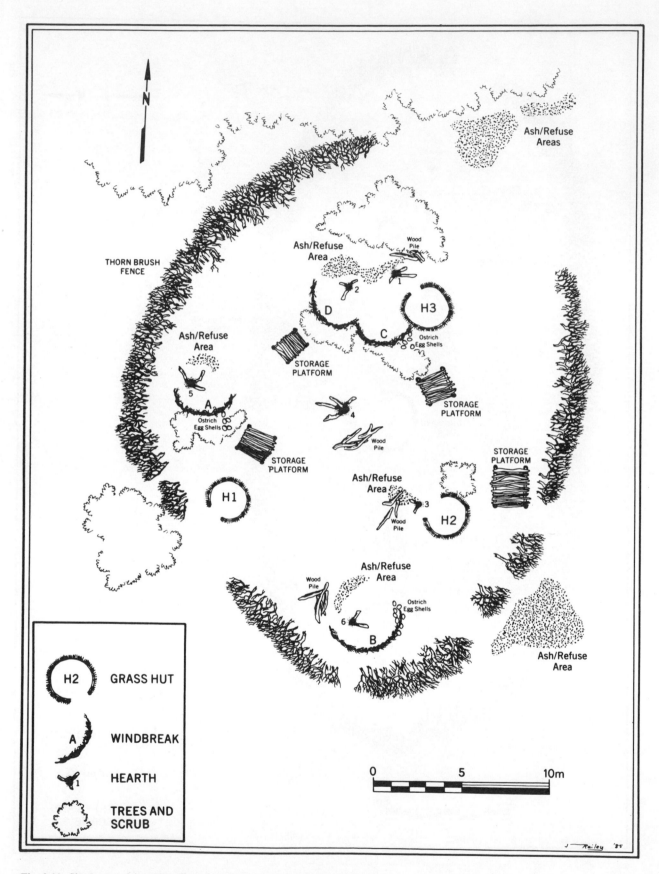

Fig. 9.11. Site 4, an anticipated medium-term but actual long-term Basarwa camp

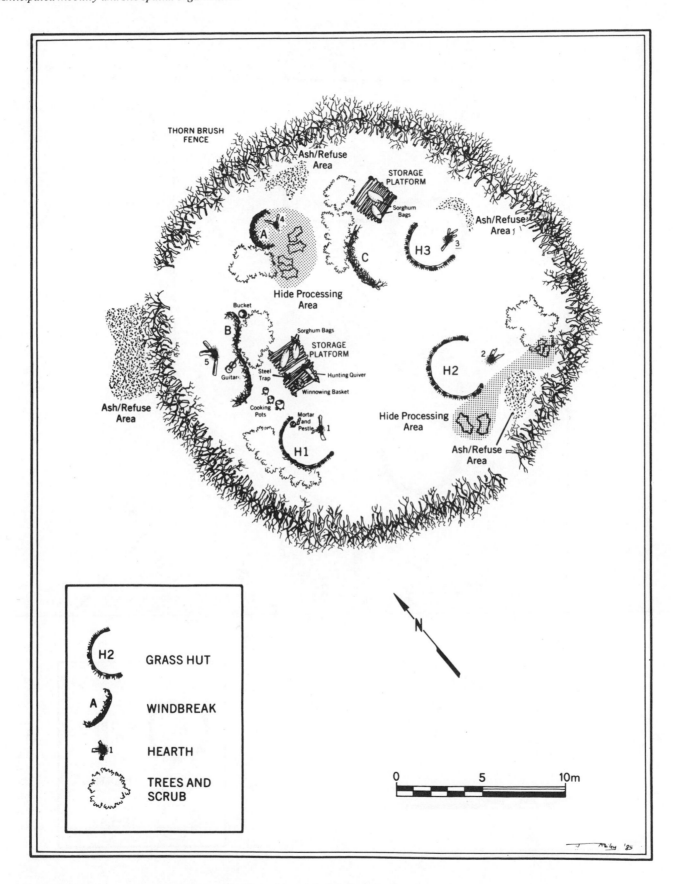

Fig. 9.12. Site 5, an anticipated medium-term but actual short-term Basarwa camp

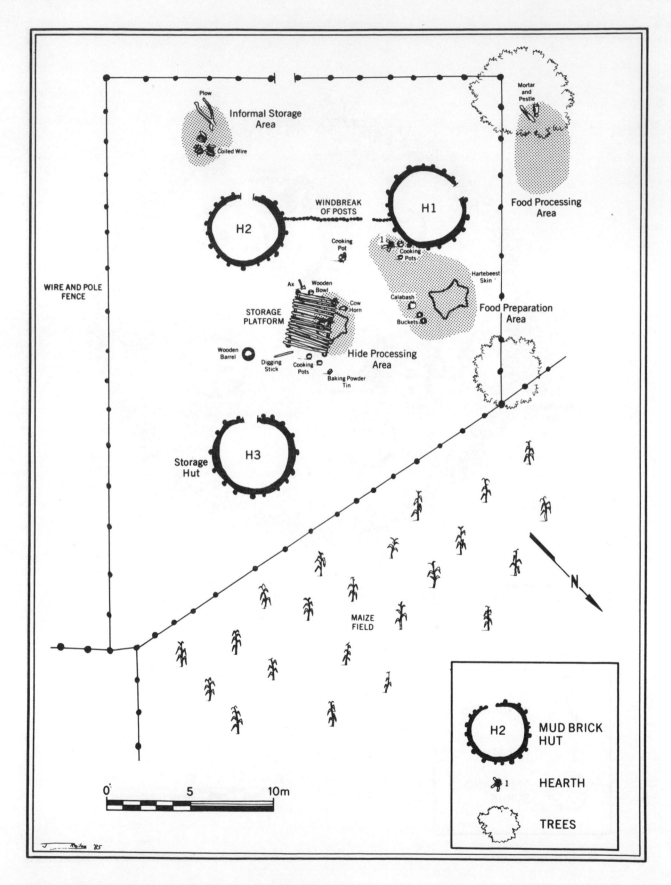

Fig. 9.13. Site 11, an anticipated and actual long-term Bakgalagadi camp

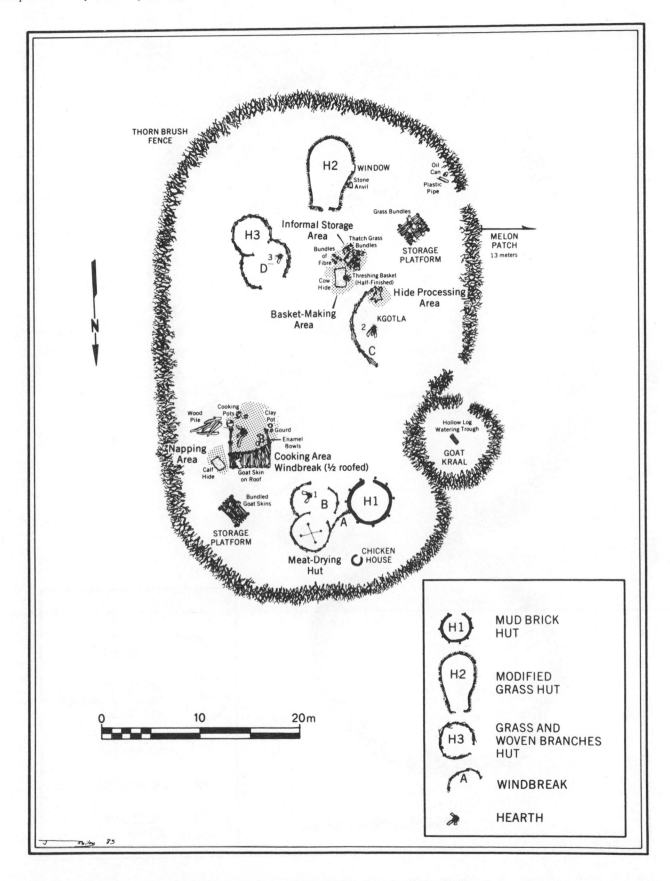

Fig. 9.14. Site 26, an anticipated and actual long-term Basarwa camp

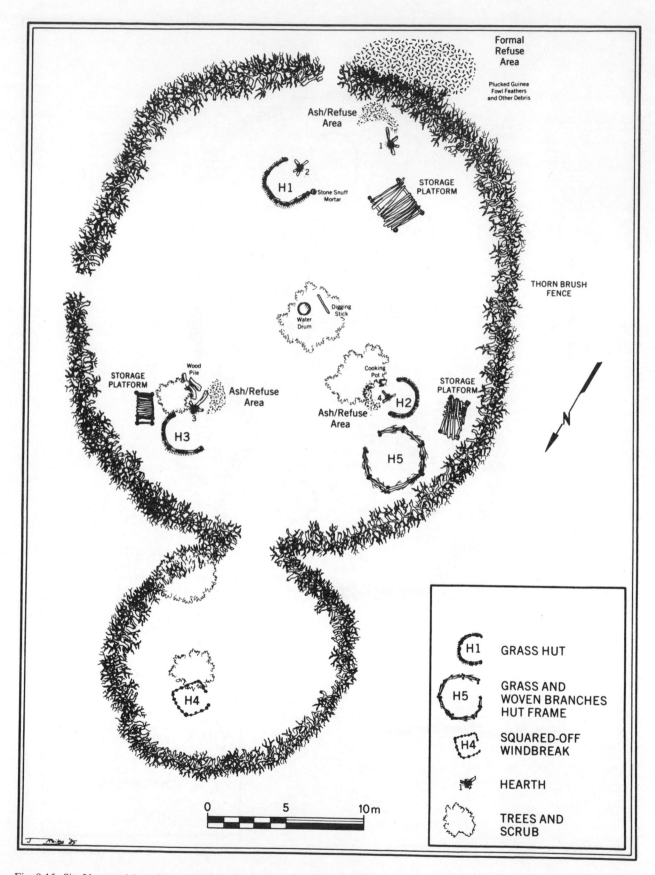

Fig. 9.15. Site 31, an anticipated long-term but actual short-term Basarwa camp

Table 9.2. *Mobility (anticipated, and actual at the time of mapping) compared with square meters per person*

Mobility[a]	Square meters per person		
	0–32.9	33–65.9	> 66
	Number of sites[b]		
Anticipated short			
Actual short	15[c]; 2	1[d]	–
Actual medium	1	–	–
Actual long	1	–	–
Anticipated medium			
Actual short	–	3	–
Actual medium	–	1	1[e]
Actual long	–	2	–
Anticipated long			
Actual short	–	–	2
Actual medium	–	–	1
Actual long	–	–	14

[a] Short = less than 2.9 months; medium = between 3 and 5.9 months; long = over 6 months.

[b] Two sites (#20 and 21) are not included owing to lack of data.

[c] Data from Yellen 1977.

[d] Anticipated reoccupation results in a site with higher m²/person value than would otherwise be the case.

[e] An old couple living by themselves without children (a relatively unusual case).

m²/person value equivalent to that of other anticipated long-term camps (e.g. #14, 17, 18, etc.) which are associated with employment and other pursuits.

We also computed m²/person values based on recalculations of Yellen's (1977) maps, and found that all of his sites, which constitute what we would classify as short-term sites, have a m²/person value of under 33.[8] Particularly interesting is that the relationship between anticipated short-term mobility and m²/person remains constant *regardless of the actual length of occupation*, be it short, medium, or long. The one exception, site 7, a Bakgalagadi short-term site where recurring seasonal occupation was anticipated, has a m²/person value consistent with anticipated medium-term sites. It is less anomalous than it may seem at first in that although the inhabitants plan to, and actually do use, the site for only short periods (a matter of days), the cumulative anticipated occupation of the site is analogous to that of sites built for anticipated medium-term stays because of its planned reoccupation.

Anticipated medium-term-occupied sites (between 3 and 6 months) all have a consistent m²/person value ranging from 33 to 65.9, independent of actual length of stay. The one exception is the unusual case of a solitary older couple mentioned earlier (site 6). Without exception the anticipated long-term sites have a m²/person value of over 66, whatever the actual length of habitation at the time of mapping. Interestingly, the only two sites (#9 and 14) with a m²/person value of over 200 both contain loci where beer is made and sold within the compound, an activity that requires more space than most. In addition, both sites were initially inhabited with the anticipation of a long stay.

Several statistical tests were used to analyze the data. Although there were too few cases to draw definitive conclusions from the analyses, they do constitute one more piece of evidence which substantiates the trends discussed qualitatively. They also add to the validity of our contention that anticipated mobility is a primary variable in site spatial organization. For example, bivariate regression analysis reveals that season and ethnic affiliation are not significantly correlated with m²/person values. Site population, or the number of occupants at a camp, explains 32 percent of the variance ($R^2 = 0.3201$), and subsistence orientation explains 31 percent ($R^2 = 0.3085$). Although both are statistically significant, anticipated mobility explains more than any other single variable, with an R^2 of 0.5187; i.e. it explains almost 52 percent of the variance (see table 9.10). Anticipated mobility and m²/person values have a linear relationship, in that the m²/person value increases with increased anticipated length of occupation. Combining subsistence orientation with anticipated mobility results in only a 5 percent increase in explanatory power over anticipated mobility used alone. The same is true when combining anticipated mobility with the number of site occupants

Table 9.3. *Actual mobility at the time of mapping compared with square meters per person*

Actual mobility	Square meters per person		
	0–32.9	33–65.9	> 66
	Number of sites[a]		
Short occupation (< 2.9 months)	2	5	2
Medium occupation (between 3 and 5.9 months)	1	1	2
Long occupation (> 6 months)	1	2	14

[a] One site is not included owing to lack of data.

Table 9.4. *Mobility (anticipated, and actual at time of mapping) compared with activity-restricted areas*

Mobility[a] and site number[b]	Informal storage area[c]	Formal storage area[d]	Hide processing area	Roasting pit	Communal area	Meat processing area	Food processing area	Beer brewing area	Cooking area	Threshing area	Kgotla	Garden inside	Formal refuse area	Special activity area[e]
BASARWA														
Anticipated short														
Actual short														
1	X		X											
20	X													
23	X				X									
Actual medium														
10			X	X										
Actual long														
2	X		X	X	X									
Anticipated medium														
Actual short														
5	X	X	X										X	
15	X	X		X										
16		X				X								
Actual medium														
6		X												
22		X												
Actual long														
4	X	X											X	
19		X	X									X	X	X
Anticipated long														
Actual short														
8	X		X	X										
31	X	X												
Actual medium														
3	X	X	X				X						X	
Actual long														
14	X	X	X			X			X					
17	X	X	X											
18	X	X	X				X					X	X	
24		X						X	X			X		
25	X	X				X	X	X						
26	X	X				X			X		X			X
27	X	X				X					X	X		
28		X	X				X							

29	X			X	
30				X	X
BAKGALAGADI					
Anticipated short					
Actual short					
7		X		X	
Anticipated long					
Actual long					
9	X	X	X	X	X
11	X	X		X	
12	X	X	X	X	X
13	X	X	X	X	X

[a] Short = less than 2.9 months; medium = between 3 and 5.9 months; long = over 6 months.

[b] Site 21 omitted as its actual length of occupation is unknown.

[c] Includes wood piles.

[d] Includes storage huts, storage platforms, open air storage cribs, and trunks.

[e] Sites 9 and 26 have a basket manufacturing area; site 19 has a mud-brick manufacturing area.

Table 9.5. *Current economic pursuits of camp compared with square meters per person*

Site economic pursuit[a]	Square meters per person		
	0–32.9	33–65.9	> 66
	Number of sites		
Hunting–gathering	3	1[b]	1
Hunting–gathering; employment[c]	–	5	1
Hunting–gathering; farming; employment	–	–	1
Farming	–	–	3
Farming; gathering	–	1	–
Farming; employment	–	–	2
Employment	1	2	10

[a] Of the 25 Basarwa camps, 5 engaged in pure hunting–gathering; 5, hunting–gathering and employment; 13, employment; 1, farming and employment; 1, hunting–gathering, employment, and farming. Of the 5 Bakgalagadi camps, 3 engaged in farming; 1, farming–gathering; 1, farming and employment. The only mixed Basarwa and Bakgalagadi camp engaged in hunting–gathering and employment.

[b] An unknown number of people is missing from this camp's count and the value may therefore not be accurate.

[c] Herding, *majako*, odd jobs, domestic and mine work, etc.

– the combination results in only a 10.2 percent increase in explanatory power over anticipated mobility examined alone.

Anticipated mobility, however, has a barely significant association with the number of types of features present at a site (see tables 9.4, 9.10, and 9.11). It accounts for 21.09 percent of the variance. Bivariate regression analysis indicates that ethnic affiliation, actual mobility, and subsistence strategy predict more of the variance in number of types of features than does anticipated mobility (27.1 percent, 26.3 percent, and 35.3 percent respectively). This can be viewed by comparing two Bakgalagadi camps, site 7, whose occupants anticipated a short use, although a recurring one, with site 13, an anticipated and actual long-term

Table 9.6. *Camp ethnicity compared with square meters per person at sites*

Ethnic group	Square meters per person		
	0–32.9	33–65.9	> 66
	Number of sites		
Basarwa	4	7	14
Bakgalagadi	–	1	4
Mixed Basarwa and Bakgalagadi	–	1	–

Table 9.7. *Camp ethnicity compared with investment in hut construction*

Ethnic group	Hut type and time invested in construction[a]		
	Less	More	Most
	Number of sites[b]		
Basarwa	22 (84%)	6 (24%)	5 (20%)
Bakgalagadi	2 (40%)	2 (40%)	2 (40%)

[a] Less = grass hut; more = grass and woven branches hut; most = mud brick hut.

[b] Some sites have more than one hut type present.

camp. The latter camp has more types of features than the former, despite a similar number of occupants – six and seven respectively (see figures 9.6 and 9.7). Also note the differences between the anticipated and actual short-term Basarwa site 1, inhabited only nine days, with the anticipated and actual long-term Basarwa site 26, inhabited for over one year at the time at which it was mapped (figures 9.4 and 9.14). Site 26 contains substantially more types of features than does site 1.

Basarwa sites 1 and 8 (figures 9.4 and 9.8) have very similar features and economic orientations (both are hunting and gathering camps). These features include grass huts requiring little construction time, windbreaks, ash/refuse or disposal areas, hearths, roasting pits, and informal storage areas, including a wood pile at site 1 (none was noted at site 8, probably because wood was plentiful and surrounded this particular camp). However, site 1 (figure 9.4) is an anticipated short-term site and site 8 an anticipated long-term site (figure 9.8). This difference is reflected in their disparate m²/person values which fall within the range of short and long occupations respectively. The other visible difference between sites beyond size per capita is the presence of a monofunctional hide-processing locus at the long-term camp.

Hut type, i.e. whether the hut is made of grass, grass and woven branches, or mud brick, is not correlated with ethnicity (table 9.7). In fact, while mud brick huts are the most substantial ones in the area and are associated with the permanently sedentary Batswana, of the seven mud brick huts in our sample five are located at Basarwa camps and two at Bakgalagadi camps. Of the eight grass thatch and woven branches huts typical of Bakgalagadi settlements, six are at Basarwa camps and two at Bakgalagadi camps. Both ethnic groups have grass-thatched Basarwa-style huts at their sites. These grass huts, requiring less construction time, are the only ones present at anticipated short-term camps, regardless of actual length of occupation at the time of mapping (table 9.8). Huts requiring more construction time are found *only* at sites at which there is a long anticipated stay, even when the camp was visited and mapped after only a few weeks of residence. Note that we are discussing only hut construction time and not style or design.

Interestingly, hut diameter varies independently of dwelling type, number of occupants, and season of use. Hut diameter varies

Table 9.8. *Mobility (anticipated, and actual at time of mapping) compared with time invested in hut construction*

Mobility[a] and site number[b]	Time invested in hut construction		
	Less	More	Most
ANTICIPATED SHORT			
Actual short			
1	X		
7	X		
20	X		
23	X		
Actual medium			
10	X		
Actual long			
2	X		
ANTICIPATED MEDIUM			
Actual short			
5	X		
15	X		
16	X		
Actual medium			
6	X		
22	X		
Actual long			
4	X		
19	X		
ANTICIPATED LONG			
Actual short			
8	X		
31	X	X	
Actual medium			
3		X	
Actual long			
9			X
11			X
12	X	X	
13	X	X	
14	X		
17		X	
18	X	X	X
24	X	X	
25	X		
26	X	X	X
27			X
28			X
29			X
30	X	X	

[a] Short = less than 2.9 months; medium = between 3 and 5.9 months; long = over 6 months.
[b] Site 21 omitted as its actual length of occupation is unknown.

Table 9.9. *Mobility (anticipated, and actual at time of mapping) compared with formal and informal storage areas*[a]

Mobility[b] and site number[c]	Informal storage area	Wood pile	Formal storage area	Storage platform	Storage hut
ANTICIPATED SHORT					
Actual short					
1	X	X			
7	X				
20	X				
23	X				
Actual medium					
10					
Actual long					
2	X	X			
ANTICIPATED MEDIUM					
Actual short					
5				X	
15	X				
16			X		X
Actual medium					
6				X	
22				X	
Actual long					
4		X		X	
19			X	X	
ANTICIPATED LONG					
Actual short					
8	X				
31	X	X		X	
Actual medium					
3			X	X	X
Actual long					
9		X	X	X	X
11	X			X	X
12	X		X		X
13	X	X	X	X	X
14	X				X
17[d]					
18	X				X
24				X	
25	X				
26	X	X		X	
27				X	
28					X
29	X	X			
30					X

[a] Informal storage occurred in and around all huts and windbreaks and, as part of these structures, is not recorded separately. Informal storage areas are discrete loci where items are regularly placed. Formal storage areas are associated with facilities such as grain storage bins and storage baskets.
[b] Short = less than 2.9 months; medium = between 3 and 5.9 months; long = over 6 months.
[c] Site 21 omitted as its actual length of occupation is unknown.
[d] Occupants of site 17 probably used some facilities of nearby site 18.

Table 9.10. *Bivariate regression analysis*

Dependent variable	R^{2a}	Prob > F^b
Square meters per person		
*Anticipated mobility	0.5093	0.0001
Number of site occupants	0.3201	0.0014
Subsistence orientation	0.3085	0.0244
Actual mobility	0.2390	0.0287
Ethnic affiliation	N.A.	0.0585
Season of occupation	N.A.	0.3014
Formal storage facilities		
*Anticipated mobility	0.2340	0.0313
Ethnic affiliation	0.2324	0.0081
Number of site occupants	N.A.	0.1969
Subsistence orientation	N.A.	0.1541
Actual mobility	N.A.	0.2300
Season of occupation	N.A.	0.6988
Feature type		
*Subsistence orientation	0.3530	0.0112
Ethnic affiliation	0.2705	0.0038
Actual mobility	0.2628	0.0190
Anticipated mobility	0.2109	0.0460
Season of occupation	N.A.	0.7397
Number of site occupants	N.A.	0.9419
Hut diameter		
*Anticipated mobility	0.3788	0.0020
Actual mobility	0.2773	0.0147
Season of occupation	0.1906	0.0179
Subsistence orientation	N.A.	0.0781
Number of site occupants	N.A.	0.2081
Ethnic affiliation	N.A.	0.6932
Number of huts		
*Number of site occupants	0.3844	0.0003
Season of occupation	N.A.	0.4948
Subsistence orientation	N.A.	0.7923
Actual mobility	N.A.	0.9304
Anticipated mobility	N.A.	0.9909
Ethnic affiliation	N.A.	0.9522

[a] N.A. = nonapplicable since the association is not significant.
[b] Because of the nature of the sample. The prob > F value should be used only as a rough guide to measure the significance of the association.
* Explains most variance.

between 1.5 and 5.7 m, with most hut sizes falling between 2 and 3.9 m. Regression analysis shows that hut diameter is not influenced by the type of structure or by the ethnic affiliation of the site's occupants. Contrary to many anthropologists' assumptions, the number of occupants in a dwelling does *not* determine hut size, as can be seen in table 9.12. One to 13 people inhabited a single dwelling and, despite the range, no pattern is discernible. The largest number of inhabitants per dwelling, 13, lived in a grass hut only 1.9 m in diameter (at site 2) whereas one and two people occupied dwellings from 1.9 to 4.2 m in size. Thus the hut size and occupants per site were compared but no association could be delineated. This lack of a relationship between hut size and number of occupants may be cross-culturally consistent, at least with the Pygmies (Fisher 1986), the Navajo (Kent 1984), and the Bedouin (Bar-Yosef 1987, personal communication). It is possible that, on a cross-cultural level, house size is partially influenced by available building materials, although our data show significant variation within the same group of people with the same access to the same building materials occupying the same environment.

Moreover, bivariate regression analysis shows that there is no association between hut size and ethnic affiliation – that is, Basarwa and Bakgalagadi inhabit huts of similar sizes (table 9.10). Neither does hut function seem to be an important variable in influencing size. In other words, habitation, storage, and meat-processing huts do not vary significantly in size. Bivariate analysis also indicates that subsistence orientation is not a significant factor in dictating hut diameter whereas anticipated and actual mobility are significant factors at the 0.01 level. A T test shows that the difference between the means of anticipated short- and medium-term sites is not significant, in contrast to the difference between anticipated short- and long-term sites ($p < 0.001$ using a one-tail test) and the difference between medium- and long-term sites ($p < 0.01$). Hut diameter becomes significantly larger at anticipated long-term sites than at short- or medium-term sites, regardless of actual mobility, number of occupants per hut, ethnicity of inhabitants, or hut function. The number of huts at a site is highly correlated with site population, although hut diameter is not (table 9.10). It appears that rather than building larger huts as site population increases, inhabitants tend to build more huts.

Anticipated and actual mobility and the organization of space

We tested the proposition that the organization of space is dictated by (1) ethnicity, (2) subsistence strategy, and/or (3) mobility, both anticipated and actual. Unexpectedly, we found that anticipated mobility dictates the organization of space using the variables we monitored, such as size of site per capita, hut investment, activity area differentiation, and others.

Our analysis indicates that all kinds of huts are found at camps of each ethnic group. Ethnicity no doubt does influence specific architectural design but it does not appear to affect how substantially constructed a dwelling will be. Of the 25 Basarwa sites 84.62 percent have grass huts which require less investment in construction time (one half to a full day), 23.08 percent have grass and woven branches huts which require more time to build (four to seven days), and 19.23 percent have mud brick huts which take the most time to build (one to three weeks, depending on whether or not it rains). (The percentages do not total 100 because some sites have more than one type of hut; table 9.7.) Each hut style is

Table 9.11. *List of sites and their associated features and mobility*

Mobility[a] and site number[b]	Grass huts	Windbreaks	Hearths	Ash and refuse areas	Informal storage areas	Roasting pits	Communal areas	Wood piles	Hide-processing areas	Storage platforms	Huts of grass/woven branches	Surrounding fences	Formal storage areas	Storage huts	Food-processing areas	Beer-brewing areas	Meat-processing areas	Mud brick huts	Cooking areas	Threshing floors	Kgotla	Goat kraals	Hen houses	Special manufacturing areas[c]	Formal gardens[d]
BASARWA																									
Anticipated short																									
Actual short																									
1	4	2	2	6	1	1		1																	
20	3	2	3		3																				
23	6	2	7		2		1																		
Actual medium																									
10	4	10	14	10		2			1																
Actual long																									
2	6	5	10	9	3	1	1	3	1																
Anticipated medium																									
Actual short																									
5	3	3	5	4						2	2														
15	1	1			1	1																			
16	8	3	6										4	1			1								
Actual medium																									
6	1	1	4							1															
22	7		3							1															
Actual long																									
4	3	4	6	6				4	4																
19	3	4	2	1						2			1											1	1
Anticipated long																									
Actual short																									
8	2	6	5	5	4	7			1																
31	3	1	4	4				1		3	1	1													
Actual medium																									
3		1	1		1				3				1	1	1										
Actual long																									
14	1	1	2		1				1					1	1		1		1						
17	2	2	2						1					1	1										
18			2	1	1					1	2	1	1		1									5	
24	2	1	1						1					1	1		1		1						1
25	8		4	4	1										3	1	1		1						
26	1	4	3		1					2	1	1				1	1	1	1	1	1	1	1		
27								1				1	1	1	1		1	2				1	1		1
28		1	1				1	1		1		1	1												
29		1	1		1		1						1												
30	4	5	4						1	2	2													1	

Table 9.11. *List of sites and their associated features and mobility* (cont.)

Mobility[a] and site number[b]	Grass huts	Windbreaks	Hearths	Ash and refuse areas	Informal storage areas	Roasting pits	Communal areas	Wood piles	Hide-processing areas	Storage platforms	Huts of grass/woven branches	Surrounding fences	Formal storage areas	Storage huts	Food-processing areas	Beer-brewing areas	Meat-processing areas	Mud brick huts	Cooking areas	Threshing floors	Kgotla	Goat kraals	Hen houses	Special manufacturing areas[c]	Formal gardens[d]
BAKGALAGADI																									
Anticipated short																									
Actual short																									
7	1	1	2		1										1										
Anticipated long																									
Actual long																									
9		2	2	1			2						1	1	1	1	1	1	1					1	
11		1	1		1				1	1			1	1	1	2									
12	3	3	2	2	1						4	4	9	4	1					2	1		1		1
13		3	1	1	1		1				1	1	1	1	1				1	1					

[a] Short = less than 2.9 months; medium = between 3 and 5.9 months; long = over 6 months.
[b] Site 21 omitted as its actual length of occupation is unknown.
[c] Sites 9 and 26 have a basket manufacturing area; site 19 has a mud-brick manufacturing area.
[d] I.e. within the camp.

Table 9.12. *Number of people per dwelling compared with hut size*

Number of people[a]	Hut diameter (m)						
	1.5–1.9	2.0–2.4	2.5–2.9	3.0–3.4	3.5–3.9	4.0–4.4	4.5–4.9 >5
	Number of huts						
1		2					
2	1	4	1		2	1	
3	1	1	1	1	1	1	1
4	1	1	1	1	2	2	1
5		3	2	1	1		1
6	1		5				
7			2			1	
8		1	2	1			
9							
10							
11			1				
12			1				
13	1						

[a] No data were available on the number of occupants per dwelling at many of the sites.

represented in equal proportions at the five Bakgalagadi sites. Hut types are associated with the anticipated length of occupation, not with ethnicity (table 9.8). Those made of grass and woven branches and those of mud brick take longer to build but are more substantial and enduring and are found only at sites where people anticipated a medium- to long-term occupation. This is the case even at sites occupied only for a few weeks if they had been constructed with an anticipation of a longer period of habitation (e.g. site 31).

Neither Basarwa nor Bakgalagadi anticipated short-term sites have fences around their camps whereas fences occur at most Basarwa and Bakgalagadi long-term habitations. In fact, all anticipated medium- and long-term Basarwa sites near livestock and all Bakgalagadi sites except sites 7 and 12 have fences around the majority of the compound. Fences usually encircle entire compounds in areas where there are large livestock populations that roam free. Cattle and goats will wander into camps to eat the grass thatching on huts, clothing, and any stored food they find, so in such areas fences become necessary deterrents at all but the very short-term camps. Fences at Bakgalagadi site 12 (figure 9.9) surround some individual huts and formal storage areas rather than enclose the entire compound, which according to Vierich is a pattern seen elsewhere in more remote parts of the Kalahari. Fences may be built around huts containing valuables in camps in the more remote areas in order to protect against witchcraft due to envy from passers-by seeing the possessions of the inhabitants, against thieves (a common fear because of the camps' isolation), and against wild animals.

Informal storage occurs in and around huts, windbreaks, and often in bushes near hearths. Specific informal activity areas tend to be located at most sites. Wood is usually informally piled at the same place, which makes it an informal storage locus, but wood is rarely stashed for long periods of time and its presence or absence at a site may indicate only the season and time of day a map was drawn – discrete wood piles are most commonly noted during evenings in the cold dry season.

Formal storage loci are not present at anticipated short-term sites. No anticipated short-term camps have formal storage areas of any kind (table 9.9). Although the small sample size presents a problem here, the absence of formal storage areas is found at hunting–gathering sites as well as at farming–gathering camps. It is interesting to note that the only anticipated long-term hunting–gathering site we have in our sample (#8) does not contain formal storage loci either. Most storage is at informal areas in trees and bushes near the huts and windbreaks. The site was mapped after only two months of occupation, although total length of occupation was 11 months. We do not know if storage areas were built later on during the occupants' stay, although Vierich's fieldnotes indicate that storage platforms, when they occur, are usually built early during an occupation. For instance, site 31, which was anticipated to be a long-term employment site, has three storage platforms even though it was abandoned after only three weeks when an expected job did not materialize (figure 9.15).

Formal storage areas including storage huts, platforms, and open-air cribs are located only at camps that have an anticipated medium- or long-term occupation (table 9.9). Storage platforms are often used to keep out of the reach of dogs and children cereal grain, grass bundles, hides, and other valuables that cannot conveniently be informally cached. Anticipated mobility is significantly associated with the presence of formal storage facilities ($p < 0.031$), but actual mobility is not ($p < 0.230$). Ethnic affiliation is also significantly correlated with formal storage loci ($p < 0.008$), although we are not sure why. As is visible in table 9.10, subsistence strategy, season of occupation, and number of site inhabitants are none of them significantly correlated with formal storage areas.

With the exception of one site where employment was the mode of subsistence, all roasting pits occur at hunting–gathering camps. Of the five sites containing roasting pits, three are at anticipated short-term camps, one at an anticipated medium-term camp, and one at an anticipated long-term camp. Clearly no pattern can be discerned. Although roasting pits are found only at Basarwa camps in our sample, they have occasionally been observed by Vierich at Bakgalagadi sites where they are used for roasting melons (rather than for meat and wild plants as they are used at Basarwa sites). However, it is doubtful whether roasting pits for meat could be distinguished from those for melons and the presence of roasting pits in general is apparently not ethnically determined.

Economic orientation is not totally passive in the organization of site space in other ways. The Basarwa in the sample did not generally farm their own land and acquired grain primarily from Bakgalagadi employers. They simply did not accumulate enough grain to warrant the use of grain storage cribs or threshing areas and such loci occur at only some Bakgalagadi farmers' camps. However, where Basarwa do possess their own fields, they do have threshing floors, as was observed at a few camps that were not in the sample mapped by Vierich.

Only three communal areas were noted where people gathered, sat, and talked, particularly when visitors arrived. Two are located at two of the three sites with the most people (#2 with 31 people and #23 with 39). The other is located at a camp (#26) with 20 inhabitants and although this represents a large number of people, compared to other sites, it is not the largest. The communal area may be a function of the number of families and people in general inhabiting the camp, but sites with 28 people like site 16 or with 25 like site 12 do not have such areas. Site 10 had the most occupants with a total of 40. However, only 28 of these lived at the camp during its entire occupation; the other 12 people (four couples, two with children) were visitors to trance dances held in an (unsuccessful) attempt to cure a sick female inhabitant of the camp. Three separate dances were held, and the visitors stayed for up to three days at a time, though the shaman stayed for a longer period. The woman's illness, and the dances, led therefore to the camp being occupied for longer than anticipated. In addition the area of site 10 was expanded to accommodate the visitors to the dances, making it larger than when the site was originally established. Even so, and with such a large number of inhabitants and longer than anticipated occupation, the site's m²/person value is well within the range established for anticipated short-term sites (table 9.1; see also below).

Meat-processing huts, where meat is dried, occur at camps where at least one person was employed in herding (# 14, 26, 16) and tend to be associated with cattle posts. The occupants of site 16 were in a patron–client relationship with a Bakgalagadi chief but were not employed as herders. Nevertheless, because of their relationship with the chief, the men were expected to process any cattle that died so that meat could be transported to the owner's camp. This entailed processing large amounts of meat at irregular intervals. Also associated with herding are goat kraals (corrals). At all sites where they occur, the goats were herded for someone else and the kraals are considered necessary by the animals' owners for the animals' protection. No kraal was located at site 5 where goats were also on loan but this is because they were kept in a kraal next to the owner's cattle kraal located 100 m from this compound (site 12; see figure 9.9).

Reasons for other specific features cannot necessarily be generalized into any patterns. The presence of a chicken or hen hut at site 26 is probably due to the fact that the poultry was being raised for someone else (see table 9.11). Such a hut not only shows the birds' owner that the chickens are being well cared for but also makes finding eggs easier and prevents the fowl from straying off to roost and potentially being lost to predators during the night. At site 12, however, the chickens are not on loan but, according to Vierich, the chicken hut may be the result of the large size of this particular compound and its remote location. In such a case, chickens could easily get lost or killed by predators if the fowl did not have a hut for nights and when brooding.

Most Basarwa and Bakgalagadi in the sample have gardens, even at anticipated short-term sites like sites 1 and 20, but only five have them within their camps (table 9.11). Many of the Bakgalagadi homesteads also have sorghum and millet fields located elsewhere. At site 12, the garden is located behind the threshing area so that a pregnant woman could tend to it more easily. In the garden at site 18 watermelon, beans, and tobacco were grown while the one at site 19 contained maize, beans, watermelons, and sweet reed. Vierich speculates that their proximity to the camp may permit more careful tending of these particular cultigens, and the occupants of site 19 said that they occasionally irrigated their gardens. Gardens at sites 24 and 27 are located within the compounds probably for similar reasons.

Discussion

This chapter confirms the proposition that mobility does affect site spatial organization and structure, and goes beyond this to demonstrate that it is not mobility *per se* that is most influential, but, specifically, *anticipated* mobility that determines site organization and structure. The data are in most cases unambiguous and the implications exciting. The square meters per person value shows that the actual length of occupation at the time of site mapping is not a crucial variable whereas the anticipation of mobility

is. Obviously there is an intimate relationship between anticipated and actual mobility, since people do not plan for things that consistently do not occur. What our analyses show is that it is anticipated rather than actual mobility that is usually crucial to intrasite spatial organization.

All but one of the 20 anticipated short-term !Kung Basarwa sites mapped by Yellen (1977) have a m²/person value of under 32.9 – i.e. one which our analysis shows to be a low m²/person value that is typically associated with anticipated short-term occupations. We think it is significant that site 1 from our sample, actually occupied for nine days by eight people, has a m²/person value of 30.50, site 23 occupied by 39 people for about four weeks has a m²/person value of 26.82, and site 2 occupied actually for six months by 31 people has a m²/person value of 18.02 (figure 9.16). The common link is that all these were anticipated to be short-term occupations. These three sites alone (along with the rest of our sample) indicate that population number and actual length of time spent at a camp are not as influential in the m²/person value as is the anticipated length of occupation.

Site 7 provides an interesting exception. This site, occupied by a Bakgalagadi family of six, is an example of a farm field house inhabited for a few days at a time during specific periods of the agricultural season when the fields need tending. Even though a short stay of a few days is anticipated, the m²/person value is within the medium range. Mapping occurred, however, during the first part of the first season of site occupation (after only six weeks of on and off recurrent habitation). It is not known whether other facilities were built later on so that the camp eventually resembled an anticipated medium-term site in more respects. Without more data, we can only suggest that an anticipated short but recurrent occupation may be similar in site investment to that of an anticipated medium-term habitation.

The m²/person value ranges consistently from between 33 to 65.9 for the anticipated medium-term sites (table 9.2). Two anticipated medium-term sites with actual long occupations fall within the same value range as three anticipated medium-term sites with actual short occupations. Moreover, these sites differ from anticipated short- or long-term sites with identical actual lengths of habitation!

Finally, the same is also true for the anticipated long-term sites – all have a m²/person value of over 66, regardless of number of occupants (from four to 25 people), economic pursuit (farming, employment, hunting–gathering, etc.), and actual length of habitation (three weeks to over 24 months). Site 31 was actually occupied for a relatively short habitation, only three weeks, as were site 15, an anticipated medium-term site, and site 23, an anticipated short-term habitation (figure 9.17). Irrespective of their similar actual length of stay, each of the three has a very different m²/person value that corresponds perfectly with their *anticipated* length of habitation but not with their actual length of habitation at the time of mapping. Bivariate regression clearly shows that there is little correspondence between actual mobility and m²/person. The fact that most sites in table 9.3 with a m²/person value over 66 are actual long-term occupations is probably a result of sample size

Fig. 9.16. Photograph of Site 2, an anticipated short-term but actual long-term Basarwa camp. Note the grass huts. (Photo by Becky Sigmon)

since all but three anticipated long-term sites are also actual long-term sites.

As table 9.10 indicates, economic pursuit does not explain the m^2/person values to the same extent as does anticipated mobility, although most long-term sites, all of which have m^2/person values of over 66, are employment camps (see table 9.5). Medium-term sites (33–65.9 m^2/person) tend to be camps at which hunting–gathering is combined with seasonal horticultural employment, the latter usually lasting between three and six months. The number of site occupants also influences the m^2/person value, though again it explains less variance than does anticipated mobility. Furthermore, combining anticipated mobility and site population explains only 10.2 percent more and combining anticipated mobility with subsistence orientation explains only 4.5 percent more of the variance than anticipated mobility used alone. The m^2/person value is not related to ethnic group, as can be seen in tables 9.6 and 9.10. One can only conclude that the m^2/person value is *directly* correlated with anticipated mobility which explains more variance than any other single variable.

Hut styles and investment in construction time are also directly correlated with anticipated mobility. Grass huts requiring less time to construct are associated with all types of sites, regardless of actual or anticipated mobility. The more substantial grass and woven branches dwellings and mud brick huts, in contrast, are found *only* at sites with an anticipated long-term occupation – i.e. none occurs at either anticipated short- or even medium-term sites. We suggest that it is the anticipation of mobility that determines how substantial a hut is. People moving to a site initially build more substantial huts if they think they will be there for longer than just a month or two. This is illustrated by site 31, which was actually inhabited for only three weeks but already had substantial huts made of grass and woven branches constructed when it was mapped during only the second week of its occupation. Site 2, with an anticipated short-term stay, in contrast, had only grass huts present even though the site was actually occupied for six months. The people at site 2 never built more substantial huts because they kept anticipating that they would move within a few days, although the move was ultimately delayed for six months.

The presence of informal storage areas is not confined to a particular type of site mobility, whereas that of formal storage areas, including storage platforms and huts, most certainly is (see table 9.9 and figure 9.18). Formal storage loci occur only at anticipated medium- and long-term sites (figures 9.19 and 9.20). None

Fig. 9.17. Hut 5 at Site 31, an anticipated long-term but actual short-term Basarwa camp. (Photo by Becky Sigmon)

of the pure hunting–gathering sites have formal storage areas, including site 8, an anticipated long-term but actual short-term camp.

More activity-restricted areas are located at farming-oriented and at anticipated long-term sites than at other types of sites, independent of the number of inhabitants present (tables 9.4 and 9.10). Bakgalagadi sites 12 and 13 have the same number of features and areas present, even though site 12 is inhabited by 25 people and site 13 by only seven. Site 17 is an exception to this; however, it was occupied by two sisters, each with young children, camping near their mother (who was living at site 18) while their husbands were working at the South African mines for eight months. Therefore, the relatively low number of features at site 17 might be the result of the inhabitants' use of some of the facilities located at their mother's camp. Site 29 may have fewer feature types than other anticipated long-term, actual long-term camps because only three people lived there – a blind old woman, her son, and a grandchild – and Vierich's interviews indicate that the people were partially dependent on relatives living at a nearby camp. These data suggest that anticipated and actual mobility, subsistence strategy, and ethnicity are all significant in determining the number of feature types present at a site while the number of occupants is not.

It is interesting to note that, with a similar number of occupants, the two Bakgalagadi sites 13, inhabited by the local chief, and #9, not inhabited by a high-status individual, have the same number of feature types present. Basarwa anticipated long-term camps tend to have fewer types of features than do Bakgalagadi anticipated long-term sites. The presence of a *kgotla* at three of the sites might be related to a family's political status (*kgotla* is where courts and other public meetings are held, usually at a chief's or other prominent person's camp). Nevertheless, the frequency of other monofunctional areas is clearly correlated with mobility, although more with actual than with anticipated mobility. In these instances, it appears that actual length of habitation is partially responsible for the frequency of monofunctional loci.

Mobile and sedentary Basarwa and Bakgalagadi hunters as farmers and farmers as hunters

There has been a tendency to assume that particular ethnic associations lead to particular symbolic and subsistence strategy associations which then lead to particular intrasite spatial patterning. Eskimo spatial patterning, for example, will differ from Basarwa or Kwakiutl spatial patterning because of their different ethnicity. Even more common is to assume that different subsistence

Fig. 9.18. Hut 3 at Site 5, an anticipated medium-term but actual short-term Basarwa camp. Note the storage platform in the background to the right of the grass hut. (Photo by Becky Sigmon)

orientations will lead to different activities which lead to site spatial organization. Hunter–gatherer camps, for instance, will have a different site structure from those of farmers because of their different economic pursuits. Ecologically oriented anthropologists have posited environmental and other ecological factors as directly associated with domestic spatial organization. More recent has been the association between type of mobility and type of internal site configuration. Nomadic people, for example, have different intrasite spatial patterning from sedentary people because of their greater mobility. Our initial study strongly indicates that spatial patterning of activity areas is primarily the result of anticipated mobility (short-, medium-, or long-term) and secondarily the result of ethnicity, economics, and mobility *per se* (or actual mobility).

Yellen (1977) has argued, using short-term Basarwa sites only with habitations varying from a few days to 20 days, that the longer one area is occupied, the greater the number of activities likely to occur and be repeated there. This may be valid not because the length of habitation exclusively affects how a site is internally organized, but because of the anticipated length of habitation. Nevertheless, the actual long (six-month) occupation of site 2 probably did result in more (in absolute numbers) activities

being performed at the camp than were performed at site 1, occupied only for nine days. However, the general trend of the influence of anticipated rather than actual mobility is in contrast to Yellen's (1977:134) conclusion that quantitative "analysis indicates that the size of . . . the outer ring, which encompasses special activity areas, reflects length of occupation." It does so only in the sense that anticipated and actual mobility usually coincide, but not in the sense that this is the principle behind the spatial patterning.

We think our data differ from those of Yellen (1977) because he analyzed only what we categorize as anticipated and actual short-term sites, whereas we studied anticipated short-term sites actually occupied for short, medium, and long periods. We additionally included anticipated medium- and long-term sites of varying actual habitation lengths. In other words, our sample includes enough diversity to delineate patterns, and those patterns all indicate that anticipated mobility, not simply the length of actual occupation, or ethnic affiliation, or economic pursuit, determines the size of habitations in terms of square meters per capita, the diversity of activity areas, and the size of huts and/or number of storage facilities at a site.

Hitchcock (1987:412–418), using data from the Nata River

Fig. 9.19. Threshing floor, grain storage racks, and a storage hut at a Bakgalagadi site not included in our sample. Note the windbreak to the left of the hut and the thorn brush fence in the background. (Photo by Becky Sigmon)

Basarwa, also states that intrasite space is organized according to a number of factors, including intensity of camp use, numbers of persons present, types of activities conducted, and *anticipated camp stay*. Our data suggest a change in emphasis is necessary in order to understand the principle structuring site spatial organization, a change in emphasis from population, actual length of stay, types of activities performed, and intensity of site use to that of anticipation of the length of site occupation. We included in our analysis population, actual length of occupation, and so on, but found that anticipated duration of occupation is more often than not the strongest predictor of site structure.

Our data do not support Binford's (1978a:331) contention that "the degree that activities will be spatially separated at any one time can be expected to vary with the number of different activities simultaneously performed by different persons." Instead, spatially segregated activity loci appear to be the result of subsistence orientation and ethnic affiliation and independent of the number of people at a camp. Nor does our research agree with his data from the Nunamiut which indicate that sites are organized primarily on the basis of logistical concerns (Binford 1978b), although we certainly would agree that these may be one variable involved, particularly in combination with specific subsistence

orientation. Even so, our study also agrees with and highlights the importance of Binford's (1987:456) work on planning depth, site maintenance, and caching.

Anticipated long-term sites have larger m²/person values than do anticipated short- or medium-term sites, because a greater investment is made in the site. It is important to realize that this is probably valid only with non-nucleated residences where there are no space or material constraints. More research is needed to determine the effect of nucleation and materials availability.

Many anthropologists today tend to be ecological determinists: our data demonstrate that this is not necessarily a valid approach, as is probably the case for all truly deterministic thinking. Unlike what has been contended in the literature, this study shows that it is anticipated mobility in the first place, and then subsistence and other ecological factors, and ethnicity, that influence intrasite spatial organization.

People do not move to a location only for ecological reasons, but also for ritual, social, political, and other reasons. One example is provided by a Basarwa family who moved to a particular location to wait until a member was released from jail. Another example is provided by the occupants of hut 2 at site 4, who moved near to a Bakgalagadi camp for a month after site 4

Fig. 9.20.   Unfinished Bakgalagadi hut with cow hide and sorghum drying on a grain storage rack at a Bakgalagadi site not included in our sample. Note the thorn brush fence in the background. (Photo by Becky Sigmon)

was abandoned in order to build a cattle kraal as retribution for stealing grain. Other examples include families who moved to a particular location primarily to be close to a clinic where a sick relative was receiving medication, and so on.

Our research has a number of implications, but one particularly important one is the further substantiation of the argument that the so-called agricultural "revolution" did not directly cause the storage revolution (also see Testart 1982). A correlation between agricultural subsistence activity and the use of specialized storage facilities is not supported by our data; the correlation is instead between anticipated mobility and storage facilities. Non-horticulturalists in our sample have storage platforms, storage huts, and formal storage loci despite the fact that they rely on employment for their subsistence.

Horticulturalists, as demonstrated in earlier chapters in this volume, are not necessarily sedentary, although semi- and completely sedentary sites are archaeologically most visible and characterize Neolithic horticulturalist residences in many parts of the world. Farmers, such as those occupying site 7, who anticipate a short-term habitation do not have formal storage areas, despite their horticultural endeavors, any more than have hunter–gatherers who also anticipate a short-term habitation. Our data

suggest that early horticulturalists had specialized storage facilities at their sites not because of their farming activities, but because the farmers anticipated a medium- to long-term occupation when they organized and built their site. One might speculate that people were in a sense pre-adapted to the horticultural surpluses common to sedentary farmers by virtue of being semi-sedentary (corresponding to the occupants of our medium-term sites) or sedentary hunter–gatherers (and fishers in some areas) and having storage facilities as an integral part of their site organization. Certainly the Natufians of the Middle East (south-west Asia) were at least semi-sedentary prior to a horticultural economic orientation, as were Archaic groups in Peru, eastern North America, and elsewhere.

As Hitchcock's study (1982; 1987) of the Nata River Tyua Basarwa suggests, and our study, primarily of Kūa Basarwa and Bakgalagadi, qualifies and quantifies, anticipated mobility is the single most important variable affecting site size per occupants, spatial organization, and hut size and existence of formal storage areas. In many cases, anticipated mobility interacts with actual mobility as well as with the economic practices or ethnicity of the inhabitants at a site, producing distinctive patterns of spatial organization and complexity.

The ecological approach, which emphasizes environmental and subsistence factors in influencing domestic spatial organization, has tended to be deterministic and reductionistic because it does not usually acknowledge other variables. We do not consider our work to be of this type since we do look at a number of variables – anticipated mobility, actual mobility, subsistence strategy, site population, ethnic affiliation, and season of occupation. Our analysis shows that in most cases anticipated mobility explains more variance in square meters per person values, hut diameters, and presence of formal storage facilities than do other variables. However, our study also shows that anticipated mobility does not account for the variance present in the number of huts or of feature types at a site. It is only by examining the variables independently of each other – anticipated mobility independent of subsistence strategy, anticipated mobility independent of actual mobility and so on – that valuable insights can be obtained concerning the factors influencing the organization of space.

It is necessary to have a variable with which one can confidently begin an analysis of intrasite spatial variability, particularly when dealing with the archaeological record. We feel that anticipated mobility is such a reliable variable. Nevertheless, it is not the sole factor, and when variance is not attributable to anticipated mobility, other variables need to be considered. However, we feel that our analysis demonstrates that anticipated mobility is an appropriate beginning for examining spatial patterning. Whether or not it is the only appropriate variable for particular spatial studies needs to be determined by the data.

In this book – which is entitled *Farmers as hunters: the implications of sedentism* – our limited cross-cultural study indicates that it is not the economics of farmers as hunters or as employees or as participants of other economic pursuits that is crucial for site spatial organization, but the implications of *anticipated* sedentism. This implies that the initial development of sociopolitical complexity may be a universal process, as Kent tries to argue in chapter 1 (this volume), that only later becomes tied to economic and ethnic orientations. Our chapter represents initial research with intriguing implications that we hope will motivate others to conduct similar studies with the same and other groups so that together we may begin to piece together the processes that affected the past, are affecting the present, and will affect the future.

Notes

We are most grateful to Garland White for his valuable assistance with most of the quantitative portion of this chapter. We also would like to sincerely thank Bill Vickers, Tom Dillehay, Sara Quandt, Mike Schiffer, Kenn Hirth, Jim Denbow, Offer Bar-Yosef and an anonymous reviewer for valuable comments on various drafts. We also appreciate the assistance of Jay Teachman and Sara Quandt who helped with some of the statistics. Jim Railey skillfully drew the figures. Any problems and shortcomings of the chapter are, however, entirely our fault. Funding for Vierich's field-work was provided by the National Research Council of Canada and the Social Science and Humanities Research Council of Canada.

1 The term Basarwa is used instead of San or Bushmen because this is the term used by the government and many groups in Botswana; see note 1 in Kent's chapter 1, in this volume.

2 Unless otherwise noted (as here), the field data on which this study is based were gathered by Vierich.

3 The terms mobility, nomadism, and sedentism, are used as described by Kent in chapter 1 of this volume.

4 The Batswana are politically dominant over the Bakgalagadi and have in the past enserfed and incorporated them.

5 This appears to differ from camp formation among the !Kung where gradual joining and breaking up of units after the establishment of the camp by a founding family have been reported. This difference might be due to the fact that at many !Kung camps of longer duration there is a 'core' of members who do not vary. This core group remains at a location, such as the Dobe pan, while other families join and then depart. With the Kūa there are, among hunting and gathering segments of the community, very few instances of a core group remaining in the same location permanently. There are instances of visitors who stay for as long as a few weeks or even months at a time at Kūa camps, but they are definitely only temporary members of a camp. Those who have a reason to stay in a locale beyond a short visit usually build their own camp near to an established one, if a camp already exists there (i.e. they do not usually merge camps).

6 Only monofunctional activity areas are listed in table 9.4 and shown on the site plans (figures 9.4–9.15), since the data do not permit a thorough discussion of multipurpose loci.

7 Site measurements include approximately 1.5 m beyond the features that mark the boundary of a site, such as fences, since that space was observed to be in use during camp occupation.

8 In order to be consistent with our own measurements, we recalculated Yellen's (1977) square meters per person figure in accordance with our own, which included 1.5 m beyond the physical features marking the boundary of a site, such as a fence.

Chapter 10

New directions for old studies

Susan Kent

The aims of this book are to employ different theoretical perspectives, different levels of analysis and different data bases from various parts of the world to study farmers as hunters and to explore the implications of sedentism. The object of the book is *not* to produce a group of essays which agree with one another in content or orientation. It is to look at the themes – farmers as hunters and the implications of sedentism – cross-culturally, diachronically, and across subdiscipline boundaries. Although archaeologists sometimes use ethnographic data and, perhaps more rarely, ethnographers sometimes use archaeological data, truly integrative studies such as the one presented here are relatively uncommon. However, by incorporating both archaeological and ethnographic data bases to pursue a common theme, we can understand the topic in greater depth.

This book represents an initial multiperspective study of hunting in horticultural societies. It explores the nature of hunting, animals, and meat in these farming societies. The book further examines the similarities and differences between food extractors (or hunter–gatherers) and food producers (or horticulturalists) to determine if the similarities and differences can be attributed to the sedentism characteristic of many farming groups who hunt.

The topics of farmers who hunt and sedentism can be viewed diachronically in terms of cultural evolution or synchronically in terms of cultural diversity. Most chapters in this volume apply both perspectives. This results in studies which have more depth and breadth than is customary. The combination of perspectives results in chapters that provide information of interest to more than one anthropological subdiscipline.

For a long time anthropologists have studied horticulturalists who hunt. In fact, some classic ethnographic and archaeological investigations have dealt with such societies. However, questions relating to the nature of animals, hunting, and meat in these societies have not been systematically investigated, nor have they been investigated from the perspective of the implications of sedentism. By directly addressing the topic of sedentary farmers who hunt from this perspective the book contributes important insights about these societies. Understanding the dynamics of these societies is more important now than ever before as once nomadic hunter–gatherers are becoming sedentary farmers who hunt and former horticulturalists who hunt are becoming incorporated within larger economic, social, and political systems.

Despite the different orientations, time periods, and geographical locations of their areas of study, the authors contributing to this volume identify some central issues that seem to underlie the topic of farmers as hunters. Most indicate that hunting has symbolic or social implications beyond the value of the protein or minerals that meat provides. These symbolic and social implications do not necessarily apply to other food resources such as fish (which is also exploited in some of these societies) or to societies with domesticated animals. In addition, the authors indicate that restricted mobility results in changes in settlement and spatial patterning of sites. These changes necessitate new strategies for the procurement of meat. In some semi- to completely sedentary groups there are interesting patterns of aggregation and dispersal, relatively large square meters per person values for sites, and reliance on communal hunting strategies.

The value of meat acquisition among farmers who hunt

In the past, studies of farmers who hunt concentrated on an individual society. However, certain symbolic aspects of animals, hunting, and meat in horticulturalist and hunter–gatherer societies become more visible when viewed from a cross-cultural perspective. After showing that meat and hunting are valued over plants and gathering cross-culturally, I suggest in chapter 1 that the reason why hunting and meat have value beyond what they contribute to subsistence is because in these types of societies animals are classified as intellectual beings. They are therefore placed in the same macro-category as humans, whereas plants and fish are not.

The macro-categorical classification of animals in these societies is manifested in the social manipulations of meat in a specific society, the Cashinahua, as described by Kensinger in chapter 2. Cashinahua men *must* hunt. They must hunt because their sense of identity, of maleness, of being contributors to society (since they cannot contribute biologically by producing offspring) are all contingent upon their worth as hunters and contributors of meat. Kensinger points out that the Cashinahua manufacture reasons to hunt if none exist by creating a perceived scarcity of meat. The concept that Cashinahua men are hunters first and farmers second is so intertwined with their psychology, kinship, and status that the delicate balance between male adult status and family, mistress, and wife all depend on hunting success. Women help perpetuate the perceived scarcity of meat by creating a perceived scarcity of sex – meat being one means of acquiring sex, among other things.

Whereas Kensinger's provocative interpretation of the value of hunting holds for Cashinahua society, it cannot be uncritically generalized to apply to other farmers who hunt. However, Rosman and Rubel (chapter 3) imply that a somewhat similar mechanism operates in New Guinea. Rosman and Rubel suggest that domesticated animals are qualitatively different from wild animals. I tried to show that domesticated animals form a different macro-category from wild animals or humans who tend to be grouped together in the same macro-category. In other words, farmers who hunt conceptualize animals in a different manner from farmers with domesticated animals. These conceptualizations are similar to those of hunter–gatherers who do not have domesticated animals. Rosman and Rubel examine a range of wild to domesticated animals, emphasizing pigs, in New Guinea horticultural societies. They show that feral and domesticated pigs differ in their symbolic, social, and ritual status. Among the Mafu-

lu, for example, one can eat only wild pigs, like other wild animals, but not the domesticated pigs raised at one's compound. Wild pigs must be used in certain rituals and domesticated pigs in others; the two are not mutually interchangeable. The non-domesticated– domesticated animal dichotomy discussed in chapter 1 is supported by Rosman and Rubel in chapter 3 who show that the dichotomy is also present in New Guinea. This observation raises some interesting questions; for example, why were pigs and not other animals such as monkeys brought by humans to New Guinea? A fruitful approach may be to view pigs as objects that were eaten as well as exchanged ritually and socially among the people who initially brought them to New Guinea in contrast to monkeys which were not. We do not know if pigs were exchanged for social, ritual, and political purposes prior to people's migration to New Guinea, but if they were, they may have had a value greater than that attached to their subsistence value alone. Such a view complements Rosman and Rubel's contention that the intensity of New Guinea pig production and horticulture is associated with large-scale ceremonial exchange systems, a fascinating proposition that needs to be investigated further.

To explore the themes of farmers as hunters and the implications of sedentism from a more empirical and ecological perspective, Sponsel in chapter 4 uses ecological principles and data to demonstrate the necessity for Amazonian cultivators to hunt when domesticated animals are not available. He shows that societies in much of Amazonia owe their existence to this mixed subsistence strategy. Hunting and horticulture of necessity appear together where fish is not a viable or year-round resource, and particularly where manioc is the staple crop. Sponsel maintains that protein is a critical factor in the Amazon and is a scarce commodity, a view not shared by other authors in the book.

In chapter 4, Sponsel points out the dilemma present among horticulturalists who hunt – in order to get their prey they have to be mobile, but mobility tends to hamper intensive farming which often needs constant supervision. One group's solution to this dilemma is the alternation of settlement aggregation with dispersal. The aggregated and dispersed mobility patterns of a semi-sedentary group of Amazonian farmers who hunt are described by Vickers in chapter 5. He convincingly demonstrates that sedentism does not necessarily have to be a horticulturalist's mobility pattern any more than hunter–gatherers have to be nomadic. This implies that there is much more diversity in the ethnographic record and, probably undetected, in the archaeological record than is usually acknowledged. However, without recognizing such diversity and by uncritically using normative categories of mobility or aggregation we can potentially mask the very diversity we seek to study.

Griffin in chapter 6 describes the relationship between horticulture and sedentism among hunter–gatherers. The Agta of the Philippines represent an interesting case. They are a group of nomadic foragers who are increasingly becoming dependent on their own horticultural endeavors, and they are becoming less mobile as a result. Their reduced mobility has serious repercussions. Griffin emphasizes the flexibility of nomadic Agta settlement patterns. He documents the sensitivity of settlement patterns to changes of any kind – be they climatic, as with different seasonal regimes; demographic, as with the encroachment of non-Agta groups; religious, as in the death of an important person; or economic, as with the reliance on a particular subsistence strategy, such as horticulture. As the economic returns from hunting diminish to an unacceptable level, some Agta have expanded their farming activities into larger-scale horticulture with the consequence of restrictions to their mobility. Griffin observed Agta groups who are still relatively mobile completely fission as the result of disagreements, with people coming together again several years later. Without formal sanctions to arbitrate disputes, fissioning is one of the few means of settling disputes available. Such an option is not possible for a sedentary group. This is not an isolated situation, as is noted by a number of researchers working around the world from the Philippines to Africa, and is one that merits further study.

Mobility among farmers who hunt

Another theme that emerges from this volume is the influence and interaction between people of supposedly completely autonomous groups. As both Griffin and Sponsel explicitly note in their chapters and as is implied by Speth and Scott, and by Kent and Vierich, few groups today or in the past have ever lived in complete isolation. For example, Griffin's chapter examines the hunting and horticultural relationship between Agta and non-Agta groups. Viewed in terms of settlement patterns, subsistence strategies, and other realms of behavior, the relationship between foragers and horticulturalists is potentially a crucial one. Some Agta groups hunt primarily to obtain meat to exchange for crops from non-Agta farmers. Elsewhere prehistoric Anasazi farmers may have had a symbiotic relationship with Plains hunter–gatherers who regularly exchanged bison meat for maize and other crops (Speth and Scott, chapter 7). Basarwa and Bakgalagadi neighbors also interact far more than researchers once thought (chapter 9). The chapters here show that the existence of pristine groups completely unaffected by their neighbors is simply not a tenable position whether applied to archaeological analyses of the past or to ethnographic analyses of the present. Nevertheless, this is a topic that has been somewhat neglected and as a result needs to be studied in depth. We need to begin to examine the relationship between neighboring peoples by incorporating more cross-cultural data into our research in general and by incorporating more regional (rather than group-specific) studies into our research designs in particular.

This volume points out that erroneous conclusions can be drawn if research is atemporal, ignoring current events which influence the people being observed. Sponsel shows the difficulties inherent in generalizing to other societies hypotheses drawn from studies of the economic returns from hunting in a society impacted by a modern highway in South America. Griffin documents mobility and subsistence changes resulting from recent encroachment of non-Agta farmers into Agta hunting territories. Kent and Vierich examine changes resulting from sedentarization among once no-

madic peoples. These chapters make it clear that, if used critically, data from such non-"pristine" societies can potentially tell us as much about past and present processes as can data from so-called "pristine" societies – sometimes more. Instead of lamenting the loss of a pristine society, or ignoring changes which have occurred, it is more productive to incorporate the changes and their ramifications into a research design. In fact, if it were not for the fact that contemporary Basarwa are currently becoming sedentary and adopting new subsistence strategies, it would not have been possible to investigate the influence of mobility and subsistence orientations on spatial organization of sites. It is important to remember that the past was never static and that population increases, deforestation, and contact with different groups all affected bygone peoples at different times in different places. The best way to study the effects of these and other events is to observe them as they occur today, not to pretend they do not exist.

Several authors point out why the adoption of horticulture and sedentism necessarily result in alterations to hunting strategies and butchering. As noted in both chapter 7, by Speth and Scott, and in chapter 8, by Szuter and Bayham, large prey tend to be hunted out of the immediate vicinity of sedentary, aggregated settlements. Speth and Scott demonstrate the need to change from local individual hunting strategies to long-distant communal hunting of large animals as a group becomes more sedentary, aggregated, and horticulturally oriented. However, their study using data from prehistoric Southwestern North American archaeological sites indicates that this shift may not always be archaeologically visible. This potential lack of visibility presents a methodological challenge. It might be possible to infer the shift from individual to communal hunting by relying on changes in species frequency and skeletal element representation at sites.

Some scholars have contended that because communal hunting has relatively low returns, it is practiced primarily when meat has a higher value than the time spent in its procurement. Speth and Scott demonstrate that this is a simplistic view of a complicated phenomenon. While stating that the adoption of communal hunting is probably related to factors resulting from increasing sedentism and horticultural commitments, Speth and Scott leave it to future research to determine the specific reasons for increasing reliance on communal hunting. Such research might study a group's division of labor or exchange networks, as noted by Speth and Scott, or its subsistence specialization, as noted by Szuter and Bayham. Communal hunting is not totally associated with sedentism because there are examples of non-sedentary hunters and gatherers who engage in communal hunting. Two examples are the semi-nomadic Plains Indians and the nomadic Great Basin Indians who communally hunted bison and rabbit, respectively. The topic of communal hunting therefore warrants further evaluation.

Concerned with a slightly different aspect of hunting strategies from Speth and Scott, Szuter and Bayham show that specialized hunting camps may be a function of increasing sedentism and population aggregation, rather than a function of population increase alone as sometimes is thought. These authors suggest that resources are depleted near sedentary base camps, necessitating special-activity sites, such as hunting camps, in areas where animals are more abundant. Contrasting faunal remains from highland and lowland Hohokam archaeological sites from Arizona, they show that sedentism and aggregation required a change in traditional hunting strategies. However, the change did not necessarily lead to communal hunting since one or a few hunters can potentially occupy a hunting site while procuring meat away from home. The authors contend that settlement patterns and animal availability may be linked to hunting strategies and horticulture in that small-scale farming is more conducive to the hunting of locally available large animals than is large-scale farming. For example, the type of lagomorphs locally hunted, owing to their slightly different ecological niches, depends on the intensity of horticulture being practiced.

The chapters in this volume highlight some of the methodological issues which need to be addressed before we can fully understand farmers as hunters and the implications of sedentism. One such issue is how we can interpret the archaeological record if horticulturalists who hunt, sedentism, and population aggregation all have an effect on hunting strategies and species exploitation in addition to their effect on butchering techniques and the representation of bones at an archaeological site. Changes in butchering are often not directly observable in the archaeological record and must, therefore, be inferred from circumstantial data. Furthermore, many archaeologists use the quantity of bones as an index of the quantity of hunting conducted and meat procured. However, it is unlikely that people would be willing to carry large carcasses over long distances to a base camp only to discard most of the heavy bones at the site. As a consequence, the amount of bones and the minimum number of individuals represented in a faunal assemblage may not always be a good index to the amount of hunting conducted or the amount of meat consumed. Once more, additional research is necessary.

Investigations of the modifications of intrasite spatial patterning which result as a group becomes more sedentary and adopts horticulture and other subsistence endeavors are also difficult to obtain from the archaeological record alone. Ethnoarchaeological research, however, has recently provided data useful in obtaining the kind of information needed to understand the process of sedentarization and the impact of subsistence strategies on intrasite spatial organization relevant for interpreting both the archaeological and ethnographic records. Kent and Vierich (chapter 9) try to document changes in site structure and spatial organization by comparing nomadic and sedentary Basarwa (San, "Bushmen") and Bakgalagadi (Bantu speakers) engaged in hunting–gathering, farming, employment, or a combination of each. By discerning variables responsible for intrasite spatial patterning, we could evaluate the proposition that increasing anticipated sedentism creates increasing site size per capita. It was found that anticipated mobility influences site structure and spatial organization more than do the occupants' subsistence pursuits or ethnic affiliation. This could imply that the initial development of sociopolitical complexity might be a

universal process that only later becomes tied to subsistence and ethnic orientations. Furthermore, site population and actual length of habitation apparently are not as influential in the organization of intrasite space as is usually thought. This is another important topic that needs to be pursued further.

New questions for old studies: farmers as hunters – the implications of sedentism

From the previous chapters we have seen how the meaning attached to hunting cross-culturally goes beyond the acquisition of meat. This appears to be the case whether one is discussing horticulturalists without domestic animals or hunter–gatherers. Does this mean then that hunting actually loses its economic significance and becomes more of a symbolic or social act among hunter–gatherers? I believe the chapters here indicate that hunting never loses its nutritional worth to a people, but instead that it is given a value above and beyond its nutritional and/or economic significance in societies without domesticated animals, be they hunting–gathering or horticultural. What is even more interesting about the value placed on hunting and meat on a cross-cultural, cross-economic level is that, regardless of the contribution of plants or fish to the subsistence of a group, and with only a few exceptions, meat is esteemed and plants are not. Whereas there are groups that rely primarily on meat, surviving without many vegetables, as in the Arctic, there also are groups that rely primarily on vegetable foods and survive without much meat. Plants provide essential nutrients just as meat does, yet the former are consistently disparaged compared with the latter. So the question is not, why are hunting and meat deemed so important, but rather, why are they considered so much *more* important than fish or plants that are also high in nutritional value?

Kensinger presents a culture-specific interpretation of this question and Kent, and Rosman and Rubel, present cross-cultural interpretations. Just one example of how this question can be explored from the different levels of analysis is provided by Rosman and Rubel's description of specific societies, such as the Maring of New Guinea, who require hunters pursuing wild marsupials to observe the same taboos as those observed in warfare. The cross-cultural material presented by Kent suggests that warfare among the Maring may be considered analogous to hunting wild animals; in other words, warfare may be perceived as the "hunting" of humans, therefore requiring the same ritual observances as does the hunting of wild animals. Is this because humans and wild animals constitute the same macro-category of intellectual being for the Maring and therefore the hunting of either humans or wild animals requires the observance of the same taboos? Might this also explain the New Guinea Keraki custom of decorating different parts of a person's body with mud when he kills either a wild pig, or, in the past, a human? Consistent with the proposition that wild animals and humans compose a single macro-category while domesticated animals form a separate category is the use of domesticated pigs for bridewealth and for payments for sociopolitical status by Big Men in New Guinea. Domesticated pigs in general then become significant as stores of wealth, as nonintellectual objects in other words, and, as such, are diametrically opposed to non-domesticated or wild pigs. Domesticated pigs are as a result categorically different from humans and wild animals and are symbolically conceived as different.

Another question that is generated by the topics covered in this book is, when do animals become categorically (on a macro level) similar to humans and dissimilar from plants and fish? At what point in cultural evolution are hunting and meat imbued with a symbolism and importance separate from or beyond nutrition? I think the chapters here indicate that hunters and gatherers and farmers who hunt always had this conception of animals and it is only with the domestication of animals that the categorization is lost. That is, hunting has social and symbolic as well as economic significance in hunting–gathering and in horticultural societies. However, with the introduction of domesticated animals, their social and symbolic significance changes: animals viewed conceptually as humans become domesticated animals viewed conceptually as objects and very different from humans. If anything, domestic animals gain in economic value and, unlike animals in the wild state, are socially and ritually important primarily because of this economic value.

As stated above, the purpose of this book is to raise as many questions as it answers. We do not purport to have all the answers, only some of the questions. However, without raising the questions, answers can never be found. One question that might be asked after reading this book is whether or not there are global patterns of mobility which affect hunting among farmers. Perhaps the question to pursue is not how does mobility affect hunting among farmers but how does mobility affect horticulture among hunter–gatherers. The different chapters indicate that while horticulturalists do not have to become sedentary (chapter 5), in practice they often do (chapter 6). In fact, Griffin shows that the intensity of horticulture affects the degree of sedentism among the once purely hunting and gathering nomadic Agta. Most of the chapters in this book underscore the dramatic changes in hunting necessitated by sedentarization. Chapters 7 and 8 discuss changes in hunting strategies which accompany that sedentism. Chapter 9 indicates the spatial changes to sites that are also affected by sedentism. By presenting cross-cultural examples, these chapters imply that there are global patterns to the way in which mobility affects horticultural societies. These patterns include reliance on communal and long-distance hunting trips, investment in intensive horticulture, and use of formal storage areas, among others. While these chapters admittedly represent only the beginning of the cross-cultural and cross-temporal studies required to substantiate these claims, they do offer a starting point from which to embark.

Although global patterns apparently exist, the rigid categories of mobility traditionally used can be potentially misleading rather than useful and need to be rethought. Mobility is not just comprised of different degrees of nomadism and sedentism but includes the dimension of aggregation and dispersal. What is the relationship between nomadism and sedentism, and aggregation and dispersal? Vickers, for example (chapter 5), shows that while the Amazonian Siona–Secoya may be considered semi-sedentary in their mobility, they retain this mobility strategy while returning to an aggregated village which is a central place (using optimal foraging terminology). They then habitually break up into a dispersed settlement pattern after only a few years.

We need to determine the social, political, economic, and religious ramifications of a society that intersperses community aggregation with community dispersal. For instance, would such a group have the same sociopolitical mechanisms in operation as more uniformly and permanently dispersed or aggregated groups? Do leaders have the same status and control during the years that a group is in an aggregated village as when it is dispersed? We know that the Siona–Secoya remain mobile even while in aggregated villages, which serve as central place base camps. Therefore, their transition to dispersed camps scattered over the landscape may not be as profound as it might otherwise be. What is the interaction between mobility and aggregation? It may be misleading to represent such oscillating societies as the Siona–Secoya as on an evolutionary continuum located between dispersed and aggregated societies. The Siona–Secoya remain aggregated for several years and then dispersed for several years, while relatively mobile the entire time, merely alternating between returning to an aggregated settlement and returning to a dispersed settlement (hence Vickers' characterization of them as "semi-sedentary"). This makes the Siona–Secoya mobility pattern qualitatively different from that of groups such as the Plains bison hunters of North America or the Shavante of Brazil who occupied both dispersed and aggregated camps within the same year on a annual basis. We need to ascertain the prevalence of this particular pattern in the past. Clearly more research is needed here.

A number of the chapters in this book deal with changes in storage practices as people become sedentary and horticulturally oriented. The entire topic of storage areas, their distribution, frequency, and use, needs to be studied in a much more systematic manner, and the essays presented here indicate directions such studies might take. For example, often the domestication of plants or animals is seen by anthropologists as the investment of a society in the perpetuation of a surplus, be it vegetable or meat. Griffin (chapter 6) and other authors demonstrate that storage is not unknown among foragers. Kent and Vierich (chapter 9) suggest that increased use of storage areas, particularly formal storage areas, may be related to restricted mobility more than to reliance on domesticated plants. This leads to such questions as whether storage areas are merely more visible at sedentary than at nomadic camps, or whether they are actually more common. When one compares sedentary hunter–gatherers such as the Northwest Coast Indians with sedentary horticulturalists, the difference is not in the use of storage areas but is rather in what is being stored. Nomadic hunter–gatherers such as the Basarwa do not often use formal storage areas; I would suggest that this is because they are nomadic, not because they are hunter–gatherers as opposed to horticulturalists. Preliminary data not yet analyzed from my recent fieldwork among Basarwa and Bakgalagadi indicate that formal storage areas are present at sedentary camps where hunting and gathering is still the subsistence mode (Kent, 1987 field notes). There is a complication in that these same people also receive government-supplied mealie meal flour, which may influence storage patterns. Storage is definitely an important area in need of more research.

The shift in subsistence strategies from purely hunting and gathering to the inclusion of horticulture occurred in many different places at many different times throughout the world and occurs today in areas where the last remnants of foragers continue to live. For some groups, such as the Siona–Secoya, horticulture seems to have replaced gathering. Nonetheless, the adoption of horticulture does not seem to have affected Siona–Secoya hunting to the same extent that it has affected hunting among the Agta. In fact, Sponsel (chapter 4) points out that foraging and farming are interdependent, complementary strategies in Amazonia. Is this valid for other parts of the world? One reason for the difference in hunting emphasis among the aforementioned groups may be the impact of mobility – the Siona–Secoya maintaining a semi-sedentary pattern while newly horticultural Agta have become more sedentary. The intensity of hunting among the Agta seems to decrease as the intensity of farming increases. Can this be attributed to the concomitant increase in sedentism?

Thus this book implies that we may have been asking the wrong questions in trying to understand farmers who hunt and the implications of sedentism. The critical variable in understanding farmers who hunt may not be hunting as much as it is farming. And it may not be farming *per se* that is crucial but mobility patterns. This is not what I thought when I first conceived of the book. However, it is what I think now after carrying out my own analysis and after reading the analyses of the other authors.

There is much more research that needs to be conducted in order to answer specific inquiries. For example, is there a negative correlation between the intensity of hunting and the intensity of horticulture? If so, how does the correlation relate to patterns of mobility? Furthermore, exactly how does plant production affect plant gathering? Do crops actually replace wild plants or simply add to the repertoire of plant resources? Does plant domestication primarily supersede wild food plants or does it equally replace all wild plants, including those used in medicine, ritual, and in the manufacture of artifacts, from baskets to clothing to housing? When do people begin to manipulate the growing of the latter nonedible plants? And when they do, is there a point at which they see nature as an entity to be manipulated rather than as something which manipulates them? With insights into these questions we may be able to proceed to build diachronic and synchronic models of extinct and current human behavior that will allow us to understand our world and the world of the past a little more fully.

I hope this book demonstrates how productive it is to have ethnographers and archaeologists with very different theoretical orientations come together and address a single issue. As a result of combining ethnographers and archaeologists in a single volume and in particular by enabling them to exchange essays and ideas, most of the chapters by the ethnographers encompass a more diachronic view than is conventionally presented and most of the archaeologists enhance their data with principles drawn from cross-cultural ethnographic studies. I think it is the collaboration of ideas and data bases that is the strength of this volume. The book will have achieved its goals if readers come away stimulated to conduct new analyses and/or research to further our knowledge and understanding of farmers who hunt and the implications of sedentism on cross-cultural and culture-specific levels.

Note

I am grateful to Lou Lombardo, Bill Vickers, Tom Dillehay and an anonymous reviewer for their excellent comments on various drafts. Any inadequacies, however, are solely my responsibility.

REFERENCES

Abruzzi, Williams S. 1979. Population Pressure and Subsistence Strategies among the Mbuti Pygmies. *Human Ecology* 7(2):183–189.

Akins, Nancy J. 1982a. Perspectives on Faunal Resource Utilization, Chaco Canyon, New Mexico. *New Mexico Archaeological Council Newsletter* 4(5–6):23–28.

    1982b. Analysis of the Faunal Remains from Pueblo Alto, Chaco Canyon. Unpublished Manuscript.

    1984. Prehistoric Faunal Utilization in Chaco Canyon, Basketmaker III through Pueblo III. Unpublished Manuscript.

Allen, Jim 1972. The First Decade in New Guinea Archaeology. *Antiquity* 46:180–190.

Altman, J.C. 1984. Hunter–gatherer Subsistence Production in Arnhem Land: The Original Affluence Hypotheses Re-examined. *Mankind* 14(3):179–190.

Anyon, Roger and Steven A. LeBlanc 1984. *The Galaz Ruin: A Prehistoric Mimbres Village in Southwestern New Mexico.* Maxwell Museum of Anthropology and University of New Mexico Press, Albuquerque.

Aspelin, Paul 1975. *External Articulation and Domestic Production: The Artifact Trade of the Maimainde of Northwestern Mato Grosso, Brazil.* Latin American Studies Program Dissertation Series 58. Cornell University.

Bahuchet, Serge 1978. Les Contraintes écologiques en forêt tropicale humide: L'exemple des pygmées Aka de la Lobaye (Centrafrique). *Journal d'agriculture traditionnelle et de botanique appliquée* 25:1–29.

Bahuchet, Serge and Henri Guillaume 1982. Aka–Farmer Relations in the Northwest Congo Basin. In *Politics and History in Band Societies*, edited by Eleanor Leacock and Richard Lee, pp. 189–211. Cambridge University Press, Cambridge.

Bailey, Robert C. and Nadine R. Peacock in press. Efe Pygmies of Northeast Zaire: Subsistence Strategies in the Ituri Forest. In *Coping with Uncertainty in Food Supply*, edited by I. deGarine and G.A. Harrison. Clarendon Press, New York and Oxford University Press, Oxford.

Baksh, M. 1982. The Impact of Increased Fish and Game Scarcity on Machiguenga Subsistence Behavior. Paper presented at the 81st Annual Meeting of the American Anthropological Association, Washington, D.C. (Dec. 4–7, 1982).

    1985. Faunal Food as a "Limiting Factor" on Amazonian Cultural Behavior: A Machiguenga Example. *Research in Economic Anthropology* 7:145–175.

Balikci, Asen 1970. *The Netsilik Eskimo.* The Natural History Press, Garden City.

Bamberger, Joan 1968. The Adequacy of Kayapó Ecological Adjustment. *International Congress of Americanists* 38(3):373–379.

Bargatzky, Thomas 1984. Culture, Environment, and the Ills of Adaptationism. *Current Anthropology* 25(4):399–415.

Bateson, Gregory 1936. *Naven.* Cambridge University Press, Cambridge.

Bayham, Frank E. 1979. Factors Influencing the Archaic Pattern of Animal Exploitation. *The Kiva* 44:219–235.

    1982. A Diachronic Analysis of Prehistoric Animal Exploitation at Ventana Cave. Unpublished Ph.D. Dissertation, Department of Anthropology, Arizona State University, Tempe.

    1986. Middle Archaic Animal Utilization in South Central Arizona. In *Prehistoric Hunter–Gatherers of South Central Arizona: The Picacho Reservoir Archaic Project*, edited by F.E. Bayham, D.H. Morris, M.S. Shackley, and contributors, pp. 315–340. Arizona State University Anthropological Field Studies 13. Tempe.

Bayham, Frank E. and Pamela Hatch 1985a. Archaeofaunal Remains from the New River Area. In *Hohokam Settlement and Economic System in the Central New River Drainage, Arizona*, edited by David E. Doyel and M.D. Elson, pp. 405–433. Soil Systems Publication in Archaeology 4. Phoenix.

1985b. Hohokam and Salado Animal Utilization in the Tonto Basin. In *Studies in the Hohokam and Salado of the Tonto Basin*, edited by Glen Rice, Chapter 9, pp. 191–210. Office of Cultural Resource Management, Arizona State University, Tempe.

Beckerman, Stephen 1979. The Abundance of Protein in Amazonia: A Reply to Gross. *American Anthropologist* 81:533–560.

1983. Does the Swidden Ape the Jungle? *Human Ecology* 11(1):1–12.

Bennett, John W. 1976. *The Ecological Transition: Cultural Anthropology and Human Adaptation*. Pergamon, New York.

Berlin, Brent and Elois Ann Berlin 1983. Adaptation and Ethnozoological Classification: Theoretical Implications of Animal Resources and Diet of the Aguaruna and Huambisa. In *Adaptive Responses of Native Amazonians*, edited by Raymond B. Hames and William T. Vickers, pp. 301–325. Academic Press, New York.

Berlin, Elois Ann and Edward Markell 1977. An Assessment of the Nutritional and Health Status of an Aguaruna Jivaro Community, Amazonas, Peru. *Ecology of Food and Nutrition* 6:69–81.

Bernard-Shaw, Mary 1987. *Prehistoric Canals and Charcos at the Los Morteros Site in the Tucson Basin*. Technical Series Report 87–89. Institute for American Research, Tucson.

Berndt, Catherine 1981. Interpretation and "Facts" in Aboriginal Australia. In *Woman the Gatherer*, edited by Frances Dahlberg, pp. 153–203. Yale University Press, New Haven.

Berry, B. and D. Dahmann 1980. Population Redistribution in the United States in the 1970s. In *Population Redistribution and Public Policy*, edited by B. Berry and L. Silverman, pp. 24–32. National Academy of Sciences, Washington, D.C.

Binford, Lewis R. 1978a. Dimensional Analysis of Behavior and Site Structure: Learning from an Eskimo Hunting Stand. *American Antiquity* 43(3):330–361.

1978b. *Nunamiut Ethnoarchaeology*. Academic Press, New York.

1980. Willow Smoke and Dogs' Tails: Hunter–Gatherer Settlement Systems and Archaeological Site Formation. *American Antiquity* 45(1):4–20.

1981. *Bones: Ancient Men and Modern Myths*. Academic Press, New York.

1982. The Archaeology of Place. *Journal of Anthropological Archaeology* 1(1):5–31.

1983. *In Pursuit of the Past: Decoding the Archaeological Record*. Thames and Hudson, New York.

1987. Research Ambiguity: Frames of Reference and Site Structure. In *Method and Theory for Activity Area Research: An Ethnoarchaeological Approach*, edited by Susan Kent, pp. 449–512. Columbia University Press, New York.

Binford, Lewis R., W.H. Doleman, N. Draper, and K.B. Kelley 1982. Anasazi and Navajo Archaeofauna. In *Anasazi and Navajo Land Use in the McKinley Mine Area near Gallup, New Mexico*, Vol. 1, Part 1, edited by C.G. Allen and B.A. Nelson, pp. 448–507. University of New Mexico, Office of Contract Archaeology, Albuquerque.

Black, F.L. *et al.* 1977. Nutritional Status of Brazilian Kayapó Indians. *Human Biology* 49(2):139–153.

Blomberg, Belinda 1981. Material Correlates of Increasing Sedentism: The Black Mesa Navajo. Paper presented at the 46th Annual Meeting of the Society for American Archaeology, San Diego, California.

Boas, Franz 1966. *Kwakiutl Ethnography*. University of Chicago Press, Chicago.

Bodley, John H. 1981. Inequality: An Energetics Approach. In *Social Inequality: Comparative and Developmental Approaches*, edited by Gerald Berreman, pp. 183–197.

1982. *Victims of Progress*. Mayfield, Palo Alto.

1985. *Anthropology and Contemporary Human Problems*. Mayfield, Palo Alto.

Boster, James 1983. A Comparison of the Diversity of Jivaroan Gardens with the Tropical Forest. *Human Ecology* 11(1):47–67.

Bostwick, T.W. and P. Hatch 1987. Faunal Material from Four

Harquahala Sites. In *Archaic Subsistence and Settlement in the Harquahala Valley: An Investigation of Prehistoric Sites in the Harquahala Valley Irrigation* Chapter 7, pp. 138–156. Northland Research, Flagstaff.

Bozell, John R. 1985. Some Observations on the Canids of Protohistoric and Historic Pawnee Villages. Paper presented at the 95th Annual Meeting of the Nebraska Academy of Sciences, Lincoln, Nebraska (April 12, 1985).

Braidwood, Robert J. and Bruce Howe 1962. Southwestern Asia beyond the Lands of the Mediterranean Littoral. In *Courses toward Urban Life*, edited by Robert J. Braidwood and Gordon R. Willey, pp. 132–146. Aldine, Chicago.

Brandon, Robert 1984. Adaptation and Evolutionary Theory. In *Conceptual Issues in Evolutionary Biology: An Anthology*, edited by Elliott Sober, pp. 58–82. M.I.T. Press, Cambridge, Mass.

Bratton, Susan Power 1975. The Effect of the European Wild Boar, *Sus Scrofa*, on Gray Beech Forest in the Great Smoky Mountains. *Ecology* 56:1356–1366.

Brookfield, H.C. and P. Brown 1963. *Struggle for Land: Agriculture and Group Territories among the Chimbu of the New Guinea Highlands*. Oxford University Press, Oxford.

Brooks, Alison and John Yellen 1987. The Preservation of Activity Areas in the Archaeological Record: Ethnoarchaeological and Archaeological Work in Northwest Ngamiland, Botswana. In *Method and Theory for Activity Area Research: An Ethnoarchaeological Approach*, edited by Susan Kent, pp. 63–106. Columbia University Press, New York.

Brown, Cecil 1985. Mode of Subsistence and Folk Biological Taxonomy. *Current Anthropology* 26(1):43–64.

Brown, James 1985. Long-term Trends to Sedentism and the Emergence of Complexity in the American Midwest. In *Prehistoric Hunter–Gatherers: The Emergence of Cultural Complexity*, edited by T. Douglas Price and James Brown, pp. 201–231. Academic Press, New York.

Brown, Lester 1985. *State of the World 1985*. W.W. Norton, New York.

Brown, Roger 1958. How Shall a Thing Be Called? *Psychological Review* 65(1):14–21.

Bulmer, R. 1967. Why Is the Cassowary Not a Bird? A Problem of Zoological Taxonomy among the Karam of the New Guinea Highlands. *Man* 2(1):5–25.

Bulmer, Susan 1975. Settlement and Economy in Prehistoric Papua New Guinea. *Journal de la société des océanistes* 31:7–75.

Bunker, Stephen G. 1984. Modes of Extraction, Unequal Exchange, and the Progressive Underdevelopment of an Extreme Periphery: The Brazilian Amazon, 1600–1980. *American Journal of Sociology* 89(5):1017–1064.

Butts, Audrey J. 1977. Land Use and Social Organization of Tropical Forest Peoples of the Guianas. In *Human Ecology in the Tropics*, edited by J.P. and R.E.J. Garlick, pp. 1–17. Halsted Press, New York.

Caperton, Thomas J. 1981. An Archaeological Reconnaissance. In *Contributions to Gran Quivira Archaeology*, edited by Alden C. Hayes, pp. 3–12. Publications in Archaeology 17. U.S. Department of the Interior, National Park Service, Washington, D.C.

Carneiro, Robert L. 1956. Slash-and-Burn Agriculture: A Closer Look at its Implications for Settlement Patterns. In *Men and Cultures: Selected Papers on the Fifth International Congress of Anthropological and Ethnological Sciences*, edited by Anthony F.C. Wallace, pp. 229–234. University of Pennsylvania Press, Philadelphia.

1967. On the Relationship between Size of Population and Complexity of Social Organization. *Southwestern Journal of Anthropology* 23:234–243.

1968a. Slash-and-Burn Cultivation Among the Kuikuru and its Implications for Cultural Development in the Amazon Basin. In *Man in Adaptation: The Cultural Present*, edited by Yehudi A. Cohen, pp. 131–145. Aldine, Chicago.

1968b. The Transition from Hunting to Horticulture in the Amazon Basin. *8th International Congress of Anthropological and Ethnological Sciences, Proceedings* 3:244–248.

1970a. Hunting and Hunting Magic Among the Amahuaca of the Peruvian Montaña. *Ethnology* 9(4):331–341.

1970b. A Theory of the Origin of the State. *Science* 169:733–738.

1973. The Four Faces of Evolution. In *Handbook of Social and Cultural Anthropology*, edited by John J. Honigmann, pp. 89–110. Rand McNally, Chicago.

1982. Comment. *Current Anthropology* 23:418–419.

1983. The Cultivation of Manioc Among the Kuikuru of the Upper Xingu. In *Adaptive Responses of Native Amazonians*, edited by Raymond B. Hames and William T. Vickers, pp. 65–111. Academic Press, New York.

Cashdan, Elizabeth 1980. Property and Social Insurance Among the //Gana. Paper presented at the 2nd International Conference on Hunting and Gathering Societies, Quebec.

1984. The Effects of Food Production on Mobility in the Central Kalahari. In *From Hunters to Farmers: The Causes and Consequences of Food Production in Africa*, edited by J. Desmond Clark and Steven Brandt, pp. 311–327. University of California Press, Berkeley.

1985. Coping with Risk: Reciprocity Among the Basarwa of Northern Botswana. *Man* 20(3):454–474.

Cauvin, Jacques 1978. *Les Premiers Villages de Syrie–Palestine du IXème au VIIème Millénaire avant J.C.* Collection de la Maison de l'Orient Méditerranéen Ancien 4, Série Archéologique 3. Maison de l'Orient, Lyon.

Chagnon, Napoleon A. 1968a. The Culture-Ecology of Shifting (Pioneering) Cultivation Among the Yąnomamö Indians. *8th International Congress of Anthropological and Ethnological Sciences, Proceedings* 3:249–255. Science Council of Japan, Tokyo.

1968b. Yąnomamö Social Organization and Warfare. In *War: The Anthropology of Armed Conflict and Aggression*, edited by Morton Fried, *et al.*, pp. 109–159. Natural History Press, Garden City.

1974. *Studying the Yąnomamö*. Holt, Rinehart, and Winston, New York.

1983. *Yąnomamö: The Fierce People*, third edition. Holt, Rinehart, and Winston, New York.

Chagnon, Napoleon A. and Raymond B. Hames 1979. Protein Deficiency and Tribal Warfare in Amazonia: New Data. *Science* 203:910–913.

Chaplin, R.E. 1971. *The Study of Animal Bones from Archaeological Sites*. Seminar Press, New York.

Charnov, E.L. 1976. Optimal Foraging: The Marginal Value Theorem. *Theoretical Population Biology* 9:129–136.

Charnov, E.L., Gordon H. Orians, and K. Hyatt 1976. Ecological Implications of Resource Depression. *American Naturalist* 110:247–249.

Christensen, O.A. 1975. Hunters and Horticulturalists: A Preliminary Report of the 1972–4 Excavations in the Manim Valley, Papua New Guinea. *Mankind* 10:24–36.

Chudacoff, Howard 1972. *Mobile Americans: Residential and Social Mobility in Omaha 1880–1920*. Oxford University Press, Oxford.

Clark, Desmond 1970. *The Prehistory of Africa*. Praeger, New York.

Cleland, Charles E. 1966. *The Prehistoric Animal Ecology and Ethnozoology of the Upper Great Lakes Region*. Anthropological Paper 29. University of Michigan, Museum of Anthropology, Ann Arbor.

1976. The Focal–Diffuse Model: An Evolutionary Perspective on the Prehistoric Cultural Adaptations of the Eastern United States. *Midcontinental Journal of Archaeology* 1(1):59–75.

Cock, James H. 1982. Cassava: A Basic Energy Source in the Tropics. *Science* 218:755–762.

Colchester, Marcus 1984. Rethinking Stone Age Economics: Some Speculations Concerning the Pre-Columbian Yanomama Economy. *Human Ecology* 12(3):291–314.

Collins, Michael B. 1971. A Review of Llano Estacado Archaeology and Ethnohistory. *Plains Anthropologist* 16:85–104.

Conklin, Harold 1957. *Hanunóo Agriculture: A Report on an Integral System of Shifting Cultivation in the Philippines*. Food and Agricultural Organization, Rome.

Coursey, D.G. and R.H. Booth 1977. Root and Tuber Crops. In *Food Crops of the Lowland Tropics*, edited by C.L.A. Leakey and J.B. Wills, pp. 75–96. Oxford University Press, Oxford.

Crocker, J. Christopher 1985. My Brother the Parrot. In *Animal Myths and Metaphors in South America*, edited by Gary Urton, pp. 13–47. University of Utah Press, Salt Lake City.

Croes, Dale 1977. *Basketry from the Ozette Village Archaeological Site; A Technological, Functional, and Comparative Study*. Ph.D. Dissertation, University Microfilms, Ann Arbor.

Crown, Patricia L. 1984. Introduction: Field Houses and Farmsteads in South-Central Arizona. In *Hohokam Archaeology along the Salt–Gila Aqueduct Central Arizona Project*, Vol. 5: *Small Habitation Sites on Queen Creek*, edited by Lynn S. Teague and Patricia L. Crown, pp. 3—22. Archaeological Series 150. Cultural Resource Management Division, Arizona State Museum, University of Arizona, Tucson.

Dallman, John E. 1983. *A Choice of Diet: Response to Climatic Change*. Report 16. University of Iowa, Office of the State Archaeologist, Iowa City.

Dart, Alan 1985. *Archaeological Investigations at La Paloma: Archaic and Hohokam Occupation at Three Sites in the Northeastern Tucson Basin, Arizona*. Anthropological Papers 4. Institute for American Research, Tucson.

Davis, Goode P., Jr. 1982. *Man and Wildlife in Arizona: The American Exploration Period 1824–1865*. The Arizona Fish and Game Department. Somers Graphics, Scottsdale.

DeBoer, Warren R. 1981. Buffer Zones in the Cultural Ecology of Aboriginal Amazonia: An Ethnohistorical Approach. *American Antiquity* 46(2):364–377.

Denbow, James 1984. Prehistoric Herders and Foragers of the Kalahari: The Evidence for 1500 Years of Interaction. In *Past and Present in Hunter–Gatherer Studies*, edited by Carmel Schrire, pp. 175–193. Academic Press, New York.

1986. A New Look at the Later Prehistory of the Kalahari. *Journal of African History* 27:1–25.

Denbow, James and Edwin Wilmsen 1986. Advent and Course of Pastoralism in the Kalahari. *Science* 234:1509–1515.

Denevan, William 1971. Campa Subsistence in the Gran Pajonal, Eastern Peru. *The Geographical Review* 61(4):496–518.

Dillehay, Tom D. 1974. Late Quaternary Bison Population Change on the Southern Plains. *Plains Anthropologist* 19:180–196.

Dillehay, Tom D. and Americo Gordon 1977. El Simbolismo en el Ornitomorfismo Mapoche; la Mujer Casada y el *Ketru Metawe*. *Actas del 7. Congreso de Arquelogía Chilena*: 303–316. Santiago.

Diong, C.H. 1973. Studies of the Malayan Wild Pig in Perak and Johore. *Malay Nature Journal* 26:120–151.

Divale, William T. and Marvin Harris 1976. Population, Warfare, and the Male Supremacist Complex. *American Anthropologist* 78:521–538.

Doelle, William H. 1980. Past Adaptive Patterns in Western Papagueria: An Archaeological Study of Nonriverine Resource Use. Unpublished Ph.D. Dissertation, Department of Anthropology, University of Arizona, Tucson.

Douglas, Mary 1966. *Purity and Danger: An Analysis of Concepts of Pollution and Taboo*. Routledge and Kegan Paul, London.

1970. *Natural Symbols*. Barrie and Rockliff, London.

1975. *Implicit Meanings – Essays and Anthropology*. Routledge and Kegan Paul, London.

Doyel, David E. and Fred Plog (eds.) 1980. *Current Issues in Hohokam Prehistory: Proceedings of a Symposium*. Anthropological Papers 23. Arizona State University, Tempe.

Draper, Patricia 1975. !Kung Women: Contrasts in Sexual Egalitarianism in Foraging and Sedentary Contexts. In *Toward an Anthropology of*

Women, edited by Rayna Reiter, pp. 77–109. Monthly Review Press, New York.

n.d. !Kung Work: A Southern Perspective. Unpublished Manuscript. (On file with author.)

Driver, Jonathan C. 1984. Zooarchaeology in the Sierra Blanca. In *Recent Research in Mogollon Archaeology*, edited by S. Upham, F. Plog, D.G. Batcho, and B.E. Kauffman, pp. 140–155. Occasional Paper 10. New Mexico State University, University Museum, Las Cruces.

1985. *Zooarchaeology of Six Prehistoric Sites in the Sierra Blanca Region, New Mexico*. Technical Report 17. University of Michigan, Museum of Anthropology, Ann Arbor.

Drucker, Philip 1951. *The Northern and Central Nootkan Tribes*. Bulletin 144. Bureau of American Ethnology, Washington, D.C.

1963. *Indians of the Northwest Coast*. Natural History Press, New York.

1965. *Cultures of the North Pacific Coast*. Chandler, San Francisco.

Duffield, Lathel F. 1970. Some Panhandle Aspect Sites in Texas: Their Vertebrates and Paleoecology. Unpublished Ph.D. Dissertation, University of Wisconsin, Madison.

Durham, William H. 1976. Resource Competition and Human Aggression, Part I: A Review of Primitive War. *The Quarterly Review of Biology* 51:385–415.

Eckholm, Erik P. 1976. *Losing Ground: Environmental Stress and World Food Prospects*. W.W. Norton, New York.

Eder, James F. 1978. The Caloric Returns to Food Collecting: Disruption and Change Among the Batak of the Philippine Tropical Forest. *Human Ecology* 6(1):55–69.

1984. The Impact of Subsistence Change on Mobility and Settlement Pattern in a Tropical Forest Foraging Economy: Some Implications for Archaeology. *American Anthropologist* 86(4):837–853.

Emslie, Steven D. 1981. Birds and Prehistoric Agriculture: The New Mexican Pueblos. *Human Ecology* 9(3):305–329.

Estioko, Agnes A. and P. Bion Griffin 1975. The Ebuked Agta of Northeastern Luzon. *Philippine Quarterly of Culture and Society* 3:237–244.

Estioko-Griffin, Agnes A. 1984. The Ethnography of Southeast Cagayan Agta Hunting. Unpublished M.A. Thesis, Department of Anthropology, University of the Philippines, Diliman, Quezon City. (Available from the Department of Anthropology, University of Hawaii, Honolulu.)

Estioko-Griffin, Agnes A. and P. Bion Griffin 1981a. The Beginnings of Cultivation Among Agta Hunter–Gatherers in Northeast Luzon. In *Adaptive Strategies and Change in Philippine Swidden-based Societies*, edited by Harold Olofson, pp. 55–72. Forest Research Institute, College, Laguna, Philippines.

1981b. Woman the Hunter: The Agta. In *Woman the Gatherer*, edited by Frances Dahlberg, pp. 121–151. Yale University Press, New Haven.

Fabian, Johannes 1983. *Time and the Other: How Anthropology Makes Its Object*. Columbia University Press, New York.

Fagerstone, K.A., G.K. Lavoie, and R.E. Griffith, Jr. 1980. Black-tailed Jackrabbit Diet and Density on Rangeland and near Agricultural Crops. *Journal of Range Management* 33(3):229–233.

Fahim, Hussein 1980. Nubian Resettlement and Nomadic Sedentarization in Khashm el-Girba Scheme, Eastern Sudan. In *When Nomads Settle*, edited by Philip Salzman, pp. 140–156. Praeger, J.F. Bergin, Brooklyn, New York.

Fawcett, William B., Jr. 1985. Communal Hunts, Human Aggregations, Social Variation, and Climatic Change: Bison Utilization by Prehistoric Inhabitants of the Great Plains. Unpublished Ph.D. Dissertation, University of Massachusetts, Amherst.

Fish, S. 1984. Agriculture and Subsistence Implications of the Salt–Gila Aqueduct Project Pollen Analysis. In *Hohokam Archaeology along the Salt–Gila Aqueduct Central Arizona Project*, vol. 7: *Environment and subsistence*, edited by Lynn S. Teague and Patricia L. Crown, Part 2, Chapter 1, pp. 111–138. Archaeological Series 150. Cultural

Resource Management Division, Arizona State Museum, University of Arizona, Tucson.

Fish, S., R. Gasser, and J. Swarthout 1985. Site Function and Subsistence Patterns. In *Studies in the Hohokam and Salado of the Tonto Basin*, edited by Glen Rice, pp. 175–190. Office of Cultural Resource Management, Arizona State University, Tempe.

Fish, S., C. Miksicek, and Christine R. Szuter 1984. Introduction. *In Hohokam Archaeology along the Salt–Gila Aqueduct Central Arizona Project*, Vol. 7: *Environment and Subsistence*, edited by Lynn S. Teague and Patricia L. Crown, pp. 3–6. Archaeological Series 150. Cultural Resource Management Division, Arizona State Museum, University of Arizona, Tucson.

Fisher, John 1986. Shadows in the Forest: Ethnoarcheology among the Efe Pygmies. Unpublished Ph.D. Dissertation, Department of Anthropology, University of California, Berkeley.

Fittkau, E.J., *et al.* 1975. Productivity, Biomass, and Population Dynamics in Amazonian Water Bodies. In *Tropical Ecological Systems*, edited by Frank Golley and Ernesto Medina, pp. 289–311. Springer, New York.

Flannery, Kent 1972. The Cultural Evolution of Civilizations. *Annual Review of Ecology and Systematics* 3:399–426.

Flores, J.F. and V.F. Balagot 1969. Climate of the Philippines. In *Climate in Northern and Eastern Asia*, edited by H. Arakawa, pp. 159–213. Elsevier, Amsterdam.

Flowers, Nancy M. 1983. Seasonal Factors in Subsistence, Nutrition, and Child Growth in a Central Brazilian Indian Community. In *Adaptive Responses of Native Amazonians*, edited by Raymond B. Hames and William T. Vickers, pp. 357–390. Academic Press, New York.

Foley, Robert 1982. A Reconsideration of the Role of Predation on Large Mammals in Tropical Hunter–Gatherer Adaptations. *Man* n.s. 17(3):393–402.

Ford, Richard I. 1968. An Ecological Analysis Involving the Population of San Juan Pueblo, New Mexico. Unpublished Ph.D. Dissertation, University of Michigan, Ann Arbor.

1981. Gardening and Farming before A.D. 1000: Patterns of Prehistoric Cultivation North of Mexico. *Journal of Ethnobiology* 1(1):6–27.

1983. Inter-Indian Exchange in the Southwest. In *Handbook of North American Indians*, Vol. 10: *Southwest*, edited by Alfonso Ortiz, pp. 711–724. Smithsonian Institution, Washington, D.C.

Fortune, R.F. 1963 [orig. 1932]. *Sorcerers of Dobu*. E.F. Dutton, New York.

Frechione, John 1982. Manioc Monozoning in Yekuana Agriculture. *Antropologica* 58:53–74.

Freeman, J.D. 1955. *Iban Agriculture*. Colonial Office, Colonial Research Studies 18. Her Majesty's Stationery Office, London.

Fritz, G.L. 1980. Appendix C: Faunal Analysis. In Past Adaptive Patterns in Western Papagueria: An Archaeological Study of Nonriverine Resource Use by Wm. Doelle, pp. 329–338. Unpublished Ph.D. Dissertation, University of Arizona, Tucson.

Garfield, Viola 1966. The Tsimshian and Their Neighbors. In *The Tsimshian and Their Arts*, edited by Jay Miller and Carol Eastman, pp. 3–70. University of Washington Press, Seattle.

Gell, Alfred 1975. *Metamorphosis of the Cassowaries: Umeda Society, Language and Ritual*. L.S.E. Monographs on Social Anthropology 51. Athlone Press, London.

Gladwin, H.S., Emil W. Haury, E.B. Sayles, and N. Gladwin 1938. *Excavations at Snaketown: Material Culture*. Medallion Papers 25. Gila Pueblo, Globe, Arizona.

Glass, Margaret 1984. Faunal Remains from Hohokam Sites in the Rosemont Area, Northern Santa Rita Mountains. In *Hohokam Habitation Sites in the northern Santa Rita Mountains*, Vol. 2, Part 2, edited by A. Ferg, K. Rozen, W. Deaver, M. Tagg, D. Phillips, Jr., and D. Gregory, Appendix A, pp. 823–916. Archaeological Series 147. Cultural Resource Management Division, Arizona State Museum, University of Arizona.

Goldschmidt, Walter 1980. Career Reorientation and Institutional Adaptation in the Process of Natural Sedentarization. In *When Nomads Settle*, edited by Philip Salzman, pp. 35–47. J. F. Bergin, New York.

Golson, Jack 1981. New Guinea Agricultural History: A Case Study. In *A History of Agriculture in Papua New Guinea: A Time to Plant and a Time to Uproot*, edited by Donald Denoon and Catherine Snowden, pp. 55–64. Institute of Papua New Guinea Studies, Port Moresby.

1982. The Ipomoean Revolution Revisited: Society and the Sweet Potato in the Upper Wahgi Valley. In *Inequality in New Guinea Highlands Societies*, edited by Andrew Strathern, pp. 109–136. Cambridge University Press, Cambridge.

Golson, Jack and P.J. Hughes 1980. The Appearance of Plant and Animal Domestication in New Guinea. *Journal de la société des océanistes* 36:294–303.

Good, K. 1982. Limiting Factors in Amazonian Ecology. Paper presented at the 81st Annual Meeting of the American Anthropological Association, Washington, D.C. (Dec. 4–7, 1982).

Gordon, Robert 1984. The !Kung in the Kalahari Exchange: An Ethnohistorical Perspective. In *Past and Present in Hunter–Gatherer Studies*, edited by Carmel Schrire, pp. 195–224. Academic Press, New York.

Gould, Richard and John Yellen 1987. Man the Hunted: Determinants of Household Spacing in Desert and Tropical Foraging Societies. *Journal of Anthropological Archaeology* 6(1):77–103.

Grayson, Donald K. 1978. Minimum Numbers and Sample Size in Vertebrate Faunal Analysis. *American Antiquity* 43(1):53–64.

1984. *Quantitative Zooarchaeology*. Academic Press, New York.

Greene, Jerry L. and Thomas W. Mathews 1976. Faunal Study of Unworked Mammalian Bones. In *The Hohokam Desert Farmers and Craftsmen*, by Emil Haury, Appendix 5, pp. 367–373. University of Arizona Press, Tucson.

Gregor, Thomas 1977. *Mehinaku*. University of Chicago Press, Chicago.

1985. *Anxious Pleasures*. University of Chicago Press, Chicago.

Griffin, P. Bion 1981. Northern Luzon Agta Subsistence and Settlement. *Filipinas* 2:26–42.

1984. Forager Resource and Land Use in the Humid Tropics: The Agta of Northeastern Luzon, the Philippines. In *Past and Present in Hunter–Gatherer Studies*, edited by Carmel Schrire, pp. 95–121. Academic Press, New York.

1985. Population Movements and Sociocultural Change in the Sierra Madre. In *The Agta of Northeastern Luzon: Recent Studies*, edited by P. Bion Griffin and Agnes Estioko-Griffin, pp. 85–101. Humanities Series 16. San Carlos Publications, University of San Carlos, Cebu City, Philippines.

Griffin, P. Bion, Agnes Estioko-Griffin, Madeleine J. Goodman, and John Grove n.d.a. Agta Women Hunters: Subsistence, Reproduction and Child Care. Unpublished Manuscript, Department of Anthropology, University of Hawaii, Honolulu.

Griffin, P. Bion, Thomas N. Headland, Navin Kumar Rai, Melinda S. Allen, and Karen Mudar n.d.b. Agta Hunting, Ecotones and Wild Pigs. Unpublished Manuscript, Department of Anthropology, University of Hawaii, Honolulu.

Gross, Daniel R. 1975. Protein Capture and Cultural Development in the Amazon Basin. *American Anthropologist* 77(3):526–549.

1982. Proteína y Cultura en la Amazonia: Una Segunda Revisión. *Amazonia Peruana* 3(6):127–144.

1983. Village Movement in Relation to Resources in Amazonia. In *Adaptive Responses of Native Amazonians*, edited by Raymond B. Hames and William T. Vickers, pp. 429–449. Academic Press, New York.

Gross, Daniel R., G. Eiten, Nancy M. Flowers, F.M. Leoi, M.L. Ritter, and D.W. Werner 1979. Ecology and Acculturation among Native Peoples of Central Brazil. *Science* 206:1043–1050.

Haeberlin, Hermann and Erna Gunther 1930. The Indians of Puget Sound. *University of Washington Publications in Anthropology* 4(1):1–85.

Hall, R.L. 1978. Analysis of Plant Remains from the Miami Wash Project. In *The Miami Wash Project: Hohokam and Salado in the Globe-Miami Area, Central Arizona*, edited by David E. Doyel, Appendix A, pp. 217–232. Contribution to Highway Salvage Archaeology in Arizona 52. Arizona State Museum, University of Arizona, Tucson.

Hall, Stephen A. 1984. Pollen Analysis of the Garnsey Bison Kill Site, Southeastern New Mexico. In *The Garnsey Spring Campsite: Late Prehistoric Occupation in Southeastern New Mexico*, edited by W.J. Parry and John D. Speth, pp. 85–108. Technical Report 15. University of Michigan, Museum of Anthropology, Ann Arbor.

Hames, Raymond B. 1979. A Comparison of the Efficiencies of the Shotgun and the Bow in Neotropical Forest Hunting. *Human Ecology* 7(3):219–252.

1980a. Game Depletion and Hunting Zone Rotation Among the Ye'kwana and Yanomamo of Amazonas, Venezuela. In *Studies in Hunting and Fishing in the Neotropics*, edited by Raymond B. Hames, pp. 31–66. Working Papers on South American Indians 2. Bennington College, Bennington.

(ed.) 1980b. *Studies in Hunting and Fishing in the Neotropics*. Working Papers on South American Indians 2. Bennington College, Bennington.

1983a. The Settlement Pattern of a Yanomamo Population Bloc: A Behavioral Ecological Interpretation. In *Adaptive Responses of Native Amazonians*, edited by Raymond B. Hames and William T. Vickers, pp. 393–427. Academic Press, New York.

1983b. Monoculture, Polyculture, and Polyvariety in Tropical Forest Swidden Cultivation. *Human Ecology* 11(1):13–34.

Hames, Raymond B. and William T. Vickers 1982. Optimal Diet Breadth Theory as a Model to Explain Variability in Amazonian Hunting. *American Ethnologist* 9(2):358–378.

Hames, Raymond B. and William T. Vickers (eds.) 1983. *Adaptive Responses of Native Amazonians*. Academic Press, New York.

Hamilton, W.J. and K.E.F. Watt 1970. Refuging. *Annual Review of Ecology and Systematics* 1:263–286.

Hanc, Joseph Robert n.d. Influences, Events and Innovations in the Anthropology of Julian H. Steward: A Revisionist View of Multilinear Evolution. Unpublished M.A. Thesis, University of Chicago, Chicago.

Harris, David R. 1972. The Origins of Agriculture in the Tropics. *American Scientist* 60:180–193.

1977. Alternative Pathways to Agriculture. In *Origins of Agriculture*, edited by Charles A. Reed, pp. 179–243. Mouton, The Hague.

Harris, Marvin 1968. *The Rise of Anthropological Theory: A History of Cultural Theories*. Thomas Y. Crowell, New York.

1974. *Cows, Pigs, Wars, and Witches: The Riddles of Culture*. Random House, New York.

1984a. Animal Capture and Yanomamo Warfare: Retrospect and New Evidence. *Journal of Anthropological Research* 40(1):183–201.

1984b. A Cultural Materialist Theory of Band and Village Warfare: The Yanomamo Test. In *Warfare, Culture, and Environment*, edited by R. Brian Ferguson, pp. 111–140. Academic Press, New York.

Hart, John A. 1978. From Subsistence to Market: A Case Study of the Mbuti Net Hunters. *Human Ecology* 6(3):325–353.

Hart, Terese B. and John A. Hart 1986. The Ecological Basis of Hunter–Gatherer Subsistence in the African Rain Forest: The Mbuti of Eastern Zaire. *Human Ecology* 14(1):29–55.

Hassan, Fekri 1981. *Demographic Archaeology*. Academic Press, New York.

Haury, Emil W. 1950. *The Stratigraphy and Archaeology of Ventana Cave*. University of Arizona Press, Tucson.

1976. *The Hohokam: Desert Farmers and Craftsmen. Excavations at Snaketown, 1964–1965*. University of Arizona Press, Tucson.

Hawkes, Kristen, Kim Hill, and James O'Connell 1982. Why Hunters Gather: Optimal Foraging and the Aché of Eastern Paraguay. *American Ethnologist* 9(2):379–398.

Hayden, Brian 1981. Subsistence and Ecological Adaptations of Modern

Hunters–Gatherers. In *Omnivorous Primates: Gathering and Hunting in Human Evolution*, edited by Robert S.O. Harding and Geza Teleki, pp. 344–421. Columbia University Press, New York.

Headland, Thomas N. 1978. Cultural Ecology, Ethnicity, and the Negritos of Northeastern Luzon: A Review Article. *Asian Perspectives* 21:128–139.

———. 1984. Agta Negritos of the Philippines. *Cultural Survival Quarterly* 8(3):29–31.

———. 1986. Why Foragers Do Not Become Farmers: A Historical Study of a Changing Ecosystem and its Effect on a Negrito Hunter–Gatherer Group in the Philippines. Unpublished Ph.D. Dissertation, Department of Anthropology, University of Hawaii, Honolulu.

Heffley, Sheri 1981. Northern Athapaskan Settlement Patterns and Resource Distributions: An Application of Horn's Model. In *Hunter–Gatherer Foraging Strategies*, edited by Bruce Winterhalder and Eric Alden Smith, pp. 126–147. University of Chicago Press, Chicago.

Henley, Paul 1982. *The Panare: Tradition and Change on the Amazonian Frontier*. Yale University Press, New Haven.

Herskovitz, P. 1972. The Recent Mammmals of the Neotropical Region: A Zoogeographical and Ecological Review. In *Evolution, Mammals, and Southern Continents*, edited by Allen Keast, pp. 311–431. State University of New York Press, Albany.

Hickerson, Harold 1965. The Virginia Deer and Intertribal Buffer Zones in the Upper Mississippi Valley. In *Man, Culture, and Animals*, edited by A. Leeds and A.P. Vayda, pp. 43–65. American Association for the Advancement of Science, Washington, D.C.

Hide, Robin 1980. Aspects of Pig Production and Use in Colonial Sinasina, Papua New Guinea. Unpublished Ph.D. Dissertation, Columbia University.

Hill, Kim and Kristen Hawkes 1983. Neotropical Hunting Among the Aché of Eastern Paraguay. In *Adaptive Responses of Native Amazonians*, edited by Raymond B. Hames and William T. Vickers, pp. 139–188. Academic Press, New York.

Hitchcock, Robert 1978. *Kalahari Cattle Posts – a Regional Study of Hunter–Gatherers, Pastoralists, and Agriculturalists in the Western Sandveld Region, Central District, Botswana*, Vol. 1. Preliminary Report to the Ministry of Local Government and Lands, Botswana.

———. 1982. *The Ethnoarchaeology of Sedentism: Mobility Strategies and Site Structure among Foraging and Food-Producing Populations in the Eastern Kalahari Desert, Botswana*. Ph.D. Dissertation, University of New Mexico. University Microfilms, Ann Arbor.

———. 1987. Sedentism and Site Structure: Organizational Changes in Kalahari Basarwa Residential Locations. In *Method and Theory for Activity Area Research: An Ethnoarchaeological Approach*, edited by Susan Kent, pp. 374–423. Columbia University Press, New York.

Hitchcock, Robert and Alec Campbell 1982. Settlement Patterns of the Bakgalagadi. In *Settlement in Botswana*, edited by R. Renee Hitchcock and Mary Smith, pp. 148–160. Heinemann Educational Books, Marshalltown.

Hitchcock, Robert and James Ebert 1984. Foraging and Food Production Among Kalahari Hunter–Gatherers. In *From Hunters to Farmers: The Causes and Consequences of Food Production in Africa*, edited by J. Desmond Clark and Steven Brandt, pp. 328–348. University of California Press, Berkeley.

Hodder, Ian 1982. Theoretical Archaeology: A Reactionary View. In *Symbolic and Structural Archaeology*, edited by Ian Hodder, pp. 1–16. Cambridge University Press, Cambridge.

———. 1987. The Meaning of Discard: Ash and Domestic Space in Baringo. In *Method and Theory for Activity Area Research: An Ethnoarchaeological Approach*, edited by Susan Kent, pp. 424–448. Columbia University Press, New York.

Holmberg, Allan 1969. *Nomads of the Long Bow – The Siriono of Eastern Bolivia*. Natural History Press, Garden City.

Holmes, Rebecca 1984. Non-Dietary Modifiers of Nutritional Status in Tropical Forest Populations of Venezuela. *Interciencia* 9(6): 386–391.

Horn, Henry S. 1968. The Adaptive Significance of Colonial Nesting in the Brewer's Blackbird (*Euphagus cyanocephalus*). *Ecology* 49:682–694.

Huckell, Bruce 1986. Late Archaic Archaeology of the Tucson Basin: A Status Report. Paper presented at the Tucson Basin Conference, Tucson, Arizona.

Huelsbeck, David 1983. *Mammals and Fish in the Subsistence Economy of Ozette*. Ph.D. Dissertation, University Microfilms, Ann Arbor.

Hugh-Jones, Christine 1979. *From the Milk River: Spatial and Temporal Practices in Northwest Amazonia*. Cambridge University Press, Cambridge.

Hugh-Jones, Stephen 1979. *The Palm and the Pleiades – Initiation and Cosmology in Northwest Amazonia*. Cambridge University Press, Cambridge.

Hurault, Jacques 1972. *Français et indiens en Guyane*. Union Générale d'Edition, Paris.

Hutterer, Karl L. 1982. *Interaction between Tropical Ecosystems and Human Foragers: Some General Considerations*. Working Paper, Environment and Policy Institute, East–West Center, Honolulu.

Ingold, Tim 1983. The Significance of Storage in Hunting Societies. *Man* 18:553–571.

Irwin-Williams, C. 1979. Post-Pleistocene Archaeology, 7000–2000 B.C. In *Handbook of North American Indians*, Vol. 9: *Southwest*, edited by Alfonso Ortiz, pp. 31–42. Smithsonian Institution, Washington, D.C.

Irwin-Williams, C. and V. Haynes 1970. Climatic Change and Early Population Dynamics in the Southwestern United States. *Quaternary Research* 1:59–71.

Jackson, H. Edwin 1986. *Sedentism and Hunter–Gatherer Adaptations in the Lower Mississippi Valley: Subsistence Strategies during the Poverty Point Period*. Unpublished Ph.D. Dissertation, University of Michigan, Ann Arbor.

Jeffers, B. and G. Childers 1976. *G ≠ wi/dom – The Borehole Community in the Central Kalahari Game Reserve*. Report to the Ministry of Local Government and Lands, Botswana.

Jelinek, Arthur J. 1967. *A Prehistoric Sequence in the Middle Pecos Valley, New Mexico*. Anthropological Paper 31. University of Michigan, Museum of Anthropology, Ann Arbor.

Jewitt, John 1815. *A Narrative of the Adventures and Sufferings of John R. Jewitt; During a Captivity of Nearly Three Years Among the Savages of Nootka Sound; With an Account of the Manners, Mode of Living, and Religious Opinions of the Natives*. Middletown, Connecticut.

Jochim, Michael A. 1976. *Hunter–Gatherer Subsistence and Settlement: A Predictive Model*. Academic Press, New York.

Johnson, Allen 1977. The Energy Costs of Technology in a Changing Environment: A Machiguenga Case. In *Material Culture: Styles, Organization, and Dynamics of Technology*, edited by Heather Lechtman and Robert S. Merrill, pp. 155–167. West Publishing, St. Paul.

———. 1982. Reductionism in Cultural Ecology: The Amazon Case. *Current Anthropology* 23(4):413–428.

Johnson, Allen and Clifford A. Behrens 1982. Nutritional Criteria in Machiguenga Food Production Decisions: A Linear Programing Analysis. *Human Ecology* 10(2):167–189.

Johnson, Allen and Timothy Earle 1987. *The Evolution of Human Societies: From Foraging Group to Agrarian State*. Stanford University Press, Stanford.

Johnson, Gregory A. 1982. Organizational Structure and Scalar Stress. In *Theory and Explanation in Archaeology*, edited by C. Renfrew, M.J. Rowlands, and B.A. Segraves, pp. 389–421. Academic Press, New York.

Johnson, Paul 1980. Archaeological Fauna from Gu Achi. In *Excavations at Gu Achi*, edited by W. Bruce Masse, pp. 359–370. Western Archaeological Center (NPS), Publications in Anthropology 12, Tucson.

Jones, Kevin T. 1984. Hunting and Scavenging by Early Hominids: A Study in Archaeological Method and Theory. Unpublished Ph.D. Dissertation, University of Utah, Salt Lake City.

Jordon, G.L. 1981. *Range Seeding and Brush Management on Arizona Rangelands.* Cooperative Extension Service, Agricultural Experiment Station. The University of Arizona, College of Agriculture, TS1121, Tucson.

Joyce, J.W. 1938. *Slavery Report of the Advisory Committee of Exports, League of Nations.* Publication 6 B:1, Slavery. League of Nations, Geneva.

Kahn, Miriam 1983. Sunday Christians, Monday Sorcerers. *Journal of Pacific History* 18(2):96–112.

 1986. *Always Hungry, Never Greedy: Food and the Expression of Gender in a Melanesian Society.* Cambridge University Press, Cambridge.

Kaplan, Hillard and Kim Hill 1985a. Food Sharing among Aché Foragers: Tests of Explanatory Hypotheses. *Current Anthropology* 26(2):223–246.

 1985b. Hunting Ability and Reproductive Success among Male Aché Foragers: Preliminary Results. *Current Anthropology* 26(1):131–133.

Kelley, Jane H. 1966. The Archaeology of the Sierra Blanca Region of Southeastern New Mexico. Unpublished Ph.D. Dissertation, Harvard University, Cambridge, Mass.

 1984. *The Archaeology of the Sierra Blanca Region of Southeastern New Mexico.* Anthropological Paper 74. University of Michigan, Museum of Anthropology, Ann Arbor.

Kelly, Raymond 1977. *Etoro Social Structure.* University of Michigan Press, Ann Arbor.

 n.d. Etoro Suidology: A Reassessment of the Pig's Role in the Prehistory and Comparative Ethnology of New Guinea. Unpublished Manuscript.

Kelly, Robert L. 1983. Hunter–Gatherer Mobility Strategies. *Journal of Anthropological Research* 39(3):277–306.

Kensinger, Kenneth M. 1974. Cashinahua Medicine and Medicine Men. In *Native South Americans: Ethnology of the Least Known Continent*, edited by Patricia J. Lyon, pp. 283–288. Little, Brown, Boston.

 1975. Studying the Cashinahua. In *The Cashinahua of Eastern Peru*, edited by Jane Powell Dwyer. The Haffenreffer Museum of Anthropology, Brown University Studies in Anthropology and Material Culture 1.

 1977. Cashinahua Notions of Social Time and Social Space. *Actes du 42ème. Congrès International des Américanistes* 2:233–244.

 1983. On Meat and Hunting. *Current Anthropology* 24(1):128–129.

 1984. Sex and Food: Reciprocity in Cashinahua Society? In *Sexual Ideologies in Lowland South America*, edited by Kenneth Kensinger, pp. 1–3. Working Papers on South American Indians 5. Bennington College, Bennington.

Kent, Susan 1975. An Analysis of Northwest Coast Combs with Special Emphasis on those from the Ozette Village Site. Unpublished M.A. Thesis, Department of Anthropology, Washington State University, Pullman.

 1983. The Differentiation of Navajo Culture, Behavior, and Material Culture: A Comparative Study in Culture Change. *Ethnology* 22(1):81–91.

 1984. *Analyzing Activity Areas: An Ethnoarchaeological Study of the Use of Space.* University of New Mexico Press, Albuquerque.

 1986. The Influence of Sedentism and Aggregation on Porotic Hyperostosis and Anemia in the North American Southwest: A Nondiet Approach. *Man* 21(4):605–636.

 1987. Parts as Wholes – a Critique of Theory in Archaeology. In *Method and Theory for Activity Area Research: An Ethnoarchaeological Approach*, edited by Susan Kent, pp. 513–546. Columbia University Press, New York.

 n.d.a. Kutse: Spatial Portrait of a Sedentary Kalahari Hunter-Gatherer Community.

 n.d.b. The Relationship between Mobility Strategies and Site Struc-

ture. [In press: In *The Interpretation of Spatial Patterning within Stone Age Archaeological Sites*, edited by T. Douglas Price and Ellen Kroll. Plenum, New York.]

 forthcoming. A Cross-cultural Study of Segmentation, Architecture, and the Use of Space. In *Domestic Architecture and the Use of Space*, edited by Susan Kent. Cambridge University Press, Cambridge.

Khazanov, A.M. 1983. *Nomads and the Outside World.* Cambridge University Press, Cambridge.

Kiester, A.R. and M. Slatkin 1974. A Strategy of Movement and Resource Utilization. *Theoretical Population Biology* 6:1–20.

Killeen, P.R., J.P. Smith, and S.J. Hanson 1981. Central Place Foraging in *Rattus norvegicus. Animal Behavior* 29(1):64–70.

Kiltie, Richard 1980. More on Amazon Cultural Ecology. *Current Anthropology* 21(4):541–544.

Klein, Richard G. and Kathryn Cruz-Uribe 1984. *The Analysis of Animal Bones from Archaeological Sites.* University of Chicago Press, Chicago.

Krause, Aurel 1956. *The Tlingit Indians – Results of a Trip to the Northwest Coast of America and the Bering Straits.* University of Washington Press, Seattle.

Kuper, Adam 1970. *Kalahari Village Politics: An African Democracy.* Cambridge University Press, Cambridge.

Lancaster, Jane and Chet Lancaster 1983. Parental Investment: The Hominid Adaptation. In *How Humans Adapt: A Biocultural Odyssey*, edited by D.J. Ortner, pp. 33–56. Smithsonian Institution Press, Washington, D.C.

Landtman, G. 1927. *The Kiwai Papuans of British New Guinea.* Macmillan, London.

Lang, Richard W. and Arthur H. Harris 1984. *The Faunal Remains from Arroyo Hondo Pueblo, New Mexico: A Study in Short-Term Subsistence Change.* Arroyo Hondo Archaeological Series 5. School of American Research Press, Santa Fe.

Lathrap, Donald W. 1968. The Hunting Economics of the Tropical Forest Zone of South America: An Attempt at Historical Perspective. In *Man the Hunter*, edited by R.B. Lee and I. DeVore, pp. 23–29. Aldine, Chicago.

 1970. *The Upper Amazon.* Praeger, New York.

Layne, Linda 1987. Village-Bedouin: Patterns of Change from Mobility to Sedentism in Jordan. In *Method and Theory for Activity Area Research: An Ethnoarchaeological Approach*, edited by Susan Kent, pp. 345–373. Columbia University Press, New York.

Leach, Edmund 1964. Anthropological Aspects of Language: Animal Categories and Verbal Abuse. In *New Directions in the Study of Language*, edited by Eric Lenneberg, pp. 23–63. M.I.T. Press, Cambridge, Mass.

Lee, Richard B. 1968. What Hunters Do for a Living, or, How to Make Out on Scarce Resources. In *Man the Hunter*, edited by Richard Lee and Irven DeVore, pp. 30–48. Aldine, Chicago.

 1972a. Population Growth and the Beginnings of Sedentary Life among the !Kung Bushmen. In *Population Growth: Anthropological Implications*, edited by Brian Spooner, pp. 329–342. M.I.T. Press, Cambridge, Mass.

 1972b. The Intensification of Social Life Among the !Kung Bushmen. In *Population Growth: Anthropological Implications*, edited by Brian Spooner, pp. 343–350. M.I.T. Press, Cambridge, Mass.

 1979. *The !Kung San: Men, Women, and Work in a Foraging Society.* Cambridge University Press, Cambridge.

 1982. Politics, Sexual and Non-sexual, in an Egalitarian Society. In *Politics and History in Band Societies*, edited by Eleanor Leacock and Richard Lee, pp. 37–60. Cambridge University Press, Cambridge.

 1984. *The Dobe !Kung.* Holt, Rinehart, and Winston, New York.

Lee, Richard B. and Irven DeVore (eds.) 1968. *Man the Hunter.* Aldine, Chicago.

Lehmer, Donald J. 1971. *Introduction to Middle Missouri Archaeology.* Anthropology Paper 1. U.S. Department of the Interior, National Park Service, Washington, D.C.

Leslie, Robert H. 1979. The Eastern Jornada Mogollon, Extreme South-eastern New Mexico (A Summary). In *Jornada Mogollon Archaeology*, edited by P.H. Beckett and R.N. Wiseman, pp. 179–200. New Mexico State University Press, and Historic Preservation Bureau, Department of Finance and Administration, State of New Mexico, Las Cruces and Santa Fe.

Lévi-Strauss, Claude 1963a. *Structural Anthropology*. Basic Books, New York.

    1963b. *Totemism*. Beacon Press, Boston.

    1966. *The Savage Mind*. University of Chicago Press, Chicago.

Levinson, David and Martin J. Malone (eds.) 1980. *Toward Explaining Culture*. Human Relations Area Files Press, New Haven.

Lewis, Gilbert 1975. *Knowledge of Illness in a Seoik Society: A Study of the Gnau, New Guinea*. L.S.E. Monographs on Social Anthropology 52. Athlone Press, London.

Linares, Olga F. 1976. "Garden Hunting" in the American Tropics. *Human Ecology* 4(4):331–349.

Lizot, Jacques 1977. Population, Resources, and Warfare among the Yanomami. *Man* 12(3/4):497–517.

Lynch, Thomas F. 1978. The Paleo-Indians. In *Ancient South Americans*, edited by Jesse D. Jennings, pp. 86–137. W.H. Freeman, San Francisco.

Lytle-Webb, J. 1978. Analysis of Pollen from the Miami Wash Project. In *The Miami Wash Project: Hohokam and Salado in the Globe–Miami Area, Central Arizona*, edited by David E. Doyel, Appendix C, pp. 243–268. Contribution to Highway Salvage Archaeology in Arizona 52. Arizona State Museum, University of Arizona, Tucson.

Madsen, Rees Low 1974. The Influence of Rainfall on the Reproduction of Sonoran Desert Lagomorphs. Thesis submitted to Department of Biological Sciences, University of Arizona, Tucson.

Malinowski, Bronislaw 1935. *Coral Gardens and Their Magic*. American Book Company, New York.

Marshall, Lorna 1976. *The !Kung of Nyae Nyae*. Harvard University Press, Cambridge, Mass.

Martin, John F. 1983. Optimal Foraging Theory: A Review of Some Models and Their Applications. *American Anthropologist* 85(3):612–629.

Mayane, Soblen 1979. Chobokwane: Notes on a New Multi-ethnic "Customary" Community. *Botswana Notes and Records* 11:128.

Maybury-Lewis, David 1974. *Akwē–Shavante Society*. Oxford University Press, London.

McKusick, Charmion R. 1980. Three Groups of Turkeys from Southwestern Archaeological Sites. In *Papers in Avian Paleontology Honoring Hildegarde Howard*, edited by K.E. Campbell, Jr., pp. 225–235. Contributions in Science 330. Natural History Museum of Los Angeles County, Los Angeles.

    1981. The Faunal Remains of Las Humanas. In *Contributions to Gran Quivira Archaeology*, edited by Alden C. Hayes, pp. 39–66. Publications in Archaeology 17. U.S. Department of the Interior, National Park Service, Washington, D.C.

McMillan, R.B. 1976. The Dynamics of Cultural and Environmental Change at Rodgers Shelter, Missouri. In *Prehistoric Man and His Environment: A Case Study in the Ozark Highlands*, edited by W.R. Wood and R.B. McMillan, pp. 211–232. Academic Press, New York.

Meggers, Betty J. 1954. Environmental Limitations on the Development of Culture. *American Anthropologist* 56:801–824.

    1957. Environment and Culture in the Amazon Basin: An Appraisal of the Theory of Environmental Determinism. In *Studies in Human Ecology*, edited by Angel Palerm, pp. 71–113. Pan American Union, Washington, D.C.

    1971. *Amazonia: Man and Culture in a Counterfeit Paradise*. Aldine, Chicago.

    1973. Some Problems in Cultural Adaptation in Amazonia with Emphasis in the Pre-European Period. In *Tropical Forest Ecosystems in Africa and South America: A Comparative Review*, edited by

Betty J. Meggers, *et al.*, pp. 311–320. Smithsonian Institution Press, Washington, D.C.

    1974. Environment and Culture in Amazonia. In *Man in the Amazon*, edited by Charles Wagley, pp. 91–110. University of Florida Press, Gainesville.

    1982. Archaeological and Ethnographic Evidence Compatible with the Model of Forest Fragmentation. In *Biological Diversification in the Tropics*, edited by Ghillean T. Prance, pp. 483–496. Columbia University Press, New York.

Meggitt, Mervyn 1958. The Enga of the New Guinea Highland: Some Preliminary Observations. *Oceania* 28:253–330.

    1964. Male–Female Relations in the Highlands of Australian New Guinea. In *New Guinea: The Central Highlands*, edited by J.B. Watson. Special Publication. *American Anthropologist* 66(4) Part 2:204–224.

    1965. *The Lineage System of the Mae-Enga of New Guinea*. Oliver and Boyd, Edinburgh.

    1977. *Blood is Their Argument: Warfare among the Mae Enga Tribesman of the New Guinea Highlands*. Mayfield, Palo Alto.

Miksicek, C. n.d. Hohokam Adaptation to the Chaparral Zone: Paleoecology and Subsistence in the ANAMAX-Rosemont Area. Unpublished Manuscript, Arizona State Museum, University of Arizona, Tucson.

Milton, Katherine 1981. Distributional Patterns of Tropical Plant Foods as an Evolutionary Stimulus to Primate Mental Development. *American Anthropologist* 83:534–548.

    1984. Protein and Carbohydrate Resources of the Maku Indians of Northwestern Amazonia. *American Anthropologist* 86(1):7–27.

Mish, Frederick 1985. *Webster's Ninth New Collegiate Dictionary*. Merriam-Webster, Springfield.

Moore, James A. 1981. The Effects of Information Networks in Hunter–Gatherer Societies. In *Hunter–Gatherer Foraging Strategies: Ethnographic and Archaeological Analyses*, edited by Bruce Winterhalder and Eric Alden Smith, pp. 194–217. University of Chicago Press, Chicago.

Moran, Emilio F. 1973. Energy Flow Analysis and the Study of *Manihot esculenta* Crantz. *Acta Amazonica* 111(3):29–39.

    1976. Manioc Deserves More Recognition in Tropical Farming. *World Crops* (July/August): 184–188.

    1980. Mobility and Resource Use in Amazonia. In *Land, People and Planning for Contemporary Amazonia*, edited by François Barbira-Scazzocchio, pp. 46–57. Cambridge University Centre of Latin American Studies Occasional Publication 3, Cambridge.

    1981. *Developing the Amazon*. Indiana University Press, Bloomington.

    1983. Mobility as a Negative Factor in Human Adaptability: The Case of South American Tropical Forest Populations. In *Rethinking Human Adaptation: Biological and Cultural Models*, edited by Rada Dyson-Hudson and Michael A. Little, pp. 117–135. Westview, Boulder.

Morren, George 1977. From Hunting to Herding: Pigs and the Control of Energy in Montane New Guinea. In *Subsistence and Survival – Rural Ecology in the Pacific*, edited by Timothy P. Bayliss-Smith and Richard Feachem, pp. 273–315. Academic Press, London.

Mudar, Karen 1985. Bearded Pigs and Beardless Men: *Sus barbatus* (wild pig) and the Agta Hunting in Coastal Cagayan. In *The Agta of Northeastern Luzon: Recent Studies*, edited by P. Bion Griffin and Agnes Estioko-Griffin, pp. 69–84. Humanities Series 16. San Carlos Publications, University of San Carlos, Cebu City, Philippines.

Mueller-Dombois, D. (ed.) 1981. *Island Ecosystems*. Elsevier, New York.

Munson, P.J., P.W. Parmalee, and R.A. Yarnell 1971. Subsistence Ecology of Scovill, a Terminal Middle Woodland Village. *American Antiquity* 36(4):410–431.

Murphy, Robert F. 1977. Man's Culture and Woman's Nature. *Annals of the New York Academy of Sciences* 293:15–24.

Murphy, Yolanda and Robert F. Murphy 1974. *Women of the Forest*. Columbia University Press, New York.

Nelson, Ben A. and Linda S. Cordell 1982. Dynamics of the Anasazi Adaptation. In *Anasazi and Navajo Land Use in the McKinley Mine Area Near Gallup, New Mexico*, Vol. 1, edited by C.G. Allen and B.A. Nelson, Part 1, pp. 867–893. University of New Mexico, Office of Contract Archaeology, Albuquerque.

Neusius, Sarah W. 1984. Garden Hunting and Anasazi Game Procurement: Perspectives from Dolores. Paper presented at the 49th Annual Meeting of the Society for American Archaeology, Portland, Oregon (April, 1984).

Norman, M.J.T., *et al.* 1984. *The Ecology of Tropical Food Crops*. Cambridge University Press, Cambridge.

O'Connell, James 1987. Alyawara Site Structure and its Archaeological Implications. *American Antiquity* 52(1):74–108.

Ohnuki-Tierney, Emiko 1974. *The Ainu of the Northwest Coast of Southern Sakhalin*. Holt, Rinehart, and Winston, New York.

Olsen, John W. 1980. *A Zooarchaeological Analysis of Vertebrate Faunal Remains from the Grasshopper Pueblo, Arizona*. Unpublished Ph.D. Dissertation, University of California, Berkeley.

Olson, Ronald 1936. The Quinault Indians. *University of Washington Publications in Anthropology* 6(1):1–190.

Oosterwal, G. 1961. *People of the Tor*. Royal Van Gorcum, Assen.

Orians, Gordon H. and Nolan E. Pearson 1979. On the Theory of Central Place Foraging. In *Analysis of Ecological Systems*, edited by D.J. Horn, G.R. Stairs, and R.D. Mitchell, pp. 155–177. Ohio State University Press, Columbus.

Ortiz, Alfonso 1969. *The Tewa World – Space, Time, Being, and Becoming in a Pueblo Society*. University of Chicago Press, Chicago.

Oswald, Dana 1987. The Organization of Space in Residential Buildings: A Cross-cultural Perspective. In *Method and Theory for Activity Area Research: An Ethnoarchaeological Perspective*, edited by Susan Kent, pp. 295–344. Colombia University Press, New York.

Oswalt, Wendell 1967. *Alaskan Eskimos*. Chandler, San Francisco, California.

Pandian, Jacob 1985. *Anthropology and the Western Tradition: Toward an Authentic Anthropology*. Waveland Press, Prospect Heights.

Pandit, T.N. 1976. The Original Inhabitants of the Andaman and Nicobar Islands. *Yojana* 20:1–6.

Paolisso, Michael and Ross Sackett 1985. Traditional Meat Procurement Strategies Among the Irapa–Yukpa of the Venezuela–Colombia Border Area. *Research in Economic Anthropology* 7:177–199.

Parker, E., D. Posey, J. Frechione, and L.F. daSilva 1983. Resource Exploitation in Amazonia: Ethnoecological Examples from Four Populations. *Annals of Carnegie Museum* 52(8):163–203.

Parkington, John 1984. Soaqua and Bushmen: Hunters and Robbers. In *Past and Present in Hunter–Gatherer Studies*, edited by Carmel Schrire, pp. 151–174. Academic Press, New York.

Peterson, Jean Treloggen 1978. *The Ecology of Social Boundaries: Agta Foragers of the Philippines*. Illinois Studies in Anthropology 11. University of Illinois Press, Urbana.

——— 1981. Game, Farming, and Interethnic Relations in Northeastern Luzon, Philippines. *Human Ecology* 9(1):1–22.

——— 1982. The Effects of Farming Expansion on Hunting. *Philippine Sociological Review* 30:35–50.

——— 1985. Hunter Mobility, Family Organization and Change. In *Circulation in Third World Countries*, edited by R. Mansell Prothero and Murray Chapman, pp. 124–144. Routledge and Kegan Paul, London.

Pettitt, George 1950. The Quileute of La Push 1775–1945. *University of California Anthropological Records* 14(1):1–28.

Plog, Fred 1980. Explaining Culture Change in the Hohokam Preclassic. In *Current Issues in Hohokam Prehistory*, edited by David E. Doyel and Fred Plog, pp. 4–22. Anthropological Research Papers 23. Arizona State University, Tempe.

Pollock, Donald K. 1985. Food and Sexual Identity among the Culina. *Food and Foodways* 1:25–42.

Pospisil, Leopold 1963a. *Kapauku Papuan Economy*. Yale Publications in Anthropology 67. Yale University, New Haven.

——— 1963b. *The Kapauku Papuans of West New Guinea*. Holt, Rinehart, and Winston, New York.

Price, T. Douglas and James Brown (eds.) 1985. *Prehistoric Hunter–Gatherers: The Emergence of Cultural Complexity*. Academic Press, New York.

Pulliam, H. Ronald 1981. On Predicting Human Diets. *Journal of Ethnobiology* 1(1):61–68.

Rafferty, Janet E. 1984. The Archaeological Record on Sedentariness: Recognition, Development and Implications. In *Advances in Archaeological Method and Theory*, Vol. 8, edited by Michael B. Schiffer, pp. 113–156. Academic Press, New York.

Rai, Navin Kumar 1982. From Forest to Field: A Study of Philippine Negrito Foragers in Transition. Unpublished Ph.D. Dissertation, Department of Anthropology, University of Hawaii, Honolulu.

Rappaport, Roy 1969. Marriage among the Maring. In *Pigs, Pearlshells, and Women*, edited by R.M. Glasse and M.J. Meggitt, pp. 117–137. Prentice-Hall, Englewood Cliffs.

——— 1984. *Pigs for the Ancestors: Ritual in the Ecology of a New Guinea People*. Yale University Press, New Haven.

Rea, A. 1983. *Once a River: Bird Life and Habitat Changes on the Middle Gila*. University of Arizona Press, Tucson.

Reichel-Dolmatoff, Gerardo 1985. Tapir Avoidance in the Colombian Northwest Amazon. In *Animal Myths and Metaphors in South America*, edited by Gary Urton, pp. 107–143. University of Utah Press, Salt Lake City.

Reidhead, Van A. 1976. Optimization and Food Procurement at the Prehistoric Leonard Haag Site: A Linear Programming Approach. Unpublished Ph.D. Dissertation, Indiana University, Bloomington.

Rifkin, Jeremy 1980. *Entropy: A New World View*. Bantam Books, New York.

Robison, Neil D. 1982. A Critical Review of Mississippian Hunting Patterns and Their Antiquity. *Tennessee Anthropologist* 1:62–74.

Rocek, Thomas R. and John D. Speth 1986. *The Henderson Site Burials: Glimpses of a Late Prehistoric Population in the Pecos Valley*. Technical Report 18. University of Michigan, Museum of Anthropology, Ann Arbor.

Rodman, Margaret 1985. Moving Houses: Residential Mobility and the Mobility of Residences in Longana, Vanuatu. *American Anthropologist* 87(1):56–72.

Roosevelt, Anna Curtenius 1980. *Parmana: Prehistoric Maize and Manioc Subsistence Along the Amazon and Orinoco*. Academic Press, New York.

Rosaldo, Michelle 1980. *Knowledge and Passion: Ilongot Notions of Self and Social Life*. Cambridge University Press, Cambridge.

Rosaldo, Renato 1982. The Social Relations of Ilongot Subsistence. In *Contributions to the Study of Philippine Shifting Cultivation*, edited by Harold Olofson, pp. 29–41. Forest Research Institute, Laguna, Philippines.

Ross, Eric B. 1978. Food Taboos, Diet, and Hunting Strategy: The Adaptation to Animals in Amazon Cultural Ecology. *Current Anthropology* 19(1):1–36.

——— 1979. On Food Taboos and Amazon Cultural Ecology. *Current Anthropology* 20(4):544–546.

Ross, Eric B. and Jane Bennett Ross 1980. Amazon Warfare. *Science* 207:592.

Ross, Jane Bennett 1980. Ecology and the Problem of Tribe: A Critique of the Hobbesian Model of Preindustrial Warfare. In *Beyond the Myths of Culture: Essays in Cultural Materialism*, edited by Eric B. Ross, pp. 33–60. Academic Press, New York.

Rowley-Conwy, Peter 1983. Sedentary Hunters: The Ertebølle Example. In *Hunter–Gatherer Economy in Prehistory*, edited by G. Bailey, pp. 111–126. Cambridge University Press, Cambridge.

Rubel, Paula G. and Abraham Rosman 1978. *Your Own Pigs You May Not Eat: A Comparative Study of New Guinea Societies.* University of Chicago Press, Chicago.

Saffirio, Giovanni and Raymond B. Hames 1983. The Forest and the Highway. In *The Impact of Contact,* edited by Kenneth M. Kensinger, pp. 1–52. Working Papers on South American Indians 6. Bennington College, Bennington.

Saffirio, Giovanni and Richard Scaglion 1982. Hunting Efficiency in Acculturated and Unacculturated Yanomama Villages. *Journal of Anthropological Research* 38(3):315–327.

Sahlins, Marshall 1976. *Culture and Practical Reason.* University of Chicago Press, Chicago.

Salati, Eneas, J. Marques, and L. Molion 1978. Origem e distribução das chuvas na Amazônia. *Interciencia* 3(4):200–205.

Sanday, Peggy 1981. *Female Power and Male Dominance: On the Origins of Sexual Inequality.* Cambridge University Press, Cambridge.

Sanford, Robert L., Jr., *et al.* 1985. Amazon Rain-Forest Fires. *Science* 227:53–55.

Sauer, Carl O. 1963. Man in the Ecology of Tropical America. In *Land and Life: A Selection from the Writings of Carl Ortwin Sauer,* edited by John Leighly, Chapter 10, pp. 182–193. University of California Press, Berkeley.

Sayles, E.B. and E. Antevs 1941. *The Cochise Culture.* Medallion Papers 29. Gila Pueblo, Globe, Arizona.

Schalk, Randal 1977. The Structure of an Anadromous Fish Resource. In *For Theory Building,* edited by Lewis Binford, pp. 207–249. Academic Press, New York.

Schapera, I. 1930. *The Khoisan Peoples of South Africa – Bushmen and Hottentots.* Routledge and Kegan Paul, London.

Schiffer, M. 1982. Hohokam Chronology: An Essay on History and Method. In *Hohokam and Patayan: Prehistory of Southwestern Arizona,* edited by R. McGuire and M.B. Schiffer, pp. 299–344. Academic Press, New York.

Schiffer, M. and R. McGuire 1982. *Hohokam and Patayan: Prehistory of Southwestern Arizona.* Academic Press, New York.

Schubart, Herbert O.R. and Eneas Salati 1982. Natural Resources for Land Use in the Amazon Region: The Natural Systems. In *Amazonia: Agriculture and Land Use Research,* edited by Susan B. Hecht, pp. 211–239. Centro Internacional de Agriculture Tropical, Cali, Colombia.

Schwabe, G.H. 1968. Toward an Ecological Characterization of the South American Continent. In *Biogeography and Ecology in South America,* edited by E.J. Fittkau, *et al.,* pp. 113–136. J.W. Junk, The Hague.

Serpenti, L.M. 1977. *Cultivators in the Swamps.* Van Gorcum, Assen, Amsterdam.

Sharp, Henry 1981. The Null Case: The Chipewyan. In *Woman the Gatherer,* edited by Frances Dahlberg, pp. 221–244. Yale University Press, New Haven.

Shostak, Marjorie 1981. *Nisa: The Life and Words of a !Kung Woman.* Harvard University Press, Cambridge, Mass.

Silberbauer, George 1981. *Hunter and Habitat in the Central Kalahari Desert.* Cambridge University Press, Cambridge.

Silberbauer, George and A.J. Kuper 1966. Kgalagadi Masters and Bushman Serfs: Some Observations. *African Studies* 25(4):171–179.

Silitshena, R.M. 1983. *Intra-rural Migration and Settlement Changes in Botswana.* African Studies Centre Research Reports 20. Leiden.

Simmel, Georg 1950. *The Sociology of Georg Simmel.* The Free Press, Glencoe.

Siskind, Janet 1973a. Tropical Forest Hunters and the Economy of Sex. In *Peoples and Cultures of Native South America,* edited by Daniel R. Gross, pp. 226–240. Natural History Press, Garden City.

1973b. *To Hunt in the Morning.* Oxford University Press, New York.

Smith, B. 1975. *Middle Mississippi Exploitation of Animal Populations.* University of Michigan Museum of Anthropology, Anthropology Papers 57. Ann Arbor, Michigan.

Smith, Eric Alden 1981. The Application of Optimal Foraging Theory to the Analysis of Hunter–Gatherer Group Size. In *Hunter–Gatherer Foraging Strategies,* edited by Bruce Winterhalder and Eric Alden Smith, pp. 36–65. University of Chicago Press, Chicago.

Smith, Nigel J.H. 1976. Utilization of Game Along Brazil's Transamazon Highway. *Acta Amazonica* 6(4):455–466.

1978. Human Exploitation of Terra Firma Fauna in Amazonia. *Ciência e Cultura* 30(1):17–23.

1982. *Rain Forest Corridors: The Transamazon Colonization.* University of California Press, Berkeley.

Solway, Jacqueline 1979. The Cattle Economy and Socioeconomic Change in Western Kweneng. *Botswana Notes and Records* 11:130–132.

1986. Commercialization and Social Differentiation in a Kalahari Village, Botswana. Unpublished Ph.D. Dissertation, Department of Anthropology, University of Toronto.

Sowls, Lyle K. 1984. *The Peccaries.* University of Arizona Press, Tucson.

Sparling, J. 1974. Analysis of Faunal Remains from the Escalante Ruin Group. In *Excavations in the Escalante Ruin Group, Southern Arizona,* edited by David E. Doyel, pp. 215–253. Arizona State Museum, Archaeological Series 37. Tucson.

1978. Analysis of the Faunal Remains from the Miami Wash Project. In *The Miami Wash Project: Hohokam and Salado in the Globe–Miami Area, Central Arizona,* edited by David E. Doyel, Appendix E, pp. 283–300. Contribution to Highway Salvage Archaeology in Arizona 52. Arizona State Museum, University of Arizona, Tucson.

Spath, C.D. 1981. Getting to the Meat of the Problem: See Comments on Protein as a Limiting Factor in Amazonia. *American Anthropologist* 83(2):377–379.

Speth, John D. 1983. *Bison Kills and Bone Counts: Decision Making by Ancient Hunters.* University of Chicago Press, Chicago.

Speth, John D. and S.L. Scott 1985. The Role of Large Mammals in Late Prehistoric Horticultural Adaptations: The View from Southeastern New Mexico. In *Contributions to Plains Prehistory: The 1984 Victoria Symposium,* edited by David Burley, pp. 233–266. Occasional Paper 26. Archaeological Survey of Alberta, Edmonton.

Speth, John D. and Katherine A. Spielmann 1983. Energy Source, Protein Metabolism, and Hunter–Gatherer Subsistence Strategies. *Journal of Anthropological Archaeology* 2:1–31.

Speth, W.W. 1972. Historicist Anthropogeography: Environment and Culture in American Anthropological Thought from 1890 to 1950. Unpublished Ph.D. Thesis, University of Oregon, Eugene.

Spielmann, Katherine A. 1982. Inter-societal Food Acquisition Among Egalitarian Societies: An Ecological Study of Plains/Pueblo Interaction in the American Southwest. Unpublished Ph.D. Dissertation, University of Michigan, Ann Arbor.

Sponsel, Leslie E. 1981. *The Hunter and the Hunted in the Amazon: An Integrated Biological and Cultural Approach to the Behavioral Ecology of Human Predation.* University Microfilms International, Ann Arbor.

1983. Yanomama Warfare, Protein Capture, and Cultural Ecology: A Critical Analysis of the Arguments of the Opponents. *Interciencia* 8:204–210.

1985. Ecology, Anthropology and Values in Amazonia. In *Cultural Values and Tropical Ecology in Southeast Asia,* edited by Karl Hutterer and Terry Rambo, pp. 77–122. University of Michigan, Center for South and Southeast Asian Studies, Ann Arbor.

1986. Hunger Rivers. Unpublished Manuscript.

Stein, Walter T. 1962. Mammals from Archaeological Sites, Point of Pines, Arizona. Unpublished M.A. Thesis, University of Arizona, Tucson.

Stern, Bernhard 1934. *The Lummi Indians of Northwest Washington.* Columbia University Press, New York.

Steward, Julian H. 1938. *Basin–Plateau Aboriginal Sociopolitical Groups.*

Bureau of American Ethnology Bulletin 120, Washington, D.C.

(ed.) 1948. *Handbook of South American Indians*. Vol. 3: *The Tropical Forest Tribes*. Bureau of American Ethnology Bulletin 143, Washington, D.C.

1955. *Theory of Culture Change: The Methodology of Multilinear Evolution*. University of Illinois Press, Urbana.

1977. The Concept and Method of Cultural Ecology. In *Evolution and Ecology: Essays in Social Transformation by Julian H. Steward*, edited by Jane C. Steward and Robert F. Murphy, pp. 43–57. University of Illinois Press, Urbana.

Steward, Julian H. and Louis Faron 1959. *Native Peoples of South America*. McGraw-Hill, New York.

Stiger, Mark A. 1979. Mesa Verde Subsistence Patterns from Basketmaker to Pueblo III. *Kiva* 44(2–3):133–144.

Styles, B. 1981. *Faunal Exploitation and Resource Selection: Early Late Woodland Subsistence in the Lower Illinois Valley*. Northwestern University Archaeological Program, Scientific Papers 3. Evanston, Illinois.

Suttles, Wayne 1974. The Economic Life of the Coast Salish of Haro and Rosario Straits. In *Coast Salish and Western Washington Indians*, Vol. 1, edited by David Horr, pp. 41–561. Garland Publishing, New York.

Swan, James 1869. *The Indians of Cape Flattery*. Smithsonian Contributions to Knowledge 220. Smithsonian Institution, Washington, D.C.

Szuter, Christine R. 1984a. Faunal Exploitation and the Reliance on Small Animals Among the Hohokam. In *Hohokam Archaeology Along the Salt–Gila Aqueduct Central Arizona Project*, Vol. 7: *Environment and Subsistence*, edited by Lynn S. Teague and Patricia L. Crown, pp. 139–170. Arizona State Museum Cultural Resource Management Section, Archaeological Series 150. University of Arizona, Tucson.

1984b. Small Sample Sizes in Faunal Interpretation: Building Blocks of a Regional Analysis. Paper presented at the Annual Meeting of the Society for American Archaeologists, Portland.

1985a. The Faunal Evidence of Environment and Subsistence at the Valencia Road Site. In *Archaeological Investigations at the Valencia Site: A Preclassic Hohokam Village in the Southern Tucson Basin, AZ BB:13:15*, edited by William Doelle, Chapter 15, pp. 249–263. Institute for American Research, Anthropological Papers 3, Tucson.

1985b. Archaic Period Taxonomic Richness and Animal Utilization. In *Archaeological Investigations at La Paloma: Archaic and Hohokam Occupation at Three Sites in the Northeastern Tucson Basin, Arizona*, edited by A. Dart, Chapter 9, pp. 155–165. Institute for American Research, Anthropological Papers 4, Tucson.

1986. Lagomorph and Artiodactyl Exploitation among the Inhabitants of the West Branch Site. In *Archaeological Investigations at the West Branch Site: Early and Middle Rincon Occupation in the Southern Tucson Basin*, edited by F. Huntington, Chapter 14, pp. 273–288. Institute for American Research, Anthropological Papers 5, Tucson.

Szuter, Christine R. and Gwen Lerner Brown 1986. Faunal Remains from the Tanque Verde Wash Site. In *Archaeological Investigations at the Tanque Verde Wash Site: A Middle Rincon Settlement in the Eastern Tucson Basin*, edited by M.D. Elson, Chapter 13, pp. 337–359. Institute for American Research, Anthropological Papers 7, Tucson.

Tagart, E.S. 1933. *Report on the Conditions Existing among the Masarwa in the Bamangwato Reserve of the Bechuanaland Protectorate and Certain Other Matters Appertaining to the Natives Living Therein*. The Government Printer, Pretoria.

Tambiah, S.J. 1969. Animals Are Good to Think and Good to Prohibit. *Ethnology* 8(4):424–459.

Tanaka, Jiro 1980. *The San Hunters–Gatherers of the Kalahari – A Study in Ecological Anthropology*. University of Tokyo Press, Tokyo.

Taylor, Ronald L. 1975. *Butterflies in My Stomach, or: Insects in Human Nutrition*. Woodbridge, Santa Barbara.

Terra, G.J.A. 1964. The Significance of Leaf Vegetables, Especially Cassava, in Tropical Nutrition. *Tropical and Geographic Medicine* 16(2):97–108.

Testart, Alain 1982. The Significance of Food Storage among Hunter–Gatherers: Residence Patterns, Population Densities, and Social Inequalities. *Current Anthropology* 23(5):523–537.

Theil, Barbara Jean 1980. Subsistence Change and Continuity in Southeast Asian Prehistory. Unpublished Ph.D. Dissertation, Department of Anthropology, University of Illinois, Urbana.

Tlou, Thomas and Alec Campbell 1984. *A History of Botswana*. Macmillan Botswana, Gaborone.

Toll, Mollie S. and Marcia Donaldson 1982. Flotation and Macro-Botanical Analyses of Archaeological Sites on the McKinley Mine Lease: A Regional Study of Plant Manipulation and Natural Seed Dispersal Over Time. In *Anasazi and Navajo Land Use in the McKinley Mine Area near Gallup, New Mexico*, Vol. 1, edited by C.G. Allen and B.A. Nelson, Part 2, pp. 712–786. University of New Mexico, Office of Contract Archaeology, Albuquerque.

Turnbull, Colin M. 1961. *The Forest People: A Study of the Pygmies of the Congo*. Simon and Schuster, New York.

1965. *Wayward Servants: The Two Worlds of the African Pygmies*. Natural History Press, Garden City.

Upham, Steadman 1984. Adaptive Diversity and Southwestern Abandonment. *Journal of Anthropological Research* 40(2):235–256.

Urton, Gary 1985. Introduction. In *Animal Myths and Metaphors in South America*, edited by Gary Urton, pp. 3–12. University of Utah Press, Salt Lake City.

Van Devender, T.R. 1977. Holocene Woodlands in the Southwestern Deserts. *Science* 198(4313):189–192.

Van Devender, T.R. and W. Spaulding 1979. Development of Vegetation and Climate in the Southwestern United States. *Science* 204:701–710.

Vickers, William T. 1976. *Cultural Adaptation to Amazonian Habitats: The Siona–Secoya of Eastern Ecuador*. Unpublished Ph.D. Dissertation, Department of Anthropology, University of Florida.

1978. Reply to Ross. *Current Anthropology* 19(1):27.

1980. An Analysis of Amazonian Hunting Yields as a Function of Settlement Age. In *Studies in Hunting and Fishing in the Neotropics*, edited by Raymond B. Hames, pp. 7–29. Working Papers on South American Indians 2. Bennington College, Bennington.

1983a. Tropical Forest Mimicry in Swiddens: A Reassessment of Geertz's Model with Amazonian Data. *Human Ecology* 11(1):35–45.

1983b. The Territorial Dimensions of Siona–Secoya and Encabellado Adaptation. In *Adaptive Responses of Native Amazonians*, edited by Raymond B. Hames and William T. Vickers, pp. 451–478. Academic Press, New York.

1984. The Faunal Component of Lowland South American Hunting Kills. *Interciencia* 9(6):366–376.

1988. Game Depletion Hypothesis of Amazonian Adaptation: Data from a Native Community. *Science* 239:1521–1522.

Vickers, William T. and Timothy Plowman 1984. *Useful Plants of the Siona and Secoya Indians of Eastern Ecuador*. Fieldiana Botany, n.s. 15. Field Museum of Natural History, Chicago.

Vierich, Helga 1981. *The Kūa of the Southeastern Kalahari: A Study in the Socio-Ecology of Dependency*. Ph.D. Dissertation, University of Toronto, University Microfilms, Ann Arbor.

1982. Adaptive Flexibility in a Multi-ethnic Setting: The Basarwa of the Southern Kalahari. In *Politics and History in Band Societies*, edited by Eleanor Leacock and Richard Lee, pp. 213–222. Cambridge University Press, Cambridge.

Vierich-Esche, Helga 1977. *Interim Report on Basarwa and Related Poor Bakgalagadi in Kweneng District*. Report to the Ministry of Local

Government and Lands, Botswana.

Vivelo, Frank 1976. The Entry of the Herero into Botswana. *Botswana Notes and Reports* 8:39–46.

Vogt, Evon 1970. Human Souls and Animal Spirits in Zinacantan. In *Studies in General Anthropology*, edited by David Bidney, Dell Hymes, P. De Josselin de Jong, and Edmund Leach, pp. 1148–1167. Mouton, Paris.

Waddell, Eric 1972. *The Mound Builders*. University of Washington Press, Seattle.

Walker, Ernest P. 1975. *Mammals of the World*. Johns Hopkins University Press, Baltimore.

Watanabe, Hitoshi 1968. Subsistence and Ecology of Northern Food Gatherers with Special Reference to the Ainu. In *Man the Hunter*, edited by Richard Lee and Irven DeVore, pp. 69–77. Aldine, Chicago.

Watson, James B. 1977. Pigs, Fodder, and the Jones Effect in Postipomoean New Guinea. *Ethnology* 16:57–70.

Watson, Patty Jo, Steven LeBlanc, and Charles Redman 1984. *Archaeological Explanation: The Scientific Method in Archaeology*. Columbia University Press, New York.

Watt, Kenneth E.F., *et al.* 1977. *The Unsteady State: Environmental Problems, Growth, and Culture*. East–West Center Book University Press of Hawaii, Honolulu.

Wedel, Waldo R. 1983. The Prehistoric Plains. In *Ancient North Americans*, edited by Jesse D. Jennings, pp. 202–241. W.H. Freeman, San Francisco.

Weiss, Gerald 1972. Campa Cosmology. *Ethnology* 11:157–172.

Werner, Dennis 1983. Why Do the Mekranoti Trek? In *Adaptive Responses of Native Amazonians*, edited by Raymond B. Hames and William T. Vickers, pp. 225–238. Academic Press, New York.

Wesson, Gary 1982. *Shell Middens as Cultural Deposits: A Case Study from Ozette*. Ph.D. Dissertation, Department of Anthropology, Washington State University, University Microfilms, Ann Arbor.

White, J. Peter and Jim Allen 1980. Melanesian Prehistory: Some Recent Advances. *Science* 207:728–734.

White, J. Peter and James F. O'Connell 1982. *A Prehistory of Australia, New Guinea and Sahul*. Academic Press, Sydney.

White, R.S. 1978. Archaeological Faunas from the Quijotoa Valley, Arizona. In *The Quijotoa Valley Project*, edited by J. Rosenthal, Appendix 1, pp. 224–254. Western Archaeological Center, National Park Service, Tucson.

Wiessner, Polly 1982. Risk, Reciprocity and Social Influences on !Kung San Economics. In *Politics and History in Band Societies*, edited by

Eleanor Leacock and Richard Lee, pp. 61–84. Cambridge University Press, Cambridge.

Wilcox, D.R. and L.O. Shenk 1977. *The Architecture of the Casa Grande and its Interpretation*. Arizona State Museum, Archaeological Series 115. University of Arizona, Tucson.

Willey, Patrick S. and Jack T. Hughes 1978. The Deadman's Shelter Site. In *Archaeology at the Mackenzie Reservoir*, edited by J.T. Hughes and P.S. Willey, pp. 149–190. Archaeological Survey Report 24. Texas Historical Commission, Office of the State Archaeologist, Austin.

Williams, F.E. 1930. *Orakaiva Society*. Oxford University Press, Oxford.

    1936. *Papuans of the Transfly*. Territory of Papua, Anthropology Report 15. Clarendon Press, Oxford.

Williamson, Robert W. 1912. *The Mafulu: Mountain People of British New Guinea*. Macmillan, London.

Wilmsen, Edwin 1978. Seasonal Effects of Dietary Intake on Kalahari San. *Anthropology and the Assessment of Nutritional Status* 37(1):65–72.

Winterhalder, Bruce 1981. Optimal Foraging Strategies and Hunter–Gatherer Research in Anthropology: Theory and Models. In *Hunter–Gatherer Foraging Strategies*, edited by Bruce Winterhalder and E.A. Smith, pp. 13–35. University of Chicago Press, Chicago.

Winterhalder, Bruce and E.A. Smith (eds.) 1981. *Hunter–Gatherer Foraging Strategies*. University of Chicago Press, Chicago.

Woodburn, James 1968. Stability and Flexibility in Hadza Residential Groupings. In *Man the Hunter*, edited by Richard Lee and Irven DeVore, pp. 103–110. Aldine, Chicago.

Wurm, S.A. 1983. Linguistic Prehistory in the New Guinea Area. *Journal of Human Evolution* 12:25–35.

Yellen, John 1977. *Archaeological Approaches to the Present*. Academic Press, New York.

    1985. Bushmen. *Science* 85:41–48.

Yen, Douglas E. 1976. The Ethnobotany of the Tasaday. Part 3: Notes on the Subsistence System. In *Further Studies on the Tasaday*, edited by Douglas E. Yen and John Nance, pp. 159–183. Panamin Foundation Research Series 2. Panamin Foundation, Makati, Rizal, Philippines.

Yesner, David 1980. Maritime Hunter–Gatherers: Ecology and Prehistory. *Current Anthropology* 21(6):727–735.

Yost, James A. and Patricia M. Kelley 1983. Shotguns, Blowguns, and Spears: The Analysis of Technological Efficiency. In *Adaptive Responses of Native Amazonians*, edited by Raymond B. Hames and William T. Vickers, pp. 189–224. Academic Press, New York.

INDEX

Page numbers in *italics* refer to figures or tables. The following abbreviations are used: Amz., Amazonia/n; hort., horticulture/alists; NASW, North American Southwest.

Hunters in Transition
Mesolithic Societies of Temperate Eurasia and their Transition to Farming

Edited by Marek Zvelebil

This book analyses one of the crucial events in human cultural evolution: the emergence of postglacial hunter–gatherer communities and the development of farming. Traditionally, the advantages of settled agriculture have been assumed and the transition to farming has been viewed in terms of the simple dispersal of early farming communities northwards across Europe. The contributors to this volume adopt a fresh, more subtle approach. Farming is viewed from a hunter–gatherer perspective as offering both advantages and disadvantages, organisational disruption during the period of transition and far-reaching social consequences for the existing way of life. The hunter–gatherer economy and farming in fact shared a common objective: a guaranteed food supply in a changing natural and social environment. Drawing extensively on research in eastern Europe and temperate Asia, the book argues persuasively for the essential unity of all postglacial adaptations whether leading to the dispersal of farming or the retention and elaboration of existing hunter–gatherer strategies.

Contributors: TAKERU AKAZAWA; PAUL DOLUKHANOV; CLIVE GAMBLE; STEFAN KAROL KOZLOWSKI; JANUSZ KOZLOWSKI; JAMES LEWTHWAITE; GERALD MATYUSHIN; PETER ROWLEY-CONWY; SLAVOMIL VENCL; MAREK ZVELEBIL

New Directions in Archaeology

0 521 26868 0

Problems in Neolithic Archaeology
Alasdair Whittle

Problems in Neolithic Archaeology is a notable contribution to the current debate about how we can write prehistory. Drawing on both processual and post-processual approaches, it reaffirms the central role of theory and interpretation while accepting as permanent the uncertainty which makes the testing of archaeological hypotheses difficult or even impossible. Dr Whittle asserts in particular the need for greater self-confidence and for the formulation of new theory and questions more appropriate to the archaeological record. The scope that exists he explores through a series of linked studies of chronology and time, settlement and space, economic activity, material culture and burial. Different kinds of prehistory are envisaged, at varying scales in time and space, and the author's approach therefore has implications for archaeologists working in all periods. The book's specific strength lies, however, in a close contextual study of the Neolithic period in western and central Europe. In this respect it provides an admirable complement to his textbook *Neolithic Europe* (Cambridge University Press, 1985).

New Studies in Archaeology

0 521 35121 9

Quantifying Diversity in Archaeology
Edited by Robert D. Leonard and George T. Jones

One of the enduring aims of archaeological research has been to explain why human material culture is so diverse, both across the world and through history. Recognising that diversity exists is not, however, to explain it nor to measure it effectively. The aim of the contributors to *Quantifying Diversity in Archaeology* is therefore to examine what we mean by diversity, to review the methods of measurement and formulae we can apply, and assess the pitfalls that exist. Richness and evenness, the two main components of the diversity measures developed in the biological sciences, are considered, as are the value of diversity measures in the study of style, ecology, cultural geography, and faunal, lithic and spatial analysis. Subsequent papers consider critically why the archaeological remains of particular cultures vary so markedly between sites, localities and regions.

Contributors: GEORGE T. JONES, ROBERT D. LEONARD, PETER T. BOBROWSKY, BRUCE F. BALL, DAVID RINDOS, KEITH W. KINTIGH, MICHAEL B. SCHIFFER, JAN F. SIMEK, CHARLOTTE BECK, DONALD K. GRAYSON, DAVID HURST THOMAS, NAN A. ROTHSCHILD, F.E. SMILEY, CATHERINE M. CAMERSON, PRUDENCE M. RICE, MARGARET W. CONKEY

New Directions in Archaeology

0 521 35030 1

The Archaeology of Prehistoric Coastlines
Edited by Geoff Bailey

The Archaeology of Prehistoric Coastlines offers a conspectus of recent work on coastal archaeology, examining the various ways in which hunter–gatherers and farmers across the world exploited marine resources such as fish, shellfish and waterfowl in prehistory. Changes in sea levels and the balance of marine ecosystems have altered coastal environments significantly in the last ten thousand years, and the impact of these changes on the nature of human settlement and subsistence is kept in mind throughout. General consideration is also given to the ways settlement may have been geared to seasonal movements of population and resource scheduling and altered over time in response to variations in resource abundance and climate.

An overview of coastal archaeology as a developing discipline is followed by ten case studies from a wide variety of places, including Scandinavia, Japan, Tasmania and New Zealand, Peru, South Africa and the United States.

Contributors: TAKERU AKAZAWA, ATHOLL J. ANDERSON, GEOFF BAILEY, SANDRA BOWDLER, BILL BUCHANAN, MARGARET DEITH, JON M. ERLANDSON, ROBERT A. FELDMAN, MICHAEL A. GLASSOW, TONY MANHIRE, MICHAEL E. MOSELEY, JOHN PARKINGTON, CEDRIC POGGENPOEL, PRISCILLA RENOUF, TIM ROBEY, JUDITH SEALY, JUDITH C. SHACKLETON, LARRY R. WILCOXON, DAVID R. YESNER

New Directions in Archaeology

0 521 25036 6

Forest Farmers and Stockherders

Early Agriculture and its Consequences in North-central Europe

Peter Bogucki

Drawing extensively on anthropological theory and ecological models of human adaptation, *Forest Farmers and Stockherders* explores the single most radical transformation in European history – the growth of a food-producing economy in the period 5000–3000 BC.

Dr Bogucki seeks to develop a coherent view of the introduction of food-production to north-central Europe, identifying new environmental zones being exploited for the first time and new ecological adaptations being adopted by both indigenous and colonizing populations. He lays particular emphasis on the strategies developed by Neolithic communities for coping with the environmental risks and uncertainties inherent in the introduction of new economic systems and the social implications of these strategies for the organization of human behaviour.

New Studies in Archaeology

0 521 32959 0

Prehistory at Cambridge and Beyond

Grahame Clark

Professor Clark's book examines the teaching of prehistoric archaeology at Cambridge and the achievements of its graduates, placing this theme against the background of the growth of archaeology as an academic discipline worldwide. Prehistory in Cambridge began to be taught formally in 1920. From the outset it focused on the aims and methods of archaeological research and the measure of its success is shown by the achievement of Cambridge graduates at home and overseas, in both the study and the field.

0 521 35031 X